WAR ON RECORD

WAR ON RECORD

The Archive and the Afterlife of the Civil War

YAEL A. STERNHELL

Yale
UNIVERSITY
PRESS
New Haven and London

Published with assistance from the foundation established in memory of James Wesley Cooper of the Class of 1865, Yale College.

Yale University Press books may be purchased in quantity for educational, business, or promotional use. For information, please e-mail sales.press@yale.edu (U.S. office) or sales@yaleup.co.uk (U.K. office).

Set in Janson type by IDS Infotech Ltd.
Printed in the United States of America.

Library of Congress Control Number: 2023932596
ISBN 978-0-300-23414-5 (hardcover : alk. paper)

A catalogue record for this book is available from the British Library.

This paper meets the requirements of ANSI/NISO Z39.48-1992 (Permanence of Paper).

10 9 8 7 6 5 4 3 2 1

In loving memory of my father

Contents

Introduction

THIS BOOK TELLS THE STORY of an archive. That archive is composed of the official records created during the Civil War and collected by the Federal government in the war's long and uncertain aftermath. Over the years, those records have exerted a powerful influence on how the war has been understood, interpreted, and represented. In some form, they are present in every work of history and in countless reverberations of historical writing in journalism, popular culture, and public memory. The enduring legacy of the Civil War and its continued hold on the American imagination make this body of records in all likelihood the most consequential archival collection to have ever been assembled, organized, and ultimately published in the United States. It is high time that it be treated as a historical subject in its own right rather than simply utilized as an object for telling other stories.

Simultaneously, this deep dive into the history of one corpus of records is also an attempt to confront the universal question of how we know what we know, or think we know, about the past. Archives (whether public or private, small or large, physical or digital) enjoy a position of unmatched supremacy in shaping historical knowledge. For most of the modern era, archival records have provided the building blocks for virtually any rigorous recounting of human affairs since antiquity. In the process, these "Houses of

Memory" have become revered and romanticized by generations of scholars who happily succumb to their irresistible promise of unmediated access to worlds long gone. In both popular and professional parlance, archival work has become synonymous with historical research, and archives have become synonymous with historical truth.[1]

And herein lies the problem. Archives are fundamentally deceptive. They present a tremendous richness of material but only rarely reveal the gaping holes in their collections. Whether on a research trip or navigating a digital collection from home, a historian is almost naturally inclined to feel overwhelmed by the offerings of the archive rather than dwell on the absence of records that simply are not there. Occasionally, a finding aid or catalog will mention missing documents, but most of the time a visitor to an archive does not actually know and can barely imagine the records which were either never created or disappeared along the way. In a similar vein, archival researchers have also cultivated a blissful ignorance of the complex mechanisms that generated the collections they sift through. "Very little notice is still given by nonarchivists to how the record is chosen and shaped, privileged or marginalized," writes Terry Cook, a leading archival thinker. "Archivists have remained invisible in the construction of social memory, their role poorly articulated and rarely appreciated." Historians like to think of themselves as the original interpreters of archival records. Yet long before they set foot in the reading room, the records they will be working with had been interpreted in ways they do not understand and cannot escape.[2]

This, of course, is hardly a revelation. Scholars in the humanities and social sciences have been contemplating the problems *of* archives and *in* archives for decades. The "archival turn," as it has become known, is part and parcel of the broader skepticism about seemingly naturalized categories and institutions. It is intimately related to the interrogation of how historical reality is mediated through language, to the historicization of scientific practices and paradigms once considered organic, to the interest in how nations use information as a technology of rule, and to the lively interrogation of books as historical subjects rather than mere vessels for the transmission of knowledge. These and other intellectual influences have inspired, as historian Alexandra Walsham puts it, an "awareness of how the archive (in a literal as well as a figurative sense) operates as a distorting filter, lens, and prism."[3]

The archival turn has had an enormous impact on many a historical field. Feminist historians have questioned the utility of state archives, where women are frequently absent from records created by, for, and about men; historians of empire have demonstrated the ways in which colonial power was dependent on archives, where knowledge of conquered peoples was not only stored but organized and remade to facilitate and legitimize imperial rule; scholars of modern nation-states have studied how shifting political systems fundamentally altered the workings of state archives. In the late twentieth century, with the breakdown of colonialism, apartheid, and other forms of state oppression, historians began examining how archives served the brutality of fallen regimes even as they reflected on how post-conflict societies can use archives as means for reconciliation.[4]

U.S. history is a latecomer to this conversation. Americanists have occasionally explored with great skill specific episodes of archival history, but it is only relatively recently that a sustained interest in the archival turn has begun to make its mark.[5] At this point, its influence can be identified mostly among historians of American and Caribbean slavery. Studying slavery poses a particularly poignant and painful conundrum. Many archives documenting the experience of African Americans in this era have all but eradicated their subjects as fully realized human beings and to a large degree reflect the gaze of white enslavers. How to use them without unconsciously replicating their violent dehumanization is a question for which there are no easy answers. Some scholars have taken the position that traditional archives for the study of slavery (like the personal papers of white slaveholders or the records of slave trading companies) should be abandoned. Others, who do not reject the archival record altogether, have tried to construct histories by taking fragments of evidence and building on them through a variety of innovative narrative methods. The crux of the matter, to quote the editors of a special volume devoted to this topic, is whether "the violence of Atlantic slavery was so great, and the limits of its archive so absolute, that no amount of historical recovery could properly describe it, let alone begin to undo its damage." Perhaps because the stakes are so high, many historians taking part in this debate have tended to use an indefinite "the archive" as they ponder whether slavery can actually be studied through the repositories purporting to document it.[6]

While the fundamental concern with history's knowability runs through these pages as well, what follows is a different kind of endeavor. Rather than dwell on archival gaps and absences, on the archive as an obstacle, this book takes one archive as its subject and reads it, to quote anthropologist Ann Laura Stoler, "along the archival grain." What this means in practice is, first, focusing on the people who managed the records: their intellectual persuasions, ideological motivations, and personal predilections; second, studying archival users: Civil War veterans preoccupied with their personal histories, family members trying to profit from selling wartime papers, and present-day historians relying on the records for their research; and third, paying close attention to archival practices: the work of assembling, organizing, cataloging, and eventually editing records and considering their profound implications. Altogether, the goal is to answer two interrelated questions: First, how did the body of records amassed by the Federal government at the end of the war operate in the war's long and volatile afterlife? Second, how did archival processes shape what we recognize today as Civil War history?

Since the term "archive" is often overused and sometimes misconstrued, a word of explanation on how it will function here seems necessary. The United States never built a brick-and-mortar archive to house its Civil War records. Nor were the documents ever concentrated in one place. But the Federal government did become the custodian of many millions of records created during the war by the vast armies who fought in the field and by the government bureaucracies supporting them. These records were placed under the charge of the War Department, where they were managed by what might be called "archival bureaus": the Adjutant General's Office, the army's regular record keeper, and two designated agencies founded specifically to handle Civil War records, called the Archive Office, established in 1865, and the War Records Office, established in 1878. Thus, in this context, "the archive" will serve as shorthand for the Federal government's holdings of Civil War records, divided as they were between different bureaus and scattered across a wide range of storage facilities in Washington, D.C.

Even as this study gets down to the nitty-gritty details of nineteenth-century archiving, it will also rely on the work of archival thinkers about the nature of written records and their meanings. This is a rich and theoretically sophisticated literature that has produced many illuminating insights. Three will figure prominently here and deserve to be stated in brief. First, archives are unstable, constructed, and susceptible to influences of every kind. As Terry Cook and Joan Schwartz frame it, "Archives have their origins in the information needs and social values of the rulers, governments, businesses, and individuals who establish and maintain them. Archives then are not some pristine storehouse of historical documentation that has piled up, but a reflection of and often justification for the society that creates them."[7] Archives and the work taking place within their confines are shaped by (among other things) national politics, institutional structures, financial exigencies, cultural mores, and individual penchants.

Second, archival records are not static objects. Their meaning —and therefore their nature—shifts every time they are used, or, as Eric Ketelaar calls it, "activated." Ketelaar, another influential archival scientist, offers one example explicating this notion particularly well: "The records created and used by German and Dutch agencies during the Second World War to account for the looting of Jewish assets were continued to be used, after the war, by German and Dutch agencies in the processes of restitution and reparation. The same record was activated again and again for different purposes, as it is today activated in the search for looted and lost works of art and other Holocaust assets. Current use of these records affects retrospectively all earlier meanings, or to put it differently: we can no longer read the record as our predecessors have read that record."[8]

Third, archives do not simply reflect the past but actually shape the present and the future. Or, in the words of historians Francis X. Blouin and William Rosenberg, "all archival records are not only themselves the product of social, cultural, and especially political processes; they very much affect the workings of these processes as well, and hence they influence the kinds of realities that archival collections reflect."[9] What happens in archives determines which events and individuals will be remembered and which will be forgotten, which facts will become public and which will be set aside. Archives have the power to make myths and hide truths, to generate cohesion and fuel resistance, to valorize war and foster reconciliation.

In what follows, all of these seemingly abstract ideas will spring into life. Washington's Civil War archive was shaped by a multiplicity of forces; its records were repurposed and recast as they moved between headquarters, warehouses, bureaus, and printing presses; and it has had a palpable impact on the process of reuniting white men who had once tried to kill each other on the battlefield.

War on Record begins with the outbreak of hostilities in 1861 and the rapid expansion of the bureaucracies that managed what contemporaries often called "this gigantic war."[10] Though the American Civil War might seem benign and provincial in comparison to the global conflicts of the twentieth century, in its own time and place it introduced a scale of warfare hitherto unknown. The two armies eventually numbered 3 million men who fought each other across an entire continent in thousands of engagements that ranged from swift encounters between small bands to the battle of Gettysburg, where more than 50,000 men became casualties. Both sides took advantage of the era's cutting-edge technologies (trains, telegraphs, ironclad ships, rifles, torpedoes, and even rudimentary submarines) and mobilized the home front to produce a vast array of goods to supply their armies. If not entirely modern (horses and mules still played a paramount role, as did traditional battlefield tactics), the war certainly heralded a new age of industrialized slaughter.[11]

Two war machines of this magnitude and complexity generated gargantuan quantities of paperwork, which were produced, managed, and preserved by countless adjutants and clerks, the war's invisible actors. The volume of wartime paperwork was commensurate with the overall growth in the use of paper in America, which rose a staggering 900-fold over the course of the nineteenth century.[12] Though it is impossible to reliably quantify this body of records, anecdotal evidence offers a glimpse of its scale. The U.S. army handled

1,200,000 telegrams during the second year of the war and 1,800,000 during the third; the Office of the U.S. Provost Marshal General created records of the physical condition of 1,014,776 men who joined the army after 1863; the war had brought the quintupling of Federal records in Washington, from 200,000 cubic feet in 1860 to over a million by the mid-1870s. Written records, in short, were no less essential to the conduct of war than guns.[13]

This vast body of records was created in headquarters, officers' tents, and War Departments in Washington and Richmond. And yet, as will become clear, the written record documenting the war on both sides was subject to two countervailing forces. It was constantly in the process of being generated, as each day brought new reams of military paperwork enabling both armies to function, yet it was simultaneously undergoing a process of destruction, as countless records were lost, while some were never produced to begin with. Losses intensified during the final weeks of the war when the Confederate government liquidated huge troves of records and could not save all those it tried to keep.

And yet at precisely the same time, Confederate records suddenly became a focal point of national attention, as they were widely presumed to be harboring crucial information about the murder of President Abraham Lincoln in April 1865. In hopes of locating evidence for postwar trials, the U.S. army undertook a massive operation of collecting the written record of the rebellion and sending it to Washington, where it was stored in a special unit of the War Department, established in July 1865 and called the Archive Office. The trials never took place. Yet for years afterward Confederate records remained a vital source in the hands of the Federal government in its legal battles with white Southerners who tried to win reparations for war damages. The records stored in the Archive Office rooms opened possibilities for some forms of account settling with former rebels, even as they foreclosed others.

Though in the immediate aftermath of the war the archive of the Confederacy took center stage, the War Department also needed to confront the much larger corpus of records produced by its own armies. This was no minor task, as the United States did not have a national archive or any other mechanism for the systematic storage of government records. The documentation of the great victory, stored helter-skelter across Washington, was constantly at risk of obliteration by fire, flood, collapsing rooftops, and voracious mice. Congress eventually found a solution to prevent the irretrievable loss of its holdings in the absence of a brick-and-mortar archive: the publication of selected records in a government-issued publication.

Meanwhile, those who cared most about the history of the war refused to wait for the Federal government to provide access to the records. The hunger for archival documentation in post–Civil War America had its origins in the information void during wartime and remained a constant in its aftermath as veterans and historical writers (who usually were the same people) sought access to records. Archival work in America was never the exclusive purview of professional historians. Long before history PhDs arrived on the scene, men and women with no formal training in research barraged the government with requests for information, preferably from original documents. The papers hidden in Washington's storage rooms were perceived as the ultimate source of truth about the Civil War, an object of yearning and a driving force in the grassroots culture of history writing after the war.

The interest in the documentation held by the government, combined with the palpable threat to the documents' material fate, moved Congress in June 1874 to authorize funding for an edited compilation of records titled *War of the Rebellion: The Official Records of the Union and Confederate Armies.* Though Congress had a long tradition of funding and distributing official publications, the *War of the Rebellion* was its largest and most ambitious project. It took a quarter century to make, cost millions of dollars, and at times seemed unlikely to ever be completed. Historians of the Civil War era probably do not need convincing as to why studying the making of the compilation—transforming the massive and messy mounds of papers strewn across the capital into a neatly bound set of 128 books—is essential. Other readers might consider the fact that from the late nineteenth century to our own day the compilation has been regarded as the most important source for the study of the sectional conflict. It has been used by historians writing on any aspect of the period and enjoys the kind of intimate recognition among specialists that has earned it the affectionate nickname "the *OR*."[14] Yet despite its unique epistemological status, it has never been studied as rigorously as it deserves. Filling this void begins here with an investigation of the decision-making process that shaped the compilation: the political, personal, and institutional agendas that determined which records would be published and how they would be presented to the reader. As will become clear, decisions made by a group of Gilded Age military bureaucrats have shaped the contours of Civil War history down to the present, but the work was also heavily dependent on the collaboration of Civil War officers who dug up their old records, provided missing facts, deciphered telegrams, and vouched for the veracity of their handwriting. Veterans also exerted influence over the making of the *OR* by being its primary audience, a fact that compilers never lost sight of and that had a tangible impact on how the project developed.

Finally, the rebellion's leaders also played an unexpected role in the making of the *OR*. The relative dearth of Confederate records in the War Department's archives compelled the editors to seek out the aid of ex-Confederates, promising in exchange that the government's official history would present a wholly impartial narrative. Despite some initial suspicion, officers who took part in the rebellion were persuaded to donate their records and over time became some of the War Department's most valuable allies. The results were manifold and far-reaching. Reconciliation between white Americans took place in many settings and in many forms, but the archive must be recognized as a central locus in this movement.

The bulk of this book is based on collections documenting the bureaus that managed Civil War records. At first glance, these are dull bureaucratic sources and have thus been lying dormant in the National Archives storage rooms for many years (on one occasion, a reference archivist referred to some as "the lonely records"). A deeper look, however, reveals extraordinarily rich collections in which the work of preserving, organizing, searching, indexing, and eventually editing wartime documents comes into sharp relief. At the same time, working from these documents poses the challenge Eric Ketelaar has referred to as the "double bind" for scholars historicizing archives.[15] If archival records are never simply objective reflections of reality, but are always the products of the processes that brought them into being, how does one consciously use them when trying to write a history of the very same processes? There seems to be no recourse but to use them, however, for the story of the Civil War archive in Washington must be told, and, to be told, must rely on the voluminous documentation left behind by the same record keepers whose decisions, habits, and sensibilities are the subject of this book. Supplementary sources have offered little help, as many were drawn from other institutional archives and thus are also the embodiment of appraisal, selection, and cataloging decisions made by archivists who shared the same professional and cultural sensibilities. Published sources, including annals of Congress, newspapers, and government reports, provide important information and additional perspective, though they too are always suspect of masking more than they reveal. The archive of the archive, in short, is as partial and inscrutable as any collection of records. In what follows, it is approached with some of the care, skepticism, and self-awareness taught by the archival turn.

In recent years, archivists are increasingly contending that historians must move beyond the "invisible archive" and confront the true nature of the institutions they rely on to craft their stories.[16] *War on Record* heeds this call and attempts a full-scale study of a body of records, starting with its creation and ending with the publication of a selection from its riches. This is neither a study of the entire documentary output of the Civil War nor a complete narrative of how historians have used these records. The first is impossible and the second is a topic for another book. Yet looking *at* Washington's Civil War archive rather than looking *through* it will hopefully cast a new light on how we know what we know, or think we know, about the past.

CHAPTER ONE

An Archive Made and Unmade

The outbreak of the Civil War famously caught the Union army ill prepared for the struggle on which it was about to embark. A minuscule force of 16,000, stretched thin across a vast frontier, it comes across as woefully understaffed and underequipped, a remnant of an era gone by. Yet this was not entirely true. As a bureaucracy, the antebellum army was remarkably forward-looking. The General Staff, seated in Washington, consisted of nine independent departments, including adjutant, inspector, medical, quartermaster, subsistence, engineer, judge-advocate, ordnance, and paymaster. These were established during the first half of the nineteenth century and had developed into what one historian has termed "a small but robust military bureaucracy."[1]

The administrative focal point of the army was the bureau of the adjutant general, which linked units in the field with the army's headquarters through an extensive network of written communications. As an 1879 history of the War Department put it, the Adjutant General's Office "is the right arm of the military establishment,—the medium of its orders and commands, the custodian of its records and archives, the guardian of its documentary and best evidence, from the muster of the humblest enlisted man to the commission of the commander-in-chief, and the orders on the field of a pitched battle."[2] Records included correspondence (sent or received and filed in books), orders (either general, published to an entire command, or special, meant only for the soldiers affected by them), returns (documenting the strength of every unit and the names and whereabouts of commissioned personnel), reports (like daily morning reports filed by each company, providing information not only on personnel but also on the activities of the company on a given day), court-martial records, muster rolls, applications, accounts, and claims. Paperwork sent from the field moved up the chain of command, accruing endorsements along the way, until it reached the Adjutant General's Office in Washington, where it was arranged, briefed, filed, and indexed. The adjutant's staff also reshaped the raw data arriving from the field into new forms of military knowledge: consolidated returns (providing information about entire commands or armies), station books (showing where each unit was stationed every month), endorsement books, memoranda books, index books, telegram books, and numerous registers of military personnel covering soldiers and officers in every shape and form, active, injured, imprisoned, missing, furloughed, discharged, or dead.[3]

The *Regulations for the Army of the United States*, which one historian calls the "Old Army's Bible," provided officers in the field detailed instructions on every aspect of military record keeping, including the issuance of orders, the correct use of communication channels, the submission of copies, and the application of printed forms.[4] The *Regulations* stipulated, for example, that "[r]olls and returns will be accompanied by a letter of transmittal, enumerating them, and referring to no other subject," and that "[c]opies of all orders of the commanders of the armies, departments, divisions, and detached brigades, and of the Superintendent of the recruiting service, will be forwarded at their dates, or as soon thereafter as practicable, in separate series, on full sheets of letter paper, or as printed, to the Adjutant-General's office." No detail was too small: officers were instructed on how to fold letter paper and how to sign their names.[5]

Meticulous record keeping also dominated the Quartermaster General Department, whose varied responsibilities included feeding, clothing, transporting, and otherwise supplying the army. It was the largest bureau in the War Department, spending a third of the army's annual total budget. From its founding in 1818 until 1860 it was run by a single officer, Thomas S. Jesup, who created a national bureaucracy long before similar mechanisms existed in the private sector. As early as 1825, quartermasters used thirty-seven standard paper forms to communicate with each other and with the department in Washington, where their reports were closely examined by Jesup's clerical staff.[6]

Thus, despite its compact size, the U.S. army had been generating an abundance of records for decades, and its personnel had developed considerable expertise in managing military paperwork. While the army may have been short on experience in fighting large battles, it was long on administrative and logistical know-how. It was an apparatus, as historian Wayne Wei-Siang Hsieh has said, that "could virtually run on institutional autopilot under inexperienced secretaries of war."[7]

The outbreak of the Civil War, however, posed a challenge of a different order. During the first year of the conflict, the army ballooned into a force of nearly 576,000 soldiers and officers. In April 1865, a million men were in active service, while another million had already been discharged.[8] The exponential growth in manpower and the phenomenal complexity of Civil War operations brought an outpouring of paperwork that overwhelmed even the most effective bureaucrats in Washington. A few months into the war, the new but highly capable quartermaster general Montgomery Meigs wrote to Secretary of War Edwin M. Stanton: "The business of the office has increased twentyfold. A larger force and great increase in the number of its clerks are absolutely necessary to the quick dispatch of business and to the proper filing and preservation of its records."[9] A year later, Meigs's sense of panic seems to have only increased. There were 1,000 regiments in the field, each with a quartermaster submitting monthly and quarterly returns; in addition, 10,000 company commanders were making monthly returns for the equipment they had been issued. The desks of his office were piled with unpaid accounts worth $105 million. Meigs was asking for 120 additional clerks, and would continue to plead for a bigger workforce until the end of the war. "We have no experience of the cost and contingencies of carrying on war on a great scale, and it is beyond any human foresight to estimate it with accuracy," he warned during the first year of the war.[10] While the quartermaster general may have been the most overburdened, other departments were also inundated by a flow of paperwork. The chief of ordnance wrote in October 1863 asking for an additional 130 clerks, stating that the previous increase authorized by Congress "has been found totally inadequate to meet even the demands of the daily business, much less to prepare and arrange the necessary data which should be always at hand."[11]

Yet despite the pressure they were under, the General Staff departments were ultimately able to master the huge influx of written records arriving from the field. Whether it was because of the increase in the clerical workforce, the competence of high-ranking officers, or the strength of the army's antebellum administrative experience, both later historians and contemporary actors saw considerable order emerging out of apparent chaos. B.W. Brice, the acting paymaster general, boasted in a November 1864 report that his 155 clerks were exhibiting "zeal, competency, and general efficiency," and voiced no complaints about the demands of the hour. Roughly at the same time, the bureaucrats of the quartermaster general had managed to get enough of a handle on the paperwork in their office to produce "from the best data" available at that moment an "estimate for the military materials, supplies and expenses of the Quartermaster's Department needed to continue the struggle on the scale of the military forces actually raised in 1864." The adjutant general, whose primary functions revolved around military paperwork, declared in his annual report of October 31, 1864, that "the difficulties springing from a sudden and vast increase of business have been measurably overcome . . . the various branches of duty have been systematized, principal and subordinate clerks have been instructed, and the business is now transacted with promptness and efficiency."[12]

Even if the expansion of military record keeping demanded by the war had grown exponentially, so did the ability of professional bureaucrats and their growing teams to manage it. In the end, Washington staff departments and their representatives in the field were able to create and maintain systems that were far from perfect but were nevertheless sufficiently functional to offer armies the logistical and administrative support they needed to win the war. Though Civil War staff departments sometimes seemed submerged under paperwork, they did not actually drown.

Out in the field, however, the state of record keeping was far more erratic.[13] Written communications were absolutely essential for the management of armies as large and far-flung as those fighting in the Civil War, and officers on all levels were required to carry out correspondence, fill out forms, submit reports, and maintain unit records in an orderly fashion. Some seem to have successfully done so by following, at least in part, the detailed guidelines laid out in the *Regulations for the Army of the United States*. Writing from Virginia in August 1864, commander of the U.S. army Ulysses S. Grant ended a letter to his wife saying he had a "full twelve hours constant wrighting to do, which I must do, before me."[14] Among other high-ranking officers, a few of the more effective record keepers were John M. Schofield, George Henry Thomas, and Gouverneur K. Warren; the last was commended after the war for being "so careful and painstaking in preserving the record of the operations that he commanded, as to make his correspondence almost a complete history of the corps which he commanded."[15] William S. Rosecrans testified that it was his "invariable rule to keep the records of my headquarters officially intact, and whenever confidential communications affecting public affairs were received, if my personal papers and public records could not both be served, preference was always shown to the official records, which were kept intact." Some units, like the headquarters of the Army of the Potomac, were noted for systematic record keeping, especially of letter and order books. Telegraphic correspondence was particularly well-preserved across the board, since operators tended to abide by an order to keep copies of every dispatch they sent.[16]

Yet many of the officers handling military records seem to have had a much harder time maintaining and preserving the papers documenting their units. Two main factors were at work. First, most company and regimental commanders were volunteers who had received no training in military record keeping and paid little attention to that aspect of their commissions.[17] Second, the chaos inherent to field service. As the secretary of war put it in 1875,

Clerks at the Army of the Potomac headquarters, Brandy Station, Virginia, February 1864. Courtesy of Library of Congress.

"Owing to the pressure of affairs during the war, the field-records were kept in a hurried and sometimes crude and careless manner."[18] Archivists who have looked into this estimate that, in total, about one-third of the operations in the Civil War were not officially documented to begin with but are mentioned in nonofficial publications like local newspapers. This was particularly true during the first year of the war for regular units and remained true throughout the conflict for actions involving state troops and irregular forces.[19]

The reality of poor to nonexistent documentation was evident while the war was still in progress. Lorenzo Thomas, the adjutant general, admitted in May 1862 that officers commanding military prisons were simply not keeping records of the prisoners received and discharged.[20] Units in the field were also failing in this regard, as was apparent in the reports submitted by the office of the inspector general to the army's chief of staff. Monthly inspections of military units covered a wide variety of topics, including the appearance and discipline of soldiers, the competence and energy of officers, the cleanliness of camps, the well-being of animals, and the devotion of chaplains. Inspectors also examined the state of units' paperwork and were often unhappy with what they found. "Regimental and company books and records very incomplete" appears in the reports on myriad units, whether they were serving on the front lines in Virginia or on the Western frontier.[21] Officers turned in their reports and returns late, left their records behind as they went on months-long campaigns, or neglected them altogether.[22] Morning reports were "made irregularly," and accounting of public property by officers and quartermasters was lax. Chaplains were also frequently reprimanded for failing to make monthly reports to regimental commanders, as required by law. On occasion, inspectors offered a glimpse into how "very incomplete" books and records were created. Lieutenant Colonel W.D. Smith, who inspected a force stationed in Lafourche, Louisiana, reported that only two officers "could give me the number of men for duty that morning. They admitted they had signed their reports but knew nothing of their correctness."[23] In a few cases, officers in the field complained that they had never received equipment for record keeping from the army, despite making requisitions. Even as some units were commended for keeping complete records, the inspector general's reports from the last part of the war reveal a habit of uneven record keeping that was as common in elite fighting forces as it was in those units that inspectors referred to as "little better than an armed mob."[24]

In the aftermath of the war, officers readily admitted to their sloppiness. Chelsey D. Bailey, an officer in the 9th Kentucky Infantry, remembered serving with the regiment from March 1863 to September 1864, sharing a tent with the regimental commander, and doing most of the work of an adjutant. "Aside from a casualty list I do not think there was an official report in extenso of the operations of the regiment during the days covered by the battle" of Chickamauga. Neither the division nor the brigade, claimed Bailey, were in the habit of making reports.[25] Oftentimes, officers on campaign did not have the means for composing a written report. William Brooke Rawle, who served with a Pennsylvania cavalry volunteer regiment, described the period around the battle of Gettysburg: "[O]ur reports were at that time few and far between. In five weeks at one time we did not see our wagons or papers."[26] An officer serving in northern Virginia in 1862 also remembered that "Brigade commanders of Reynolds' division were not called upon for reports of this campaign: and if this was the case it was doubtless due to the fact that the Division and Brigade commanders were entirely destitute of every convenience for so doing on account of their separation from their baggage."[27] Robert H. Milroy, one of those brigade commanders, confirmed Bailey's assessment about the lack of reporting yet cited different reasons. According to Milroy, he was never called upon to report and besides was too preoccupied with active operations and "had no taste for spending time in making reports." It would be reasonable to suspect Milroy, who was soundly defeated in this campaign, for having intentionally avoided creating a record of his failures. Yet the rich correspondence of the War Department with officers in the postwar period reveals little correlation between an officer's performance and his penchant for creating a documentary record.[28]

Orders given while battles were in motion rarely became formal records, since commanders handed them down verbally or wrote them in pencil on slips of paper. William T. Sherman was known to have communicated with his subordinates mainly through pencil notes, which were never copied and survived the war only if the officers on the receiving end kept them.[29] Philip Sheridan, who commanded an intense campaign in Virginia's Shenandoah Valley in the fall of 1864, ran a headquarters that left "next to nothing . . . either in the way of matter sent or received." Even in relatively well-managed commands, like that of the Army of the Potomac, the rule was not to enter into formal books orders written under fire issued to field commanders. "If they were preserved at all, it was due to the extra official care or thoughtfulness of the commanding general, or of some person associated with him at the Corps' Headquarters," wrote George B. Davis, a War Department bureaucrat who would spend years chasing down the missing records. At times, Davis confronted inexplicable record-keeping decisions by officers, like General James McPherson, who at some point in the war was "placed in charge of the railroads, and from an examination of his papers I should say that he had kept a duplicate way-bill of every pound of freight that went over the railroad in either direction." On the other hand, there were no "indications of the existence of any of the important reports of General McPherson's commands . . . for example, he made no report of the siege of Vicksburg—a somewhat remarkable omission, as he was an engineer officer himself, and the operations against Vicksburg were those of a character in which a military engineer would be interested. If he made any report it has simply disappeared."[30]

Yet even when records were created and reasonably kept, there were virtually limitless opportunities for their loss or destruction. Union commands were constantly on the move, from one battlefield to the next, from one theater of war to the other. Records were carelessly packed and unpacked, loaded on wagons caught by the enemy, or sent to headquarters never to be seen again.[31] "There was much confusion at the time," wrote Davis to one officer looking for a report on the Nashville campaign. "Many regimental reports never advanced any further on their way to the [War] Department than the headquarters of the post, brigade or other command to which they were attached."[32] Sometimes, veterans could recount exactly how their records had disappeared. General Henry W. Slocum lost his papers while he was serving out west: "They were forwarded to me from Vicksburgh but never received." Yet often officers simply remembered making a report and sending it up the chain of command, and had no idea what happened to it.[33]

The disappearance of records could become a deeply personal issue. The 6th Corps of the Army of the Potomac, which had participated in much of the war's hardest fighting, barely left a paper trail. The War Department assumed that it was simply "very remiss in the way of preserving records" or that "some headquarters" along the way was to blame for the loss of the records. But Martin M. McMahon, an assistant adjutant general who served with the corps, vehemently objected. "[T]he records of the 6th corps during my connection with it and until the end of its service were duly sent to the Adjutant General's Office in Washington," he wrote the War Department. McMahon claimed he "was very much disappointed and disgusted" when he found out "how incomplete the papers were, and I have reason to believe that some of them were destroyed or removed at a certain time at the close of the war." McMahon offered an educated guess for why the unit's papers had gone missing. The corps commander, John Sedgwick, "was not a favorite with the great war secretary and whenever he had anything to say in his reports he said it. Some of those reports are now missing and it is a great pity." His own collection of wartime records was " 'expended in action' or otherwise disposed of."[34]

Large battles were particularly ripe opportunities for administrative chaos. When commanding officers were wounded or killed, which was far from unusual, they left no one to report on events and often lost their set of unit records in the process. "I was wounded a few days after the battle of Cedar Mountain at Rapidan Station," explained Samuel S. Carroll, who was actually a West Point–trained career officer, "and absent from the said command until after termination of that campaign, and I can find no data from the papers in my possession on which to found any report." Napoleon T. Dana, also a career officer, told a similar tale of being "carried from the field, wounded at Antietam—was promoted and appointed to other commands—and did not take away with me a single paper belonging to that Brigade and never saw it again." Sustaining battlefield wounds could potentially serve as a convenient excuse for poor record keeping even during quieter times. Oliver O. Howard, who could not find a report documenting the operations of his command during the monthlong siege of Yorktown in the spring of 1862, explained that the siege led up to the battle of Fair Oaks, where he was severely wounded and relinquished his command. "I am inclined to believe that no report was made for the period above referred to." Those officers who emerged unharmed were exhausted and distracted, and frequently paid little attention to the regulation demanding a detailed report. The result was that some of the war's central military engagements were not documented in real time and some of the most active units in the field were left destitute of records.[35]

This became increasingly true as the war ground to a halt. The Appomattox Campaign was barely documented both because of the intensity of the fighting and because, after the surrender, U.S. officers "seemed to be satisfied with the great fact that the war had closed, and so as a rule reported their operations less fully than had been the case." No one filed an official report of Robert E. Lee's surrender ceremony. A few weeks later, when Joseph Johnston surrendered in North Carolina, many officers on the victorious side did not even bother listing the names of Confederate parolees and simply submitted the numbers of men they had captured.[36] The list of gaps and losses goes on and on. The U.S. war machine generated a vast written record, but that record was disjointed and imperfect, defined by what was missing as much as by what was written down.[37]

As in many other areas of governance, record-keeping practices in the Confederacy closely resembled those of its enemy. At the outset of the war, the South's military leaders were largely veterans of the Old Army, including Samuel Cooper, the adjutant general, who had served the United States in the same capacity during the 1850s. The chapters dealing with record keeping in the *Regulations for the Army of the Confederate States* are virtually indistinguishable from the equivalent ones in the *Revised United States Army Regulations of 1861*, and so was their implementation by military bureaucrats on all levels. The existing documentation of the Confederate War Department, probably the most complete set of government records to survive the rebellion, comprises the usual assortment of nineteenth-century official records, organized in a familiar fashion: letter books, telegram books, endorsement books, order books, appointment books, and all other manner of rolls, reports, returns, certificates, and memoranda.[38]

While the Confederate government did create a national bureaucracy, it strove to maintain, in the words of one of its clerks, "a rigidly economical administration of the duties of each department" and hired as few clerks as possible.[39] The result was an immense workload, especially in the War Department. Massive quantities of papers began to pile up from day one, as attested to by John B. Jones, a department clerk. By the time the Confederate government moved from Montgomery, Alabama, to Richmond, Virginia, on May 27, 1861, he was astonished by "how vast a volume of papers accumulates in a short space of time," and continued commenting on "the immense mass of business accumulating" as the War Department settled in its permanent rooms in the building formerly known as the Mechanics' Institute.[40] A few months later, Secretary of War Judah P. Benjamin asked Congress for an addition of twenty clerks to the department's workforce, citing unreasonable hours, a mountain of unpaid bills, and correspondence in arrears in all staff bureaus.[41]

Despite the challenges of setting up new governments, both Confederate departments and state administrations took care to maintain governmental records and keep them in rooms that functioned as rudimentary archives. The Provisional Congress kept complete records, as did the Confederacy's elected Congress, though more so when it sat in open rather than secret session. Enough documentation from the State and Treasury Departments has survived to prove that record keeping and archiving were standard in Richmond. On the state level, the government of the Commonwealth of Virginia continued functioning and maintained ordinary record keeping in its executive and legislative branches.[42]

Another record-keeping feat was accomplished by the Army Intelligence Office; the office is little known today because, ironically, its own records did not survive the war. Founded during the blood-soaked summer of 1862 by the chaplain William A. Crocker, it aspired to provide accurate information about sick, wounded, and dead Confederate soldiers in Richmond. As Crocker wrote decades later, he first conceived of the idea after having visited convalescent soldiers "scattered over the city in various tobacco factories which were used as hospitals," and encountered thousands of family members who had arrived in town to care for them. Crocker drew up a plan that received support from the secretary of war and the surgeon general and was allocated resources in the shape of disabled soldiers who served as clerks. There was no precedent for an agency of this kind—when he approached the Quartermaster Department with requisitions for stationery and office space, "the old army officers in charge looked at them askance and asked 'What new thing is this?' " Once Crocker and his team set up shop, they embarked on the daunting task of obtaining the names and commands of the 30,000 wounded men then hospitalized in Richmond. Soon enough, with the commencement of the Seven Days Battles, thousands more piled up. Crocker opened a book for each state and placed a clerk in charge. Every day reports arrived from the city's hospitals and were passed around the office. "[E]ach clerk checked off and recorded the names belonging to his state. The name, command, number and ward of hospital, when admitted, discharged, removed, or died, was carefully entered." The same system, which Crocker defined as "the most important record of our office," was set up for dead soldiers from every branch of the Confederate army. His clerks perused the quarterly reports of field and hospital surgeons filed in the Surgeon General's Office and wrote them down in "large and substantial ledgers prepared, one for each state[;] . . . could these records have been preserved, they would have been greatly prized by every surviving soldier of our armies."[43]

The value Confederate administrations placed on records became evident every time the U.S. army arrived at the gates of a Southern capital. During the Peninsula Campaign of 1862, when a huge Union force was approaching Richmond from the Virginia coast, the Confederate secretary of war, George W. Randolph, ordered the secret removal of the War Department's archives by wagons at 9:00 p.m., from a back door, to avoid panic. The Confederate governor of Arkansas cleared out of Little Rock with the state archives when U.S. forces were deemed too close, as did the governor of Tennessee after Fort Donelson had fallen and Nashville was no longer considered safe.[44] When Ulysses S. Grant was tightening his grip on Vicksburg in the spring of 1863, his Confederate counterpart, John C. Pemberton, wrote Mississippi's governor and advised removing the state archives from Jackson.[45] While we have little detailed knowledge of how these archives were organized and kept, the fact that governments on the run took pains to carry their archives along with their treasuries reveals that records were sufficiently extensive and organized to be considered as important to Confederate governance as the specie with which it paid the bills.

Though Confederate armies were smaller than those of the United States, they were equally geographically dispersed and equally reliant on written communications for their operations. Among rebel officers there were those who followed War Department regulations diligently and created complete documentary records of their units, like Samuel Lockett, an engineer who served in some of the war's most critical campaigns and testified to have maintained "very full and extended" records from the very beginning of the war to the very end. Robert Ould, the Confederate commissioner for prisoner exchange, claimed to have kept every piece of paper he had received from Federal agents as well as copies of the papers he had sent them. Samuel H. Stout, the medical director of hospitals for the Army of Tennessee, also claimed to have been a diligent record keeper. "It was my habit throughout my official career, never to destroy any official paper. They were all, when not needed for reference, packed away in boxes."[46] General Albert Sidney Johnston, commander of the Confederacy's Western Department, was killed in action in April 1862 but by then had already accumulated a collection of roughly 8,000 documents, which were later considered a complete record of his command. Johnston had been meticulous about preserving documents addressed to him personally as well as the hefty letter books of his headquarters. His collection included letters, telegrams, orders, reports, returns, memoranda, and even newspaper clippings and Bank of Kentucky statements.[47]

Despite the evidence for attention to record keeping and an acute awareness of their importance, the realities of an upstart nation fighting for its survival and the peripatetic nature of Civil War fighting ensured that the Confederacy's written record would be both messy and full of gaps. Adjutant General Cooper admitted in December 1863 that his office did not hold a collection of company muster rolls, since company commanders did not send them, though they were required to do so by army regulations. "The failure to receive them is attributable partly to the neglect of the officers, but often, no doubt, results from losses incident to sudden movements of troops, conflicts with the enemy, and other difficulties in the way of their transmission to the Department." Various Confederate officers confirmed his observation in hindsight. The assistant adjutant general for General Patrick Cleburne admitted that the latter had made only one report during the entire Atlanta-Dalton campaign of 1864, and even that report was incomplete because Cleburne was constantly on the move and never finished it before his death in the battle of Franklin on November 30 that year. Yet officials who were entirely stationary also proved lackluster record keepers. At the outset of the war, state adjutant generals did not send in muster rolls of the various companies and regiments organized in their states, leaving the Confederate adjutant general in the dark as to the actual organization of the army and the names of the troops. An enrolling officer appointed in South Carolina in the summer of 1863 found "more or less confusion in the mode and manner of keeping the rolls and records" due to the short supply of books and the frequent changes in personnel.[48] Repeated pleas by the adjutant and surgeon generals to maintain better records of individual soldiers fell flat, making it frequently impossible to ascertain the very fact of a particular soldier's death in the field.[49]

As the Confederacy's prospects darkened, the difficulties of creating and preserving records overpowered even the most disciplined officers. The worsening shortage of books and papers, the hasty retreats in the face of superior U.S. forces, and the growing sense of despair all contributed to the virtual collapse of record making and keeping in the Confederate army. The Federal War Department later estimated that by the final stages of the war most Confederate commanders no longer bothered with making regular returns, rolls, and reports and limited their written notes to the number of men actually present for duty.[50] As one historian has shown, the Army of Northern Virginia's internal inspection reports in 1865 lamented the fact that company and regimental records were either woefully incomplete or entirely missing.[51] Years later, George B. Davis summarized the matter to an ex–Confederate general: "The constant movements of troops during the last year and a half of the war, the difficulties of transportation and communication, the want of time and opportunity to keep regular books of record and the extreme difficulty of preserving those that were kept" meant that fewer documents were being created, and even fewer than that would survive the collapse of the Confederacy.[52]

In the aftermath of defeat, some former Confederate officials blamed the Federal government for the loss of their papers during the war's final months, when policies toward Confederate property were hardened. W.C. Falkner, William Faulkner's grandfather, claimed his records were burned when Federal forces set his house on fire in 1864. John Mosby, the infamous cavalry raider, explained that his papers were taken during a raid on his home in Virginia when "a negro man then living at the house took advantage of the presence of the Federal cavalry to seize these papers, stow them in a corn sack, and leave with the troops."[53] Christopher G. Memminger, the Confederate secretary of the treasury, said he had lost the copies of Treasury Department records in February 1865, when his home in Columbia, South Carolina, burned during the great fire set by William T. Sherman's army, whose soldiers did not spare the capital city of the state that stood at the vanguard of secession. While the U.S. commander who raided Mosby's house had no recollection of ever seeing the papers, and it is doubtful that Memminger had actually sent home many copies of official Treasury documents, the result was the same: the records were gone.[54]

The concluding days of the rebellion brought an all-out destruction of records, from individual documents to entire archives. The Civil War did not end in one great battle but rather in a series of winding retreats in which Confederate armies gradually fell apart. This had a devastating effect on the preservation of records since the wagons loaded with books and papers were often the first to be given up when armies needed to travel light. During the Appomattox Campaign, the ten-day retreat of the Army of Northern Virginia from the trenches in Petersburg to the courthouse where Robert E. Lee surrendered, the army lost, according to one estimate, between 200 and 300 wagons carrying records. Testimonies from the campaign abound with images of papers and record books strewn along the army's path.[55] On April 11, Lee answered a request for a statement on the strength of his army right before he surrendered by saying he was unable to give one since "all company + regimental records + papers have been lost or destroyed." This was not actually true, and many papers would eventually turn up. Lee, in fact, would provide a number the following day when he wrote a report to Jefferson Davis narrating the fateful events of the previous week. Nevertheless, the destruction of entire trunks and wagons loaded with papers is an indisputable fact.[56]

State records often suffered the same fate. The military records of Arkansas were "lost or destroyed, at some point near the Red River, at the close of the war." The records of South Carolina were similarly "lost or burnt at [the] close of the war." In some states, only fragments of the records were discovered. From North Carolina, what survived of state documents were two letter books, one comprising 640 pages and one comprising 69 pages.[57] The Georgia records suffered a more peculiar fate. Henry C. Wayne, the Confederate adjutant general for the state, claimed to have adopted a "system in practice in the offices of the War Department as to recording, indorsing, indexing, filing, and boxing each year's records and papers being separately boxed with the year, in large numbers, painted on the boxes. These boxes were secured by locks and screws." Wayne insisted that at the end of the war he had turned into the hands of a Federal officer "every paper, document, and record referring to the military action of the State of Georgia beginning January 1st 1861" and was receipted for them. But by 1888, the Georgia adjutant general informed the War Department that "the records are sadly misplaced or missing, as I can not find them either in this office or among the archives of the State."[58]

The largest and most crucial repositories of Confederate records were located in Richmond, and events there, more than anywhere else, determined what would remain of the Confederacy's official record for posterity. Jefferson Davis and his cabinet abandoned the capital on the night of April 2, 1865, after learning that Lee's army had proven unable to hold its defensive line and that the U.S. army was moving on the capital. The first telegram conveying the news arrived at 10:40 a.m. and caused tremendous alarm all over town. Yet for many Confederate bureaucrats, these dire tidings did not come as a total surprise. Rumors that the government might have to abandon its seat had been circulating for weeks, and well-informed Confederate officials knew just how precarious Lee's position was. Secretary of the Navy Stephen Mallory, describing the preparations for departure that Sunday, noted that "this contingency had long been anticipated, and, to a large extent, provided for." Various departments had made some preparations for sending their records to a place of safety. A few days earlier, on March 28, William J. Bromwell, a clerk for the State Department, left Richmond with three boxes of his department's records and arrived in Danville, a tobacco town 140 miles southwest of the capital, where he located seven more boxes that had already been sent there and kept at the local women's college. These boxes included diplomatic correspondence, records of negotiations with foreign governments, papers on the operations of Confederate agents for the purchase of arms abroad, and more. Though the boxes were made of soft pine and repeatedly fell apart, he was able to transport this entire charge to Charlotte, where it remained safely hidden even after the arrival of the U.S. army.[59]

War Department staff began boxing up records in early March and sending them to Lynchburg, one of the last destinations in Virginia considered safe from enemy invasion.[60] But Robert Kean, the Confederacy's head of the Bureau of War, started packing papers in his office only after receiving Lee's telegram announcing that his lines had been broken ("labored hard all day," he remarked in his diary). By six o'clock that evening he was at the depot with the records and boarded a government train for Danville, along with hundreds of Confederate officials. Train after train left the station and, as one Confederate remembered, "[o]ne bore the archives and employees of the Treasury Department, another those of the Post Office Department, another those of the War Department."[61] Upon arrival in Danville, Kean promptly reopened the Bureau of War for business, though not for long. The Confederate government decamped from Danville on April 10 after learning that Lee had surrendered, and Kean transported the records to Charlotte, North Carolina, where they were eventually turned over to Union authorities. Kean kept special watch over two packages with particularly important documents: recent letters from the Confederacy's senior commanders to the secretary of war and reports made by bureau heads in the department late in the war. He carried these bundles on his person when he left Charlotte and brought them intact back to Virginia, where he turned them over to a Federal officer, who forwarded them to Washington.[62] The most important records of the Treasury Department, Justice Department, and Post Office Department were also transported out of the capital before the arrival of the Union army, and some were later retrieved from various locales along the government's route of escape. Judah P. Benjamin, the Confederate secretary of state, seems to have burned some particularly sensitive records, and the rest were sent out of town and eventually hidden in Washington, D.C. All in all, it is obvious that the provisions made in various departments during the long weeks of stalemate preceding

Lee's surrender paid off and ensured the survival of many valuable records.[63]

Yet it is equally clear that the hurried departure from Richmond and the ensuing retreat of the Confederate government wreaked havoc on the documentary record of the rebellion. Examples abound: Albert H. Campbell, one of the Confederacy's senior topographers, remembered placing on the night of April 2, "in charge of an engineer officer and a draughtsman upon an *archive* train bound for Raleigh, North Carolina, a box or two containing all the original maps and other archives of my office . . . This officer in charge never has reported to me the fate of this property, nor his own fate. It is supposed it was burned with the train, or pillaged, for fragments of some of the maps were reported to have been seen along that route in North Carolina." Federal archivists later determined that the records of entire War Department bureaus, like the Engineer Bureau, the Ordnance Bureau, and the Niter and Mining Bureau, though removed from the capital in time, disappeared on the road.[64]

The Treasury records, which were moved with the government's leftover specie and were thus well cared for, were also gradually dwindling, as the officer commanding the Treasury train, marching on foot through the Carolinas, "lightened ship," in his own words, by throwing away books and papers from his cargo. A. Roane, head of the Produce-Loan Office in the Treasury Department, claimed without further explanation on July 27, 1865, that "all the books, papers, and records of the office were lost or destroyed at the time of the evacuation of Richmond." At Fort Mill, North Carolina, civilians observed the destruction of "[a] great many valuable papers belonging to the Confederate States . . . large boxes were broken open at the depot and books and papers belonging to the Post office department scattered on the ground." From Greensboro through Charlotte, Fort Mill, Chester, Abbeville, and Washington, the government's path of escape from Richmond was strewn with archival wreckage.[65]

Even more spectacularly, Richmond itself was the scene of epic documentary losses during the final days of the rebellion. Government clerks began burning papers on April 2, when it became apparent that there would not be enough time to pack and send all that was left in the different departments.[66] But the fires set to destroy papers were a minor prelude to the vast fire that engulfed large parts of the city that same night. Before leaving, the Confederacy's leadership, determined to prevent its remaining military assets from falling into Federal hands, ordered the destruction of the city's bridges, military and naval stores, and tobacco and cotton warehouses. It was a catastrophically bad decision. As military authorities torched the city's warehouses and arsenals, the wind began blowing, and the fire spread across the city's business district and government buildings. Between 800 and 1,000 buildings burned, including the city's financial institutions, newspaper offices, and railroad depots. At the same time, the city's efforts to get rid of its liquor supply created a literal stream of alcohol flowing through the streets at a moment in which government authority was all but absent. The result was a drunken mob hell-bent on availing itself of stores that had been in short supply for years. As one Confederate described it to his wife, "[T]he city on Sunday night presented a horrible spectacle. Almost every store was broken into and robbed and literally sacked by men of the worst description—negroes and white men, drunk with the liquor they got (which in some places ran in a stream in the gutters)—the worst mob you ever imagined of."[67]

While Capitol Square, Virginia's seat of government, was largely spared, some key government buildings also caught fire, most critically the Mechanics' Institute, where the War Department had been housed. This accounts for many of the gaps in the records of the Confederate war effort. Among the War Department bureaus whose records were mostly or entirely consumed by the fire were the Surgeon General's Office, the Commissary General's Office, the Signal Office, the Army Intelligence Office, and the Bureau of Indian Affairs. The records of the Confederate Navy Department were also largely lost. Many fragments of these archives would eventually reappear, through the diligence of either U.S. officers who were charged with locating enemy records or individuals who were affiliated with those agencies and had kept papers elsewhere. And yet the losses of institutional archives during the tail end of the war were enormous.[68] Contemporary accounts show that this was evident while events were still in motion. Charles Page, a reporter for the *New York Tribune*, wrote that "acres of ground, and all the streets, and the very air, were thick with paper—flying in the wind, picked up by the curious, gathered in baskets by negroes; papers and letters, papers and letters everywhere." Constance Carry Harrison, a Richmond writer and avid Confederate, remembered streets lined with piles "like street-sweepings, of papers torn from the different departments' archives of our beloved Government."[69]

Records stored in buildings that survived the fire became casualties of Richmonders' new enthusiasm for memorabilia from their now defunct rebellion. Most of the records of the Treasury and State Departments were gone by the time the Federal army entered Richmond, but as an officer described it in early May, "The records and papers which were left behind were plundered by the people and by relic-hunters after occupation of the City." In the small room occupied by the clerk of the Senate, Federal officers found that the papers that were not removed "had been culled over by visitors before access to the room was prohibited. In many cases, the signatures of the different officials were found to have been torn off, as autographs or memento's."[70]

The best-documented process of archival destruction involved the papers of Jefferson Davis, which were considered a prized possession at the time and would remain in high demand for decades. Davis famously received Lee's first telegram while attending church services on the morning of April 2. His office seems to have been woefully unprepared for this eventuality. First, Davis's papers were highly disorganized to begin with. As Burton N. Harrison, his private secretary, reminded him years later, important letters arriving from the field "often remained, for months, on your own table, in the office occupied by *you* and were then generally carried by you to your house," where they were placed on "piles of other letters which had accumulated on the table in the room near your bedroom." Second, his aides seem not to have made advance preparation for a hasty departure despite the precarious military situation. Only Harrison, who had already left town on March 30 as an escort to the president's wife, Varina Davis, had packed the papers in his office. Otherwise, the boxing of Davis's presidential records only began after Lee's telegram arrived, principally by Micajah H. Clark, the chief clerk of the Executive Office, and Colonel John

Taylor Wood, a Davis aide. Clark and Wood claimed that they had packed every piece of paper they found in the Executive Mansion, but the pressure of that morning prevented them from doing so with any system.[71] The Federal officer who later captured some of the boxes remarked that papers were not endorsed or arranged, but were evidently "swept from his private desk rather hastily . . . [t]he haste and disorder in which they were packed is shown by the fact that letters of different dates and different subjects are frequently thrown together, in some cases mixed with ordinary visiting cards." Some official records were actually packed in Harrison's private trunk, which was left in the Executive Mansion after his departure.[72]

In any case, the boxes packed up at the Executive Mansion were loaded on the president's train in Richmond, unloaded in Danville during the week spent there, and then reloaded as the government continued its flight into North Carolina. After a short stay in Greensboro, what was left of the cabinet continued by wagon and horseback to Charlotte, where the fugitives received the news that General Joseph Johnston had also surrendered. At that point, even the most ardent Confederates lost hope. The cabinet and its entourage began to break up, as each officer, politician, and clerk made his own plans for getting home or leaving the country. Davis continued to Abbeville, South Carolina, where he held his last council of war and finally came to terms with the fact that his official duties were over. This meant that there was no longer any sense in traveling with a cumbersome wagon train. Davis would continue on horseback and try to leave the country, while his aides would attend to his belongings.[73]

Here, in Abbeville, began the wholesale disintegration of the presidential archive. Clark, Wood, and another aide, William Preston Johnston, set out to "reduce the trains" and therefore "opened and destroyed many unimportant papers," as Clark described it. The papers that survived were left at the home of refugees from Kentucky, in the care of a Mrs. Leovy. On their next stop in Washington, Georgia, the archive was once again divided. Davis kept some of the papers in his own valise. Clark left the trunk belonging to Burton N. Harrison in the hands of a Mrs. Robertson with whom Harrison had stayed a few days earlier when he came through town with Varina Davis. Another bundle of important letters and message books was left at the home of Colonel Armistead Burt. Clark, who was now in charge of the Treasury train, continued with the rest of the papers along with the gold to Florida, and ended up leaving them with the family of the Confederate senator David Yulee, who was staying in a farm so remote it was considered safe. The family then transferred the boxes to the home of a Unionist friend in nearby Waldo, without telling him what they contained.[74]

Each of these collections suffered a different fate. Some, like the boxes left in Waldo and the papers Davis carried in his suitcase, were captured by Federal troops and sent to Washington; Harrison would eventually have his trunk, including the Davis papers stored there, sent to him when he settled down in New York; and Jefferson and Varina Davis received the baggage left with Burt.[75] The greatest destruction was inflicted on the papers left in Abbeville. In August 1865, Micajah Clark returned to the home of Mrs. Leovy, found the papers intact, "and went through the whole of them, a work of a week, destroying all useless papers, court-martial records, applications for transfer, promotions +c+c, to reduce their bulk." While Clark saved the papers he considered important, including "every letter from Generals, Governors, Senators, +c+c.," the loss was immense.[76] Additional losses continued for years after the war. Some crucial documents, like private letters from Lee to Davis, disappeared from Harrison's trunk after it had reached New York. They were most likely retained by Charles C. Jones, an ex-Confederate colonel and historian, who had convinced Harrison to place the trunk in his custody for safekeeping and then stole its contents.[77]

Even as Davis's archive was disintegrating, Davis continued to generate written records of some import. In Danville, on April 4, he published a declaration urging Confederate citizens not to give up the fight despite the loss of the capital; two weeks later, he solicited from his cabinet members their written opinions on the proposed armistice between Confederate General Joseph E. Johnston and U.S. General William T. Sherman, which was signed on April 18 in Durham Station, North Carolina. While the circumstances of the Davis papers were particularly complicated, they were not unique. Across the vast expanse of land over which the Civil War was fought, the official record of the war effort was always being unmade even as it was being made. At any given moment, reams of paper were created to allow both sides to manage the war: forms were printed, reports written, letters endorsed, and telegrams transmitted. These documents were the engines of both war machines, as critical to their successes and failures as the guns that fired on the battlefield. Yet simultaneously papers were constantly going missing. Some were never generated to begin with, while others disappeared into the vortex of war or were lost in its long aftermath. Production, fragmentation, and dissolution took place simultaneously, molding the body of official records left behind. Generations of historians would delve into this gargantuan mass of paper, revel in its riches, and bemoan its gaping holes.

In April 1865, however, the war was only beginning to move from present to past, and official records assumed widely different meanings across the sectional divide. While Union records were stashed in the trunks of officers going home or sent for storage at the adjutant general's rooms, Confederate records were perceived as a threat to national security and evidence of treason. As the rebellion came to a close, Northern politicians and military commanders trained their eyes on the records that did survive the conflagration in the capital and the flight of the government. These documents might now offer some answers to the pressing questions of the postwar era.

CHAPTER TWO

Revenge in the Archive

THE ARCHIVE OF THE CONFEDERACY was on the minds of Federal officials from the moment it became clear that the war had finally ground to a halt. Yet initially there was no immediate plan for how to handle the archive and no clear vision of what purpose it would serve. A plan only evolved over time and was conditioned by the changing tides of the postwar era. Ultimately, the Federal repository of Confederate records would play an instrumental role in the legal and political battles that continued to rage in Washington for decades, with enormous consequences for the people involved in them and for the country as a whole.

On April 5, 1865, forty-eight hours after the U.S. army entered Richmond, Secretary of War Edwin M. Stanton issued an order to the commanding general in the conquered capital to send "immediately by special messenger . . . all papers, letters, and correspondence, private or public, found in the post-office or elsewhere at Richmond." He also sent down to Richmond his personal emissary, Assistant Secretary of War Charles A. Dana, and instructed him to supervise the collection and transmission of records to Washington. Dana complied but was skeptical about the prospect of finding anything of value. The records of the government and Congress had been removed before the evacuation, he told Stanton, "and during the firing the capitol was ransacked and the documents there were scattered." Regardless, on April 7 the adjutant general ordered all Union officers occupying Confederate locales to "collect and forward to this office any papers left behind by the rebels which may be of public use or interest."[1]

Despite War Department directives, during those early days of April, searching for Confederate records was not the first priority for U.S. forces attempting to gain control of a region wrecked by war, short on food, and reeling from the social revolution of slave emancipation. This changed on the night of April 14. Shocked and enraged, Federal officials assumed the Confederate government had been complicit in the assassination of Abraham Lincoln and set out to prove it. Suddenly, collecting government records in the South became a critically important task. On April 22, General Henry W. Halleck, who had served as the army's chief of staff during the latter part of the war, arrived in Richmond as the new commanding officer. It was hoped that his extensive administrative experience would enable him to govern the volatile Confederate capital.[2] Halleck, a master of paperwork, immediately appointed Colonel Richard D. Cutts as keeper of the public archives and ordered rooms cleared in the Custom House for storage and arrangement of "all captured papers, books, maps, and public documents." In a stern order issued by his headquarters he directed ex-Confederates, civilians, and Federal personnel to deposit any type of papers in their possession and threatened violators with arrest and imprisonment. Cutts was strictly prohibited from allowing anyone to remove material from the archive without a direct order from Halleck.[3]

Yet, as Halleck readily acknowledged, this may have been too little and too late. "[V]ery little care had been taken to secure and preserve the documents and archives of the rebel government," he wrote Stanton on May 11. "Many which had escaped the conflagration had been plundered and carried off by relic hunters." His predecessors in Richmond had not "considered the importance of preserving all official and private papers of the rebel leaders for future reference and as evidence against them and their coadjutors, here and at the North." He assumed most of what was being sent to Washington was worthless, but still hoped some documents

Custom House, Richmond, Virginia, April 1865. Courtesy of Library of Congress.

would contain "much evidence in regard to plots of assassination, incendiarism, treason, &c."[4]

Hard at work in the Custom House, Cutts shared Halleck's pessimism about the potential value of the material under his charge, calling the books and papers "merely as the debris saved and collected" since the issuance of Halleck's order. The rest had been carried off, burned, or plundered. Nevertheless, Cutts was making frequent shipments to the War Department in Washington, comprising dozens of boxes. Every possible type of state paperwork was present: correspondence, reports, returns, telegrams, requisitions, orders, scrapbooks, pamphlets, circulars, and statutes, along with financial, medical, and congressional records.[5]

Those still hoping to find incriminating evidence against the Confederate government were encouraged by the fact that seemingly relevant records were turning up all over the South. On May 14, the books and papers of the Orange and Alexandria Railroad were located in Lynchburg, Virginia, along with the private trunk of the Confederate agent George N. Sanders, who had organized a Confederate raid in Vermont and was widely believed to have been involved in Lincoln's assassination. The following day the papers of Confederate politician Robert M.T. Hunter were discovered, including an envelope, marked "confidential," with correspondence from Beverly Tucker, a Confederate envoy to Europe and Canada, who was also assumed to have played a role in the assassination. Halleck was hopeful: "[B]y comparing these papers with others of Tucker's and Sanders' additional links in the chain of evidence may be supplied."[6]

A more substantial breakthrough took place the next day, May 16, when General John M. Schofield, the commanding general in North Carolina, reported the discovery of the Confederate War Department's papers, which had been left in Charlotte by the fleeing Confederate government. Confederate officials had done their best to prevent the destruction of these records, considered "essential to the history of the struggle," and were willing to see them fall into U.S. hands if that would ensure their preservation. There are conflicting versions of how the documents were discovered—Morris C. Runyan, an officer with the 9th New Jersey Infantry Regiment, claimed he discovered them accidentally. He had been ordered to take charge of the ordnance left in Charlotte and was tipped off by a civilian about the existence of additional stores hidden somewhere in town. After some inquiries he arrived at a warehouse where he found boxes full of flags and documents. The Confederate general Joseph E. Johnston confirmed that this was indeed the War Department's archive. In an official report, Schofield offered a different account, claiming Johnston voluntarily disclosed the existence of the archive after he surrendered to William T. Sherman on April 26.[7] At any rate, Schofield's superiors seemed confident that this was what they had been waiting for. "It is very important to have the rebel War Department papers here immediately for use on the present trials," wrote Stanton. "Preserve every piece of paper, however unimportant it may appear," instructed Halleck. "We have the key to their ciphers." On May 17, Schofield forwarded to Washington eighty-one boxes weighing ten tons.[8]

Between April and July, Federal forces were able to locate a host of other records along the Confederate cabinet's route of escape: post office records in Chester, South Carolina; treasury records in Weldon, North Carolina; and a variety of other documents in Salisbury, North Carolina.[9] On June 6, Schofield dispatched to Washington "thirty-seven boxes containing records and papers of the rebel Senate, district court, and Post-Office Department." Records emerged deeper down south: From New Orleans came six boxes containing bonds, treasury notes, and the correspondence of Louisiana state officials with the Confederate government and other Southern states. The commanding officer in Macon, Georgia, forwarded the complete records of the Confederacy's Provisional Congress and records of the Treasury Department, which had been abandoned by the fleeing government in Washington, Georgia.[10] The provost marshal in Savannah sent the papers of Confederate generals Pierre G.T. Beauregard and Gideon Pillow, along with some additional records from Macon and unspecified "papers of value."[11]

Everyone involved in the search for Confederate records understood what was at stake: discovering written proof of plots and crimes that went beyond the mere act of secession and war. They held on to every lead. "The box marked 'Senate' contained a paper showing that a bill passed the rebel Senate in secret session authorizing the formation of companies for the destruction of Northern property by land and sea," wrote Schofield in a note accompanying a shipment. There was particular interest in records relating to prisons, which could serve as fodder for trials against Confederate officials who had abused Union prisoners of war, and in financial records, which could expose the Rebels' trade partners and benefactors overseas.[12]

The most tantalizing discovery of the postwar spring was the papers of Jefferson Davis. Federal forces got hold of two parts from the decomposing Davis archive: the trunk and boxes hidden in Waldo, Florida, by the Confederate senator David Yulee and the fleeing president's personal baggage. Both contained a mix of personal effects with official records. The officers who seized the baggage went through the papers, hoping to find the smoking guns the government was after. The search yielded meager results. The most important papers in the Waldo trunk, according to Israel Vodges, the commanding officer on the scene, offered the opinions of Confederate cabinet members about the terms of armistice signed by William T. Sherman and Joseph Johnston on April 18. The rest were private letters, blank note paper, and what were defined as "miscellaneous papers."[13] The papers found in Davis's private baggage were more numerous but hardly more useful for U.S. officials. They consisted mostly of the correspondence between Davis, his wife Varina, his aides, and cabinet secretaries during the last weeks of the war, all revolving around the logistics of the flight from Richmond and the breaking up of the Confederate government.[14]

Back in Washington, the absence of any useful documents was clearly aggravating the notoriously cantankerous Stanton, who was determined to locate evidence against the Confederacy's leadership for the trials then in motion of the accomplices in Lincoln's assassination. On June 25, as the Waldo trunk and boxes were making their way up the coast, he warned General Quincy Gillmore, commanding the Department of the South at Hilton Head, South Carolina, to transfer the captured Davis papers from Florida "immediately under guard, with instructions not to have them handled or inspected until turned over to the Adjutant-General. There has been great negligence, delay, and misconduct in some departments in regard to official papers, which will not be overlooked."[15] Upon reception of the containers, the War Department determined they had been "opened & ransacked," and sent Vodges a long list of questions demanding to know how they had been handled while in his custody. Vodges explained that he had opened the boxes and trunk in a private room with a couple of senior officers, examined their contents, and returned the items as they were. Vodges was confident that no papers were retained, left out, exhibited, or copied by anyone. The papers had been found "in a deranged state, apparently having been thrown in hurriedly." But knowing their importance to the War Department, he had been "particularly careful to see that all papers and effects were replaced and sent forward."[16] Stanton would suffer additional disappointments. Charleston and Columbia, two secessionist hotbeds, produced next to nothing in terms of official records, despite stringent orders stipulating a thorough search and despite the fact that historical documents of great import "literally carpeted the floors of the old Court House" in Charleston. A journalist found letters by Revolutionary generals, the official report of the 1832 nullification convention, and legal documents from the eighteenth century. Yet of the Confederate government's alleged clandestine actions no trace could be found.[17]

By mid-May it had become obvious that the sheer quantity of documents accumulating in Washington and the prospect that important information might nevertheless be hiding somewhere required a more meticulous examination than commanders in the field were able to conduct. Stanton started searching for an appropriate person to take charge of the work. His first choice was the Boston newspaper editor and lawyer Horatio Woodman, who declined, citing the "sheer impossibility to release myself from engagements." A week later Stanton approached renowned historian George Bancroft, asking to have "the benefit of your judgement in regard to those which may be useful as illustrating the history of the rebellion." Bancroft's response, if there was one, has not survived. Meanwhile, Ulysses S. Grant was lobbying for one of his subordinates, General Benjamin Alvord. Stanton, still looking for a man of letters rather than a military officer, seems to have ignored Grant's suggestion. Finally, in mid-July, he offered the job to Francis Lieber.[18]

Lieber, born in 1798, was a Prussian émigré who had arrived in the United States in 1827 after a stormy youth in Europe. As a teenager he had fought in the Napoleonic Wars and then in the Greek war of independence. Despite having been identified as a dissident and barred from most universities in Prussia, he was able to obtain a doctorate in math from the University of Jena. Yet consistent government harassment, including two prison terms, convinced him he had no future on the continent. He fled to London in 1826 and then emigrated to the United States, where he hoped to find freedom and opportunity. He tried unsuccessfully to introduce gymnastics to American schools and served as an American correspondent for German periodicals. Despite knowing next to no English when he landed on American shores, two years later he began publication of the *Encyclopedia Americana*, a local version of the highly popular

Francis Lieber, chief of the Archive Office, 1865–1867. Courtesy of Library of Congress.

German-language encyclopedia titled *Conversations-Lexikon*. The *Americana* was a commercial and critical success but did not bring about the grand prize Lieber was pining for—a professorship in a Northern university. However, in 1835 a job materialized at South Carolina College. Lieber moved with his wife Matilda to Columbia and spent more than twenty years teaching young Southern men history and political economy. Lieber's two decades in Columbia were a complicated time. On the one hand, he was intellectually productive, churning out foundational works in political science, as well as a range of shorter essays in other fields, and cementing his reputation as a leading political theorist and legal thinker. He read widely and became intimately acquainted with Southern scholars, incorporating their ideas into his work along with those of Northerners and Europeans. But he never assimilated into Southern society and experienced life in Columbia as a prolonged exile.[19]

Slavery posed a particular challenge. Lieber purchased an enslaved mother with her daughter a few months after relocating to South Carolina, justifying the purchase as a lesser evil than hiring slaves or allowing the mother and daughter to be separated by the slave market. During his time in South Carolina, he remained a slaveholder and made additional purchases of human beings. Yet he was genuinely horrified by the evils of slavery and never came to terms with his complicity in the institution or with its very existence as part of American life.[20] In 1856, Lieber left South Carolina for New York and the following year was finally able to secure a position at Columbia College as a professor of history and political science. He spent the war in New York, an ardent nationalist increasingly radicalized by the conflict. Publicly and privately, he advocated for a strong Union, Lincoln's reelection, Republican Party unity, and the prosecution of a hard but fair war.[21]

Lieber was also involved in the war effort more directly, offering the administration his opinions on some of the thornier legal challenges posed by the war, like prisoner exchange, the parole system, and guerrilla warfare. In the fall of 1862 he approached Henry W. Halleck, himself an expert on the laws of war, and suggested composing a comprehensive legal guide for the army. Lieber had met Halleck in the 1840s, and the two grew closer during the sectional crisis. In December, Halleck heeded Lieber's appeals and appointed him to a special committee charged with producing a code for the U.S. army. The result was entitled *Instructions for the Government of Armies of the United States in the Field* and was issued by Abraham Lincoln as General Orders no. 100 in April 1863. It would remain the fundamental document expounding the laws of war for the American army until the end of the conflict and for decades to come. Undergirding the code was the notion that in wartime, extraordinary means were permissible if they brought an end to hostilities. Lieber sought to bring order and system into the Union army's sprawling operations but in a way that would allow soldiers and officers to prosecute the war vigorously, regardless of the suffering inflicted on combatants and noncombatants alike.[22]

After the publication of the code, Lieber continued to furnish advice to government officials on legal questions relating to the war. In the immediate aftermath of victory, he wrote an influential opinion piece stating that ex-Confederate soldiers could be tried for treason once the state of war had concluded and they no longer enjoyed the status of prisoners on parole. On July 15, he submitted a memorandum explaining why Jefferson Davis should be tried for his crimes in civil courts rather than by a military tribunal. He argued that it would make no sense to try Davis for any specific war crime, since his fundamental crime had been committing "plain, broad, and wide treason." While other Confederate officials should stand before military tribunals for offenses like murdering prisoners of war, Davis "and a few others might with perfect propriety be singled out for trial for treason, to set a seal and stamp on secession and rebellion, and let it stand there stamped in history for future generations."[23]

Lieber's uncompromising approach toward the leaders of the rebellion may have also had something to do with the war's harrowing impact on his own family. All three of his sons had enlisted. His eldest, Oscar, had stayed in South Carolina after his parents left and became a Southern nationalist. He joined the Confederate army and died in the battle of Williamsburg in May 1862, where a second son, Norman, was fighting on the other side. A third son, Hamilton, also fought for the United States and lost an arm in the battle of Fort Donelson, in Tennessee, in February 1862. Lieber went west to look for him and, "walking through the hospitals, peering in the ambulances," experienced war for the first time as a father.[24]

This was the man who would take charge of the captured Confederate records—a radical Republican, a proponent of rigorous warfare, a grieving father, and a staunch believer in the necessity of putting secessionists on trial. As he put it at the time to a friend in Europe, he took part in the Civil War "with my whole soul, my whole mind, and my whole family." His appointment reflected the Federal government's appreciation of his scholarship and sound legal counsel. It also reflected the agenda of leading Northern politicians in the summer of 1865: finding the appropriate evidence that would enable legal action against those who had tried to break up the United States and caused the country untold suffering and loss.[25]

Lieber received news of his appointment from Stanton with mixed feelings. He had been interested in getting a government job for a while, but the position of archivist had some drawbacks. Stanton, he wrote Matilda from Washington on July 14, was "appointing me to establish a sort of bureau to classify +c +c the Rebel papers. I do not know what to say. I hate coming hither frequently." But on July 25 he accepted the appointment, including the pay of a colonel of cavalry plus an allowance for fuel and quarters. Crucially, Lieber was able to secure his son Norman, a lawyer and judge advocate in the U.S. army, a position as his assistant.[26] The order establishing the bureau that Lieber was to oversee defined its tasks as "collection, safe keeping, and publication of the Rebel Archives that have come into possession of this Government." While this broad definition obscured the government's goals for the office, the regulations published a month later made clear that the material deposited in the Archive Office was considered sensitive and possibly at risk. The adjutant general was to appoint a "vigilant guard" to protect the office "by day and night." Moreover, the orders stipulated that "the business of the office will be strictly confidential. No person, not connected with the office, will be permitted to visit it, or inspect any paper or document, without written permission." Similarly, no information from the papers in the office, or the "state or condition of the business of the office," could be advertised without written permission from the secretary of war.[27]

The Liebers and their staff began work immediately and spent a sweltering August going through the contents of 500 boxes, barrels, and hogsheads full of papers, some still covered in Richmond street dirt.[28] Lieber, the pampered academic, had a hard time. "The three weeks I spent in the hottest season in dusty, dirty Washington, in the hardest and dullest work every day from 9 to 5 without interruption are, taken all in all, perhaps the most ploughing and swetting days I have passed in my life," he wrote Halleck.[29] In mid-September he reported to Stanton that his staff had examined and classified 428 boxes, 71 barrels, and 120 mailbags. These contained a dizzying array of documentation, from the records of War Department bureaus and the papers of various field headquarters (including those of Robert E. Lee, which were thought to have been lost), to books and records from the Confederate Post Office Department and the Treasury Department, to local records of different states, courts, hospitals, arsenals, banks, and more.[30] By that point, Lieber had returned to New York, and his son Norman took charge of the work in Washington. The staff continued to search for potentially incriminating information against the Confederate government by examining the journals of the secret sessions of the Confederate Congress and the papers of Jefferson Davis, but they simultaneously worked to rein in the overall chaos by creating complete files of General Orders, organizing the papers of various Confederate bureaus, arranging battle reports, and making inventories. It was a daunting task, requiring the staff to sift through enormous quantities of paperwork in a state of "utmost confusion." There were 118 boxes and barrels of second auditor accounts, 126 others filled with quartermaster accounts, and 24 boxes of rosters and payrolls, which Lieber described as "having evidently been scattered about and collected again, many apparently swept together in the streets." In a letter to Halleck he suggested using "the bonfire as one of my archive agents."[31]

As the search for the smoking gun continued, Lieber hung on to every scrap of evidence he could find. A promising avenue was the secret operations of the Confederacy in Canada, which amounted to very little in practice but were thought to have posed a genuine threat to cities in the northernmost reaches of the United States. On September 15, he sent Judge Advocate General Joseph Holt "5 sheets of note paper, containing writing by a K.J. Stewart, a correspondent of Jeff. Davis, from Canada; showing the perfect connection of Jefferson Davis with the *raiders* c—if, indeed, this connection were not already proved."[32] The Archive Office also provided information for congressional committees investigating the abuse of U.S. prisoners of war by Confederate officials, including evidence for the trial of Major John H. Gee, commander of Salisbury Prison in North Carolina, where thousands of Union soldiers had perished—though this proved insufficient to convict Gee or to provide the basis for indictments of higher-level Confederate officials.[33]

Reading through the Confederacy's archive, Lieber found plenty of fuel for his fervent hostility toward the leaders of the rebellion. In correspondence with friends, he recounted tidbits of Confederate depravity found in its official record: the "fiendish ferocity" toward Southerners suspected of being deserters, the various plots of destruction against the North contemplated by Confederate officials, the ugly designs proposed for the Confederate flag. He railed against what he saw as Confederates' ruffianism, faithlessness, and impudence. "I do not believe that a more contemptible set of noisy bombastic mischief-makers can be found in all history," he wrote Halleck.[34] But even as he reveled in the documentation of the South's cultural and moral inferiority, Lieber was also honest about the fact that the incriminating evidence he was assigned to dig up on Davis and others simply was not there. "*Entre nous* very little of any special importance has been found," he admitted to Halleck on September 10.[35]

Lieber's official reports on the findings in the archive reflected the same truth. In May 1866 he was asked to submit to the Senate's Judiciary Committee all evidence "of a circumstantial character" that could confirm the Confederate government's complicity in Lincoln's assassination, evidence that Jefferson Davis had personally "entertained propositions to assassinate Abraham Lincoln and the most prominent men of the North," and evidence that the shady characters the Federal government had identified as working in Canada for the rebellion were indeed accredited Confederate agents.[36] Lieber had more to offer on the latter point, as the men who were trying to wreak havoc north of the border had left something of a paper trail. But evidence pertaining to the direct involvement of the government in the Lincoln assassination amounted to highly tangential communications and newspaper reports concerning the routes of the Confederate army's signal corps, which were allegedly used by John Wilkes Booth in his escape from Washington. Despite having sorted through 270,000 letters, Lieber could not tie Jefferson Davis personally to the assassination beyond showing that he had received and endorsed several letters proposing assassination schemes. There was no evidence showing that Davis or any other Confederate official ever initiated or took part in what some of their constituents were suggesting.[37]

The disappointment Lieber suffered in locating evidence against Davis as a coconspirator was compounded by the diminishing prospects for a treason trial, which at the closing of the war had seemed like a foregone conclusion and which Lieber saw as crucial to the future of the Union. At first, there were legal obstacles. Attorney General James Speed refused to bend the rules and insisted that if a trial were to take place, it would have to be by civil court and in the place where the crime was committed. But the civil courts in Virginia were still closed and it was not clear when they would open. Then there was the real possibility that holding the trial in Richmond would result in an acquittal by a Virginian jury. Lieber understood this well, predicting to Halleck that the trial "would be a terrible thing—volumes, a library of the most infernal treason will be belched forth—Davis will not be found guilty and we shall stand there as completely beaten. The time was lost and can never be recovered." This was true in more than one way. As the war began to recede into the past, enthusiasm for legal proceedings against Davis was waning among the victors too. As Cynthia Nicoletti has shown, by 1866 the tide of public opinion had begun to turn, and a variety of influential figures publicly supported freeing Davis, a fact that his lawyer adroitly exploited. The leader of the rebellion was released on bail on May 13, 1867.[38]

The political realities of early Reconstruction also weighed heavily on Lieber, who remained an unwavering radical Republican. "Our affairs here are not in as good a condition as they should be after such a great victory," he wrote a German friend in March 1866. Indeed, ex-Confederates did not perceive their defeat on the battlefield as evidence that the ideology underlying the rebellion was proven wrong. Within a few short weeks of surrender, most whites in the South were taking part in a multipronged effort to build a social order that would largely approximate a system of slavery. Though they had lost the war, they remained firmly in command of crucial resources, first and foremost the land from which Southerners of both races made a living. This simple fact enabled them to re-indenture most freedpeople and to eradicate emancipation on the ground. They combined the effort to create a pseudo-slavery on plantations with rampant violence and draconian legislation passed in statehouses, which were back in business and under the control of the same political leaders who had spearheaded the bid to create a slaveholding republic. Men of Lieber's convictions demanded that the government take assertive action, yet the executive branch was under the control of President Andrew Johnson, who had no interest in doing so. A conservative Tennessean, Johnson was the only senator from a Confederate state who rejected secession and remained loyal to the United States. He had served as the military governor of Tennessee and was selected as Abraham Lincoln's running mate in the election of 1864 to signal that the administration was open to reconciliation with Southerners who would accept the authority of the Federal government. Once in office in the aftermath of Lincoln's assassination, it became apparent that, despite the ferment of the past four years, his pro-Southern leanings had remained intact. He pursued lenient and conciliatory policies toward ex-Confederates, pardoning men in the thousands and allowing seceded states to reenter the Union with few preconditions. Though he disliked the institution of slavery, he was a firm believer in white supremacy and rejected granting civil rights or government protection to freed slaves. In a letter to Halleck, Lieber was unequivocal about the president and his impact: "Things in general stand badly, and the rebels have again their heads up like killing snakes. Johnson has revived them." The election of 1867, in which the Republican Party's radical wing took a beating, did nothing to mitigate his despair at the shifting mood in the North. "Did you observe in the papers that Beauregard was called the ex-Rebel Beauregard. Why not call every pardoned thief, an ex-thief?"[39]

Lieber was concerned that the new winds blowing in Washington would spell disaster for the huge trove of Confederate material under his charge. A detailed report he submitted to Stanton in January 1866 on the contents of the Archive Office, including some of his juicier findings about the Confederacy's malicious conduct toward its own people, was never made public. By his own account, Lieber was also denied permission to publish anything out of the information amassed in the Archive Office. Writing discreetly to Halleck, he predicted that once Stanton was replaced as secretary of war, "my archives will be dilapidated—destroyed."[40] In August 1867 he was discharged of his duties as chief of the archive, having been told that he had accomplished his goal of carefully arranging the papers, though in reality that was hardly the case (an 1880 report described the papers in the Archive Office as still unarranged and unindexed). The *Boston Daily Herald* interpreted his dismissal as the president's way of closing down the Archive Office and removing a man "whose uncompromising loyalty has long been a stumbling block" to Johnson's sinister intentions. In his parting words to the interim secretary of war, Ulysses S. Grant, whom he tried and failed to see in person before leaving Washington, Lieber warned that the time might come when the army so quickly disbanded after the war would be needed again to "protect a people's national character, their country and their liberty against 'an aggressive executive.'" To Lieber, both the archive and the republic seemed fragile and endangered by postwar fatigue, budding reconciliationism, and Republican weakness.[41]

And yet, at least as far as his fears concerned the archive, Lieber turned out to be wrong. Within a few short years of his departure, the Archive Office would become a crucial resource in the hands of the Federal government as it entered a new era of legal wrangling with ex-Confederates over property lost during the war. The trash swept from the streets of Richmond in April 1865 would turn out to be worth its weight in gold.

One feature of the Civil War's long aftermath was a fierce contest between the Federal government and thousands upon thousands of Americans who demanded compensation for financial damages they had incurred during the conflict. Most losses were rooted in the harsh realities of a prolonged land war, in which millions of U.S. soldiers fighting across the Confederate states consumed huge quantities of the goods required to sustain armies in the field and destroyed or confiscated whatever could potentially aid the Confederate war effort. At times, Federal policies were a reasonable means for winning an otherwise unwinnable war. At others, the soldiers were stunningly brutal, even sweeping away the meager property of enslaved families who happened to live on their path. As soon as it became possible, Southerners from all walks of life began approaching the Federal government demanding restitution. Applicants included men and women, Blacks and whites, freedpeople and free people, the rich and the poor. All made claims on the Federal treasury based on the same principle: civilians who had remained loyal to the United States were owed payment for property the Federal army had taken from them to supply its wartime needs.

Americans first acted on this proposition while the war was still in progress, turning to local military officials, to special military boards created for this purpose, and to congressional claims committees.[42] In 1864 Congress limited the right to file a claim to citizens of loyal states, despite the objections of border state politicians who supported their constituents' efforts to receive compensation and argued for their persistence and courage as Unionists residing in contested territory.[43]

With the end of the war, Southerners continued to press their case, appealing to every officeholder from the president down to commissary officers. As Susanna Michele Lee has shown, appeals to Congress "dominated the legislative calendar, accounting for an estimated one-half to one-third of the legislation passed in the 1860s and 1870s."[44] Another important forum for considering appeals was the Court of Claims. The court was established in 1855 as an advisory body to Congress, but owing to the pressure of wartime circumstances, it was expanded in 1863 and granted authority to adjudicate claims. It dealt mainly with demands by Southerners to receive compensation for cotton confiscated under the Abandoned and Captured Property Act, which gave the U.S. army license to seize property in the rebellious states for sale by the Treasury Department. By 1888, it had paid Southern loyalists nearly $10 million in compensation for lost cotton.[45]

Northern and Western Republicans in Congress were fiercely opposed to these payments, yet the shifting circumstances of Reconstruction soon left them little choice. The return of representatives of the former Confederate states to Congress provided a critical mass of supporters for those who had been advocating for the payment of Southern claims and convinced some Northern Republicans that they would be better off creating a mechanism for adjudicating claims while they were still in power.[46] On March 3, 1871, Congress authorized the president to appoint a three-person board of commissioners for two years to "receive, examine, and consider the justice and validity" of claims for "stores or supplies taken or furnished during the rebellion for the use of the army of the United States."[47] Its decisions would have to receive final approval from Congress, which gave Republicans some assurance that they still controlled part of the process. The creation of the board was a compromise between Democrats and Republicans, between those who did not believe in the existence of Southern Unionists and those who sought to funnel money into the South by paying as many self-proclaimed loyal Americans as possible. The three commissioners, selected by Grant, now president, were Asa Owen Aldis, who had served on the Vermont Supreme Court and as a U.S. consul at Nice; Orange Ferriss, a congressman representing New York and a fierce critic of Andrew Johnson; and James B. Howell, a lawyer, politician, and editor from the Northwest who was then filling a vacancy in the Senate and was generally unsympathetic to Southern claimants.[48]

The Southern Claims Commission (SCC) ended up considering 22,298 applications for a total of $60,258,140. While claims could be filed for two years only, the commission took an entire decade to judge them. Claimants had to prove, above all else, that they had indeed remained loyal to the United States throughout the war and were willing to tender their active support to the cause of quashing the rebellion. This was no easy task, as residence in a seceded state in and of itself was considered proof of disloyalty. Claimants provided written and oral testimonies by friends, families, and neighbors and answered detailed questionnaires about their whereabouts, sentiments, and associations during the conflict. The commission employed an exacting standard for judging loyalty and used a variety of means to discover fraudulent claims. Fifty-six percent of the claims submitted were rejected on account of disloyalty; the total sum paid to claimants amounted to less than $5 million, roughly 6 percent of what had been claimed.[49]

In addition, the United States took part in two international commissions, one for adjudicating claims by British nationals and one for settling cases with Mexico. The Mexico-U.S. commission was founded following a convention signed in July 1868 to adjudicate claims of citizens from both countries since the end of the Mexican-American War in 1848, including claims for property confiscated or destroyed during the Civil War.[50] The Mixed Commission on American and British Claims, created by treaty in May 1871, was authorized to hear cases emerging out of the war period. It heard a total of 496 cases, the vast majority of which were filed by British citizens. It ended up accepting 181 British claims, paying claimants $2 million, and rejecting all American claims. Even though the number of claims filed was minuscule compared to the volume of business handled by the SCC, the claims, many of which were filed by companies for extensive losses, brought the total sum applied for to $60 million, the same as the SCC total. With interest, it grew to a staggering $96 million.[51]

Thus, by the early 1870s, the United States government was defending itself against an avalanche of demands for payment made in multiple claims commissions, the Court of Claims, and congressional committees. Requests for reimbursement ranged from $100 for one mule taken from a farmer to millions of dollars' worth of cotton confiscated from a British trading company. Though every imaginable kind of ware had fallen prey to invading armies, the most common claims were for food, animals, cotton, and wood. Yet regardless of size or nature, the potential success of any claim hinged first and foremost on a claimant's track record of loyalty to the United States during the war.

The onset of the claims era in the Federal government's relationship with Southerners reconfigured the Archive Office and gave its work a new direction and a new meaning. Though the collection of papers lying in its rooms had failed to provide the evidence required for sensational war trials, it proved extraordinarily useful when it came to establishing the Confederate affiliation of numerous individuals, companies, and properties. Once again, archival records proved their potential to shape the relationship between winners and losers in the bitter aftermath of civil war.

Even without a new chief (Lieber was never replaced), the War Department bureaucrats entrusted with the Archive Office not only kept charge of the papers but actively encouraged the government to use them. Before the establishment of the Southern Claims

Commission, they followed debates in Congress and offered unsolicited information about claimants. In March 1869, Bezalel Wells, the chief clerk, wrote the adjutant general about a resolution that had passed the previous day in the House to pay one Blanton Duncan. "I desire to state that Mr. Duncan was a vindictive Rebel, that he raised in Kentucky a regiment for the Rebel Army, and was subsequently printer of Treasury Notes at Columbia, S.C. He manifested during the war the utmost hostility to the United States. The records of this office contain a great number of letters from him." Wells also tried to pressure the War and Treasury Departments to act on the information he found about a large piece of property, seventeen and three-quarter acres of land in Bibb County, Georgia, that had been sold to the Confederate government and was thus legally the property of the United States.[52] Additional evidence for Confederate ownership of land, factories, and railroads continued to resurface occasionally over the next decade and was forwarded to the War Department, often in an implicit attempt to coax the government into taking advantage of the spoils to which it was entitled.[53] The Court of Claims was more adept at using the War Department's files, since the attorney general and his staff, as trained lawyers, understood the value of archival evidence for legal proceedings better than congressmen did. Clerks from the Archive Office sent information upon demand and appeared occasionally in court on behalf of the government to showcase documents from their collection, duly authenticated to conform to what was defined by the court as "the ordinary rules of evidence."[54]

The establishment of the Southern Claims Commission brought a considerable increase in the business handled by the Archive Office and required a systematic working relationship between the two agencies. The three commissioners were inherently suspicious of anyone who had spent the war as a resident of the Confederacy and employed a variety of means to root out fraudulent claims. They appointed three traveling agents in 1872 to collect evidence concerning larger claims and called witnesses into oral questioning. The names of claimants were advertised in their communities to encourage accountability and to make sure claimants were willing to publicly defend their record as Unionists.[55] The SCC also took advantage of claimants' own blunders, like admitting that they had asked for a presidential pardon after the war or inadvertently providing testament to their grudging adherence to various Confederate policies. But in some ways the most important resource in the hands of the SCC was the Archive Office, with its trove of incontrovertible evidence for wartime interactions between the Confederate government and its citizenry.

As soon as claims began pouring in, the Archive Office got to work on the lists of names sent over from the commission. "A search for evidence is being rapidly pushed forward," confirmed Wells to the adjutant general in May 1871. This was highly challenging work. The volume of paper stored in the Archive Office was huge, and some records were still unsorted as late as 1879. Another problem was identifying the right individual, especially when the SCC provided only the names of claimants. "We have already sent copies of papers which, although bearing the same names as those of the claimants, did not prove to refer to them," wrote the chief clerk in June 1871. "This has arisen from our having so little to base our opinion upon as to the relevancy of the subject matter."[56] If evidence was discovered, the incriminating information was assembled on special slips, which became part of the permanent record of disbarred claims.[57] The office regularly transmitted briefs of evidence to the claims commission and often sent additional evidence discovered while searching for information on other cases.[58]

Whether working on applications pending before claims commissions, the Court of Claims, or Congress, the clerks of the Archive Office located proof of disloyalty everywhere in the sprawling record of the Confederacy. A claimant by the name of Jonas P. Levy argued he was owed $10,000 for stores confiscated by the Union army merely because he had gotten stranded in Wilmington, North Carolina, on his way to Mexico, where he had large investments. Levy swore under oath that he had never served the Confederacy nor offered aid, comfort, or information to the government or its officers, and denied ever having communicated with Confederate authorities. Yet the Archive Office had located a number of letters from Levy to various government officials, including the secretary of war, reflecting his allegiance to the Confederacy. (In one letter to the secretary of war, he asks for special permission to transport to Richmond 100 kegs of baking soda over railroads that were being used exclusively by the government, "in such quantities as you will deem prudent and not be an injury to the cause of our confederacy.") Levy denied the allegations and claimed that his signature had been forged by a one-legged clerk named Charles Miller, by then deceased. The commissioners interrogated him mercilessly, forcing him into making a clearly preposterous argument that the original letters they were showing him were written in a handwriting different from his own and telling other improbable lies about his wartime life. Albert P. Tasker, the new chief clerk of the Archive Office, testified in the hearing, certifying that the papers implicating Levy were in the boxes sent from Richmond at the end of the war. The following day, the Archive Office forwarded additional papers pertaining to Levy, though the point was already moot. The commissioners rejected his claim, calling him a "shameless traitor."[59]

Numerous other Southerners who had sworn under oath that they were fervently loyal to the United States throughout the war were confronted with documents bearing their names and demonstrating their support, or at least acceptance, of Confederate authority. Some were on record for petitioning the Confederate Congress and executive departments for various allowances or exceptions;[60] others appeared in the vast cache of quartermaster, ordnance, and commissary paperwork, selling the army necessities like fodder, rope, tents, mules, horses, corn, cattle, salt, and shoes.[61] There were those who turned up on Confederate muster rolls and those who were discovered to have subscribed to the Confederate cotton loan, one of the financial instruments used by the rebel government to raise money for the war effort.[62] Southern corporations—railroad companies, steamer lines, manufacturers—which asked for relief from the Federal government or filed claims for losses incurred were found to have played a part in the Confederate war machine by contracting with the government or receiving aid to improve their services.[63]

The high stakes involved in the claims filed by British companies made the search for information about the ties between these entities and the Confederate government a crucial task, all the more so since claimants asking for millions of dollars brazenly denied their involvement in the war. This was the case in the suit filed by both the proprietors of the firm S. Isaac, Campbell & Co., which served as one of the major suppliers of Confederate military equipment, and Thomas Stirling Begbie, a London shipowner and broker, who built and operated blockade runners.[64] The firms had sued the U.S. government for the cargo of ships seized during the war, claiming they were not headed toward the Confederacy. The Archive Office produced evidence for the relationship between these businessmen and the Confederacy: a contract between the Confederacy's European emissaries and Begbie for furnishing eight blockade-running steamers in addition to the four he had already provided, plus documentation of purchases made by the Confederacy's liaison from S. Isaac, Campbell & Co. amounting to more than a million pounds. These documents, declared Robert S. Hale, the Federal agent at the Mixed Commission on American and British Claims, saved the government "beyond question half a million of dollars & upwards in the claims of these parties." An even larger claim, for $4,415,900, was filed by an English merchant by the name of Leslie. The staff of the Archive Office, learning about the filing, presented documents showing "that he was very extensively engaged in furnishing the Rebel Govt. with supplies."[65]

Congress in the 1870s also continued reviewing large-scale claims, which now enjoyed the support of white Southern representatives, who had retaken their seats in both chambers. A particularly infamous case was that of Southern mail contractors, who had lost their jobs once the Federal government stopped providing postal services to the seceded states in 1861. Claims for compensation for services rendered before that date but left unpaid were submitted to Congress as early as 1871, and bills for payments were passed starting in January 1872.[66] The Archive Office provided proof that 1,133 claims for the same lost wages had been submitted to the Confederate Post Office Department, for a total of $773,444.17, and that the Confederate Congress had passed laws to pay them. The Archive Office was also able to produce evidence that particular states had paid mail contractors out of their own budgets.[67] The issue remained alive for over a decade as Southern congressmen continued to advocate on behalf of their constituents. On January 12, 1874, Robert Vance, a Democrat from North Carolina, introduced a bill in the House of Representatives to compensate certain mail contractors in the state. When learning about this development, the staff at the Archive Office wrote the secretary of war, reminding him that these claims had already been settled by the rebel post department. "This fact has been already reported to the Honorable Post Master General and by him to the Committee of Appropriations in the House." Always using suitably official language, but nevertheless nudging the secretary to act, they asked that he alert the relevant officials "lest this bill . . . might pass without due consideration having been given to the fact that these parties presented claims and were paid by the Confederate government."[68]

At the same time, the staff in the War Department was also aware of its own limitations. While the reports of the Confederate postmaster general showed conclusively that $564,544.22 had been paid to mail contractors, only eighteen receipts of payment to particular individuals survived. Arguing against the payment of one A.C. Crawford, who had carried mail in Mississippi before the war, the adjutant general wrote the Senate Claims Committee that Crawford had continued to carry mail for the Confederacy on the same route, "and it would seem fair to infer that his claim was paid by C.S. Govt., notwithstanding the fact that his receipt for the amount is not on file."[69] On the other hand, the archive included other useful documents for the struggle in Congress over mail contractors. In February 1878 the issue was once again up for debate when Alfred Waddell, another Democrat from North Carolina, submitted a bill along the same lines. He enjoyed enthusiastic support from none other than John C. Reagan, the Confederate postmaster general, who had returned to Congress representing Texas. Reagan testified that the United States had suspended postal operations in the South on May 31, 1861, and that the Confederacy had instructed postmasters to settle their accounts with the United States and to return the money and postage stamps still in their possession. After the debate, Representative Edwin Willits, a Republican from Michigan and an experienced prosecutor, retrieved from the Archive Office several official documents showing the Confederacy had assumed the debts of all postmasters to the United States. The highlights of his discovery were a proclamation by Reagan himself instructing postmasters to retain the money in their possession and a document showing that Reagan had personally reimbursed the contractors for their pecuniary losses. Reagan claimed he had forgotten all about the payment and tried to salvage the situation by suggesting that the bill be sent back to committee. The Archive Office saved in its files clippings from pro-Republican newspapers celebrating Reagan's humiliation and lauding the archive's great utility to the government.[70]

The vast store of Confederate paperwork was also useful for defeating claims by ex-Confederates who sought pensions from the Federal government. Pensions were big business in the late nineteenth century, as the government gradually expanded benefits to include all Civil War veterans and their widows and paid them generous monthly sums. Southerners were generally excluded from this rare display of government largesse toward needy individuals, including not only those who fought against the United States, of course, but also ex-Confederates who had served in the U.S. army before the Civil War and had received pensions prior to secession. Two thousand Southern veterans were dropped from the rolls during the war, and in its aftermath many tried to win their way back. Ex-Confederates were hardly the only ones attempting to take advantage of a generous and loosely regulated system. As Theda Skocpol has shown, while nothing certain can be said about the total number of illegitimate applications, 40 percent among claims reexamined in 1874 were found to be fraudulent, and the rate was 28 percent between 1876 and 1879.[71]

And yet claims by ex-Confederates were subjected to an investigation in the Archive Office, where the clerks searched for proof of rebel affiliation and, in many cases, found it. Caty Shaw, a ninety-four-year-old widow from New Orleans, was eliminated from the pension rolls after it was discovered that during the war she had signed a petition to the congress in Richmond asking that the Confederate government take over payment of her pension. Shaw presented a sworn testament before a clerk of the U.S. Circuit Court that "she never applied to the so-called Confederate Government for a pension in lieu of that received from the United States Government: that she never authorized anyone to make such application for her, and never expressed even a wish to do so . . . so far from it, that she always expressed herself content to wait and abide her time, feeling satisfied that it would all come right in the end, and the Federal authority re-established." She also submitted a letter of support from Frank Morey, her Republican congressman. But the clerks in the Archive Office compared her signature on the petition with the one appearing on her letter to the commissioner of pensions and found "that there is no doubt whatever as to the genuineness of the signature." Shaw, along with other signatories of the same petition, was dropped from the rolls in December 1871.[72]

Comparing signatures became a crucial tool—indeed, practically the only way to confront claimants' flat-out denials that they had ever sought payment from the government of the rebellion. Clerks in the Archive Office quickly developed an expertise in reading the handwriting of Southern individuals that had made its way into the written record. Louisa H.P. Screven, the widow of Lieutenant Colonel Richard Bedon Screven, a Georgian who had fought in the Mexican-American War and took part in the infamous removal of the Cherokee Nation known as the Trail of Tears, applied for the renewal of her pension and similarly swore that she had never signed a petition to the Confederate Congress. But she too was on record asking the Confederate secretary of war to bring her case before Congress. James H. Baker, the commissioner of pensions, asked that her signatures be compared. "She signs herself 'Louise P. Screven widow of Lt. Col. R.B. Screven 8 Infy'—In this signature the middle initial 'H' is omitted but the character of the hand writing is evidently the same," the War Department responded.[73]

Other applicants surfaced in the ubiquitous muster rolls that populated the Archive Office's rooms. Despite the frenzied process of assembling these records at the end of the war and the Confederacy's lax record-keeping practices, enough information survived to invalidate the claims of some soldiers who attempted to disavow their Confederate service.[74] In some cases, it was a close call. William F. Riley, a Tennessean, had served as a volunteer in the Mexican-American War. At first, a search for evidence of Confederate service yielded nothing. One day later, it turned out that a single muster roll of Tennessee regiments had been overlooked, and going over it, the clerks found a record of Riley's enlistment on November 1, 1861, in Jonesboro. Some claimants admitted to having served the Confederacy but argued that they had been forced to enlist, prompting the commissioner of pensions to ask for the "dates of the actual commencement of conscription in the Confederate States." The Archive Office provided the statute books of the Confederate Congress where conscription laws appeared but had trouble offering more precise information because of how little had survived from the documentation of the Confederacy's Conscription Bureau and because of the murkiness of conscription policies across the different states.[75]

Finally, the archival record of the Confederacy played a role in one additional form of postwar account-settling between loyal and disloyal states: government appointments. Once again, the clerks in the Archive Office did not simply wait to be approached by other official entities but followed government policy closely and offered information they thought had gone unnoticed or ignored. When an R.L. Hearth was nominated in early 1870 by President Ulysses S. Grant for the position of U.S. marshal for New Mexico, Bezalel Wells wrote Adjutant General Edward D. Townsend to remind him that Hearth had written "a very disloyal letter" in April 1861. "The letter is on file in this office. You have already seen it." Later that year, Wells approached Townsend about Ralph Abercombie, whom President Grant had sought to appoint as consul. "If this man is the Abercombie who was formerly of the U.S. Army, I must respectfully state that he has imposed on the President. Ralph Abercombie resigned from the Army during the war, went South and professed loyalty to the 'Confederate States.' He wrote in a letter to the Rebel authorities that he had always been opposed to Mr. Lincoln and Republicanism and that his sympathies were for the South."[76]

The best-known case of evidence from the Archive Office hampering the prospects of a candidate for government office was the nomination of the Massachusetts politician and diplomat Caleb Cushing for chief justice of the Supreme Court in 1873. Cushing's appointment encountered resistance to begin with because of his mixed record in supporting the United States and its policies during the war. In his confirmation hearing, senators spoke for and against his appointment until a document found in the Archive Office was pulled out and passed around the room. It was a letter Cushing wrote to Jefferson Davis in March 1861 recommending a friend for a position in the Confederate ordnance department, which amounted to a legitimization of the Confederacy. Cushing did not deny writing the letter but argued that he had done everything he could to stop secession and by communicating with Davis was merely recognizing an existing reality. But it was to no avail. His nomination was withdrawn, a fact celebrated by a Republican newspaper as an "escape" from a "terrible calamity."[77]

Even as the government's Confederate archive profoundly shaped the dynamics of the claims era, the impact flowed both ways. As the stash of papers lying in the Archive Office emerged as the Treasury's best and often only defense against fraudulent claims, it was reconfigured in several important ways. The documents that had been considered prize possessions during the Lieber period—the correspondence of senior figures in the Confederate government and pieces of evidence pointing to crimes and conspiracies—lost their significance. The records that mattered now were those that had been considered useless before—tedious financial paperwork and mundane communication of the Confederate government with citizens from all walks of life. Quartermaster vouchers, receipts, records of the auditors' offices, muster rolls and payrolls of otherwise nondescript units, petitions and letters to Confederate officials—all assumed a new and unexpected import. Any Southerner was potentially a claimant, regardless of what their standing was in the Confederacy. Women were as prominent as men, anonymous supply officers more valuable than celebrated battlefield leaders, and records of routine commissary purchases more useful than the annals of Gettysburg or Vicksburg. The claims era brought a new calculus to the work of preserving and mastering the Confederacy's written record.

Under these circumstances, the government now had a new motivation to expand its archival holdings and a willingness to spend large sums of money to purchase collections of papers from private parties. One major acquisition was the records of the Confederate Trans-Mississippi Department's cotton bureau, which were offered for sale by its chief clerk, J.P. Broadwell. The bureau had been established by the Confederate general Kirby Smith in 1863 in an effort to preserve the cotton left west of the Mississippi and use it to purchase military supplies in Mexico. Its head was William A. Broadwell, a cotton factor and Confederate supply officer from New Orleans, who employed his brother and left him the papers upon his death.[78] J.P. Broadwell first approached the Federal government in 1869, but only in early 1872, when the exigencies of the claims era had become evident in Washington, did efforts to buy the records get underway. The collection contained documentation of Southern cotton shipments from cities on both sides of the Mexico-U.S. border and of business dealings with scores of individuals who took part in the Confederate cotton trade. Albert P. Tasker, the chief clerk of the Archive Office, lobbied a variety of officials to move forward on the purchase, stating that "these papers properly belong to this office and would be of great money value to the Government. The few papers which we have of this character have already defeated a number of cotton cases." Broadwell had originally asked for $25,000, but by 1871 was willing to settle for $10,000. Robert S. Hale, the Federal agent dealing with British claims, urged the Treasury and War Departments to spend the money, stating that they would be "worth ten times their cost to the government."[79] In early 1873 the secretary of war finally sent Tasker down to New Orleans to examine and make an inventory of the records. Once Tasker completed his evaluation, Broadwell made a final push for a deal, telling Tasker that he would accept only $10,000 and only during the next month. "The amount named would be *small* compared with their value to *others*. It is therefore suggested that you act in this matter promptly if you desire to accomplish this acquisition to the government archives at the least expense." A month later, the commissioners of claims, who held the authority to spend congressional money on the purchase of rebel records, authorized the payment of $5,000 for the papers, which Broadwell seems to have accepted, despite his earlier warnings.[80]

While the commissioners were unwilling to spend the full amount requested by Broadwell, $5,000 still stood out as a significant sum compared to what other sellers approaching the Federal government received at the time. The new hierarchy of archival knowledge created by the claims era meant that collections of papers useful mainly for historical purposes were considered less valuable than those that might serve the different statutory and legislative bodies confronting claims. While Tasker was down in Louisiana, he also examined a collection belonging to the headquarters of the Trans-Mississippi Department and offered by an attorney in Shreveport on behalf of an anonymous client. The papers were deemed historically significant, as the Archive Office had very little documentation of the Confederacy's Western armies, but not valuable enough for defeating claims. The government was willing to pay only $2,500.[81] Likewise, when John Bell Hood, one of the Confederacy's best-known generals, offered his papers for sale in 1879, War Department staff suggested paying him $12,500 (his asking price was $20,000) even though the records were of "greater historical value" than other collections purchased during the 1870s. However, as the bureaucrats wrote Townsend, "other collections possess a value in connection with claims against the government of which the Hood collection is destitute."[82] Thus the claims era shaped the government's Confederate archive first and foremost as a legal and financial tool. As Commissioners Aldis and Ferris explained in a public letter, "[T]he vast amount of claims against the government before Congress, the departments, the Court of Claims and the Commissioners of Claims" meant it was essential to secure all "contemporary written evidence furnishing proof of the disloyalty of claimants. One can never tell what claims may be made upon the government, or from what source they may spring, and such preparation for the defence of the Treasury is, within reasonable limits, as essential as to sustain a navy or an army for the contingencies of war."[83]

The same considerations drove the government's most expensive and most notorious acquisition of Confederate papers. In the summer of 1872, the Treasury Department paid $75,000 for the rebel State Department records. The authority for spending the money was granted to the Treasury Department by Congress, which appropriated $150,000 in June 1872 "to collect captured and abandoned property of the United States, and to collect, procure, and preserve all vouchers, papers, records, and evidence."[84] The four trunks comprising the collection were originally removed from Richmond in the final days of the war by the chief clerk of the department, William J. Bromwell, who placed them in a barn outside Charlotte, where they had never been discovered by the U.S. forces hunting for records.[85] The purchase drew considerable attention for two reasons. First, the seller was John T. Pickett, a highly questionable character who had served as the Confederacy's ambassador to Mexico and done such a poor job that he ended up fleeing Mexico City. He apparently came by the papers after the Confederate secretary of state, Judah P. Benjamin, got into a dispute with Bromwell and disclosed their location to Pickett. It was never made clear what claim Pickett held to the papers and by what authority he was transacting the sale and pocketing the money, a vast sum by any standard and all the more so in the cash-poor Reconstruction South. Pickett endured the wrath of ex-Confederates, while the government met severe criticism in the press for succumbing to the demands of a former rebel and for making an unauthorized payment for property that was rightfully its own as the victor in the war.[86] The commissioners of claims, who made the final call to buy the collection, explained that it contained thousands of names of individuals who had dealings with the Confederacy and was thus indispensable for fighting claims. "Contemporary written evidence," they wrote, was sometimes the only means to determine a person's loyalty when "the lapse of time, the death of witnesses, and unwillingness to give information against one's neighbors" undermined other ways of obtaining proof.[87]

While the collection known as the "Pickett Papers" never made it physically into the Archive Office (it was retained by the Treasury Department and moved to the Library of Congress in the early twentieth century), this monumental purchase comprised an important addition to the Federal collection and characterized the government's attitude toward Confederate records as tens of thousands of claims were piling up on desks across Washington. If the government wanted to avoid paying millions to undeserving claimants, it needed to expand its holdings of Confederate records, even at considerable cost and even if doing so meant foregoing the principle that official rebel paperwork belonged to the United States just like captured Confederate warships and cannons did. At least in writing, Federal officials never explained why they were incapable of following the law and confiscating collections of Southern records they knew were available. Perhaps the same lack of political will to confront former rebels on all matters, which paved the way for the reinstatement of a slavery-like regime of oppression in the aftermath of emancipation, also limited the options of the War Department when it came to enemy records. Perhaps Federal bureaucrats feared lengthy legal proceedings that would ultimately deny the government access to the records while the pertinent cases were pending. Regardless, the result was one and the same. If ex-Confederates were determined to hold on to their records, the Treasury and War Departments had to pay up.

Another important shift brought on by the claims era was the growing politicization of archival work. The sectional character of the Archive Office was nothing new, of course. From the outset, collecting Confederate paperwork was a tool for avenging the crimes of secession and treason. Yet the public deliberations about thousands and thousands of claims, sometimes accompanied by dramatic depictions in the press of Southerners being humiliated in courtrooms by archival records, turned the very work taking place in the Archive Office into a political act. Searching for documents, verifying names, comparing signatures—all became means for the Federal government to confront the onslaught of Southern claimants and thus the efforts of those in the former Confederate states to wrest some cash from the Federal Treasury. For white Southerners and their allies in Congress, the great repository of Confederate records, the clerical force staffing it, and the professional methods developed to locate claimants in the sprawling and messy archive amounted to a sectional and partisan attack on the interests of the South.

This had been evident already by 1867, when Lieber was discharged and President Johnson was accused of attempting to shut down the Archive Office and destroy the records.[88] The growing visibility of the office's work during the 1870s ensured that it would remain a contentious issue amidst the partisan struggles raging in Washington. In 1876 the budget of the Archive Office was facing a dramatic cut that would have reduced its workforce to three copyists. Edward D. Townsend, the adjutant general, learned about the reduction from a draft of the appropriations bill recommended to the House and wrote the chairman of the Committee on Appropriations, the powerful and conservative Pennsylvania Democrat Samuel J. Randall, asking that he reconsider. Townsend described the heavy workload in the Archive Office, which required more staff, but he did so in a clearly bipartisan language, most likely to appease a staunch enemy of congressional Reconstruction: "Questions are constantly coming from the Pensions office as to soldiers who were prisoners of war and treated in Southern hospitals. Evidence is furnished as to claims. Enquiries are answered from persons North and South as to friends whose fate is unknown and as to property lost or destroyed. Questions asked in regard to military movements, resolutions of Congress go there for reply +c +c."[89]

If he received the letter, Randall must not have been impressed by the attempt to portray the Archive Office as strictly bipartisan and professional. In a House debate he supported the reduction, ignoring the claims of other congressmen about the great utility of the Archive Office in saving the government money by discrediting claims, and argued that "three copyists are quite adequate for the purpose of the government in connection with these claims and the searching of the rebel archives." He also accused the clerks in the office of receiving their salaries from two different budgetary sources and of secretly employing family members as extra help. In the end, the appropriation bill did include additional funding for the Archive Office, but the debate in Congress reaffirmed the fact that the Confederacy's archival material remained a deeply divisive issue more than a decade after Appomattox. While most white Americans had moved on from the ferment of secession and war, the clerks of the Archive Office were still busy digging up old crimes of disloyalty and refreshing Southerners' memories of their wartime careers. That had not gone unnoticed by political actors who were eager to leave the sectional conflict behind and minimize its transformative impact.[90]

In this regard, despite all that had transpired since the frantic days of April 1865, the Archive Office continued to function in the late 1870s as a repository of Confederate culpability, a weapon of the Federal government against those who had betrayed it in its moment of need. Though the Archive Office had failed to reveal the dark secrets and tantalizing scandals many were seeking at the close of the war, its records did contain abundant evidence for the warp and woof of rebellion, the small acts of treason conducted in plain sight. Even as the leaders of the rebellion never faced charges, the archive enabled the United States to settle scores with thousands of ordinary men and women who had participated in the war effort and then attempted to wipe the slate clean.

And yet, even as the material stored in the Archive Office functioned consistently as a weapon of retribution, it was never a static stockpile of papers but a dynamic, shifting body of knowledge, cast and recast through the political and legal circumstances of the postwar era. It grew in size as the Federal government began investing money in large acquisitions; its internal hierarchy changed as paperwork once thought useless turned out to be worth millions of dollars; its staff abandoned the focus on leaders of the rebellion and developed an expertise in their constituents, locating faceless men and women in the deep recesses of the archive, unearthing their histories, and verifying their identities. These transmutations created an archive fit for the demands of the claims era, a time of intense litigation involving thousands of individuals and countless documents. But the changes did not preclude other configurations of the collection, which evolved to reveal the multivalent nature of the Confederate archive, along with the broader archival interests of the United States government.

CHAPTER THREE

Archiving without an Archive

THOUGH CONFEDERATE RECORDS SERVED as an indispensable tool in the postwar legal battles between Southerners and the Federal government, it was obvious from the outset that preserving the South's written record was also part of the Federal government's broader historical mission. Even during the tense aftermath of Lincoln's assassination, when every piece of Confederate paperwork could potentially provide the government with evidence for indictments, the newly appointed Federal commander in Richmond, General Henry Halleck, ordered the careful collection of all existing Confederate papers because, regardless of their legal merit, "they will prove of great value to those who may hereafter write the history of this great rebellion."[1]

Once he became chief of the Archive Office, Francis Lieber also saw his mission as creating an archive that would serve as a historical repository rather than simply a legal tool. In his 1866 report to the Senate's Judiciary Committee, he warned that "[t]oo great precautions cannot be taken for the preservation of records which are of the last importance to the faithful history of this Rebellion." Lieber also assumed that the material he was charged with would eventually become available for scholars, telling one of his correspondents, "Whatever may ultimately be done concerning the documents in this office," once the work of arranging and registering them would be complete, "the archives will, no doubt, be open for proper use by the student of history." Acutely aware of the gaping holes in the collection, he suggested importing Confederate states' archives to Washington and assembling printed documents, Southern newspapers, and "other works, not official," which could make up for the paucity of records from military commands and government bureaus. As Lieber understood, the government had inadvertently established a national archive for the Confederacy, which would benefit from being as comprehensive as possible if it were to serve its historical purpose.[2]

At times, Lieber laid out an even grander vision for the collection, hoping it would eventually become the ultimate resource for the history of the rebellion, a "General American War Archives" rather than merely a Confederate repository, and was encouraged by the fact that the agency's name was fixed as the neutral "Archive Office of the War Department," even if in practice it was still commonly referred to as the Rebel Archives Bureau. In September 1865, the records of the United States 13th Corps were sent to the office, which both Lieber and his deputy and son Norman erroneously interpreted as an initial step in that direction. Norman followed up with a formal letter to Adjutant General Townsend suggesting that the records of the volunteer forces that made the bulk of the U.S. army in the war be handed over to his agency. The Liebers clearly saw the potential of concentrating wartime records in one place and assumed their superiors saw it too.[3]

Yet the records of United States units never arrived in the Archive Office, nor was there ever any intent to send them there. In fact, at that point in time, the idea of a central storehouse for Civil War records was entirely foreign to the Federal government's archival culture. In that sense, the United States was an outlier among up-and-coming nations in creating a centralized storehouse of records. Archives had been instrumental to the growth of Europe's nascent nation-states since the early modern period. As historian Jacob Soll puts it, "To centralize a government, one first had to identify and centralize its archives. From the Middle Ages onward, power was about the mastery of paperwork."[4] Granted, this had never been a straightforward process. It was always plagued by conflict and resistance from competing forces (clerics, merchants, and local magistrates, among others) and preexisting systems of knowledge, which hardly disappeared with the rise of the state. Yet the explosive growth of written documentation from the sixteenth century onward, combined with the expanding reach of European governments, created a new need for and a new attention to the preservation of records in a central location. King Philip II of Spain (1556–1598), also known as "The Paper King," established during his long reign what is considered the first proto-modern state archive to house the voluminous records through which he governed his enormous empire. In France in the seventeenth century, a number of powerful administrators in the royal courts of the *ancién regime* set up repositories and engineered information systems to serve the state's growing desire for control over its subjects. In locales as remote as Venice and Sweden, storage practices were being invented, archivists appointed, and records brought under one roof.[5]

The nineteenth century brought another archival boom. As modern states solidified, archives were an important tool of nation building. Revolutionary France took the lead with the establishment of the Archives Nationales in 1789, Prussia founded its state archive in 1803, and Britain set up its Public Records Office in 1838. By 1900 most European and American countries had followed suit. These new institutions served two distinct goals: they facilitated the task of administrating large territorial units by central governments, and they helped foster much-needed illusions of organic states with shared histories. National archives embodied the claims to a glorious past and the expectations for a glorious future.[6]

At the same time, these nations were also hard at work managing their expanding colonial holdings, an undertaking that relied in many ways on the gathering of information about faraway lands and the peoples inhabiting them. These monumental bodies of knowledge served state officials struggling to make sense of realities they could never quite control or even understand. They also served as the source material for self-narrations of imperial states in which the colonized and their histories were silenced or reimagined to fit the needs of colonizers. In the words of Nicholas Dirks, who studies the British rule of India, "Colonial conquest was about the production of an archive of (and for) rule. This was not an archive that was imagined as the basis for a national history, for it was only designed to reap the rewards and to tell tales of imperial interest."[7]

The growing centrality of archives as tools of state authority increased the demand for archivists and for the dissemination of their professional know-how. In 1821, France opened a professional school for archivists-paleographers, the École des Chartes, which was always conditioned by the country's shifting political circumstances but which still created a cohort of men trained in the classification and evaluation of documents who went on to serve in the nation's archival facilities. By 1841, French archivists had codified the concept of *respect de fonds*, which meant preserving documents according to the organization that had created and accumulated them. A second principle, *l'order primitif*, stipulated that documents should remain in the same order in which they had been kept before being transferred to the archive. As these ideas made their way across Europe, they solidified into the bases of modern archiving and shaped a host of increasingly professionalized state archives. In 1891, a group of Dutch archivists created the first professional organization in the field and appointed a committee to produce guidelines for record keepers across the Netherlands. The result was what has been called the *Dutch Manual*, the first attempt to systematically compile the record-keeping methods that had taken root in Europe since Napoleon.[8]

Meanwhile in the United States, chaos reigned. Despite its new status as an emerging global power, by the late nineteenth century effective mechanisms for the preservation of public documents were few and far between. This is not to say that the importance of keeping a historical record of America's past was entirely lost on its citizenry. Revolutionary-era historians like Jeremy Belknap began collecting state papers as early as 1774 and founded the Massachusetts Historical Society in 1791 in order to keep the documentary record of the struggle for independence from disappearing in private homes and disorganized government bureaus.[9] Though these efforts were moderately successful, they did not mature into consistent policies. Archiving in the different states was haphazard at best; the state historian of New York referred to local conditions as a "tragedy": important public records were intentionally burned, sold to junk dealers, or lent to private individuals never to be seen again. Some of New York City's most critical records were kept in a dungeon in City Hall and composed "about as filthy a jumble as the eye ever rested on" when finally extracted and sent for classification.[10] Another known and notable loss were the records of New York State's Bureau of Military Statistics, an agency founded during the Civil War by Governor Edwin D. Morgan to document the contribution of the then-largest state to the war effort of the United States. The bureau's chief, Lockwood Lyon Doty, was a forward-looking administrator particularly interested in the lived experience of the common soldier. He distributed a one-page form to be filled out by each soldier with information about his civilian and military history. In Doty's first year only, he distributed 125,000 forms. Yet the vast majority of these filled-out forms, along with the bureau's other records, have been lost.[11]

Southern states habitually lost records when their capitals relocated, which occurred multiple times over the first decades of statehood. But the destruction of records continued even once the seat of government had been selected. Tennessee's archival woes have been particularly well documented but are typical of Southern official record keeping more generally. Government papers were concentrated in a few rooms in the State Department, but when space ran out, they were removed and ended up in the Capitol's basement. Here, according to local historian Robert A. Halley, they "lay piled in masses on the stone floors, among old paint barrels, ashes, trash of every description, dirt and grime." Some were eventually burned because they were "wet and nasty" while others were sold as waste paper. At one time, the secretary of the Tennessee Historical Society accidentally discovered the original manuscript of Tennessee's constitution from 1796, signed by its framers, lying covered in dust in a closet. It had, in his estimate, been lying there for three or four decades. Asked what the condition of the state archives was like, he responded that he could not see how it could be worse. States in the North and South would eventually create history departments and fund public archives, but not before the twentieth century.[12]

The Federal government was equally remiss, failing to create a central repository or implement a uniform method for preserving its records even as these began to proliferate during the Civil War. (Between 1789 and 1860, the total accumulation of archives of the executive departments amounted to only 108,000 cubic feet. Between 1861 and 1916, that number grew to 923,000.) Each division, bureau, or executive department stored its own paperwork and developed its own filing system, which often simply meant having no system at all. Government papers were stored in more than one hundred different locations, which included, according to a contemporary observer, sticking them in "cellars, and subcellars, and under terraces, in attics and over porticos, in corridors and closed-up doorways, piled in heaps upon the floor, or crowded in alcoves." Others had been moved to rented structures like "abandoned car-barns, storage warehouses, deserted theatres." John Franklin Jameson, a founding father of the American historical profession, described one warehouse where the papers of the Treasury Department had been sent for storage. The records "have simply been dumped on the floor—boxes, bundles, books, loose papers—till the pile reaches well toward the ceiling; and no man knows what it contains, or could find in it any given book or paper."[13] These conditions left the records in constant danger. Fires destroyed multiple government buildings in Washington during the nineteenth century and consumed the records lying about, like those of the Revolutionary War, which were lost when the British army burned the War Department in 1814. But the country's written record also suffered from damp and dust, extreme heat, lack of ventilation, and vandalism.[14]

These facts were generally known to the powers that be. Congress occasionally allocated money for the construction of fireproof record rooms, and presidents expressed interest in the matter but did little else. In the 1870s, as department heads repeatedly complained that their offices were inundated with records they could neither destroy nor protect, Congress began to entertain plans for a central hall of records. In 1878, Quartermaster General Montgomery Meigs even drew up a plan that Secretary of War George McCrary and President Rutherford Hayes recommended, but by the beginning of the twentieth century, no actual steps had been taken by either of those branches of the Federal government.[15] At that point, the absence of a national archive had become a source of embarrassment for historians who had spent time in Europe and visited state repositories. Speaking in 1913, Charles M. Andrews, a Yale historian of early America and another fierce advocate for a national archive, called the Federal government's neglect of its records "so serious as to warrant the charge of indifference due to inferior intelligence and in this respect a ranking among the backward nations of the earth. Such a position no first-class state can long endure." Despite historians' appeals to popular jingoistic sentiments, it would take another two decades before a feasible program for a national archive got off the ground.[16]

Civil War records were in better shape than most, since the War Department concentrated many of its records under the aegis of the adjutant general. Even so, each bureau of the War Department (quartermaster, ordnance, engineer, paymaster, surgeon, signal) managed its own wartime paperwork, while other related records belonged to the collections of the Treasury, Navy, State, and Post Office Departments. In line with standard professional practice in the Federal government, Civil War records needed for daily consultation were kept within reach, while others were scattered in buildings all over Washington and beyond. Regardless of where they were situated, they were in constant danger of being burned, lost, or broken up into fragments.[17] This applied even to rare and expensive wartime documentation, like the collection of roughly 4,000 negatives purchased for $25,000 from the renowned photographer Mathew Brady in 1875. Three years later, a War Department bureaucrat noted they were "fast going to disintegration for want of a care that, for lack of the proper means, cannot be bestowed upon them. At present there is not even space for their proper storage." Despite these warnings, negatives from the collection kept breaking and disappearing over time.[18]

Confederate records, ironically, were better preserved, centralized as they were in one repository and supervised by a devoted staff that did its best to stave off demands by other government entities to receive parts of the collection and kept a detailed log of documents on loan. In one exchange revolving around a request to remove the records of U.S. prisoners who died in the South from the Archive Office to the relevant division in the Adjutant General's Office, chief clerk Albert P. Tasker refused to set a precedent for breaking up the collection and added on the margins of his official response: "It is my own belief that the importance of keeping these records together cannot be over-estimated."[19] Yet even these valued records were exposed to the same dangers as other archives were. As early as November 1865, Norman Lieber warned that despite his best efforts, the material in the Archive Office was vulnerable to fire or theft. The previous night he had discovered that some papers had been eaten by mice. Lieber suggested moving the most important documents into safes and strengthening the floors in the building, but with little success. Over the years, other custodians of the Archive Office complained of leaky roofs and of water entering the storage rooms during storms. But in nineteenth-century Washington, adequate facilities to preserve papers safely were few and far between. Most of the time, the vigilance of bureaucrats and dumb luck were the only safeguard against the destruction of records.[20]

Under these circumstances, archival losses in Civil War records were inevitable. A particularly well-documented case involves the records of the Freedmen's Bureau, a vital source on the history of African Americans, emancipation, and Reconstruction. Founded in 1865 by Congress under the title Bureau of Refugees, Freedmen, and Abandoned Lands, it was a pathbreaking institution in American governance, devoted to providing relief to impoverished Southerners of both races and to easing the transition from a slave society to one based on freedom for all. Its work touched on all aspects of African American life, and its agents often served as the only shield for freedpeople from the wrath and abuse of their former enslavers. A welfare agency sympathetic to the needs of Black people, it was always an awkward fit with America's racist and individualist political culture. By the early 1870s it had run out of friends in Congress and the Federal government and, on June 10, 1872, was formally abolished. The last few months of the bureau's life were grim; aggressive defunding left it with only a skeletal staff, and Commissioner Oliver O. Howard had been sent to Arizona by the secretary of war on an unrelated peace mission with Native Americans. Howard was gone for months and had little control of the affairs in the bureau or over the decision by Congress to close it down. In a rush to speed up the process, lawmakers set the date of July 1, 1872, for transferring the bureau's responsibilities and attendant records to the Adjutant General's Office, leaving little time for preparation.[21]

Transferring records in Washington was always potentially catastrophic for the integrity of archival collections. Waldo G. Leland, a future president of the American Archival Association, offered a bleak picture of what happened to records once in motion. As government offices were abolished and new ones created, their records "have been transferred from one department to another, their functions have been modified or redistributed, and while in theory and law the records have followed the office or the function, they have in practice frequently failed to do so, and in some instances have been lost sight of for years, or even appear to have dropped out of existence altogether." Among the medical records of the army, for example, other archivists found many "in disorder" that appeared to be "fragments of files . . . It appears also that the contents of a number of the boxes were spilled at one time or another, probably in the course of moves, and put back in no order."[22]

This was more or less what happened to the crucially important records of the Freedmen's Bureau, a loss historians are still mourning today. What exactly went wrong is hard to determine, since officials from the bureau and the Adjutant General's Office offered sharply different accounts of the same events. An initial disagreement centered on the state of the bureau's records before they were moved. Assistant Adjutant General Thomas M. Vincent painted an unflattering picture of the archive he inherited: "[t]he books and files of the different offices being promiscuously intermingled, the desks full of papers belonging to the files, and the files themselves in general disorder." Papers from different states, times, and divisions of the bureau were thrown together, with no system of reference and no account of actions taken. Some records were entirely missing, and Vincent raised the possibility that assistant commissioners and agents had taken them home against orders when discharged from duty. He also expressed open suspicion that soldiers claiming money from the Freedmen's Bureau were "defrauded, extensively," by agents, and highlighted minor irregularities in the bureau's accounting as proof. As far as Vincent was concerned, the state of the records bespoke a poorly run, most likely corrupt agency, which he was now charged with putting in order.[23]

Howard responded to these allegations with a searing rebuke, claiming that his office was "always arranged in the most systematic order," as were the papers of the different divisions, which he claimed to have inspected "almost daily." Whatever confusion could be found in the papers resulted from circumstances beyond the bureau's control. Local agents were unable to keep systematic records because of the peripatetic nature of their work. Going "from place to place," they did "what they could to ameliorate the condition of the slaves set free. Many were wounded, some were killed. Their records were letters to me, which are on file; they often made no others." Then came the bureau's defunding, which left only enough clerks to "receive and answer important communications," leaving other business to accumulate. Howard also defended his chief disbursing officer, General George G. Balloch, against Vincent's charges of corruption, declaring that he had run a "well kept" office and employed "diligent and able clerks." Whatever disorder there was in the disbursed records, Howard claimed, was the result of the recent appointment of inexperienced clerks who had not been part of the bureau's staff over the years and were not familiar with its work.[24]

Then there was the actual handover. According to the agreed upon plan, records were due to be transferred from Howard University to their new home in a building near the War Department on the corner of F and 17th Streets on June 28. In hindsight, it seems clear that the stage was set for a debacle. No one seemed to know which agency was in charge of the process, and even Howard admitted that his own clerks, mostly students at the school, were "irritated and disappointed, having been suddenly cut off from government employment, and, as it seemed to them, treated as if in disgrace." But Howard placed most of the blame on the messengers, laborers, and clerks that Vincent had sent to pick up the archives. "Books and papers were taken with little regard to order, and tumbled into carts. We picked up important papers *en route* to the new office, and books were found on the stairs and on the ground." Once the records were in transit, Howard added, they were stolen or destroyed, or they simply vanished. In his autobiography, he added that the adjutant general's clerks burned what they considered unimportant records before they were properly arranged and that other records were missing because they did not reach Washington from the South.[25]

Vincent vehemently rejected Howard's narrative of the move, arguing that except for one clerk, his staff was not even present during that first day and that once his office took charge of the work, it was executed carefully over the course of a few weeks.[26] The two agencies even disagreed on how the material was packed. Howard claimed that "the men employed by the War Department remov[ed] the books and papers loosely in baskets and wagons instead of tying up and labeling each set separately when taken from the file-cases." Vincent's chief clerk responded that he had secured specially made boxes and high-quality baskets for the move and that cases were removed without disturbing their contents; record books were appropriately labeled, and bundles of papers were "secured with gun bands or twine, and these bundles were tied together with strong cord in packages convenient for packing."[27]

Yet even as the sparring between Howard and Vincent reached the specifics of whether twine was used or not, the state of the Freedmen's Bureau records clearly embodied the larger issues behind the closing of the groundbreaking agency that stood as the hallmark of the Federal commitment to freedpeople. Howard's response to the accusations hurled at him by Vincent revealed that he recognized the dangerous potential of record keeping to inflict damage on his reputation in the volatile political climate of Reconstruction. The bureau had been defunded and abolished despite his pleas to Congress for another appropriation, and after it closed, he was repeatedly barred from access to its records. "Any ordinary business man would be troubled at a sudden transfer of all his papers and accounts into new hands," he wrote. "Much worse it is for me. I had hoped to be permitted to put my own office into shape, but neither the appropriation was granted, nor the permission given me to do so." Howard suspected that Secretary of War William W. Belknap was personally hostile to him and to the mission of his bureau, and he defined as "unfriendly" the way he had been treated by Congress. "It seemed to me at this time that there must be some concerted plan to treat my office with contempt, and bring it into disgrace." The chief clerk of the bureau, John H. Cook, who wrote his own account of the transfer, told how Howard had been anxious about being unable to secure an appropriation that would have allowed him to leave the records "in such condition as that the history of its entire work might be intelligible on the most casual examination." He also recounted Howard's "signal failure to secure either sympathy or interest, or to obtain the necessary money for the purpose." In a letter directed at Howard, he invoked "the frequent expressions of fear on the part of your friends that eventually you would be severely criticised, censured, and placed in an unenviable light before the country for not having done what you were prevented from doing."[28]

And so he was. As he worked to sort out the Freedmen Bureau's archives, Assistant Adjutant General Vincent did not let go of the matter and repeatedly brought up the possibility that Howard was responsible for the missing funds in the bureau's accounts. In December 1873, Secretary of War Belknap reported the department's suspicions of Howard to the House of Representatives, which authorized President Grant to appoint a court of inquiry to investigate the charges, including gross financial mismanagement and the transfer of "confused and incomplete records." After long deliberations Howard was found "not guilty upon legal, technical, or moral responsibility, in any of the offenses charged." It was a gratifying result for Howard and his former subordinates, but for the records lost or destroyed during the move, it was too late.[29]

The saga of the Freedmen's Bureau lays bare two important facts. First, in the absence of a central archive, records are vulnerable. The importance of the bureau's documentation was never in doubt, both as evidence of its unique work and as a record of the millions of dollars paid in bounties to African American soldiers. Yet this was not enough to ensure the collection's safety and integrity. Second, archiving was used as a political tool in the intense power struggles of the postwar era. By 1872, Howard knew enough about Washington to surmise that any irregularities in the records of the bureau would come back to haunt him. He and his staff had been vilified and denigrated at every turn by white Southerners and Northern Democrats, and the bureau's future was always in doubt. A meticulously kept archive could shield Howard from accusations of corruption and overspending and would leave a transcript of the great undertaking to bring freedom south. That is why he fought to regain access to his records and felt such frustration at the insistence of Congress that he could not. In the heat of Reconstruction, archival losses turned out to be as meaningful as archival finds had been at the end of the war.

The same dangers that lurked in Washington also jeopardized the multitudes of records that never made it into the capital. Though General Order no. 60, issued on April 7, 1865, stipulated that all military records should be forwarded immediately to the adjutant general, officials on all levels carried their personal archives home when discharged from duty.[30] Even Secretary of War Edwin M. Stanton disregarded his own order and, according to a War Department official, "took with him a great many official papers, relating to the operations of the Department and armies in the field," of which no copies existed and which were sorely needed by the government in the years after the war.[31]

With records scattered all around the country in homes, offices, hotels, and military bases, losses occurred on a regular basis. General Philip Sheridan, who claimed to have kept "a very full set of retained papers," lost all of them in the burning of his headquarters in Chicago, "blotting out at once all the correspondence that he preserved between himself and Corps and Division commanders." General Arthur Ducat, though a renowned expert on fire prevention, also lost his wartime documents to the Chicago fire of 1871.[32] The same year, General John Pope claimed to have lost his record books to a fire in the Lindell Hotel in St. Louis, Missouri, where they had been kept in a safe.[33] Other officers recounted documents that "disappeared somewhat mysteriously," were "lost or destroyed," and were "lost, or stolen" over the years.[34] William T. Sherman, who stayed in active military service after the war, made sure to move his records as he changed headquarters, but even that was no guarantee of their safekeeping. On one occasion he was unable to locate a particular report in which he criticized his superior officers for their actions during the siege of Corinth in 1862. Sherman had left the report along with some other papers in his private office in 1869 and never saw them again, "though every effort has been made to find them." He strongly suspected they had been purloined.[35]

While many of these losses would become known only gradually, by 1874 even the most historically oblivious policy makers in Washington realized that proactive measures were required to prevent irreparable damage to the written record of the Civil War. The plan Congress settled on to avoid this calamity was publishing a comprehensive collection of contemporary documents from both sides of the sectional divide. Publishing original documents was a time-honored tradition in America, which often made up for the dearth of public archives and also made the records accessible to a broader public who could not travel to brick-and-mortar facilities anyway. It was also in step with similar projects undertaken at the time by other nations and for similar purposes.

Like archival preservation, the publication of state records in America dated back to the onset of the Revolutionary War. In 1774, Ebenezer Hazard, an antiquarian, bookseller, and future postmaster general, devised a plan to publish a compilation documenting the colonies; with some funding from Congress two volumes eventually came out in the 1790s.[36] In the early nineteenth century, the United States was swept by what one historian has called "documania." One hundred and ten historical societies were founded during this period, and most devoted their efforts to publishing original documents. Meanwhile, Congress contracted with several editors and funded substantial projects of historical publication, among them the twelve-volume *State Papers and Public Documents*, published in 1819 by Thomas B. Wait; the twelve-volume *Diplomatic Correspondence of the American Revolution*, published in 1829 by Jared Sparks; the thirty-eight-volume *American State Papers*, containing legislative and executive documents of Congress and spanning the years 1789 to 1832, published between 1831 and 1861 by a private party but with active editorial involvement of congressional staff; and the nine-volume *American Archives*, a documentary history of the Revolutionary era, which was supposed to be a much larger project but was never completed.[37]

The increasing involvement of Congress in sizeable and expensive publication projects opened the door to widespread overspending and fraud, which drew enough public scrutiny to force action. In 1852 lawmakers appointed a superintendent for public printing, who was supposed to oversee all contracts and publication processes, but when even that turned out to be an insufficient means to stem the tide of corruption, Congress took charge of the whole process in 1860. In March 1861 the Government Printing Office in Washington was opened under the leadership of John Dougherty Defrees, a printer and newspaper publisher from Indiana. Thus, even in the absence of a national archive, the Federal government did employ a mechanism for preservation through publication and had a decades-old habit of investing public money in historical collections.[38]

In that sense, the United States partook in a trend common among nineteenth-century nation-states, who used a range of publication projects as another means of forging national narratives to promote unity and a sense of shared national goals. As Oz Frankel has shown, the British Parliament also published extensive records of its deliberations, as well as a range of investigative reports and documentary projects meant to represent the country to its subjects but also to create monuments in print for the government itself.[39] Outside the English-speaking world, The *Monumenta Germaniae Historica* began publication in 1826, at the initiative of a Prussian minister with the motto "The Holy Love of the Fatherland Gives Encouragement." The medieval laws of Norway were published starting in 1846, a project approved by Parliament, and the *Monumenta Hungariae Historia* began publication in 1857.[40] In one congressional discussion about publishing Civil War records, Senator Charles Sumner mentioned that the French emperor Napoleon III had commissioned a collection of his uncle's writings, which was meant to include "every scrap, military, diplomatic, or personal, which can be found proceeding from the late Emperor of France, the first Napoleon." The work was edited by a special committee composed of the "first men" of France, Sumner added, and "if we shall undertake our work, I think we ought certainly to do as well by it as the Emperor of France does by the work of his uncle." In an age of fierce national competition, a well-made historical series was seen as reflecting a government's aptitude and the importance it assigned to its founders.[41]

Europe's expanding nation-states were also intimately involved in large-scale publication projects undertaken by academic institutions, like the *Corpus Inscriptionum Latinarum*, initiated in 1853 by the Prussian Academy of Sciences in Berlin, and the *Carte du Ciel*, launched in 1887 by an international congress hosted at the Paris Observatory. The first was a compilation of 180,000 Latin inscriptions, collected from the entire territory of the ancient Roman empire; the second was a set of 20,000 photographic plates of the night sky as captured by eighteen observatories. Both took decades to complete and occupied teams of scholars working within state-sponsored institutions. Both, as Lorraine Daston has shown, were monumental archiving projects, which "proudly took their place among the other monuments, including temple-like national museums and libraries, erected to prove the superiority of the self-proclaimed *nations civilisées* or *Kulturnationen* to other cultures far away and long ago."[42]

Closer to home, the leaders of the women's rights movement also embarked on an ambitious historical venture in an effort to shape the legacy of their struggle. By 1876 that struggle was a generation old, beset by internal strife, and facing a hostile public climate. As a response, Elizabeth Cady Stanton, Susan B. Anthony, and their collaborator Matilda Joslyn Gage began collecting material for a work that would end up comprising five 1,000-page volumes under the title *History of Woman's Suffrage*. The compilation was a portable archive, explicitly aimed at compensating for the absence of state repositories and for the marginalization of women in the historical documentation that did exist. The editors loaded the volumes with all manner of original documents to amplify its appeal as an "arsenal of facts," creating an extraordinarily rich source that impressed even some enemies of women's suffrage. As Lisa Tetrault points out, deeming women's history worthy of preservation and publication was a deeply radical proposition, perhaps no less so than women's suffrage. Yet for all its uniqueness, it was also very much in step with the prevailing habit of editing and publishing original sources as a form of shaping public perceptions of events present and past.[43]

The notion that Civil War records should be selected, arranged, and made publicly available was also rooted in the huge accumulation of information during the war and the new challenges that accumulation posed. Attempts to gather and systematize wartime paperwork got their start in the Medical Department early on. The surgeon general, William Hammond, began overhauling his record-keeping system as soon as he assumed his post in April 1862, and his successor, Joseph K. Barnes, continued improving on it by expanding and transforming reporting from the field. These records included, among others, numerical reports of wounds, accidents, injuries, and surgical diseases, submitted monthly and after every military engagement; quarterly reports of the wounded, surgical operations, and sanitary conditions, as well as extracts from case books; and reports and essays on new methods of treatment, innovations in surgery, and new modes for transporting the soldiers in ambulances. By the end of the war, as Assistant Surgeon General J.J. Woodward put it, the extent of materials received from medical personnel was "simply enormous . . . the accumulation of a mass of facts and observations in military surgery of unprecedented magnitude."[44] The records were not only voluminous but remarkably useful. As Shauna Devine has shown, the detailed reporting by doctors in the field and the centralized collection and processing of medical information transformed American medicine in real time and dramatically improved the care offered to sick and wounded soldiers.[45] The next logical step, as Barnes put it, "in justice to humanity and to the national credit," was to make this vast trove of information permanently available to the public. Plans for a *Medical and Surgical History of the War* were announced as early as June 1862, and the first of six volumes came out in 1870 in 5,000 copies, with funding from Congress.[46]

A similar initiative got underway for military records in November 1863, when Henry W. Halleck, then in his position as general in chief of the army, recommended that all official documents and reports received by the War Department since the outset of the war be collected and published in chronological order. Halleck seems to have struggled in making his annual report to the secretary of war and was frustrated by the gaps and errors he discovered. Some documentation of military engagements was entirely missing, while other records were present and even published by Congress, "but they are so incorrectly printed and badly arranged as to be almost useless as historical documents."[47] Halleck would know. Not only was he a master military bureaucrat, but his background in archival work was much deeper. As secretary of state in California after the Mexican-American War, he devoted himself to collecting all available land records in the state so the new government could determine land ownership in the transition from Mexican to American rule. Congress printed 100,000 copies of his report, and the collection he assembled became the first archive in California. He continued to do research in land records as a lawyer in private practice, with great success.[48]

Halleck's proposition was well received by both chambers of Congress. On April 21, 1864, Senator Henry Wilson, a prominent radical Republican from Massachusetts serving as chairman of the Senate Committee on Military Affairs, brought a resolution stipulating that "it is to be the duty of the Secretary of War under this resolution to transmit, from time to time, to the Superintendent of Public Printing, copies of all official reports, and of all telegrams and dispatches . . . relating to the movements, engagements, and operations generally, of the armies of the United States." The documents were to be arranged chronologically with titles indicating to which engagement they pertained. After some deliberations in the House and discussions with John Defrees, the public printer, it was agreed to add a complete index and to limit the number of pages in each volume to 800.[49] The actual work of locating and arranging the documents was entrusted to Edward D. Townsend, the assistant adjutant general. Townsend reported in October 1864 that the work was progressing, but failed to note that the volumes his office was producing were rather far removed from what Congress had asked for. He selected only reports by commanding officers, the most easily available records, and left correspondence for later volumes. The documents were riddled with errors, and the indices that were considered essential to make the volumes usable were never produced. When Defrees received the first eight volumes, he refused to print them.[50]

Though there was broad agreement that publishing military records was a sound idea both for the army's professional needs and for historical reasons, the crush of events during the last year of the war set it aside. With the end of hostilities, the issue resurfaced and Congress took it up in May 1866. First, there were the treasures of the Archive Office. While Lieber, to his great frustration, was not allowed to print any of his findings, the orders establishing the agency defined its role as "the collection, safe keeping and publication of the Rebel Archives that have come into possession of this government," and according to an internal report composed by the staff of the Archive Office, the storage and examination of the records was done "with a view of their classification for reference and publication."[51] As Lieber's staff was hard at work, Senator Wilson, still chairman of the Military Affairs Committee and still interested in the publication project, brought up a new resolution. Wilson acknowledged that the effort undertaken in 1864 had failed and that the current volumes assembled by the War Department were "very defective indeed." But that was no reason to give up, especially now that the war had concluded the way it did. In the aftermath of the Union's great victory, the "proud record" of its armies needed to be made public. Wilson, who would go on to publish a three-volume magnum opus on the history of slavery, considered the project as a politician as well as a scholar. He made the critical editorial suggestion to publish records according to context rather than according to type: "All the public papers and telegraphic dispatches and reports in regard to it—should all go together because they illustrate each other." He also stressed the importance of producing a well-made compilation: "[I]f the work is to be of real historical value, if it is to be any credit to the country," it had to be published "in a compact, convenient, and permanent form of what may be termed the official military history of the rebellion."[52]

Unlike the discussion in 1864, which was brief and did not arouse serious objections, this time senators were not as easily convinced. Neither Wilson's passionate arguments for the project nor his estimates of cost, length, and feasibility were taken for granted. The idea of publishing every paper pertaining to the war, as stipulated by the 1864 decision, seemed absurd now that it was over. "Everybody can see," said Senator William Fessenden of Maine, that the current plan "will go to an interminable length, and that we shall be publishing a vast amount of material that is not of the slightest use in the world." Senator Charles Sumner brought up the sore topic of *American Archives*, the congressionally funded series that was supposed to offer a comprehensive documentary history of the Revolutionary War but never went beyond 1776. The crux of the matter, senators agreed that day, was finding the right editor, someone who would take the vast mass of paper lying about in Washington and make a coherent and serviceable collection by selecting, arranging, and indexing the most relevant papers. But they were skeptical that such a man even existed. "Who is the competent man?" asked Sumner. "I do not know him. I dare say he would come to light, perhaps, if we went about with a candle after him."[53]

Another question the senators pondered that day was the publication of Confederate records, which the original resolution, passed in 1864, obviously did not include. Though Wilson spoke of the project as a monument to victory, as the debate moved into the specifics of what should be printed and how, senators displayed an interest in publishing the Confederate records assembled in Washington along with those generated by the United States. Senator Fessenden suggested that "all that we have of the confederate documents on the same subjects ought to be printed in juxtaposition, so that the whole subject-matter might be seen," a suggestion to which Wilson readily agreed. Though this was a majority-Republican, fiercely anti-Southern chamber, its members assumed the role of publishers and consciously chose to make public the written record of an enemy government for the sake of creating a usable historical compilation.[54]

Perhaps because they now had a better grasp of the project's actual scope, the senators agreed to send the resolution back to committee and work out a better plan before advancing any legislation. In late July, Congress passed a joint resolution ordering the secretary of war to appoint a "competent person" to prepare a plan for publication and an estimate of its cost. The resolution made no mention of Confederate records and referred only to the "official documents relating to the rebellion and the operations of the Army of the United States." But this was ultimately of little importance. Though a compiler was named—Peter H. Watson, a former assistant secretary of war—he never actually filled the position, and his appointment expired in 1868 without any progress having been made.[55]

This is where matters stood for a few years. In his annual reports as secretary of war, William W. Belknap, who served in this role between 1869 and 1876, repeatedly asked for funding to embark on the project, but none was forthcoming. Finally, in June 1874, Congress allocated $15,000 in an amendment to a sundry civil expenses bill, to "begin the publications of the official records of the war of the rebellion, both of the Union and of the confederate armies."[56] The decision by Congress to finally spend some money on the project after dragging its feet for a decade seems to have been made for a combination of reasons. First, veterans' organizations like the Loyal Legion and the Grand Army of the Republic had lobbied the War Department and Congress, where they found receptive ears among a host of veterans in influential positions, like Secretary Belknap and Congressman James A. Garfield of Ohio.[57] Second, a growing awareness of the passage of time and the dangers to the papers in their present condition created a sense of urgency that had not existed before. As Congressman John Coburn of Indiana put it, the records were "in buildings where they are liable any day to be destroyed by fire or other accident; they are liable to be abstracted or lost." Congressmen also seem to have been convinced by Townsend's appearance before the Committee on Military Affairs, where he claimed that a large part of the documents had already been copied and were ready for publication.[58]

Archiving governmental records and publishing them in curated volumes were hardly the same thing, of course. In fact, storing records in the original order in which they came into being is very much the opposite of selecting certain documents and placing them in a new context created by an editor. Yet both projects for preserving records—storing and printing—served the same goals. Both ensured that the written record of the war would not disappear. Moreover, both answered a widespread demand for a truthful recounting of the events that had touched, disrupted, and remade millions of lives. In the long Civil War era, both the raw records stored pell-mell and the neatly bound volumes that would eventually come off the press were the means with which numerous Americans contended with the legacy of the war.

CHAPTER FOUR

Official Records and the Search for Truth

OFFICIAL RECORDS PERVADED the public landscapes of Civil War America. Throughout the war, newspapers on both sides regularly ran copies of reports, orders, dispatches, and telegrams culled from the armies' sprawling communication networks. Readers were accustomed to consuming information about the war through original documents, sometimes penned by the war's main actors, sometimes by obscure officers and adjutants. The predilection for records as a form of knowledge about wartime events was undoubtedly part and parcel of a broader turn toward realism in American culture and the growing demand for unmediated facts as a means of accessing reality. These changes were expressed in many different forms, including the growing prominence of science in public discourse, the rising popularity of journalistic reporting, and the advent of realistic fiction. As David Shi puts it, "Realists of all sorts—scientists, philosophers, writers, artists, architects, and tastemakers—muscled their way onto center stage of American culture and brusquely pushed aside the genteel timidities, romantic excesses, and transcendental idealism then governing affairs of the mind. By the end of the century, the various reality-seeking systems of discourse and artistic expression seemed triumphant."[1]

But the prevalence of original documents on the pages of the nation's numerous organs was also specific to the nature of the sectional conflict and its highly frenzied news culture. In the motley mix of facts, rumor, and guesswork that made up a Civil War paper, official records, printed in their original form, stood out as seemingly rock-solid sources for reliable knowledge about the progress of a vast, sprawling, and often incoherent conflict. At a time of overwhelming uncertainty, they seemed to offer the most precious of commodities: the truth.[2]

Publishers looking to turn a profit identified this need and acted accordingly. In the fall of 1861, New York's G.P. Putnam began issuing what would become an eleven-volume series named *The Rebellion Record: A Diary of American Events*, edited by journalist Frank Moore. An assortment of fiction and nonfiction, each 800-plus-page volume contained scores of battlefield reports, political speeches, legislative acts, and proclamations. Moore vowed to furnish readers with "a Digest of all verifiable FACTS; accurate copies of all essential documents, and a reliable transcript of all notable and picturesque INCIDENTS." As Alice Fahs has remarked, the *Rebellion Record* "reflected Victorian optimism that the war could be made, quite literally, legible if enough 'facts' connected with it were gathered together."[3]

The Federal government, which had been in the business of publishing documentary collections for decades, disseminated a variety of texts throughout the war to meet public demand for evidence-based information. These included a compilation on the highly controversial subject of prisoner exchange, a report by General George B. McClellan on his equally controversial tenure commanding the Army of the Potomac, and an account by the judge advocate general on the execution by Confederate forces of United States soldiers from North Carolina. Commissioned and published by Congress, these were hefty anthologies running to dozens and at times hundreds of pages and encompassing a wide variety of original documents from the files of executive departments.[4]

Publishing documents also figured in the political warfare of the early postwar period when the Republican Party in Congress and President Andrew Johnson jockeyed for control of Reconstruction policies in the South. In 1866 Congress put out two volumes of military correspondence gathered by the Joint Committee on the Conduct of the War, an ad hoc congressional body that was often at odds with the Lincoln administration. The committee had held hearings during the conflict and had published its proceedings, but the two supplemental volumes, no longer necessary for congressional oversight, were issued for no other reason than contributing to the historical record. Roughly at the same time, Congress printed and distributed tens of thousands of copies of a report written by General Carl Schurz of the U.S. army on the situation in the former Confederate states. Schurz had been sent south by President Johnson, but when Johnson realized the condemnatory nature of the report and Schurz's support for assertive government action, he asked Schurz to keep it to himself. The printing and circulation of the report was an act of defiance by a radicalized Congress, but one that would not have made any sense in the absence of an audience eager to read a lengthy report.[5]

Yet the thirst for official records could hardly be quenched by what Congress or the War Department chose to print and distribute. In the aftermath of the war, Americans laid claim to the raw material stored in Washington and demanded access to the wealth of information imprinted on its pages. Despite the absence of a central repository, they had a clear sense of the Federal government as the nation's record keeper and insisted on their right to utilize its archival holdings. National governments on both sides of the Mason-Dixon Line had invaded the lives of Americans in unprecedented ways during the sectional conflict; seeking access to the records documenting this collective effort constituted a demand for reciprocity and an expression of entitlement by Americans who took part in the war, akin to the sentiments driving the avalanche of claims inundating the Federal government in the postwar decades and to the hugely successful drive to pay veterans generous pensions.[6]

The practice of applying to the government directly for information can be traced back to wartime conditions. In Washington, the outward flow of classified documents from the War Department was such that Secretary of War Edwin M. Stanton issued a threatening circular in the summer of 1864 prohibiting his subordinates from "exhibiting any table, statement, or paper belonging to the official records, or giving any information, copy, or extract from the same . . . to any person whatever not on duty." The only exception would be for civilians approaching the government for information about the wounded and the dead. "All such information is to be furnished to such persons as freely as before."[7] This was an unavoidable concession. In the absence of regular mechanisms for informing families of battlefield casualties, petitioning the government was often the only means at the disposal of relatives racked by anxiety. Richmondites developed similar habits in their relationship with the Confederacy. As local residents described it, "news gatherers" would regularly assemble "for the latest tidings" around the War Department and post office, especially when there was reason to believe major events on the front lines were afoot.[8] The superintendent of the Confederacy's Army Intelligence Office, the aforementioned clearinghouse for information about casualties, remembered "streams of visitors" pouring in as well as "great packages of letters" arriving from all parts of the Confederacy every day from mothers, wives, and other "anxious friends."[9]

Families continued searching long after the guns fell silent, and they continued approaching the War Department for leads. Sarah Chenoweth, who declared that she had "furnished three sons to the defense of our glorious Union," asked to learn what happened to her fourth, who enlisted in Arkansas in the Confederate army. She did not believe he was alive, but still wanted to ascertain how he had died.[10] Requests for information about those missing in action arrived from Northerners and Southerners, in independent appeals, and through congressmen, lawyers, and family friends. Like Chenoweth, most applicants were looking for peace of mind. They often had some vague knowledge about the whereabouts of their relations and wanted to confirm what they thought. They asked that records be searched "to relieve my mind of its solicitude and uncertainty," to alleviate their "extream anxiety," to help a widow who "is very anxious to find out" how her husband had died.[11]

The arrival of Confederate documents in Washington was a potentially important development, since, once sorted and cataloged by the Archive Office, they could help fill the information void created by the collapse of the rebellion. Yet more often than not, the office was of no help to families searching for men who had disappeared. Exact locations and dates of Confederate war deaths or of United States prisoners of war who perished in the South were hard to come by, forcing the bereaved to live with lingering doubts. But the appeal of the Archive Office for those looking for closure was irresistible. Even Francis Lieber, after retiring from his post, eventually turned to the office and asked for information about the military career of his beloved son Oscar, who had fought and died for the Confederacy. Lieber actually knew how Oscar had fallen, but wanted to learn whatever he could about his service before the fateful battle. Bezalel Wells, the chief clerk who took charge of the archive after Lieber's departure, was able to locate a few letters revealing Oscar's ambition to serve as an engineer and, speaking like the true white Southerner he had become by 1861, his demand for "the position of a gentleman."[12]

Other correspondents with the Archive Office were looking for a host of documents, books, and personal effects lost during the war. Wade Keyes, who had served as an attorney general for the Confederacy, asked that the office search for "four or five bundles of letters, written to me by my wife, a small revolver and a pair of slippers" packed with the records of the last session of the Confederate Congress; Josephine LeConte, wife of John LeConte, a former colleague of Lieber's at South Carolina College, wrote asking whether some of her husband's papers had reached the rebel archives. "All of his mss., notes, papers, letters, etc, etc, were placed in a trunk and given in custody of Dr. O'Connell (the Catholic priest) of this city for safety. Dr. O'C. was robbed and his house burnt; and it is probable that all of our valuables were *destroyed.*" But since she had heard that the house had been pillaged before it was burned, LeConte hoped that some of the documents may have survived and made it to Washington. Lieber responded laconically, stating "there is nothing of the kind here." A former professor at the College of William and Mary was convinced a trunk full of personal effects, including clothing, family silver, and also a "manuscript commentary on the Antigone of Sophocles & a copy of my edition of the Philippics of Demosthenes," had been shipped to Washington along with the records of the Confederate Tax Bureau. "The war has left me stark poor and among strangers," he added, pleading that a search be conducted. Perhaps hoping to induce in Lieber some sympathy for a fellow scholar, he said that the manuscript was the product of "a long study, with which I hoped to benefit the cause of classical education."[13] George W. Munford, Virginia's secretary of state, pleaded that a search be conducted for an insurance policy issued by a New York company, which he had packed with state records. Munford was also worried that a half-finished draft of a novel entitled "You be switched," which he had written "for my own amusement at odd time[s]," would be published by the Federal government. "I should dislike very much to have it printed," he wrote the adjutant general.[14] Requests for papers and artifacts of legal, monetary, or sentimental value continued pouring in for years. The Rebel Archives Bureau was often the only hope for those looking for what they had lost in the war. It was a repository for the history not just of a fallen government but of its conquered constituents too.[15]

While those looking for missing persons or lost baggage were men and women of all stripes, the majority of applicants turning to the Federal government asking to consult its archives were veterans searching for historical facts. The desire for original records was very much a part of their larger commitment to debating, commemorating, and reflecting on the war. Though most veterans reintegrated into civilian life, they remained deeply preoccupied with their wartime experiences and took part in a great variety of shared activities. They joined hundreds of veterans' organizations, from regimental associations to national bodies—namely, the Grand Army of the Republic (GAR), which was founded in 1866 and peaked in 1890 with a membership of more than 350,000 men, and the United Confederate Veterans, which was founded in 1889 and had a membership estimated at 80,000 in 1903.[16]

Veterans took part in a wide variety of commemorative activities, of which the most visible and well known were battlefield reunions. But they were also deeply engaged in literary pursuits. They subscribed to specialized newspapers, wrote personal recollections, and published thousands of unit histories.[17] They read *Century Magazine*'s popular Battles and Leaders series (1885–1887), which gave voice almost exclusively to renowned officers, and penned their own

Civil War veterans of the 40th New York Infantry Regiment and two women at a reunion at Devil's Den in Gettysburg, Pennsylvania, 1888. Courtesy of Library of Congress.

narratives for the *National Tribune*, which was founded in 1877 and became the leading periodical on veteran affairs. Running weekly after 1881, it featured a column entitled Fighting Them Over, where rank-and-file soldiers could share war stories and hash out different perspectives on events on the battlefield.[18]

A defining feature of veterans' writing was their passion for detail. They compiled exhaustive chronologies, debated the specifics of every minor engagement, and corrected each other's real or perceived errors. Historians have offered drastically different readings of this widely shared tendency. In his study of Civil War memory, David Blight has been sharply critical, calling veterans "America's first Civil War buffs." As he puts it, the "ceaseless accumulation of campaign detail" played a number of roles in the lives of veterans: it served deep psychological needs by displacing the memories of horror and tragedy, it granted recognition for painful sacrifices, and it allowed them to set the record straight. Yet in Blight's mind, what veterans who engaged in the careful study of wartime history failed to understand was that by focusing on minute factoids they were erasing the war's larger meaning as a battle for the soul of the nation. A contravening interpretation sees the insistence on detail not as mere hairsplitting but as an expression of veterans' commitment to historical truth. Veterans understood well that no recollection was perfect, but they cared a great deal about presenting to future generations an accurate version of an event they knew to be transformative, not just in their own lives but for the country at large.[19]

The reasons behind veterans' fixation on the war were most likely shifting and complex, defying a single characterization. Yet regardless of their motivations, from the summer of 1865 and into the twentieth century, those on a quest to ascertain the truth bombarded the War Department with requests for information from official records. Who commanded a particular unit and at what rank? How many soldiers fought on either side of a given engagement? What was the order of battle on a certain occasion? When was a particular general appointed to a particular post? What was written in a telegram sent on this or that day? Was there a battle report on hand about a particular occasion and could one consult it? What part was taken by Native Americans in the war? Which Confederate congressmen voted for the "Twenty Negro Law"? Was there a map of a specific fort one could copy? Did the department own a complete set of Confederate Statutes at Large? Were there muster rolls of a particular unit on hand? Could the department provide a copy? The list goes on and on. Veterans expected the documents stored in Washington to settle disputes, dispel myths, save reputations, support arguments, and soothe gnawing doubts. In short, they expected the archive to resolve the questions left open at the end of the war.[20]

The ease many clearly felt in requesting archival access was partly the product of the ubiquity of official records in the public sphere, but it may have also resulted from the fact that the department's archival bureaus—the Adjutant General's Office, the Archive Office, and the War Records Office—were staffed with veterans who shared many of the same affiliations and sensibilities of the men seeking closure in the archives. Major Robert N. Scott, who headed the War Records Office between 1878 and 1887, had served in the Army of the Potomac and the Military Division of the James, first as a field officer and then as senior aide-de-camp to General Henry W. Halleck. Colonel Henry M. Lazelle studied at West Point and was a professional soldier, but during the war he was colonel of the 16th New York Volunteer Cavalry. Other senior archival functionaries had not only served but were active participants in the world of historians-veterans. Joseph W. Kirkley served with the First Maryland and wrote its unit history, as well as a field guide to the Chickamauga and Chattanooga National Military Park and a data-driven study of the Gettysburg campaign.[21] Even more visible was Captain George B. Davis, who managed Civil War records for six years starting in 1889. Davis would rise to become judge advocate general, teach law, and publish important legal tracts. But he was also a veteran of the Army of the Potomac who took part in commemorative activities even as he supervised the preservation and publication of government documents. During his tenure as compiler, he voluntarily became involved in battlefield preservation work, visiting different grounds and attempting to create markers and memorials for visitors. On the other side of the sectional divide was Marcus J. Wright, a former Confederate general who served in the Western theater. Starting in 1878, he spent decades working as the War Department's agent for the collection of Confederate records while writing numerous articles and several books on Civil War history.[22]

Over the years, archival staffers fielded hundreds of applications from veterans of all ranks, from both sides of the sectional divide and spanning every branch of service. Whether they were household names crafting soon-to-be bestselling memoirs or lowly privates laboring over a speech for their local GAR post, all sought to consult the original records, and most exuded a sense of polite entitlement to the information stored by the Federal government. John Bresnahan, a veteran of the 27th Indiana Infantry Regiment, asked for the original reports written by his officers as he prepared remarks for the regiment's upcoming reunion. His first letter had gone unanswered, which he clearly felt was unacceptable. "I lost

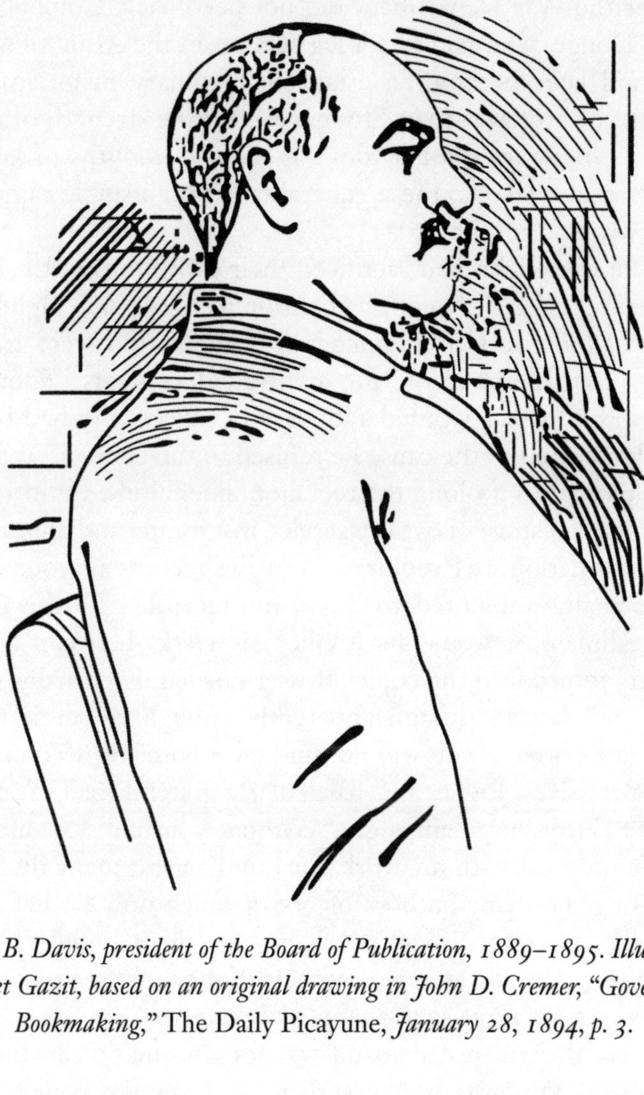

George B. Davis, president of the Board of Publication, 1889–1895. Illustration by Ayelet Gazit, based on an original drawing in John D. Cremer, "Government Bookmaking," The Daily Picayune, *January 28, 1894, p. 3.*

my right arm at Chancelleorsville [*sic*], while serving in the above named organization. For these, and other reasons not necessary to mention, I sincerely hope you will be able to comply with the request contained in this letter." A better-known one-armed veteran, General Oliver O. Howard, wrote from his headquarters in Omaha, Nebraska, asking for material about Gettysburg for an article in *Century Magazine.* Howard desired "to obtain all official data in existence" on the first day of the battle and asked to keep whatever the War Department did not need back. Colonel Theodore A. Dodge, who had lost a leg serving in the Army of the Potomac and later became an established military historian, wrote with a list of no fewer than fifty queries on the strength of opposing forces in a variety of battles. "It requires months of labor, of one person, to make up these general tables for a single campaign," Lazelle wrote in response.[23]

While those who had sacrificed their own limbs in the service of the American government had reason to assert their right to the records of their service, Confederate veterans too were frequent and enthusiastic applicants for archived documents. Thomas L. Rosser was a former Confederate cavalry officer who had been so zealously devoted to the cause he refused to surrender at Appomattox and plotted to prolong the rebellion indefinitely. Yet in 1884 he was writing a history of cavalry service in Virginia and appealed for "such information as I required from the records in your office," which actually amounted to 2,000 muster rolls. By the department's estimate, it would have taken six clerks between one and two years to produce the copies Rosser needed. Eventually, he settled for much less, though apparently enough to merit writing Scott that he hoped "you will not find me a bore" on account of his frequent missives. Rosser was particularly grateful for U.S. records from the Gettysburg campaign. "Without your aid, I would make but little progress with my work, for I find a great many discrepancies among the many authors of books which now lie before me. I find the greatest difficulty existing on the Confederate side. Strange to say hardly any two captains of the same regiment in the Southern armies agree as to *time place* or *numbers.*"[24]

Indeed, the greatest demand was for information in the form of numbers. This was hardly surprising. Over the course of the nineteenth century, statistics had assumed a position of utmost importance in American public life. The ascendence of numbers was already manifest in the antebellum era, with the 1839 establishment of the American Statistical Association, the 1844 founding of the Federal Bureau of Statistics, and the great proliferation of statistical publications covering any and every aspect of the human condition in America.[25] In wartime, as Drew Gilpin Faust has shown, numbers functioned as a crucial means of confronting the horrors of the conflict: "Statistics offered more than just the possibility of comprehension. Their provision of seemingly objective knowledge promised a foundation for control in a reality escaping the bounds of the imaginable. Numbers represented a means of imposing sense and order."[26] Yet the yearning for precise numbers may have also been particularly strong because they were so hard to come by. Reports about battles habitually misstated the tallies of dead, wounded, and captured. When it came to the war's mass engagements, even the most informed participants struggled to assess their true human cost. In the aftermath of Gettysburg, when an array of confused and confusing reports reached Richmond about the number of casualties, a newspaper editor publicly commented on one such story, which stated that 40,000 Union soldiers had been taken prisoner, by saying, "Forty Thousand is a phrase in telegraphic language equivalent to X in algebra. It means that the reporter does not know how many."[27]

The hunger for exact numbers did not abate with Appomattox but may have actually intensified as postwar controversies raged on. First and foremost was the hotly debated question of why the North won. Robert E. Lee made the case that his army was "compelled to yield to overwhelming numbers and resources" in his famous and widely distributed farewell address, written on the day of his surrender. The notion that the Confederacy was defeated merely because its armies were smaller would go on to become the foundation of the Lost Cause myth and would be instrumental in the glorification of Southern men as heroes who fought for their independence and lost for no fault of their own. The pervasiveness of this notion and its constant appearance in both public and private debates pushed actors across the sectional divide to try and establish accurate estimates for both armies in total and for individual units and battles that were thought to have played a decisive role in determining the final outcome.[28]

Veterans, in their obsession to nail down the finer details of history, were particularly devoted to numbers. Statistical tables and numerical calculations were a staple of post–Civil War literature and appeared in many of the unit and campaign histories that started coming out as soon as the fighting ended, like Hermann Everts's *A Complete and Comprehensive History of the Ninth Regiment, New Jersey*

Vols. Infantry: From Its First Organization to Its Final Muster Out (1865). The next few decades saw the publication of massive and meticulously researched statistical works like Frederick Phisterer's *Statistical Record of the Armies of the United States* (1881); William F. Fox's elaborately titled *Regimental Losses in the American Civil War, 1861–1865: A Treatise on the Extent and Nature of the Mortuary Losses in the Union Regiments, with Full and Exhaustive Statistics Compiled from the Official Records on File in the State Military Bureaus and at Washington* (1889); Thomas Livermore's *Numbers and Losses in Civil War America* (1900); and Frederick H. Dyer's *A Compendium of the War of the Rebellion Compiled and Arranged from Official Records of the Federal and Confederate Armies* (1908).[29]

Despite the growing availability of data in a variety of publications, those who sought to do their own research went straight to the source. A typical appeal to the War Department reads, "Have you any printed thing which shows the number of men in the Confederate armies, giving the number called into service from time to time, the numbers drafted, the numbers of substitutes furnished, the numbers of men killed in service, the numbers of men wounded in service and the like?" Colonel Judson W. Bishop, who commanded the 2nd Minnesota Infantry was perturbed by the fact that a book by General John B. Turchin on Chickamauga included casualty figures for his regiment that were different from those published elsewhere, and concluded that "there must be or maybe some such official list on file in your office. If so I shall be very much obliged for a literal copy of it with the name of the officer signing or making it, date & c." Henry Capehart, a colonel in the U.S. army and recipient of the Medal of Honor, asked for the number of killed and wounded in the brigade of General Thomas Jonathan Jackson (known as Stonewall Jackson) during the first battle of Bull Run in July 1861. "I wish to ascertain how strong a stonewall it took to resist any attack made upon him on that day." Ephraim C. Dawes, a brigadier general in the U.S. army and active historian, wrote: "I want to get from the War Department *complete* copies of the returns of the Army of Northern Virginia May 31 1863 and July 20 1863." He was unhappy that "[o]ther parties have been furnished copies," including none other than one of Robert E. Lee's aides. Henry Brainerd McClellan, a former Confederate officer and the author of

The Life and Campaigns of Major General J.E.B. Stuart, was looking for figures from May 1863 in the hopes of proving his claim that the Confederacy's elite fighting force was smaller than had been previously thought. "I am struggling with the 9,356 effective total of the cavalry division, A[rmy] of N[orthern] V[irginia] 31st of May, 1863. I am honest in the belief that this number exaggerates the strength of that command; and I think that I can show that it does." McClellan was looking for a way to deduct the number of unserviceable horses and ineffective men from the total number appearing in Confederate returns. As that figure simply did not exist, he asked to consult the equivalent figures on the U.S. side and be provided with the "average to the regiment or company of unserviceable horses."[30]

In letter after letter, applicants wondered about "Confederate strength and losses," "relative numbers of troops in the Union and Confederate Armies," "the number of men & of regiments furnished by the different states to the *Confederate* army." Time and again, the War Department responded that it was unable to provide the information applicants needed since it simply did not exist in the documents under its charge. As George B. Davis put it in one communication, "[T]he data are incomplete in all fields of statistical inquiry, and so incomplete in some as to make any compilation out of the question."[31] Yet Davis was not consistent in his answers and seems to have tried to steer clear of potential trouble by evading the question of Confederate military strength. Otherwise, it would be difficult to explain why occasionally he did offer some figures after all. "From the information at our disposal," he wrote William R. Holloway, a veteran and the author of *Indianapolis: A Historical and Statistical Sketch of the Railroad City*, "we fixed the maximum number of enlistments at, at least, one million." Davis also referred questions to private publications like Fox's *Regimental Losses in the American Civil War*, which he defined as an "unusually reliable authority," one based on official records. In some exchanges he discreetly admitted that an exceptionally high numerical estimate of Confederate forces that appeared in *Century Magazine* and set the number at 1,500,000 men had actually originated "in this office, based upon the best obtainable data at the time it was made." Davis understood full well the meaning of attaching the War Department's name to such an explosive figure, which would suggest that the Confederate army was in fact larger than many in the South wanted to believe. Just like his interlocutors, he recognized the privileged status of information deriving from original records stamped with official approval.[32]

Another deeply fraught figure was the number of prisoners of war and, more specifically, the number of men who died while interned. During the war, few topics aroused public sentiment like the fate of the men languishing in prisoner of war camps. Some sites of incarceration, particularly the Confederate camp in Andersonville, Georgia, became synonymous with suffering and death. The only Confederate official tried and executed by the Federal government in the aftermath of the war was its notorious commander, Henry Wirz, a symbolic gesture that spoke volumes about Northern bitterness toward those who were deemed responsible for the horrors of the camps. While prisoners' personal histories were often considered too gruesome for a broader public, ex-prisoners did write and speak about their experiences, and death rates in Confederate prisons remained a hot-button issue in the North for years.[33] The publishers of a volume entitled *Narrative of Prison Escape* asked the War Department for "war statistics which might be characterized as interesting and valuable" to supplement their story, particularly ones that will "relate to Federal Prisoners of war or some other matter or subject of equal interest to Ex soldiers, Prisoners & their friends the Public generally."[34] On one occasion, Davis was approached directly by Alcinus Ward Fenton, a veteran of the 6th Ohio Infantry Regiment who was active in its postwar commemorations. Fenton had sent in a newspaper clipping with some statistics attributed to the War Records Office, including figures comparing death rates in Andersonville and Elmira, a prison in New York where Confederate soldiers were known to have died in great numbers. Davis took the time to respond to his queries, but first made sure to clarify that the report was false. "[N]o such statistics have been prepared. So far as I know, there are no data in the Department for preparing them, and in the absence of exact data, there is certainly no disposition on the part of the War Records Commission to speculate or theorize in such a dangerous field of endeavor." As to the actual question of which side in the war lost more prisoners, Davis claimed cryptically, inexplicably, and perhaps dishonestly, that "[t]he total number of Confederate and Union prisoners who died in prison has long been known to have been nearly the same."[35]

In 1886 the War Department had occasion to provide official records to none other than Francis Amasa Walker, one of the country's leading social scientists. Walker at the time was president of the American Statistical Association, the American Economic Association, and the Massachusetts Institute of Technology. But he was also an active Union veteran who had experienced combat as a rank-and-file soldier in the Army of the Potomac; he had been captured and imprisoned and then promoted and appointed adjutant for General Winfield Hancock, eventually attaining the rank of brigadier general. The war continued to preoccupy him for decades despite his other obligations and growing eminence both at home and abroad. He wrote an 800-page *History of the Second Army Corps in the Army of the Potomac* and a biography of Hancock and was not above arguing on the pages of *Century Magazine* over whether his beloved commander had had the authority to command the artillery force of his corps at Gettysburg and whether he had commanded it well. Walker's *History of the Second Army Corps*, as he put it in the preface, "has come to embrace a vast amount of statistical and personal mat[t]er, in addition to the narrative of battles and marches which was contemplated at the outset," and could not have been written without the active assistance of the War Department's archival staff, especially Robert N. Scott, chief of the War Records Office, whom he singled out as being "due more than words can express." The War Department clearly went out of its way to provide Walker with precise information. Its top archival bureaucrats repeatedly went over his numerical and nominal tables, correcting mistakes, and adding and subtracting names and figures based on the information found in the archive. "We get nearer the exact truth every time," Scott noted proudly in one of their exchanges.[36]

Though Walker was surely a U.S. veteran of particular standing, his devotion to the unit he served in and his commitment to creating a written record of its deeds were typical of Civil War veterans, who wrote thousands of unit histories in the aftermath of the war. As Brian Matthew Jordan has shown, unit historians were meticulous researchers who attempted to gather all available sources and ascertain every available fact.[37] This included consulting original documents in state repositories as well as in the Federal War Department. And while lesser-known writers than Walker did not receive the same personal attention from the staff in Washington, they too wanted access to the archival collections stored in its rooms and used every means at their disposal to gain it. Christopher C. Andrews, who had commanded the 3rd Minnesota Infantry and was writing its history, had visited the War Department in person and later wrote to ask for "all Confederate reports and correspondence" pertaining to a little-known engagement in Arkansas called the battle of Fitzhugh Woods.[38] A.L. Gusman, writing the history of the 1st and 2nd Louisiana regiments, asked to be furnished "data, figures, statistics and information" from the department's archives, but also offered something in exchange. Understanding the value of original records, he revealed that he was about to receive "important documents, records and reports" he was sure "your bureau has never seen," as well as "matters of interest from Genl. Kirby Smith," and would be willing to share them if the War Department would "lend me the aid I now request of you for the second time."[39]

Some approached the War Department equipped with a reference from their former commanding officer asking that they receive access. "The bearer, Maj. L.H. Evarts, my adjutant during the war, is desirous of looking over some of the records of your office with reference to publishing a history of the 4th division of the 15th army corps," read a typical letter of introduction. This was such a widely known practice that when Ephraim C. Dawes, a notable speaker and historian in his own right, desired access to the coveted returns of the army of Northern Virginia in the summer of 1863, he casually remarked, "I presume a line from Gen. Sherman would obtain them." It did. The clerk Dawes hired was allowed to enter the archive and copy the records.[40]

It probably did not hurt that some of the applicants requesting access to original documents were unit commanders or their adjutants, who were therefore actually looking for records of their own making or those pertaining to their own military careers. Some merely needed a particular piece of information, like the date of their promotion or an order authorizing one of their actions. Others made extravagant requests for entire volumes of records, which the department could not accommodate.[41] Often veterans were most interested in battle reports, and for more than one reason. Battle reports were useful tools for anyone interested in wartime history because they comprised coherent summaries of complex events, written by prominent actors. But they were also deeply personal creations, shaped by emotions, interests, and exigencies. A substantive report enabled an officer to craft a narrative of a battle, including, of course, his own part in it; it gave him a chance to cover up his mistakes, explain decisions, and commend particular subordinates and units that had performed well or condemn those who did not. It was a medium for laying blame, settling accounts, and burnishing reputations. It was, in short, a highly subjective depiction masquerading as clear-cut facts.

Perhaps because veterans were intimately familiar with military paperwork, they understood the limitations of battle reports. Thus, even as they sought them out, some veterans had a specific preference for documents by field officers rather than by generals. Edwin E. Marvin was "getting up a little sketch" of the 5th Connecticut Infantry on behalf of the regiment's reunion association and asked for an assortment of battle reports, including those written by Confederate officers, "the lower in rank the better." He also specified that on the U.S. side he preferred a report by a brigade commander, "as it would necessarily come closer to us each time than a division report." Colonel William E. Merrill, one of the Federal army's senior engineers, found that most of the reports sent to him upon request from the War Department were unusable. "What I wanted was *detailed* information, such as would be found in reports of blockhouse commanders," he emphasized in an exchange with Davis. Henry Brainerd McClellan, one of the department's regular correspondents, was wondering about a certain report that had already been published in the aforementioned *Rebellion Record* but did not appear in the War Department's own publications. "Why not?" he asked. "Is there any doubt as to its authenticity?"[42]

Yet, at the same time, veterans eagerly reclaimed their battle reports for their own narratives or as mementos. William E. Potter, a highly regarded staff officer from New Jersey who served in some of the U.S. army's busiest units, sent a detailed and specific list, which reflected his deep knowledge of what reports were actually drafted and by whom—for instance, "[t]he official report of Col. Thomas H. Smyth, 1st Del. Vols, temporarily commanding 2d Division 2d Army Corps, during its operation north of the James, August 1864." Edward C. Walthall, a former Confederate general and United States senator from Mississippi, was "very anxious" to see a short report he had made on the battle of Missionary Ridge, where he was known to have served gallantly. When the War Department could not locate its own copy, he had the original sent from his home in Mississippi and politely encouraged Scott to make a new copy for the archive.[43] War Department staffers also seem to have understood the importance of regaining ownership of battle reports for the men who had written them. Even when the lists that veterans sent were lengthy, they made an effort to locate every report and respond to follow-up questions. When Charles Sheldon Sargeant, an acclaimed subordinate of William Tecumseh Sherman, wanted his own report on the fall of Atlanta, George B. Davis tellingly answered that he regretted, "extremely" that none was on file.[44]

Applicants to the War Department asked for information on wartime stories large and small, famous and obscure. Inevitably, the most highly sought records were those pertaining to the battle of Gettysburg. The three-day engagement in Pennsylvania had assumed mythic proportions even before the war was over and became a focal point of postwar reckoning among winners and losers alike.[45] Yet since the battle was seen as having decided the war, ex-Confederates were uniquely invested in understanding what had happened and who was to blame for its outcome. Much was at stake in these bitter debates: the reputations of revered military leaders, of course, but also the legacies of elite units and the states from which they hailed. Most famously, Virginians had accused North Carolinian brigades of fleeing in the face of a stubborn U.S. defense during the crucial hours of the third day, in what is known as Pickett's Charge. This version of the story began to circulate through Richmond newspapers in the summer of 1863 and became Southern dogma shortly thereafter. Veterans of the maligned divisions tried to offer an alternative narrative, and turned, among other places, to the War Department. In 1876, William R. Bond, a former staff officer from North Carolina and the most active champion of Tar Heel virtue, asked to know how many men one of the Virginia brigades in question had "carried into the battle. How many they had the day after the battle and how many they had as soon as they crossed the Potomac. It was reported in the army that they were all killed in their charge; but by some miracle the most of them came to life as soon as the river was crossed." Bond was clear about his motivations. "The average Virginian has never been able to tell the truth about this fight and I don't think ever will."[46] In 1879 a group of former Confederate officers petitioned Congress "to compile and publish, in text form, the knowledge by which the positions and movements of troops were laid down on the Engineer maps of that battle."[47]

Edward Porter Alexander, who commanded the Confederate artillery forces during the crucial hours of the third day, requested records documenting "how many rounds of artillery ammunition per gun were carried in the reserve ordnance with Lee's Army" as well as figures on artillery casualties for an article he was writing on the battle. Though Alexander was leading a busy and successful life after the war as an engineer and executive, he remained engaged with the controversies roiling his former comrades and wrote extensively about his own experiences and the larger questions of Confederate history. When he approached the War Department in late 1897, Alexander was living in Nicaragua, where he was demarcating that country's border with Costa Rica and where he finally sat down to write his recollections of the war. "I am away off from home with no access to records," he explained. The War Department responded by sending a range of reports, returns, and lists of casualties, which he used in his *Military Memoirs of a Confederate*, still considered one of the most effective eyewitness histories of the Confederate war effort.[48]

Though the great majority of veterans writing the War Department's archival bureaus were interested in official documents to ease their minds, win arguments, and set the record straight, their historical pursuits often developed in unexpected ways. The intense preoccupation with original sources, the drive for precision in writing their own accounts, and the endless fact-checking of each other's work fostered historical practices and attention to method that have usually been identified with professional historians.

Indeed, in interesting ways, the proliferation of Civil War historical writing and the evolution of history as a profession occurred more or less simultaneously and were more closely related than one might think. Like many other areas of knowledge, history underwent a profound if gradual transformation in the late nineteenth century from a genteel hobby, open to anyone with time, resources, and literary skills, to a vocation, regulated by institutional demands, defined by its commitment to empirical research, and restricted to (mostly white) men. In the United States, important benchmarks in this process included the granting of the first history PhD in 1882 to James Franklin Jameson by Johns Hopkins University, the establishment of the American Historical Association in 1884, and the inauguration of the *American Historical Review* in 1895. By 1907, nearly 250 history PhDs had been granted, and a second professional organization, the Mississippi Valley Historical Association (forerunner of the Organization of American Historians), had been established.[49]

According to the standard narrative of the American historical profession, a hallmark of academic history was a new commitment to archival research and to source criticism—the careful reading, comparing, and evaluating of original documents. Originating in German universities, these practices arrived in the United States through the auspices of American scholars who had studied in Germany and returned to create the country's nascent history departments. They are usually associated first and foremost with the larger-than-life figure of Leopold von Ranke (1795–1886), a professor at the University of Berlin. Ranke has been credited both with elevating the archive to a position of epistemic supremacy in historical writing and with teaching generations of students to work with original records through a new pedagogical tool called the seminar. Both the archive and the seminar, in this telling, were attempts to emulate scientific practices of field and laboratory work at a time when science was at the height of its prestige. The adulation of science also spurred historians to remake their craft as a field of "objective" inquiry. As Peter Novick has argued, contemporary historians understood science as "rigidly factual and empirical, shunning hypothesis." Historical writing was expected to be devoid of opinions and passions; the scientific historian adopted the stance of an omniscient narrator, observing events from a safe distance and telling, in the words of one formulation, "a truth that would be acceptable to any other researcher who had seen the same evidence and applied the same rule."[50]

In recent decades scholars have debunked this heroic narrative through and through. Nineteenth-century historians claiming to be narrating objective truths were in fact acting out gender, class, and ethnic biases. Scientific history, in the words of Bonnie Smith, served as a platform for "the quest of middle-class men for competence and achievement, their will to professional power." Though they conceived of archival records as receptacles of fact and detail, the records were also the objects of intense desire, and the obsession with archival research blurred the line between science and delusion. James Turner has argued that despite the strong identification of nineteenth-century historians with the natural sciences, the real provenance of modern history was the ancient discipline of philology.[51]

Ranke's contribution has also faced increasing scrutiny. Anthony Grafton has shown that the footnote, popularly identified with the German historian, was actually first introduced in the *Historical and Critical Dictionary* by the French philosopher Pierre Bayle, published in 1696 and used extensively by eighteenth-century scholars. Suzanne Marchand points to the importance of German scholar Christoph Meiners, who in 1775 argued that the way to write ancient history was to examine contemporary historians' use of sources and to read them as products of their own time. There are sharp disagreements over the nature of Ranke's own work and historical vision and the question of whether American historians understood him correctly.[52] Eileen Ka-May Cheng has complicated the story further by showing that a small but significant group of antebellum intellectuals had already implemented many of the tools considered unique to "scientific" historians by the mid-nineteenth century. Though shorn of PhDs or a German education, they relied on primary sources, used careful citations, and were deeply devoted to the idea of impartial truth.[53]

Yet even if historians of an earlier generation had already espoused the principles that would later become identified with professional history, they had all belonged to a small and privileged milieu closely affiliated with universities and journals and situated in the Northeast. That was not the case for veterans and their family members who were writing the War Department from every corner of America. These men and women were teachers, ministers, lawyers, homemakers, merchants, engineers, professional soldiers, and army pensioners. Their devotion to using, comparing, and verifying original records shows that the culture of the fact and the insatiable hunger for truth created by the war generated a homegrown, grassroots interest in original records and their archival afterlives, which remained largely divorced from the realities of scholarly history, wherever it was practiced. Just like established historians, Civil War history writers turned to the archive as their locus for working through agendas and fixations, conscious or not.[54]

Examples abound. Some researchers were not satisfied with receiving copies from the War Department and asked to do their own research in the government's archival collections. Richard B. Irwin, a former adjutant and postwar author, asked to examine reports in manuscript in person for an article in *Century* on the Red River Campaign of 1864 "as there are several points on which accuracy would otherwise be impossible." Occasionally, a veteran entered Washington's chaotic storage spaces and discovered records that were thought to have disappeared. Luis F. Emilio, an officer with the 54th Massachusetts Colored Troops, found a crucial report chronicling the part taken by his regiment in the famous assault on Fort Wagner, in which Black soldiers fought heroically and suffered terrible losses. Emilio received permission to conduct his own search and located the document in the regimental headquarter books, filed with other records of Colored Troops in the Adjutant General's Office. Senator Joseph R. Hawley of Connecticut asked if he could consult records for what amounted to a rudimentary form of peer review. He wondered if he could, "on coming to the Dept., be allowed to look over the various reports" of the battle of Olustee, in which he had commanded a brigade. He had been asked by *Century* to read an article by a former Confederate officer, "look it over, and make any necessary suggestions or corrections."[55]

Every once in a while, the War Department encountered a correspondent who thought of its collections not merely as a resource but also as a repository other researchers would use. Robert McAllister was an officer in the Army of the Potomac who had meticulously documented his wartime experience in daily letters to his family. A generation after the war, he set about reassembling the official record of his service with the same attention to detail. Yet along with itemized lists of queries and requests to the War Department, he also offered to donate documents. "I have copy of my Brigade Report 3rd Brig 3rd D^{iv}. 2nd Corps from March 29 to April 14 1865—which you don't appear to have. If it is of value to have all these reports & you desire it I will be glad to send you a copy to aid completeness of the Records." On another occasion, he told War Department staff that he had just found reports of his regiment's movements. "Part was written by myself and part by Lt Col Schoonover—If you have not got these I would be glad to send you copies of the same." The reports were particularly important, McAllister argued, because "the Brigade reports are missing—and of course these throw light on the movements & battles of the 3rd Brig . . . and I would like them to be in the archives." McAllister was no doubt interested first and foremost in recording the contribution he and his soldiers had made to crushing the rebellion. Yet in the late nineteenth century there were numerous ways to commemorate and publicize the services of a hard-fighting brigade. McAllister seems to have realized the larger benefits of depositing records in the hands of the government and completing its collection for future reference.[56]

Emily Van Dorn Miller, a rare female correspondent of the War Department, was similarly disposed when she sent some papers belonging to her brother, the late Confederate general Earl Van Dorn. Van Dorn, a notorious womanizer, was shot to death by a jealous husband in 1863 at his headquarters in Tennessee. While his reputation was in tatters, his papers were nevertheless in demand. Official copies of his records, prepared by his staff for his own use, were discovered in his personal trunk and passed on to the Mississippi historian and politician John F.H. Claiborne, who was working on Van Dorn's biography and a history of the Civil War. When Claiborne passed away, his daughter sent them to Miller, who forwarded them to the War Department. As Miller explained, "I sent them to you hoping the memoranda might furnish some broken links in the historical records you are endeavoring to collect & preserve."[57] Yet Miller also had her own use for her brother's official records. In 1902 she pseudonymously published his biography, *A Soldier's Honor: With Reminiscences of Major-General Earl Van Dorn*. The book is peppered with original documents, including letters to family members, newspaper clippings, and an assortment of War Department records. A flowery narrative with a strong Lost Cause bent, it is also heavily archival, with orders, correspondence, service records, and reports supplementing the text. Miller may have actually taken a page from her brother. The book opens with a quote by Van Dorn from the proceedings of a court martial he stood following his disastrous performance at the battle of Corinth, Mississippi, in 1862. "These extended remarks are not meant alone for your ears," Van Dorn told the court. "The accusations against me will take an enduring form by becoming part of the archives of the nation, and the jealousy with which a soldier guards his reputation prompts me to place by their side an antidote to the poison they contain."[58]

One of the War Department's most savvy interlocuters was William Preston Johnston, who was both the son of the Confederate general Albert Sidney Johnston and a former aide to Jefferson Davis. Johnston was a highly educated lawyer and the former chair of the English and history department at Washington and Lee University in Virginia. In early 1878 he approached the War Department and offered to sell a large collection of his father's official papers for $15,000. There was a considerable measure of audacity in this proposition, since General Johnston died at the battle of Shiloh in April 1862, which meant that the collection covered only the first year of the war. Nevertheless, his son made a compelling argument for the collection's archival value. He stressed the fact that "[t]he collection is believed to be *absolutely complete*"—as it was when it was turned over to the family by the Confederate government—and "has certainly suffered no loss, detriment, or subtraction of documents since." The collection was large, comprising "8000 or 10,000 documents," but Johnston did not claim each and every paper was valuable in its own right. Rather, "it is in their *cumulative* character as *evidence*, affording the means of *positive verification* of any given point, that they have their chief value [;] . . . in a collection of *Mss*, each of the parts of which is *unique*, the aggregate value is much enhanced by the fact that it is original and complete." The War Department ended up buying the collection for a hefty $10,000 and reaffirming Johnston's argument about its merits as a self-contained archive.[59]

A few of the War Department's most frequent correspondents were clearly devoting their lives to historical pursuits or were working on rigorous, demanding historical projects. Dozier Herbert of Galveston, Texas, was a Confederate veteran and an archivist in his own right. As secretary of the town's historical society, he maintained control of the local repository, which aimed at ownership of "all possible information pertinent to the history of the state for the benefit of the future historian & of all persons inquiring after truth." In the late 1870s Herbert was working on a history of the war west of the Mississippi and was asking for copies of muster rolls and battle reports on file in the Archive Office, where the records of the Confederacy were kept. He submitted rigorously detailed lists of required muster rolls, insisting on the "latest dated rolls showing the most faithful names" of the soldiers serving out west.[60]

John Johnson of Charleston, South Carolina, was a Protestant minister and the engineer in charge at Fort Sumter who oversaw its defenses during a fifteen-month bombardment by the United States navy. In 1890, he published *The Defense of Charleston Harbor, Including Fort Sumter and the Adjacent Islands, 1863–1865*. The 500-page tome was based on Johnson's own wartime records, including notes, sketches, a personal diary, and official reports. He supplemented his collection with other officers' post-books and a wide range of published sources, from unit histories to official records of both governments. Unsurprisingly, he was also an enthusiastic user of the War Department's archives. A self-described "collector of *data*," Johnson did his own research in the Archive Office and located reports in the file room of the chief clerk. He kept up an active correspondence with Robert N. Scott, on whom he relied for missing records, and thanked him for providing telegrams and reports that gave "a completeness to the *data* that I had scarcely hoped to acquire."[61] Eventually, when the book was published, it opened with an endorsement from Pierre G.T. Beauregard, Johnson's commanding general. Beauregard, perhaps attempting to take some of the credit for Johnson's rigorous and learned study, attached to his remarks an original record, Special Order no. 109, dated April 19, 1864, in which he instructed his subordinates to establish a historical board of five for compiling a "military history of the siege of Charleston, S.C." Beauregard also noted that the book had undergone a review process by Johnson's peers. Two of the other designated members of the board, Beauregard assured readers, had "accepted and approved" the work before publication.[62]

The interest in archiving Civil War material was also manifest in the founding of private repositories devoted to preserving the material legacy of the conflict. The Southern Historical Society (SHS) was established in 1869 in New Orleans by a group of former Confederate officers committed to propagating their version of the war.[63] Four years later the society moved to Richmond and embarked on a campaign to create a Southern archive of Confederate materials, a competing effort, in many ways, to the one undertaken in 1865 by Francis Lieber and the War Department. The society's stated object was the "collection, classification, preservation, and final publication, in some form to be hereafter determined, of all the documents and facts bearing upon the eventful history of the past few years." The SHS tried to impress on its audience the urgency of reassembling the South's written record before it was too late. "It is believed that invaluable documents are scattered over the whole land, in loose sheets, perhaps lying in the portfolios of private gentlemen and only preserved as souvenirs of their own parts in the historic drama." These precious records were in danger of becoming waste, unless sent to Richmond, where they would be "industriously classified and arranged, and finally deposited in the central archives of the society, under the care of appropriate guardians." The society took an exceptionally catholic approach to its collections and solicited not only the obvious military records and statistical reports but also travel logs, ballads, speeches, sermons, and virtually any other type of document reflecting the lives of white Southerners during the Civil War.[64]

There is a fascinating contradiction between the larger goals of the Southern Historical Society and the means it used to achieve them. These former Confederate officers were as far removed as one could be both from the world of academic history and from the circles of well-read Northern intellectuals like Jared Sparks, George Bancroft, and William Prescott. They took up historical pursuits for one reason and one reason only—to shape their personal legacies and the legacy of their defeated cause. And they viewed the history of the war in traditionally Protestant terms, a view that was falling out of favor among historians as the nineteenth century wore on. Collecting facts and documents, the society postulated, would enable discovering the "secret thread . . . running through all history, upon which its single facts crystalize in the unity of some great Providential plan." Even so, the SHS couched its appeal for contributions in language very much in line with the idea that archival records, properly analyzed, would produce an indisputably true account. "It is not understood that this association shall be purely sectional, nor that its labors shall be of a partisan character," it promised. The ultimate purpose of its archival enterprise was to enable future generations to write an unbiased history of the war. History could not be written "in the midst of the stormy events of which that history is composed, nor by the agents through whose efficiency they were wrought." Only the "disinterested" next generation would be able to perform this work. But it was the duty of the living to make sure there were no "gaps in the record." And thus, the archive would form the basis of a history that would vindicate the rebellion and the men who had led it.[65]

In New York, Thomas S. Townsend, a hard-of-hearing, wealthy collector who did not serve in the war, single-handedly created a private archive of Civil War documents, which he began assembling even before hostilities broke out. Townsend documented the conflict in real time, preserving, as he boasted to the War Department, "every document available for every reference, that has been made public through the press from 1860" and in the succeeding generation.[66] Though in practice Townsend mainly collected material from New York papers, the result was a behemoth: ninety extra-large volumes, running 54,000 pages, with each page comprising four columns of printed matter. It contained a dizzying array of records: journalistic reports of military actions, the ubiquitous official records that filled the pages of the press, "facts and figures from every state," congressional records from both sides, and speeches of "public men." But like the Southern Historical Society, by aspiring to create a complete record of the war experience in America Townsend also preserved accounts of civil organizations, grassroots politicking, poetry "both serious and humorous," and much more.[67]

In order to make this compilation of original documents usable, Townsend created what he called a "compendium or digest," a work of thirty volumes, "in which reference is made to volume and page where every item mentioned in the main compendium is found." He then went on to prepare an accompanying index, which he defined as "the key to the whole work." Searching the library entailed starting with the index and working back through the compendium to the journalistic collection. No less an authority on reference than John Cogswell, who stood behind the founding of New York's Astor Library and served as its first superintendent, attested that this system actually worked and the library was searchable despite its size. "Its voluminousness might render it inconvenient in use, but for its *perfectly systematic arrangement*, which, *with its minute and complete index*, OBVIATE ALL OBJECTIONS on that score, and RENDER THE WORK as *easy to be consulted as if it were comprised in a single volume*."[68] If one were to believe Townsend's own testimony, he received numerous requests for information from generals and privates alike.[69] Congress, too, expressed interest in this enterprise. The Joint Committee on the Library recommended allocating $30,000 to buy the collection, making the argument that "the careful preservation of historical records is a subject of commanding interest and of national importance" to every American. The work was eventually purchased by Columbia University, but not before Townsend used it to publish a history of New York State's part in the Civil War.[70]

In many ways, Townsend's library epitomized the era's unique relationship with original documents. Townsend was an unpaid amateur relying on the availability of records in the public sphere. Spending by his own estimate a small fortune on the venture and devoting untold hours of labor, he created an independent archive in which he stored, classified, and indexed the records available to him. The result of his efforts was a collection that aspired to be as comprehensive as possible and aimed to serve a wide variety of researchers. Though the Federal government refused to purchase it, Townsend was at least rewarded with endorsements from a long list of Civil War grandees. One particularly enthusiastic validation by a former Confederate officer, Duncan K. McRae, reads like a promotional pamphlet trying to answer every need and desire of Civil War researchers. Townsend's library, McRae declared, was "a better source of supply for a history of the war than simply the official records, for he has many (the minutest often of those) and in addition his contemporaneous journalistic narrative, data and statistics, worked up with such elaborate and systematic method and detail, affords every facility for accurate history. Its fairness, impartiality and completeness cannot be too highly extolled." No wonder Townsend, when approaching the War Department in 1878 in an attempt to draw its interest to his library, attached McRae's endorsement to his letter. And yet by that point the War Department was already deeply engaged in its own monumental compilation project, very much like Townsend's, which would finally answer public demand for easy access to the war's official record.[71]

CHAPTER FIVE

"Simply the Facts"

When all was said and done, the *War of the Rebellion: The Official Records of the Union and Confederate Armies* had cost the Federal government roughly $3 million (about $100 million in current terms) and had taken an entire generation to make. While initial funding for the project was granted by Congress in 1874, the last of 128 volumes did not come out until 1901. The concluding volume included a celebratory preface signed by Secretary of War Elihu Root, who tried to convey the "magnitude of the labor involved" in transforming the impossibly vast body of official paperwork stored in Washington into a set of neatly bound volumes. "The papers examined were well-nigh beyond computation, being counted not by documents or boxes, but by tons, roomfuls or the contents of buildings." Though most records would not be published, all "had to be carefully read and considered, paper by paper, and, if deemed proper for publication, copied and compared." In addition, War Department personnel handled "thousands of individual contributions of original documents," some of which were collections "of formidable dimensions. In all such cases, thorough examination and consideration were required to prevent duplication of matter and to establish not only the accuracy of copies but the authenticity of original documents." Finally, the staff conducted "exhaustive correspondence and other research" to provide the "missing links" that would enable them to complete the collection.[1]

Another point of pride for Root was the War Department's editorial method of printing the original records intact and without commentary. "The Department has striven to present the papers as they were actually written and acted upon officially, leaving to the student and historian the task of investigating controversies and deciding disputes."[2] Over the years, users of the *War of the Rebellion* (*OR*) have largely accepted Root's statement at face value and have shared his enthusiasm for this seemingly forthright source. Practically every historian working on any aspect of the Civil War has relied on the *OR* for essential knowledge. This was true for the gentlemen amateurs of the late nineteenth century writing military history and is still true of academically trained women writing on gendered experiences in our own time. Examples are virtually limitless, so two will suffice. Bruce Catton, the hugely popular, Pulitzer Prize–winning author of a number of mid-century Civil War narrative histories, began the bibliographical note for his 1953 *A Stillness at Appomattox* with the casual statement that "chief reliance of course has been placed on the invaluable *War of the Rebellion.*" Thavolia Glymph, in her 2020 universally acclaimed and award-winning *The Women's Fight*, uses the *OR* and its sister publication documenting the war's navies to reconstruct the trials of enslaved women caught up in the havoc of war. Glymph combines the *OR* with a wide variety of other sources to create a multidimensional picture of events on the ground, but it is obvious that the compilation is a crucial element in her research.[3]

The *OR* has also inspired two supplementary compilations, the first being the *Official Records of the Union and Confederate Navies in the War of the Rebellion*, authorized by Congress in 1884 and published in 30 volumes. The second is a commercial enterprise called *Supplement to the Official Records by the Union and Confederate Armies*, numbering 100 volumes and printed between 1994 and 2001 by Broadfoot Publishing in Wilmington, North Carolina. The *Supplement* includes documents discovered after the *OR* had been completed and donated by private archives. Published an entire century later, it takes after the original in organizational scheme and exterior design, both of which have become staples of Civil War history, instinctively recognizable to every researcher in the field.[4]

The *OR* can easily be mistaken for an exhaustive compilation of the government's Civil War records. In hard copy, its sheer bulk is pleasingly daunting, and the elegance of its neatly bound volumes, embossed in gold, exudes an aura of reassuring authority. Online, the wealth of results generated by almost any search amplifies the allure, seemingly obviating additional research in collections of voluminous manuscripts stored in the National Archives. The subtitle's reference to "The Official Records" hints that these are, in fact, *all* the official records of the U.S. and Confederate armies, a misconception that took root early on. The *National Tribune*, celebrating the completion of the work in 1901, told its readers that the "War Records are a collection of all the accessible official documents, whether reports, returns, letters, telegrams, or what not, relating to the rebellion."[5] Given the size of the compilation, this has seemed like a credible assumption, and it has misled even critical and well-informed scholars who are far more skeptical toward other types of sources. As recently as 2020, Stephen Cushman, a prominent literary historian, articulated a common understanding of the *OR:* "If we imagine a spectrum with an ideal of pure written transcription of Civil War events at one end and an ideal of pure literary invention at the other, then it should be obvious that *The War of the Rebellion: A Compilation of the Official Records of the Union and Confederate Armies* (1880–1901) would be closer to the first end."[6]

For those who have never used the *OR*, a word of explanation might be in order at this point. The volumes of the publication are organized spatially and chronologically, with each volume covering a particular area during a particular period. For example, the fourteenth volume of the first series, published in 1885, covers operations on the coasts of South Carolina, Georgia, and middle and east Florida between April 12, 1862, and June 11, 1863. The volume opens with a "Summary of the Principal Events" for this period and then moves on to the documents. The first type of document is the all-important battle report. Events are introduced by name and date—for example: "March 9, 1863—Skirmish near Saint Augustine, Fla.," and each event is followed by a list of reports. On page 320 the volume shifts gears and moves to other types of military records: correspondence, orders, and returns. Union records appear first, followed by Confederate. The documents are rich and varied—letters showing the back and forth between officers in the field, along with extracts from official journals, memoranda, returns, orders, and exchanges with the War Department. Taken together, they generate a rather eerie sense of transporting the reader back into the reality of wartime. Here is one tidbit from this volume: on April 22, 1862, David Hunter, commanding the United States' Department of the South and stationed in Hilton Head, South Carolina, ends a letter to Secretary of War Stanton with "I inclose a note this moment received from Beaufort. The enemy have also appeared in force on Pinckney Island." The note in and of itself is a theatrical piece of writing, beginning with "All Quiet—We received not a word of news yesterday by telegraph from any quarter up to dark. A profound quiet seems to have rested over armies at all points for the last few days. It may be and probably is the awful stillness that precedes the storm." A few pages later, on May 31, Hunter, who played an important if controversial role in early efforts to recruit enslaved men in the South for military service, is pleading with Secretary Stanton to allow active operations to continue over the summer. Arguing that his forces would be able to occupy the entire coast, he adds: "[T]he slaves would flock into our posts, and the enemy be thus injured as much as in any other way. According to my experience they would rather lose one of their children than a good negro."[7] As any historian who has worked with the *OR* can testify, these men often write like they want to be quoted, and their quips appear in sources that are original, unedited, and published under the authority of the Federal government. The effect is hard to resist.

Yet despite the understandable allure of the *OR*, it is important to keep in mind that this body of knowledge, like any body of knowledge, is also a complicated creation, a product of its time and place. The archival and editorial processes Root described—selecting, authenticating, verifying, arranging, and supplementing the records—were never simply the neutral work of a professional military bureaucracy (if any bureaucracy is ever actually neutral). Every step of the process was informed by prevalent ideas about fact, truth, and history and shaped by a complex and shifting web of political, personal, and institutional constraints. All of these are crucial background for any user of the *OR* and to some degree for anyone who has consumed the historical knowledge based on the *OR*—which means practically anyone who has ever read a book about the Civil War.

The War Department got to work on compiling Civil War records shortly after Congress made its first allocation of $15,000 in June 1874. Secretary of War William W. Belknap appointed his chief clerk, Henry T. Crosby, to take charge of the work alongside the almost retired and largely uninterested Adjutant General Edward D. Townsend. He assigned some of the department's most experienced and trusted staff members to the delicate work of selecting documents for publication "from the immense mass of papers on hand." Once selected, as a contemporary report describes it, records were "copied, compared, and put to press, at the Department; the proof being carefully read and compared with the original papers, and each document, letter, report, telegram, and paper . . . being printed separately." By early 1876 the department had compiled more than thirty volumes of records arranged chronologically and segregated according to their type—reports, correspondence, and so forth. The purpose of this initial step was to save original documents from destruction by creating multiple printed copies of each document and dividing the volumes between government agencies.[8]

In July, a new secretary of war, J. Donald Cameron, appointed another senior bureaucrat, William T. Barnard, as superintendent of the work. Barnard pressed forward on multiple fronts: he increased the workforce of copyists and printers, conducted research in the War Department to discover publishable documents that had eluded his predecessors, and expanded the outreach to retired officers in search of missing records.[9] Yet he quit his job as superintendent after only a few months and was replaced by one of his colleagues, Thomas J. Saunders. In the aftermath of the 1876 elections, Cameron turned over the War Department to a new appointee, George McCrary. While the compilation process was moving ahead and Congress had allocated an additional $110,000 in several installments, the work, as Elihu Root later described it, was still being carried out "spasmodically, without system," and it was still "in an inchoate and unsatisfactory condition" more than three years after it was begun.[10]

For reasons that remain unknown, Saunders too resigned a few months later, and at that point Secretary McCrary decided to address the project's chronic disfunction. More than any of his predecessors, he appreciated the importance of salvaging the War Department's precious archives and was ready to act. In mid-December 1877 he took the crucial step of appointing an officer whose sole responsibility was to serve as compiler of records and reorganize the workforce of which he was in charge.[11] The politicians and bureaucrats who had led the project up to that point had been able to make progress, especially in terms of collecting Confederate records. But in many ways, work on the *OR* only began in earnest once McCrary appointed Major Robert N. Scott to the job and established a new agency called the Publication Office, War Records, which would come to be known as the War Records Office (WRO) and would serve as the headquarters for the Federal government's greatest historical project.[12]

Scott was a natural choice for the position of compiler. Born in Tennessee to a Presbyterian minister, he had moved to California as a teenager and joined the army in 1857 at the age of nineteen as second lieutenant of the 4th Infantry (United States). He was wounded in the battle of Gaines' Mill in June 1862 and was out of commission for two months. Upon his return, he was appointed acting assistant adjutant general and then became senior aide-de-camp to no less than General Henry W. Halleck, the army's master bureaucrat and the officer who first suggested compiling and printing Civil War records. In 1863, he created a record-keeping medium for noncommissioned officers and privates called "The Soldier's Book: A Pocket Diary for Accounts and Memoranda." The booklet, published by D. Appleton & Co. in New York City, was meant to allow the army's rank and file to keep an account of their pay and allowances while doubling as an informal ID card in case of a soldier's serious illness or death. At the same time, Scott wrote in the preface, it was also a "simple means for recording your military history." If properly kept, it will, "in after years, be of interest to you and yours as a memento of the *times* when you were braving the hardships of war to preserve, unbroken, a free government."[13]

After the war Scott remained in Halleck's service but simultaneously applied repeatedly for positions of assistant adjutant general. Despite recommendations from prominent politicians and generals, including Ulysses S. Grant, a promotion remained elusive. Scott was not shy about his desire to move up, touting his own "arduous service" as acting assistant adjutant general during wartime and lamenting the fact that his peers had enjoyed a quicker progression through the ranks.[14] Yet despite his disappointments, he remained a productive officer during the postwar years and published the 522-page *Analytical Digest of the Military Laws of the United States* as well as other pamphlets on legal questions. Scott, in other words, brought to the job of *OR* compiler three essential skills. He was an experienced military bureaucrat who understood how information flowed through official channels; he was historically aware and valued the preservation of original documentation; and he was an active legal thinker. No less important, he was also eager to prove his talents and, once appointed as compiler, threw himself into the work.[15]

Scott's influence on the *OR* cannot be overstated. He created an entirely new plan for the compilation, which went far beyond his predecessors' efforts to collect and arrange documents, and introduced the system, method, and vision that had been sorely lacking before his appointment. Though he has remained largely anonymous to posterity, Scott, more than anyone else, shaped the contours of the compilation that has underpinned historical knowledge of the Civil War ever since.

The first challenge facing Scott was one of organization. Within a few months of his appointment, he made the crucial decision "that the correspondence, orders, and reports relating to any battle or campaign should be arranged so as to give a complete history of the events to which they relate."[16] No longer would records be segregated according to type, as was the rule until then. Under the new scheme, each document would appear along with other records to which it was immediately connected, thus presenting every military event "not as an isolated fact but as an incident to the campaign to which it belonged." Scott also decided to divide publishable matter into four series: the first and largest would cover military events and include reports, correspondence, orders, and returns; the second would embrace records on prisoners of war; the third would encompass United States records on other war-related issues that did not fit into the first series, like the correspondence between the Federal and state governments and special reports by the army's senior leadership; the fourth series would do the same for the Confederacy.[17]

Robert N. Scott, chief of the War Records Office, 1878–1887. Illustration by Ayelet Gazit, based on an original drawing in John D. Cremer, "Government Bookmaking," The Daily Picayune, *January 28, 1894, p. 3.*

Meanwhile, Scott was preoccupied with the monumental question of which records were worthy of publication. The 1874 congressional act to which he was bound mandated the copying of "all reports, letters, telegrams, and general orders not heretofore copied or printed." Yet if the act was literally interpreted, Scott argued, "the official records must be clogged with thousands of pages of correspondence of no historical value and much of which, officially published, would be exceedingly mischievous to the memory of the dead and the credit of the living." Selection would thus have to be a major part of his job. Within weeks of his appointment, Scott filed a recommendation to leave out several classes of documents, including applications for appointments, contracts, charges of disloyalty, claims, tenders of troops, and unsolicited advice. Critically, he also suggested excluding "ordinary routine business of the bureaux and departments."[18]

Next, Scott set the criteria for what constituted a publishable record. First, it had to be contemporaneous; that is, it had to have been created during the war. Second, it had to meet Scott's fixed definition for the term "official," which designated "all communications designed to influence official action, or having that effect, as official documents." Third, records had to be "duly authenticated." And last, they had to appear "to be of historical value." A strict adherence to these standards, Scott seemed to believe, would ensure that the compilation would offer its readers the "historical truth," a notion he was committed to above all else.[19]

But what was the historical truth for a Gilded Age War Department bureaucrat? Scott's interpretation of this most uncertain term drew on his expertise in military law as well as on contemporary ideas of history, which were profoundly influenced by legal thought to begin with. Mid-nineteenth-century law aspired to the discovery of truth in court through the examination of evidence. Though truth-seeking methods were undergoing significant changes, like the introduction of cross-examination, their overarching goal remained the quest for veracity. The legal process, as scholars like John Fabian Witt have shown, was a "fact finding mission" for the sake of deciding between conflicting narratives. A similar disposition prevailed in historical writing. Historians in this era, explains Eileen Ka-May Cheng, were committed to the ideal of impartiality, which "prescribed that like a judge, the historian was supposed to hear both sides of a case. And like a judge, the historian was supposed to be unprejudiced in his assessment of historical testimony."[20] The legalistic mindset undergirding the War Department's work might have also received additional thrust from the fact that Confederate records were being heavily utilized as legal evidence in claims commissions cases even as they were repurposed as historical records for publication. For the duration of the *OR*'s making, the same bureaucrats selecting and copying battle reports and correspondence for the Confederate portions of the publication were digging up obscure documents and comparing signatures to prove the culpability of Southerners in court. Yet regardless of whether they perceived their work in terms drawn from history, law, or both, the men who created the *OR* saw their mission as laying out all the relevant evidence and enabling future students of the war to reach informed verdicts on issues large and small. That is why it was critical to present the records in their original form, without correction or commentary. The department's "invariable rule," as one compiler put it, was "to omit any construction, and to state simply the facts." Or, in the words of another staffer, the compilation process was undertaken in the "spirit of historical fidelity and impartiality."[21]

Having laid down the ground rules, Scott, together with the staff of the War Records Office, set out to make the compilation. Though he reflected on his work only rarely, his 1879 annual report to the secretary of war offered a glimpse into the demands placed upon the staff as it took on the herculean task of sorting through the records. The work, Scott wrote, was moving along steadily, but "the amount of labor involved in examining the mass of records stored in this city, in making judicious selections from them, and in the verification of the copies made, can hardly be appreciated by those not immediately connected with the War Department." Scott never said more in writing about what the work of "making judicious selections" actually meant, or about how he and his aides determined which records deserved to see the light of day in a published compilation and which would remain in the War Department's messy storage spaces.[22]

One way to gain a partial understanding of how the selection process worked is to examine the raw records and observe which documents were published. Luckily, the War Records Office imprinted each document selected for copying with a stamp reading "WAR RECORDS 1861–1865 COPIED." Two different stamps were used, but neither the stamp nor any other notation on the original records says when a document was reproduced and by which staff member.[23] Since the compilation process proceeded chronologically, and since compilers were credited in individual volumes, we know who was in charge of putting each volume together and sending it to the printer.

We know Robert N. Scott compiled the first twenty-six volumes and prepared enough matter for an additional ten volumes published after his untimely death in March 1887 to receive credit as their compiler.[24] But we do not know whether he or one of his deputies was going through the originals and determining which ones would be copied. Also, many of the records marked as "copied" do not actually appear in the published compilation. Someone, somewhere along the way, decided that they did not meet the criteria for publication, but we do not know who, when, and why. With these caveats in mind, a look into a small sliver of Civil War records reveals much about the selection process and the nature of the compilation.

The corpus examined here is 200 pages from the Letters Sent book of the adjutant general of the U.S. army in the months of January to May 1862. The handwritten pages in the letter book contain roughly 800 orders, dispatches, and telegrams, most of which are run-of-the-mill exchanges about the daily life of the army. But routine as they are, they provide a genuine reflection of war making. The Adjutant General's Office was to the army what the central nervous system is to the human body. Its letter books, therefore, embody the complex and sprawling nature of the Civil War as well as any written record can.[25] Even in this small fragment of documentation, the Adjutant General's Office is on record addressing a wide variety of subjects involving a diverse array of actors: humans and animals, generals and privates, soldiers and civilians, men and women, Black and white. Letters were addressed to posts, headquarters, and bureaus spread from coast to coast and range from hurried one-line dispatches to longer, carefully phrased missives. The signatories were the adjutant general of the army, Lorenzo Thomas, a fifty-eight-year-old career officer and experienced bureaucrat, and his deputy, Edward D. Townsend. Thomas was known for his troubled relationship with Secretary of War Stanton and would be effectively ousted from his position in May 1863 and sent to recruit African Americans in the Mississippi Valley. Townsend was of a similar background—a West Point graduate with years' worth of experience in the Adjutant General's Corps. Townsend would take over from Thomas when the latter left Washington, and his substandard work compiling the first iteration of the *OR* was a major reason for the project being delayed for years. Yet as the officers signing the communications from the War Department, their personal circumstances and professional mishaps are largely invisible. The language in the records is strictly official, as one might expect from bureaucrats whose job was to manage the army through an elaborate system of correspondence.[26]

The WRO staff who went through the Letters Sent book copied a range of records reflecting the warp and woof of war making: orders mandating the movement of troops, the shipment of arms, the use of ex-slaves as laborers, and the appointment of officers of all ranks. At times, the staff's copying policy is unfathomable. One copied letter, to a civilian, relates to a junior officer who was suspected of mishandling a check for $50. Another copied letter simply orders a Major Benton "to report in person at this office without delay." Many of these selections do not appear in the final compilation. Perhaps they were copied for another purpose than publication in the compilation, but it is impossible to say for sure.[27]

Among the records that ended up in print are some obvious choices, including dispatches announcing the forward movement of the Army of the Potomac on March 10, 1862, which signaled the beginning of the Peninsular Campaign, the army's first sustained (and failed) attempt to capture the Confederate capital. Another inclusion is a dispatch to the secretary of the navy, Gideon Welles, dated March 13, 1862, written four days after the first battle of ironclad ships, one of the war's most dramatic and iconic moments. The dispatch directs the blocking of a channel to prevent the Confederate vessel from coming out again, conveying in a few short lines the sense of urgency during those suspenseful days.[28] Some documents are particularly rich, like a letter to the same Major General David Hunter, who reported from Hilton Head but, before taking a post in South Carolina, was commanding the Department of Kansas. The letter informs Hunter that Brigadier General James H. Lane had convinced the president and the secretary of war to authorize an expedition "to be conducted by him against the region west of Mississippi and Kansas, . . . the outline of his plans were stated by him to be in accordance with your own views." Lane, who represented Kansas in the Senate, was a charismatic politician and a ferocious fighter against slavery in the West. In the 1850s, he had been deeply involved in the brutal conflicts between pro- and antislavery factions in the state and had distinguished himself sufficiently to earn the dubious sobriquet "The Grim Chieftain." For a few months starting in mid-1861, a brigade he had assembled operated independently in Missouri and Kansas to fight slaveholders, as some described his tactics, or to commit unspeakable atrocities against innocent civilians, as others described them.[29] In any case, in February 1862 he was in search of a new commission, which Lincoln and Stanton were willing to offer. They sent down an instruction giving Lane command of thousands of cavalry and infantry troops and authorizing him to "raise about 8,000 to 10,000 Kansas troops and to organize 4,000 Indians." Clearly trying to ease Hunter's mind about the plan, Thomas assured him that "a command independent of you is not given to General Lane, but he is to operate to all proper extent under your supervision and control, and if you deem proper you may yourself command the expedition which may be undertaken."[30]

It is hardly surprising that Scott and his team gave preference to moments of high drama, to military action per se, and to officers of high rank who made decisions and shaped events in the field. These were the records considered "historically valuable" by the bureaucrats and by the *OR*'s intended users. But war is an extraordinarily complex undertaking involving actors beyond armed forces and events far removed from the battlefield. Scott understood this and designated room in the third and fourth series of the *OR* for records generated by state governments and Federal bureaucracies connected to the armies. In the first series of the compilation, however, which is by far the largest (80 volumes out of 128) and which was presciently expected to be the most popular among readers, the focus is decidedly on military action. This meant the exclusion of revelatory and intriguing records populating the pages of the adjutant general's letter book that could offer insight into the complicated relationship between the armies and the societies with which they were intertwined.[31]

Often these missives touch on subjects that evidently did not seem "historically valuable" to nineteenth-century bureaucrats but are at the center of attention for historians today. There are more than a few exchanges about the Far West, especially on the problems plaguing communication with the region on account of Native

American resistance. "Send daily a stage load of soldiers" to "each station in the Indian country, where depredations are committed," Adjutant General Thomas telegraphed to General James W. Denver, commanding the district of Kansas, for "the Secretary desires everything in your power to be done, to give the fullest protection to the overland mail route." It is obvious, as scholars increasingly emphasize, that the American West remained a violent and volatile expanse during the war years, and events taking place from Kansas to California were inextricably intertwined with whatever was afoot in the East. And yet, to the War Department official leafing through the adjutant general's records in the 1870s, these links were invisible and events out there largely irrelevant. The Far West does not even figure as an independent theater of war in the compilation.[32]

Another class of records present in the letter book but virtually absent from the edited compilation are exchanges with civilians, who wrote the War Department on any number of subjects and received responses from the adjutant general. In a war fought by an army of citizen-soldiers, official action often meant dealing with soldiers' family members and managing the delicate relationship between uniformed men and the home front. But Scott's early decision to omit all "applications" from the published compilation effectively both silenced the voices of women and men approaching the government and omitted its replies. Thus, for example, the *OR* does not properly reflect the citizenry's preoccupation with the fate of the war dead. As Drew Gilpin Faust has shown, when battle casualties began to mount in 1862, the Federal government was confronted with both the vast logistical challenge of dealing with the dead bodies and the humanitarian challenge of determining who their loved ones were to make sure they were properly interred.[33] The adjutant general's records reflect this unfolding crisis, though none of the documents touching on it from the raw records examined here were copied for publication. Responding to an application from Judge Daniel Agnew of Pennsylvania to disinter a soldier from his state and send him home in a coffin, Thomas acknowledged that "there have been many requests made similar to this but I regret to say the Department cannot comply with them in full without injury to the service." According to Thomas, coffins were unavailable south of Baltimore and the labor required to obtain them could not be expended. John B. Alley, a Massachusetts congressman, was told that "it is not practicable for the Government to transport the remains of such of its brave soldiers who have fallen in battle . . . [A]t this time such serious inconvenience would result from permitting persons not connected with the armies to visit the sections of country where military operations are going on that passes are denied except in rare instances." Applicants of lesser stature were simply informed that "it will not be possible at this time to have the body removed."[34]

The disinterest of *OR* compilers in civilians as wartime actors drove the exclusion of other significant records from the compilation, like a letter to Charles E. Sherman, a Washington lawyer who presented himself at the War Department and demanded to be seen by Adjutant General Thomas despite an order forbidding admission of unannounced civilians "which had appeared daily in the city papers for a month past." Despite having been sent home once, Sherman arrived again and used "improper" language with one of Thomas's assistants when the latter insisted he could not come in. The nature of Sherman's business with the War Department is not stated, but a few months later, an attorney by the same name petitioned Congress to receive monetary compensation for eight African Americans who had been set free by the congressional act of April 1862 that banned slavery in the District of Columbia. In his petition, Sherman expressed confidence that the condition of things was "but temporary" and that the value "of such servants will be much enhanced when existing disturbances are closed." Though it is perfectly obvious why the WRO did not publish a document berating a civilian for showing up in the War Department and swearing at the staff, this brief exchange with a bellicose proslavery lawyer is an important testament to the relationship between the War Department and the civilians who besieged it throughout the conflict.[35]

Another document that did not make it into the *OR* is a telegram to Colonel John W. Geary, an energetic and ambitious Pennsylvania politician who had served as governor of Kansas during the stormy 1850s and would go on to govern his home state after the Civil War. Geary was suspected of authorizing a junior officer "to address a communication to the Associated Press dated from Snickersville, March 13th, concerning the movements of your command." Writing Geary the following day, Thomas did not mince words: "The Secretary of War directs me to ask you on what military principle or for what military purpose you authorize subordinate officers in your command to report military operations for the press." The same Colonel Geary was involved in another unpublished but tantalizing record, dated April 22, 1862, and addressed to Major General Nathaniel Banks, commanding the Department of the Shenandoah. "Major Henry S. Turner has just returned here from the neighborhood of The Plains, Fauquier County, Va, and reports an excitement there on account of outrageous rapes committed there by a party from Geary's camp, as it is said consisting of two soldiers and a negro, upon two highly respectable white women named Garrett, a widow and her young daughter." The document ends with an order by the secretary of war to conduct an inquiry and bring the culprits to justice.[36] Sexual abuse of women in the Civil War is notoriously underdocumented, and even when its traces do appear in writing, the explicit word "rape" is rarely used. The fact that this document was deemed unpublishable exemplifies just how different the notion of "historically valuable" was for the men who made the collection compared to that of some of the compilation's later users.[37]

This specific exclusion also raises the possibility that the staff intentionally left out records that reflected poorly on the armies. The files of the War Department's archival bureaus contain no evidence of conscious obstruction or collusion. Dallas Irvine, a long-serving National Archives specialist in Civil War records, believed that "there cannot have been much such tinkering" simply because compilers had their hands full reining in the huge quantities of paper in front of them; he attributed compilers' omissions to "human stupidity" rather than nefarious intentions. And yet there is no way of knowing what was ordered or agreed on verbally, either face to face or by telephone (Scott had a telephone line installed in the War Records Office in May 1880).[38]

One person who had grounds to suspect the compilers was Annie Heloise Abel, a pioneering historian of Native Americans and a nationally renowned authority on research in government records. Abel received her PhD from Yale in 1905, winning wide acclaim for her dissertation and subsequent works. In 1913 she received a presidential appointment as the official historian of the U.S. Bureau of Indian Affairs, and in 1919 she published *The American Indian as Participant in the Civil War.* Abel relied heavily on the first series of the *OR*, but she also examined unspecified papers from the War Department's archival files. By her own admission, her research in these records was "not by any means" exhaustive. And yet enough was examined, she writes, "to show reason for disparaging somewhat the work of the editors of the *Official Records.* Apparently, the editors . . . proceeded upon a principle of selection that necessitated courtesies of omission."[39]

Finally, reading through the 1862 letter book brings into sharp relief the extent to which the raw records offer a different sense of the war than the published volumes do. The majority of the records inevitably fall under the rubric of "mere routine" because, in a four-year war, the day-to-day workings of an army are mostly the stuff of routine. Compilers of the *OR* consciously obscured this fact by publishing those records that "carry on the narrative of military operations," as George B. Davis once put it, and leaving out others that conveyed the mundane realities of war on and off the battlefield.[40] The boredom, the pointless movements, the unrelenting, backbreaking labor that went into keeping nineteenth-century armies in the field is imprinted on every page in the raw material still stored in the archives but is largely lacking in the published compilation out in the world.[41]

The second series of the *OR*, on prisoners of war, has its own history. The decision to allocate an entire series to prisoners was made by Scott, who, as usual, did not explain it in writing. The first reasonable assumption is that he was sensitive to the widespread and intense demand for information about this deeply painful subject, shared by Americans on both sides and from all walks of life.[42] A second reason may have resulted from the modes of managing prisoners during the Civil War, which left a substantial paper trail. Despite the many innovations and "firsts" for which the war is widely known, when it came to prisoners of war, both the United States and the Confederate States initially adhered to the traditional practice of paroling and exchanging enemy prisoners. Soldiers who surrendered in battle, for example, were not supposed to be imprisoned until the end of the conflict but would be released on parole after taking an oath that they would not return to arms until properly exchanged for soldiers of equal rank. This was a convenient and humane system, which commanders on both sides implemented often without direction from the central government. Ultimately, though, it could not withstand the conflict's increasing brutality and rising stakes. When African American men joined the U.S. army in droves, the Confederacy refused to give them quarter and resolved to treat them as slave rebels, to be shot on the spot or re-enslaved. The United States, in a rare show of solidarity with its Black soldiers, refused to comply with this distinction and was willing to see exchanges stop altogether until the issue was resolved. Another source of pressure on the system was the undeniable fact that by negotiating with the Confederacy over the exchange of prisoners, United States officials were granting its government de facto recognition and undermining their own claim that secession was an illegitimate rebellion whose leaders were not to be treated as heads of state. Finally, prisoner exchanges also faltered as U.S. leadership gradually came to the understanding that it was wiser to exacerbate the Confederacy's personnel deficiency by keeping its prisoners from going back to service, even if that meant leaving Federal prisoners behind Confederate lines. Under these circumstances, the system of exchanges broke down repeatedly and was entirely suspended during the latter part of the war. The result was gruesome prison camps where disease, hunger, and human degradation of every sort killed thousands while destroying the bodies and souls of those who survived.[43]

Yet for as long as the exchange system lasted, it generated a great deal of paperwork. The officers managing exchanges communicated in writing, and each transaction required multiple documents. Most of these are highly mundane missives, providing the details facilitating individual exchanges. A typical order from the adjutant general in May 1862 to a commander of a prison reads, "[Y]ou are authorized and directed to transfer Col. R.F. Baldwin, Twenty-first Virginia Regiment . . . now in your custody, to General Wool, at Fortress Monroe, to be held by him for exchange of Colonel Corcoran, now a prisoner at Richmond." This order is accompanied by one to General John E. Wool, whose post at Fortress

Monroe in eastern Virginia, on the border between the United States and the Confederacy, placed him in charge of the actual handover. The order stipulated that upon Baldwin's arrival "you will notify the rebel officer nearest to you that he is there to be exchanged for Colonel Corcoran, now a prisoner at Richmond, and upon the arrival of the latter at Fortress Monroe you are authorized to release Colonel Baldwin." The second series is full of similar records, relating to men of every rank. Apparently, when it came to prisoners of war, the term "historically valuable" was more capacious and embraced records describing the fates of individual men and the day-to-day administration of the prison population. Many of these records may surely be considered "mere routine," yet they are in print.[44]

Why and how did the second series attain its expansive, verbose character? One explanation might hinge on the notion that men who had endured incarceration would expect to see their experiences represented in full and that imprisonment and the structures that governed it were anything but routine. As one War Department official put it, "[N]o doubt many thousands of surviving prisoners on both sides, and the heirs of others deceased would be very greatly interested to see the official records relating to cartels, exchanges, prisons and prison treatment." A look through the adjutant general's Letters Sent book shows that almost every record concerning prisoners was copied. As it is impossible to know when copying took place, it is at least conceivable that these "routine" records were copied for publication during Scott's tenure as compiler and by the same person or persons who copied the records on military operations for the first series. If that was indeed the case, then it is the cultural significance of Civil War imprisonment that accounts for the decision to incorporate records that might not have been included in other series, reflecting a broad sense that the experiences of individual prisoners merited documentation.[45]

A different explanation centers on the individual who served as compiler. The second series was compiled during the 1890s, after the War Records Office had gone through a major reorganization. In March 1889, Congress mandated replacing the head of the WRO with a Board of Publication, which consisted of one officer who served as its president and two civilians. The first president

Joseph Kirkley, compiler of the third and fourth series of the Official Records. *Illustration by Ayelet Gazit, based on an original drawing in John D. Cremer, "Government Bookmaking,"* The Daily Picayune, *January 28, 1894, p. 3.*

appointed was George B. Davis, who managed the clerks, conducted the official correspondence, and organized the distribution and sale of the printed books. The civilian who took charge of the third and fourth series was Joseph W. Kirkley, an experienced War Department clerk and published historian who had been involved in the compilation work from the outset and was considered a mainstay of the WRO by all.

The civilian who receive exclusive authority over the second series was Leslie J. Perry, a newcomer to Washington and to the War Department.[46] Perry was a writer, newspaper editor, postmaster, printer, and Republican operative from the Midwest, where he

Leslie J. Perry, compiler of the second series of the Official Records. *Illustration by Ayelet Gazit, based on an original drawing in John D. Cremer, "Government Bookmaking,"* The Daily Picayune, *January 28, 1894, p. 3.*

had led an active and sometimes turbulent life. If one were to believe the *Topeka State Journal*, a Kansas newspaper, he beat a hundred applicants for the position in the War Records Office with the support of congressmen from Wisconsin and Kansas. Perry was a Civil War veteran and an ex-prisoner. He had served with the 2nd Wisconsin Infantry and was captured and held twice, in 1861 and 1864, spending a total of twenty months in two of the Confederacy's most notorious penitentiaries, Andersonville in Georgia and Libby Prison in Richmond.[47] Perry, therefore, brought to his WRO job the instincts and interests of a newsman, rather than a lawyer or a career soldier, and the experiences of Civil War imprisonment, which few who had been through them were ever able to forget.[48]

Though he did not have previous experience as a War Department bureaucrat, Perry seems to have enjoyed considerable leeway as compiler. He received his orders orally from the new secretary of war, Redfield Proctor, appointed in 1889. Proctor was a Vermont politician and businessman who divided the work between the members of the newly formed board and instructed them how to go about the compilation. A no-nonsense administrator with a strong background in business, he seems to have had little interest in the new administrative body established by Congress and told George B. Davis he wished "the work should go on as if there were no board."[49]

Beyond the minute documentation of individual prisoners, Perry made some other editorial decisions that evinced his independent interpretation of the task he was assigned. The second series incorporates records with little relevance to prisoners of war. It opens with extensive documentation of events in Texas in 1861 that eventually led to soldiers of the U.S. army becoming prisoners of the Confederacy, but the narrative exposition provided by the records Perry published is so long and detailed, it is decidedly outside the scope of the volume's stated purpose. In volume IV Perry included an 1862 report by William P. Dole, the commissioner of Indian affairs, with multiple supporting documents, describing the misery of loyal Native Americans in Kansas who had been pushed out of their lands in Arkansas by "rebel whites and Indians" and "dispersed in every direction." These records make for gut-wrenching reading, offering an unfiltered look at the plight of Native Americans caught in the maelstrom of war. But the subject of the report are refugees, and it is hard to see why they belong in the series.[50] Perry also took the term "prisoner" to mean political prisoners and devoted an entire volume, the second in the series, to the "treatment of suspected and disloyal persons, North and South." The volume incorporates, among other things, records from the Department of State, correspondence with Federal prosecutors, and appeals by civilians. Few of the documents actually fall into the category of military records.

Eventually, Perry's catholic compilation style drew the attention of his colleagues in the War Records Office and the Office of the Secretary of War, instigating a sharp controversy over the compilation process and over Perry's interpretation of the ambiguous term "historical value." At first, the newcomer seems to have gotten on fine as a War Department employee. Though it took him nearly five years to complete the first volume in the series, his work was considered satisfactory and in line with the overall policies of the War Records Office in the new decade. In July 1891, two years after the board was appointed, its president, George B. Davis, reported optimistically that "the records and files of the War Department and the Confederate Archives are being carefully and critically examined, under the direction of Mr. Leslie J. Perry, and a large amount of interesting and valuable matter relating to the Second Series has been copied and prepared for compilation." Davis seemed content not just with the nature of Perry's editorial work but also with the pace in which it was proceeding. "In the preparation of this Series," he added, "the board has found it to be not only desirable, but necessary, in justice to all concerned, to go over the whole ground with extreme care and accuracy before sending any volumes to press."[51] Perry seemed confident in his own compilation strategy and freely critiqued earlier compilers, whom he saw as having been unnecessarily rushed. "The first few volumes were too hurriedly printed, and very much new and valuable matter has been found since their issue which should have been included in them," he wrote the Kansas congressman Edward H. Funston in 1892. Perry planned for the second series to comprise seventeen books, of about 1,200 pages each.[52]

Things seemed to have taken a turn for the worse with the departure of George B. Davis in July 1895 and the appointment of the confusingly named George W. Davis in the same role as president of the Board of Publication. A native of Connecticut, the latter Davis had volunteered for service during the Civil War and stayed in the regular army in its aftermath. He also doubled as a military engineer and took part in the construction of the Washington Monument. Davis would later play a prominent role in America's imperial project by serving as governor of Puerto Rico and commander of the American forces in the Philippines, as well as by taking part in a variety of mining and construction projects.[53]

Davis held different notions from those of his predecessor as to what should be included in the *OR*. Charged with submitting the final volumes of the first series to the printer, he found that "a great deal of matter is contained in this series that it has seemed to me is of little or no historical value." His judgment of the second series, which was still in the process of compilation, was even harsher. In a report written to Secretary of War Russell A. Alger in June 1897 he admitted that "it was some time after I came upon this duty before I was familiar with the scope of the work, but I soon became convinced that a considerable part of the letter press of Volumes I and II of Series II was either not 'records of the Union and Confederate armies' or was without historical value." Davis disagreed sharply with Perry's vision for the series. As far as he was concerned, it should have consisted of no more than five volumes, with records limited to "the principal correspondence, reports, &c., that concern the general subject, sufficient to throw the fullest light upon it, and especially upon the charges that barbarous and inhuman treatment of prisoners were sanctioned or permitted." Simultaneously, Davis wanted to omit "a vast amount of detail and repetition as possesing [*sic*] no historical value," which Perry was intent on publishing. The superfluous material, as far as Davis was concerned, included reports that had already been printed in the first series, reprints of public documents, and records pertaining to political prisoners and privateers that had little to do with the military. As Davis saw it, the slimmer five-volume series would still "include everything that will prove to be of permanent historical value." It is hard to glean from the available sources to what extent Davis was driven by personal animosity toward Perry. The three compilers, as Davis put it, "never met as a board, decided questions by vote, nor kept a record of proceedings." The board was not even holding formal meetings. But at least in writing, Davis spoke of Perry respectfully and asked that his opinion be heard, adding that he had no doubt that Perry had "endeavored to conscientiously interpret" the verbal instructions he had received from the secretary of war when appointed to his position. "The only difference between us is our disagreement as to what constitutes 'historical value' in these records."[54]

On July 17, 1897, Alger delivered his decision. The second series was to consist of eight volumes, and they had to be in print by the end of the fiscal year. This was a devastating blow to Perry, who was forced, he claimed, "to make anew my entire compilation" and to meet a deadline he defined as an "impossibility." Perry admitted that reducing the series by this much was "treble the labor of ordinary straight work." But he also made the argument that the reduction "requires the sacrifices of a large amount of valuable historical matter just at the most critical period of the war." Unwilling to accept the decision as final, he continued to lobby for a series consisting of at least twelve volumes.[55]

As bad as things were for Perry, they were about to get much worse. On June 1, 1898, George W. Davis was formally relieved of his duties, and the War Records Office came under the control of Colonel Fred C. Ainsworth, chief of the Pension and Records Office of the War Department. Ainsworth was a bureaucratic genius who had revolutionized the department's record-keeping practices. An army surgeon by training, he began his career in administration as head of the Record and Pension Division of the Surgeon General's Office, which was responsible for providing the medical histories of soldiers to the commissioner of pensions. In this role he invented the index card system, which created the nineteenth-century version of a personal service file. Each time a soldier's name appeared in a record, a new card was created. The cards were assembled in a jacket, and the jackets were arranged by name, regiment, and state, thus obviating the incredibly slow and tiring process of searching through the huge hospital registers for every single pension claim. The success of this system in resolving the chronic backlog of pending pension cases instigated its expansion into nonmedical records, eventually generating 62 million cards in which every phase in the military life of every soldier was documented.[56] Next, his system was implemented for the correspondence of the War Department in its entirety, replacing the cumbersome letter book. Letters were now entered by date into individual cards, allowing clerks to process and consult multiple records simultaneously instead of passing around a single letter

Frederick C. Ainsworth, chief of the Record and Pension Division, who took charge of the War Records Office in 1898. Courtesy of Library of Congress.

book. With this and other innovative business methods, Ainsworth launched the War Department into the world of modern information management, single-handedly demolishing the problem of arrearage and creating a durable and easily searchable database of soldiers' service records.[57]

In the wake of his extraordinary achievements, Ainsworth was promoted and made chief of a newly established Record and Pension Office, which put him in charge of all military, hospital, and pension records, as well as "other business of the War Department connected therewith." That other business included the War Records Office, where work had been moving along since 1878 but was not close to done when he arrived. Ainsworth was a forceful and zealous administrator who had no qualms about eliminating inefficient employees and driving hard those who were retained. He was not one to sit around and "talk war," as compilers were wont to do.[58] Apparently appalled by the state of affairs in the War Records Office, he wrote a scathing report to the secretary of war in August 1898 with immediate suggestions for action. Unsurprisingly, much of his report focused on the second series and its hapless compiler. The series was "much further from completion than the third and fourth series," Ainsworth noted, on account of Perry's reluctance to cut the series down to eight volumes as he had been required to do. Yet his insistence on adding material was at odds with Ainsworth's view that "volumes III and IV contain so much matter that is of no historical value, or does not pertain to the series, or is a duplication of matter printed in other series, that all of the pertinent and historically valuable matter in the two volumes, consisting of 1854 pages, could easily have been printed in one volume of about 1000 pages." Ainsworth unequivocally recommended firing Perry, "not only because his further employment is unnecessary, but because his discharge will remove one of the principal obstacles in the way of the early completion of the work in accordance with the orders of the Secretary of War."[59]

A month later, the acting secretary of war, George D. Meiklejohn, issued new and stringent orders, which read as if they had been written by Ainsworth. The publication had to "be completed without further unnecessary delay," and the officer in charge would assign duties to employees regardless of "any order that has heretofore been issued assigning any person to the charge of any particular branch of the work." The secretary also mandated which records would be printed from now on: only records pertaining to military prisoners; only records generated by armies; no records pertaining to an individual "unless he be a very distinguished one, or unless his case is intimately connected with some important subject of general historical interest." No correspondence would be printed "relative to a subject that can be fully, clearly and fairly explained by printing official reports, orders or statements." The publication would include "nothing that is unimportant, or that has little or no historical value." In short, the second series would be limited to what officers and politicians governing the War Department saw as historically valuable. Perry's comprehensive editorial policies, which left room for low-rank soldiers, incorporated the histories of civilians, and offered richer contextualization, would be abolished.[60]

A few months and some legal footwork later, Ainsworth, aided by Meiklejohn in his capacity as assistant secretary of war, dissolved the Board of Publication. Joseph W. Kirkley, whom Ainsworth considered "an expert in war records work in every sense of the term," remained in the War Records Office. Perry was out of a job, and the prisoner series was limited to eight volumes. In a story covering the fallout from Perry's dismissal, the *New York Times*, clearly informed by someone in the War Department, faulted Perry for being "tardy" and "inclined to disregard economy of time and space." The *Times* also speculated that the work had slowed down because, after such a long time, compilers were animated by "something like a reluctance to part with an old friend."[61]

Ainsworth was less charitable in his depiction of how things were going in the War Records Office. "This work has been in progress almost a quarter of a century, and has cost more than two and one-half millions of dollars. It is useless to speculate as to how much of this time and money has been wasted, but it is high time that vigorous and aggressive measures should be taken to prevent further waste of either." Ainsworth, the ferocious bureaucrat who was famous for needing a few months to overcome seemingly insurmountable record-keeping challenges, interpreted the pace of *OR* work as evidence of incompetence and laziness. He was unable to see the decades-long compilation process as the product of careful and thorough editorial work, a scholarly enterprise that did not adhere to the iron rules of speed and efficiency he had instilled in the clerks handling service records. It is, in fact, impossible to estimate whether the work could have been finished sooner and whether WRO staff had been lethargic, but the scope of the project on the one hand and the standards of accuracy and completeness employed by the staff on the other raise a distinct possibility that it was simply a gargantuan task requiring many years of work.

In any case, Ainsworth was uniquely unqualified to entertain this notion. Even before he took charge of the compilation, he had gained a reputation for being hostile toward historians and historical work. In February 1897, as head of the Records and Pensions Office, he pushed for new restrictions on access to the adjutant general's records by outside parties. Limiting the entry of researchers into the War Department was driven mainly by concerns for office space and clerical personnel, both of which were in short supply during the 1890s. Yet what this meant was the de facto closing of archival collections that had been accessible to most scholars for a generation. When Ainsworth became adjutant general in 1904, he tightened his grip of the department's archives even further, restricting access to the records under his charge to anyone not officially connected with the War Department. By the time he left the army in 1912, he had become so reviled a figure in the eyes of the emerging historical profession that his tenure as adjutant general proved a major impetus for the movement to finally build a national archive, where records would be placed under the jurisdiction of an archivist rather than an officer.[62]

Though Ainsworth probably did not need other reasons to bulldoze the *OR* into completion beyond his own disdain for inefficiency, he was far from the only Washington insider who felt the compilation process was moving at an unacceptable pace. Ainsworth, as Dallas Irvine described him, was the "executioner" appointed in 1898 once the project had been "sentenced to death" by others.[63] The displeasure of politicians with the War Records Office had accompanied its work from the outset. As early as 1878, congressmen were complaining about the unnecessary expenditure of keeping printing presses in the War Department, compelling the adjutant general, Edward D. Townsend, to elaborate on his great commitment to frugality: "The dilapidated state of most of my office furniture in use by the clerks for fifteen years, will show we have no tendency to useless expenditure." As the years passed, concern with cost was compounded by a sense that the compilation was inexplicably plodding along. As Henry M. Lazelle, who headed the WRO from 1887 to 1889, put it, "[O]ne of the irritating arguments unceasingly brought forward against the War Records publication is the extreme slowness of its advancement toward completion." Lazelle had a ready answer for the accusations: the compilation would move forward much faster if Congress were a little more generous. The appropriation for 1888 was a mere $36,000, which enabled the office to publish no more than four books. Two years later the Senate passed a resolution asking the secretary of war to report on "what steps, if any, are in his judgement necessary to be taken so to expediate the work that the entire publication may be completed within three years." The president of the Board of Publication at the time, George B. Davis, similarly responded that it was only a matter of funding and would require more than twice the appropriation approved that year.[64] The refusal of Congress to allocate resources on the one hand and its demand to publish more quickly on the other were major thorns in the flesh of War Department staff during most of the quarter century the project was in progress.[65]

Lawmakers also intervened in the compilation process in a variety of other ways that weighed down on the staff and involved it in the partisan warfare of the late nineteenth century. In June 1882 Congress responded to veterans' lobbying and debated a bill authorizing the secretary of war to allow the correction of errors in the original documents and to accept, for a period of one year, postwar reports by officers who had failed to find the originals. The plan was to publish these in a separate volume, but Scott objected vehemently, and the bill was tabled.[66] Four years later the pendulum had swung in the other direction, with an act mandating that the publication consist exclusively of "contemporaneous events" and stipulating one specific exception.[67]

In early 1888 Henry M. Lazelle ended up in the crosshairs of Congress when Republicans, seizing on a mistake made at the Adjutant General's Office, accused Lazelle of knowingly publishing a nonofficial document in volume 20 of the first series. A West Point graduate and lieutenant colonel in the regular army, Lazelle had fought in the Civil War and filled a variety of typical combat and administrative roles in its aftermath. Arriving in Washington, he faced an uphill battle. Not only did he have to measure up to the late Scott, but he also had the misfortune of serving during the presidency of Grover Cleveland, the first Democrat to occupy the White House since the Civil War. Heading the War Records Office was a professional appointment and should not have ensnared him in politics, but it did. Though he was eventually exonerated, the obloquy he suffered in congressional hearings and in the press for the nonofficial paper that had snuck into the *OR* shaped his term as compiler and poisoned his relationship with the War Department. He was dismissed after two years and transferred back to field service in the West, a decision he welcomed. "I am sick and tired of the debris of the Rebellion which I have been rolling in for so long," he wrote a friend before leaving.[68]

As part of the campaign against Lazelle, congressmen also added a clause to the appropriation funding the War Records Office, mandating that the secretary of war personally examine the volumes and certify that every document slated for publication was indeed contemporaneous, a demand which Lazelle rightfully saw as preposterous and likely to ensure that publication would effectively cease. In the end, Congress settled on replacing the head of the War Records Office with that three-man Board of Publication comprising two civilians and an officer. There was no real logic to this move beyond the desire to hassle the staff of the War Department, and it ended, nine years later, with the admission that the board was dysfunctional, the firing of Leslie J. Perry, and the takeover by Ainsworth.[69]

As what was often called the "great work" was nearing completion in August 1901, Ainsworth was given credit for accomplishing the feat of seeing the project through. Elihu Root, the incumbent secretary of war, wanted to add a paragraph to the celebratory preface opening the final volume "relating specifically to your own administration, the successive reduction in the number of employees, and the special vigor and efficiency employed in bringing the work to a conclusion instead of allowing it to drag along." Ainsworth, who seems to have drafted the introduction, graciously declined, asking "to avoid the appearance of discrimination against my predecessors in charge of the work," but conceded he did not mind if his achievements were singled out in the secretary's annual report to Congress.[70]

Despite appearances and regardless of the self-congratulatory claims by War Department officials, the compilation never was a neutral aggregation of primary sources, a written reflection of reality. To begin with, the records available to the War Department were never more than a fraction of what an actual transcript of events on the ground might have theoretically comprised. Second, once the process of assembling the *OR* began, it embodied the historical sensibilities of military bureaucrats and their contemporary if sometimes conflicting notions of what was "historically valuable" and "mere routine." (Compilers at times also admitted to self-doubt about the selection process. As George B. Davis noted on one occasion, "[I]t is often very difficult to decide" whether a record is "historically valuable.") Third, the work of compiling also bespoke the agendas and priorities of various secretaries and assistant secretaries, senators and congressmen and the policies they enacted, from the undertaking of huge publication projects, on the one hand, to the reduction of appropriations in times of fiscal retrenchment, on the other. All of these played different and shifting roles in eventually determining which records would see the light of day. The second series would have comprised seventeen volumes if it had been up to Perry and five volumes if George W. Davis had had his way. The first series could have incorporated documents on any number of other subjects beyond those that made it into print. The scheme of four series, with one devoted exclusively to battles and campaigns, was the brainchild of a specific compiler, and the organization it imposes on the records is by no means obvious. The 137,309 pages of the *OR* are hardly the sum of all valuable or important records generated by the huge conglomerates that fought the Civil War. It is merely a compilation reflecting the men who made it, the moment when it was made, and a variety of affordances—technological, financial, intellectual, institutional—that factored into its making.[71]

How have all these shaped Civil War history, a gigantic scholarly field with considerable influence on important national conversations? Answering this question is necessarily an exercise in speculation, since it is impossible to know what stories scholars would have told about the Civil War had the *OR* never been published. In all likelihood, the popularity of other well-worn sources, from Ulysses S. Grant's memoirs to unit histories to collections of Confederate papers that did not make it to Washington, would have ensured that the field would retain some of its defining features regardless. It is also highly unlikely that the gender and racial characteristics of Civil War history, in terms of both practitioners and subjects, would have been significantly different until the second half of the twentieth century. But it is reasonable to assume that a source so authoritative, so immersive, and so universal in its appeal has swayed the literature about the Civil War era in *some* form. A few thoughts on this question may therefore be in order.

First, compilers of the *OR* were all white, male, and, with the exception of the cashiered Leslie J. Perry, members of the military establishment, whether they were civilian bureaucrats like Joseph W. Kirkley and Albert P. Tasker or career officers like Scott, Lazelle, and the Davises. Dallas Irvine, the aforementioned National Archives and Records Administration archivist (also a white man), referred to the compilers as a "close-mouthed 'militaristic' bureaucracy commonly at odds with professional historians." While these facts may seem self-evident, historians have tended to use the *OR* without considering them. Scott, the most critical figure in the shaping of the *OR*, has remained largely anonymous to all but the very few. Critically, the *OR* is habitually cited in footnotes without any reference to its editors, as if the compilation were a disembodied source materializing in the War Department in the late nineteenth century by some magical feat.[72]

The identities of the compilers are also meaningful when considering the exclusion of nonwhite, nonmale participants from the compilation. African Americans, whether enslaved or free, played a variety of crucial roles in the service of the U.S. army, as combatants, informants, guides, and laborers. Yet they rarely appear in the records and virtually never by name. Likewise, some of the most important documentation of the army's dealings with white Southern women, like the records of provost marshals in U.S.-occupied areas, has also been left out. It also bears mentioning that by including the types of records that the editors (and the politicians who funded them) were most interested in, the *OR* excludes Americans from the working classes. Military rank and socioeconomic status were closely intertwined in both armies. Since privates and noncommissioned officers did not write battle reports or send telegrams, they too are invisible in the compilation, appearing only as casualties or as nameless extras in the narratives crafted by their commanding officers.[73]

In recent decades, the *OR* has been repurposed by historians studying the experiences and population groups neglected by its compilers. Armed with digital searching and scholarly ingenuity, contemporary historians are reading the volumes "against the grain" and excavating information on the wartime histories that Gilded Age bureaucrats did not know existed or did not think worthwhile. The same scholars have also discovered and incorporated innumerable kinds of other sources that have fundamentally reshaped the field, and have moved the focus from high-ranking officers to everyone else. And yet it is still important to realize that using the *OR* has meant elevating a particular perspective on the Civil War: white, male, institutional, and, to some degree, elite. These inherent biases in the compilation have been greatly amplified by the incredible facility of using the *OR* in the digital age. The online *OR*, therefore, exerts both less and more power on the scholarship than its hard-copy twin.

Second, the easy availability of such a gargantuan quantity of archival sources, printed, organized, and published by a seemingly authorized source, has given thrust to the uniquely intensive preoccupation with the Civil War as a military event. Surely, the infatuation with the battlefield was conspicuous before the *OR* was published, as evidenced by the huge popularity of other publications, like *Battles and Leaders of the Civil War*, and the wider culture of Civil War study. But it may very well be that in the twentieth century, once veterans and their immediate kin had stepped off the stage, the *OR* facilitated the unmatched focus by scholars on the military aspects of the war.[74] One person who certainly thought so was the enormously influential Southern historian Douglas Southall Freeman, who wrote the four-volume Pulitzer Prize–winning *R.E. Lee: A Biography* (1934–1935) and the three-volume *Lee's Lieutenants: A Study in Command* (1942–1944), both classic works that remain in use today. As Freeman put it in 1939, the *OR* is "the most notable publication of its kind in America or, for that matter, in the world . . . [I]f it be true that the War between the States is now, with a few regrettable omissions, the most thoroughly studied military conflict of modern times, the reason is the availability of the *Official Records*."[75]

Yet popularizing the military aspects of the war is only part of the story. An equally important question is *which* military aspects of the war actually appear in the *OR*. By editing out routine matter and focusing only on the most stirring episodes of the war, WRO staff manufactured a condensed and fast-moving version of wartime reality. While the necessity of excluding most records to create a usable compilation of reasonable size is self-evident, its implications must be recognized and taken into account. The narrative in the first series, as its compilers had intended, moves inexorably forward, operations following one another in quick succession, thus masking the true nature of army life and the actual pace of events on the ground, which was often painfully slow.

An even finer distinction is between different types of military events. Dallas Irvine has estimated that fully one half of all the military engagements in the Civil War do not appear in the *OR* or are mistakenly identified owing to the careless manner in which the editors copied their information from existing documents in the Adjutant General's Office. This feature has given further prominence to the better-documented big-name battles at the expense of small-scale, localized, sometimes irregular fighting, though in reality the latter made up much of the day-to-day reality of the war in large swaths of the South.[76] While the Civil War generation had a particular emotional investment in Gettysburg and other iconic battles, the continued hold of these events on the imagination of historians many decades later must be considered in connection with their outsized place in the *OR* and therefore in the historical literature and its by-products. The Civil War has been dramatized and glorified in American culture more than any other episode in the country's history. There are many factors underlying this phenomenon, including the fact that the war was, indeed, a uniquely gripping historical episode that ended in the defeat of chattel slavery and its defendants. And yet scholars of contemporary Civil War memory who debate the causes and consequences of the public obsession with the war might have overlooked the ways the ubiquitously popular *OR* has shaped how the historical profession understands the war and interprets it for a broader audience.[77]

Before the *OR* could begin to make its mark, however, it needed to be completed. Even as the staff of the War Records Office was preoccupied with making selections from the overwhelming abundance of wartime records, it was also grappling with the countervailing problem of archival scarcity. The work of closing the gaps and finding the missing links would require enormous energy and ingenuity. It also had its own unforeseen and far-reaching impact on the final product.

CHAPTER SIX

Missing Links

THE ORIGINAL SINS OF LAX record keeping during the war and the absence of regular archiving protocols in its aftermath left indelible marks on the archive and haunted the staff of the War Department from the moment work on the *OR* got underway. Compiler William T. Barnard, who was appointed by Secretary of War William W. Belknap in 1876, spent much of his short tenure as head of the project in trying to procure missing records. On August 1 he issued a form letter, which was sent to individual veterans around the country, asking them to send an "authentic copy" of particular documents they were thought to be holding. Barnard also politely urged them to contribute "any official documents relating thereto, which may be in the possession of yourself or acquaintances, of which you may have reason to believe the Department does not already possess originals or copies."[1] Compilers continued to agonize about completeness for as long as the compilation was in the works. They regularly commended certain records for being "wonderfully complete," referred to an absent document as an "ugly gap," and thanked contributors for "your thoughtful kindness and for the completeness of the information which you have supplied." In one exchange, as he was chasing after a proclamation made by Governor Francis Pierpont of West Virginia in 1863, Robert N. Scott admitted that "this proclamation may be of little or no importance, but I am anxious to make the records . . . as complete as possible."[2]

The first and obvious targets for locating missing records were government officials on both state and Federal levels, who varied considerably in their record-keeping habits. In some cases, soliciting records amounted to an effortless transaction—for example when Scott approached the hyper-efficient quartermaster general Montgomery Meigs for the volumes covering the early period of the war. Meigs sent a package of 556 records "connected with the most notable events of the campaigns of those two years, which were kept separate from the general files of the office and were placed upon special files properly labeled for quick and convenient reference at the time." He also offered to send the letter books containing "all correspondence relating to the supply of the armies during the year 1861," as well as telegrams, orders, and instructions sent from his office. In contrast, the commissary general of subsistence curiously responded by saying there were "no reports or letters, of record in this Bureau, relating to the War of the Rebellion, deemed by me to be of sufficient importance and historical value for publication."[3] Some states also posed insurmountable obstacles to completing the record of the war because their archives were in disarray. The adjutant general of California was able to provide an "incomplete roll of the officers and men" published in 1865, copies of which he had located in a secondhand book store in San Francisco and in the attic of the state library. Other state adjutants could not even come up with that.[4]

Then there were the numerous records strewn from Maine to California in personal collections of varying sizes and conditions. Though many records were lost in the peripatetic and dangerous world of the late nineteenth century, enough survived to necessitate an extensive outreach effort, as the Federal government had neither the will nor the means to force veterans to surrender their papers. When Scott took the reins, he initially misread the department's holdings of United States records as being as "complete as they can ever be." Yet before long, he too was attempting to discover the whereabouts of numerous documents that were supposed to be in the War Department's archives but were not. Assembling them would continue for the rest of the century and would require weaving a vast web of communication with hundreds of officers and their families in every corner of America and beyond. In written reports, War Department officials tended to describe the making of the *OR* as the work of the department's archival bureaus. Yet in reality it was a crowdsourced effort that relied on the good will, good health, and good record keeping of numerous individuals who were the custodians of documents the War Records Office could not do without.[5]

Many of the WRO's partners in the compilation process were celebrity generals, like William T. Sherman, who provided records and maps from his private archive. After his death, the department continued to consult his papers, which remained in the custody of his son and were considered important enough to justify a house visit by one of the staff.[6] General Joseph Hooker was asked in 1878 for his field orders and "generally your correspondence while commanding the Army of the Potomac" during the battle of Chancellorsville in 1863, where he suffered a disastrous defeat. Scott was "anxious to have" a crucial letter from Lincoln to Hooker, which was not on file in the War Department. Hooker complied, providing the letter despite it containing "grave reflections upon my character as a soldier in the War, and allegations as groundless as they are untruthful."[7] The War Department also negotiated with the literary agent of George B. McClellan, who commanded the Army of the Potomac early in the war until removed by Lincoln on account of his failures, and tried to salvage the remnants of Philip Sheridan's papers, mostly burned in the Great Chicago Fire of 1871.[8]

Unsurprisingly, Gettysburg received particular attention from compilers, who spared no effort in locating records about the battle as they prepared the relevant installments. Joseph W. Kirkley, who led the effort, was commended for "the completeness and excellence" of the volumes, the result of "infinite pains" and the "labor of years."[9] A key informant was Colonel George Meade, whose father commanded U.S. forces in the battle and took home his papers. Meade provided dispatch books and telegrams, which, as the staff put it, "cannot be secured from other sources," and responded to numerous inquiries.[10] The department was able to discover some specifically valuable documents, like a battle report by Colonel Alexander Moore, who played an important role at Gettysburg. A clearly excited George B. Davis called it "an extremely valuable contribution to the literature of that battle," one that "throws considerable light upon a point about which there has been a great deal of controversy."[11] In the 1890s, even though the Gettysburg volumes had long been published, George B. Davis was troubled by the absence of specific records pertaining to the battle and continued to search for them. On one occasion he wrote General Oliver O. Howard (he of the Freedmen's Bureau records fiasco) to search for a telegram by Lincoln to Meade "in which he takes exception to the failure of the latter to follow up and attack General Lee after the Battle of Gettysburg." Based on "allusions to it in the records of the Army of the Potomac," Davis surmised that Meade passed the letters on to corps commanders in the Army, one of whom was Howard.[12]

The department also approached the widows of generals, patiently explaining that "often historically valuable records have been retained by prominent actors in the war and they have forgotten it, or their heirs have no idea of the value of the contents of some forgotten chest or trunk."[13] Louise Weitzel was the custodian of papers left by General Godfrey Weitzel, who played a major part in the Virginia theater during the last year of the war. George B. Davis pleaded with her to send in the general's papers, guaranteeing that he was making "this request in an earnest desire to see your gallant husband's record made as full and complete as possible in order that future historians may have the material which will enable them to do full justice to his memory." When Mrs. Weitzel did not respond, he approached another correspondent of the War Records Office from a neighboring town, asking him "to see Mrs. Weitzel, and beg of her to send me the General's official papers, with the least possible delay."[14] Ella M. Grover sent a bundle of papers retained by her late husband, General Cuvier Grover, which Davis defined as being of the "greatest value. Some of them, I am sure, are not on file in the War Department."[15] On the other hand, Elizabeth B. Custer, the devoted widow of George Armstrong Custer, who had distinguished himself in the Civil War but met his end fighting Native Americans in the notorious battle of the Little Bighorn, claimed she was "so anxious to aid anyone who writes of my husband" but was "powerless to be of any use to you. What few official papers I have are in Michigan stored where I cannot even direct any one to look for them." Libbie Custer was living in New York at the time, where she was making a living as a writer while also mounting a successful public relations campaign to immortalize her husband as a war hero. "I am overwhelmed with work I have promised," she apologized. Davis did not give up, or maybe he did not believe that the savvy Mrs. Custer had actually left her husband's papers behind in the West while devoting her life to his legacy. Two years later he contacted her again, using a version of his standard line about the existing records failing to properly represent a veteran's heroism, and asked her to examine the "General's papers in your possession" in search of "orders, telegrams, letters or dispatches."[16]

In the early years of the compilation process the War Department was so desperate to get hold of the records it was missing that it was even willing to purchase collections of papers considered particularly valuable. These ended up being largely the records of the Confederacy's Western armies, whose histories presented the greatest lacuna in the government's Civil War collection. Making money from selling historical records to the War Department required good timing, good connections, and a fair amount of gall. After all, these records were the property of the Federal government, and the great majority of contributors to the *OR* gave away their papers for free. Among the handful who were able to receive compensation was the aforementioned William Preston Johnston, the son of the Confederate general Albert Sidney Johnston, who secured $10,000 for his father's papers. Unsurprisingly, a few months later he came back and offered for sale the records of other senior officers in the Western theater. Leonidas Polk and Braxton Bragg were failed battlefield commanders but decent record keepers who left substantial collections of papers to their heirs. Johnston believed he could convince the government of their value, but by that point the process of making the *OR* had kicked into high gear, and Secretary McCrary had become reluctant to spend public money on records that were otherwise coming into the department's hands gratis. Despite repeated attempts by Johnston, including an implied threat directed at Robert N. Scott that Congress would not allow the publication to go forward if the

War Records Office did not concede to his demands, no further allocation was made for the records he was peddling.[17]

While the War Records Office expended much of its energy in assembling the records of generals who both shaped events in the field and generated a substantial paper trail in the process, the staff also tried to reach lower-rank officers and enlisted men who might have come into possession of battle reports and other papers of importance. In the summer of 1889 it became apparent that the archive was missing many of the records for the crucial battle of Chickamauga, which took place in September 1863 in the Western theater of the war. George B. Davis, then a newly appointed compiler, advertised in newspapers across the country a list of "those regiments and batteries from which no official reports of the battle of Chickamauga have been received." He was "very anxious to secure such of these originals as may be in private hands, or such copies as were made from the originals and can be vouched for as correct."[18] Dozens of former soldiers and low-ranking officers responded, some of whom did have original records at home.[19] Perhaps this is what moved Davis, two years later, to claim he was "every day more strongly convinced that there is still much matter extant which should probably appear in the volumes . . . I feel sure that many orders & dispatches, sent and received during active operations in the field, are still in the possession of individuals—held perhaps as valued souvenirs of events in which they took an important part." Writing Ephraim C. Dawes, a brigadier general, historian, and regular correspondent of the War Department from Ohio, Davis asked Dawes to "kindly draw the attention of the gentlemen of the Ohio Commandery to the matter."[20]

Even when groups of records were relatively complete, compilers were dependent on participants in the war to provide what they called the "missing links," particular documents that had been part of an exchange but disappeared along the way.[21] The staff at the War Records Office kept entire collections of records on their desks to facilitate the careful work of closing gaps in the correspondence by cross-searching different papers for a missing dispatch, telegram, or report that might have appeared in more than one file.[22] Compilers often admitted how perturbed they were by the absence of particular documents and spared no energy in searching for them. "I am anxious . . . to supply missing links for 1861 as soon as may be," wrote Robert N. Scott as he was preparing to complete the work on the first volumes of the series in 1880 and celebrating the reappearance of a lost document. "I cannot say how gratified I am to get it," wrote George B. Davis to an officer on receiving an 1863 letter kept in a private collection. "[I]t is one of the most important links of information in the entire campaign."[23]

Aside from providing the raw material from which the *OR* would be compiled, the same men performed a host of other crucial services in the compilation process, like verifying the accuracy of records selected for publication. The *OR* was supposed to include only originals, but a copy was acceptable if it was "certified to by someone competent to certify that it is an exact copy of the original." Compilers strongly preferred doing the verification independently and attempted to retain possession of as many records as they could. This entailed cajoling officers to leave their precious wartime mementos with the War Department for years and often took some effort. As George B. Davis explained to General James D. Cox, his dispatch book was necessary because "the copying was done a number of years since, and the copies are liable to contain small mistakes, and errors of transcription, which would give great annoyance to you, and to us, if they appeared in the published volumes of the War Records." Each dispatch "is compared with your book as the proofs come from the public printer. In that way we are certain that the printed volumes will contain the dispatches in the precise form in which they were sent. You will see how important it is that the correspondence of an officer, holding so high a command as yours, should be most accurately and correctly printed."[24] On numerous other occasions the WRO relied on wartime actors to help clear up misunderstandings and fact-check the records: Which Pennsylvania regiments fought under a particular officer at Gettysburg? Was a certain dispatch by a certain general sent during the battle of Fredericksburg or the battle of Chancellorsville? Where were the keys for the ciphers used in telegrams transmitted between the War Department and the Army of the Potomac?[25]

In the quest to complete the record, compilers took full advantage of the popular fascination with Civil War facts and the wealth of original documents available for public consumption. The War

Records Office kept subscriptions to a number of historical magazines and followed up when a missing document appeared in print elsewhere.[26] The staff mined Frank Moore's wartime *Rebellion Record* for documents that never reached the War Department and sent texts to their original authors for verification.[27] Compilers also turned for help from writers like Thomas Van Horne, who received a cache of official papers from General George H. Thomas for his two-volume *History of the Army of the Cumberland* (1875).[28] Ignoring the fact that the records were supposed to have been delivered to the government at the closing of the war, Scott asked politely to receive "several important documents that cannot be found among the records in the custody of the War Department" and promised to return them and pay for postage.[29]

A few civilians with Civil War backgrounds proved to be key assets for the War Department during the quarter century it took to make the compilation. The previously mentioned Ephraim C. Dawes served as an informal liaison to former comrades and family members who were in possession of useful records. In one particularly effusive exchange, Davis expressed "our sincere thanks to you for the invaluable services which you are constantly rendering as the volumes are published . . . I cannot say how much we are indebted to you for them." Henry Brainerd McClellan, a former Confederate and a historian, compared War Department records with his own sources and offered corrections: "On Page 51, Confed. Reports Nov. 15, 1862 to June 3, 1863, in Fitz Lee's report, someone has made a mistake in copying. Acting Sergeant Major E.W. Price and Bugler Drilling, were not killed on that day to my certain knowledge:—but I well remember that Colonel T.H. Owen, of the 3rd Va. Cavalry commended them for gallantry. The report ought to read after the manner of the enclosed slip." U.S. Colonel Henry Stone went over entire volumes and sent packets of "precious" error slips, for which Davis was deeply grateful and which were put into immediate use.[30]

On its part, the War Department reciprocated by placing its collections at the disposal of those who were working on their own historical projects, especially if they had a military background. Though the government never formally opened its archives to the public, as republican France ceremoniously did in 1792, those defined as "historical writers" enjoyed free access to the records selected for publication starting in the late 1870s.[31] When veteran-and-historian Richard B. Irwin, another friend of the War Department, was offered a chance to see advance copies of *OR* volumes for his own research needs, he declined and asked instead to come into the office and take advantage of "the same privilege I have more than once before enjoyed, of examining the manuscripts of the volumes covering the operations on the Red River and in the Shenandoah and making notes from them, and, perhaps afterwards asking for copies of such as I may find necessary."[32] General William F. Smith also visited the office "various times" and was considered a heavy enough archival user to have borrowed a map, which he failed to return. Others received plate proofs of soon-to-be-published volumes or copies of the War Department's limited-edition unpublished preliminary printing of battle reports and correspondence. Users were generally slow to hand back the material they borrowed, and the staff sent reminders. "The demand being constant here," Wyllys Lyman wrote one senior officer, "it would perhaps be better to return the Chancellorsville sheets now, and send for them again when you have more opportunity to use them."[33]

The *OR* was thus a collaborative enterprise involving the work of officers who had assumed the role of compilers on behalf of the War Department and numerous others who were historians, history buffs, or veterans and family members with access to original records. The fragmentation of the war's written record in the aftermath of the war necessitated this close cooperation between the War Department and veterans, and the *OR* is immeasurably more usable for it. But it is worth considering that the formal-sounding "Official Records" project was undertaken by a group of military men with Civil War backgrounds who were aided by numerous individuals who either wrote the records being collected or were represented in their contents or had inherited them through close ties with their original owners. All involved were therefore, to some degree, interested parties, who lent their support to a project in which they had a personal stake. Inevitably this was bound to make some difference.

Veterans cared enormously about how they would be represented in the *OR*. Over the course of its life, the War Records Office received hundreds of appeals from those who worried about the records that had been printed, were going to be printed, were going to be excluded, or were no longer in existence. When George B. Davis published the list of regiments whose reports from the battle of Chickamauga were missing, dozens of unit representatives wrote in, some on the very same day. J.H. Mauzy, captain of Company D, 68th Indiana Infantry, was appointed by his fellow veterans to locate the regimental report that had gone missing. "I am in correspondence with many of the officers of the 68th Ind. Inf. Regiment and we are making every effort to find an 'official' copy of Maj. Finn's report of the Battle of Chickamauga," he wrote Davis. "We are very anxious to have our proper place in History and would be pleased to know the limit of time allowed to find the report." Davis gave the 68th two months. Mauzy spent a few weeks making "diligent efforts by correspondence with nearly all the line officers and other sources" but eventually gave up. George E. Dolton, who served with Battery M of the 1st Illinois Light Artillery, also wanted "to see our Battery receive the credit it is entitled to, for the part it played at Chickamauga." Dolton had documented his wartime experience meticulously in field diaries and in letters to his wife. Offering these documents to Davis along with "letters from various Generals to confirm all that is claimed for," he tried to argue for the logic of using them since he was "present and wrote from actual knowledge at the time." Gustavus A. Wood, who commanded the 15th Indiana Infantry, was trying to help friends in the 10th Indiana make up for the fact that their colonel had perished in the battle and his replacement did not make a report. "This regiment was composed largely of men whom I had known from boyhood," he explained, and enlisted the help of the regiment's founding officer, General Mahlon D. Manson, who "will assist by all means in his power, in completing the record of his old regiment, hoping that the honorable deeds of no soldier shall remain unrecorded."[34] Another officer was distraught over the absence of a report documenting the operations of his command during the siege of Port Hudson in 1863. This was a matter of great importance, he urged, "in justice not only to the gallant men who were killed & wounded during this long & tiresome siege but also to those who shared the fatigues, hardships & dangers of it & survived." When a search did not yield results, he wrote to "beg at least that this letter be published in the place where my report should come in, in order that the survivors of that siege & the relatives of those who fell may see that I am not to blame for the missing report."[35]

Other correspondents of the War Records Office were singularly preoccupied with how the published records would reflect on their personal reputations. Some demanded to clear any misunderstanding about their particular role in the war or to make sure their promotions and medals would be mentioned.[36] Others were bothered by their choice of language in the documents they wrote decades before, arguing that a certain word gave "an appearance of cold bloodedness which did not exist" or that a report was written in a "4 of July style" of which the author was "heartily ashamed."[37] Bradley T. Johnson, a Confederate Marylander who took part in the notorious raid on Chambersburg, Pennsylvania, in July 1864, was flummoxed by the language he had used in his report. Johnson had openly argued with his commanding general, John McCausland, over the burning of the town when its residents refused to pay the invaders a ransom of $500,000. Now he was having second thoughts. "My Chambersburg report is very, very harsh on our own people," he wrote Marcus J. Wright. Though the charges he made in the report "were strictly true," Johnson felt he "must see some of my comrades Early, Lee, Payne etc. before I direct to put it on record. I read it once a month ago & it was harsher than I thought." In wartime, officers had written reports and dispatches in haste, rage, or indifference. Now their heedless scribbling was about to become public and be entered into the permanent record of the war.[38]

Beyond semantics, there were virtually infinite possibilities for military records to impinge on the good name of an officer. Colonel Henry A. Hambright, who had commanded the 79th Pennsylvania Infantry, contacted the War Records Office in 1889, announcing that he was working with a committee of officers and "those who kept intelligent record of events" to prepare "such matter of record as may be considered competent to pass the muster that is expected it will have to undergo." From that moment on, he fretted over his portrayal in the *OR*'s 1864 volumes, visiting and writing the War Records Office multiple times and enlisting the attorney general of

Pennsylvania and the renowned Civil War collector John P. Nicholson, both of whom wrote the office on his behalf. George B. Davis called the 70-year-old Hambright "a delightful old gentleman" whose feelings he was eager to spare, but at some point his patience ran out. "Col. Hambright complains of the tone of a dispatch from General Sherman *to* him, or *about* him, just which I do not remember," he wrote Nicholson. "He came to see me about it nearly two years ago and left with me some documents received, I think, from General Thomas, which were calculated to reply to, or neutralize the effect of, the messages of which he complained. I cheerfully assured him that I would put them in, if we came upon any messages from General Sherman of the kind that he feared. He has repeatedly applied to me about it and I have as frequently reassured him. The fact is he has brooded over it so much that he is no longer sane on the subject."[39]

Hambright may have suffered from an acute case of *OR* anxiety, but the overall sentiment was shared by many. Numerous wartime actors, distraught by the contents of documents, tried to exert some influence on the compilation process. Perhaps none had better reason to do so than Fitz John Porter, the U.S. general whose career and reputation were destroyed when he was dismissed from the army for disobeying orders by General John Pope in the second battle of Bull Run in August 1862. Porter, an experienced and competent officer, had probably fallen victim to political power plays and was an easy target for those looking for someone to blame for the army's humiliating defeat in the battle. Convinced that he had been wronged, Porter spent the next two decades fighting to reverse the verdict and eventually succeeded when a board of officers appointed by President Rutherford B. Hayes in 1878 ruled in his favor. For a few years starting in the late 1880s he was a constant correspondent of the War Records Office, furnishing compilers with useful records from his own collection and from the estate of his deceased friend and former commander of the Army of the Potomac, George B. McClellan.[40] Porter did not conceal his motives for working closely with compilers to make sure the records were as complete as possible. "With this I mail you, in the best shape I have, copies of many despatches which bear immediately on the true history of the campaign in Northern Va, at the close of August and beginning of Sept. 1862," he opened one missive to George B. Davis. Leaving little to chance, the records were accompanied by explanatory notes driving home their importance: "my despatch shows what little attention was given to reopening our communications with Alexandria."[41]

Gouverneur K. Warren was another well-regarded U.S. general who was dismissed from his command by his superiors and later exonerated by a board of inquiry. Warren, a career officer and notable engineer, had been accused of moving too slowly with his corps during the battle of Five Forks in the final days of the war. Unlike Porter, he was not cashiered from the army but reassigned to a different post. But he never forgot the dishonor he suffered and demanded a reexamination of his case. It took until 1879 for a court to be convened, and by the time it reached a decision in his favor Warren was dead. At the War Records Office, George B. Davis was invested in obtaining his private papers to counter the documents in the War Department's collections, which reflected the hostility toward Warren in the higher echelons of Civil War command. It was important, he said, to make "General Warren's record as complete as possible in order that the historian may not be misled by the absence of material data."[42] If Warren had still been alive, he probably would have agreed. According to a contemporary biographer, he cared a great deal about his archival legacy and was known to have said it was "all-important that a soldier's record shall be perfect in the cold, dry files of the War Department." Warren's widow, Emily F. Warren, was reluctant to let go of her husband's records, but agreed to send the War Department several books of correspondence, thanking George B. Davis for his "disinterested desire to do justice to Gen Warren's memory. I hope you may find among the papers satisfactory explanations of Gen Warren's military movements." Mrs. Warren added that she should have liked to meet Davis in person, "as much is cognizant to me, though unwritten. I however understand that this is not necessary to your work."[43]

While Fitz John Porter and Emily F. Warren were explicitly motivated by their quest for justice in the archive, the books they sent in clearly met the War Department's criteria for publication. Other concerned veterans refused to abide by the strict policy of using contemporaneous material only and petitioned to add ex post facto statements or insert corrections into documents they felt did not represent their service faithfully. On turning in reports of Chickamauga, veterans of the 9th Ohio Infantry Regiment wrote to "respectfully ask the privilege of adding a few facts, which were omitted, in the original record, as also in the company records." Compilers insisted time and again in their communications with contributors that "the statute under which the work is carried on limits us to matter of strictly contemporaneous character" and "that *facts written up now*, could not be published." But men fearing the judgment of history were not so easily deterred.[44]

This was especially true for senior commanders, who had the most to worry about since the records bore their signatures and recounted their performance ad hominem in events of decisive importance. George H. Gordon, who commanded a brigade during the U.S. army's humiliating defeat in the Shenandoah Valley in 1862, sent in a printed narrative of the campaign, "with particular reference to my brig[ade]," and asked that it be included in the publication. The narrative was rejected, a response Gordon was reluctant to heed. "From information believed to be authentic," he wrote Secretary of War James D. Cameron in 1876, "reports of mil[itar]y operations in the late war but compiled long since the war, had been filed as official documents." Not only that, Gordon claimed, but "originals have been enlarged & materially altered by such additions and explanations," including "a totally false report" that had been "incorporated into an original official document, or added to it, wh[ich] reflects upon my brigade—if I am misinformed I shall be glad to know it; but if I am correct, that new matter is received, there could be none more fully authenticated by & from official reports and memoranda taken in the field at the time, than the narrative I sent to you." Just in case, Gordon left his text with the secretary.[45]

Another anxious correspondent trying to salvage his reputation was General Lew Wallace (future author of *Ben Hur*), who had long been held responsible for the United States' defeat on the first day of the brutal battle fought in Shiloh, Tennessee, in April 1862. For reasons that would forever remain disputed, Wallace and his division were late to reach the battlefield where other U.S. forces were being cut to pieces by the rebels. Since that fateful day, Wallace had expended a great deal of energy in trying to clear his name, claiming that he had been made "the scapegoat of the disaster which befell our army."[46] Upon learning that the Shiloh volume was nearing completion, Wallace telegraphed the secretary of war, Robert Todd Lincoln, asking to publish some supplementary records dating from 1865 to 1878. A few were already on file in the War Department and others Wallace wanted to add posthaste. Most were statements by officers on his staff coming to his defense, a typical move by a Civil War general fighting for his reputation. But one postwar exchange with Ulysses S. Grant, who commanded the army at Shiloh, seemingly cleared Wallace of the blame that had been attached to his name for the past twenty years. Robert N. Scott urged Secretary Lincoln not to give in, citing precedent and advocating for adherence to "the established rule" of publishing contemporaneous records only. The secretary of war accepted his position and apologized to Wallace for "the disappointment which will be caused you by the course which my duty in this matter compels me to take."[47]

Veterans also tried to get around the principle of publishing only records defined as "official." The 1874 mandate by Congress clearly authorized the secretary of war to publish "official records," and Scott had fixed a meaning for the term earlier on, defining it as communications that had either effected or were meant to effect official action. Nevertheless, veterans rebelled against a designation that seemed to ignore the realities of wartime record keeping and condemn to oblivion numerous deserving soldiers. Eli Sherlock, captain of Company A, 100th Indiana Infantry Regiment, was deeply frustrated by what seemed like an arbitrary designation of official status. As his regiment had marched with William T. Sherman across the South in 1864, Sherlock kept detailed records of his movements, taking special care to mark correct distances. "I furnished Lieutenant Col. Heath of the 100th Indiana at his request with a copy of each of these itineraries to attach to his regimental report, but he left the regiment and the itineraries were never sent in." Now this small feat of wartime record keeping was not considered official and would be excluded from the compilation. "It seems to me that it is due to the officers and men of the command that these accounts should appear some-where in the war record," he wrote compilers, but to no avail. General Julius White, unable to locate a particular report, asked to submit a statement on the same events verified by himself and another officer as a substitution. White argued that including postwar material was a necessary measure considering the sloppiness of senior officers in reporting the heroism of their soldiers in full. "There is frequent and just complaint made by subordinate officers, and enlisted men, of the neglect of their superiors to forward the reports of subordinates, during the war, and while it may not be possible to supply these deficiencies in official form, I respectfully submit that it is due to the rank and file, if to no others, that all obtainable *facts*, duly verified, be fairly considered in recording the history of the war, even though not in strict official form."[48]

Another challenge to the term "official" came from officers who wanted to withhold records from publication since they contained what they considered private matters. In wartime, many had unwittingly vented their frustrations and resentments in correspondence with friends or included private comments in dispatches of an operational nature. Exchanged between two men in official capacities, these missives were filed by clerks at headquarters or kept by recipients as part of their wartime archives. Reaching the War Department, they were deemed publishable material, a designation for which their authors were not always prepared. Thomas Jordan, former Confederate general, was particularly bold in asserting his prerogative as author. Jordan had gained access "by a mere accident" to "some proof sheets of a volume of the Rebellion Records that cover the latter part of 1862, and which have not yet been published," he wrote the War Records Office in 1885. "In these sheets, I was surprised to find three *private letters* of mine addressed to General Beauregard." Jordan had served as Beauregard's chief of staff and the two had become friends. "Now, clearly, these letters are stamped with the character of private communications. There is nothing official about them . . . they are the offspring wholly of the close, personal relations which existed between the General and myself." Jordan claimed he was "not ashamed of these letters either as to manner or matter—nor will any friend of mine be ashamed of them, should they see the light!" Yet he was still protesting "the publication of these three private letters . . . as being in no way 'official' communications." Scott refused to accept the notion that documents containing nonofficial content should not be published. Responding to a request by Secretary of the Navy William Chandler to reconsider publication of a letter between two naval officers since it involved "much that is personal,"[49] Scott emphatically responded that the record was "clearly official, and, in my opinion it is important as indicating the relations between the commanders of the land and naval forces. A great deal of the official correspondence coming under my observation 'contains much that is personal' and I submit that that is not sufficient reason for omitting it."[50]

As in this instance, Scott and his successors—namely Henry M. Lazelle and George B. Davis—mostly stood firm against the pressures exerted by the authors of records and their attempts to influence the makeup of the *OR*. But things became more complicated when the same policies clashed with the exigencies of the compilation process and with compilers' own preferences.

There is no shortage of evidence in the files of the War Records Office showing that the department violated its own rules in response to a variety of challenges it encountered during the compilation process. Though these violations did not fundamentally alter the nature of the *OR* as envisioned by its makers, they reveal the tentative nature of editorial work even as compilers were doing their best to enforce the policies they had crafted and which they believed were essential to create a compilation that would stand the test of time.

The first and most obvious example is the stipulation that records published in the *OR* be contemporaneous. This should have been easy to carry out. Yet what "contemporaneous" actually meant was dubious to begin with. Battle reports were often written months after the events they were describing and at a point when their consequences had become clear. As U.S. General William F. Smith reminded the War Department on one occasion, "[S]ome generals who having blundered into a success write a report afterwards in which the *plans are made to confirm to the results*." In addition, the Civil War ended officially on August 20, 1866, when President Andrew Johnson declared "the insurrection at an end."

The sixteen-month gap between the end of large-scale fighting and the presidential proclamation allowed officers to claim that records created in the aftermath of events could still be considered to have been written during wartime.[51]

War Department bureaucrats were aware of this problem, yet given officers' tendency to put off writing battle reports, and in their desire to make the *OR* as complete as possible, compilers used an expansive definition for "contemporaneous." They defined publishable records in one iteration as "made within a reasonable time subsequent to the occurrence which they narrate" and in another as "made during the war or very shortly thereafter."[52] And so the records pertaining to Lew Wallace and his performance in the battle of Shiloh, which took place on April 6–7, 1862, embraced exchanges from July and September 1863, including Wallace's request for a court of inquiry, an outcome of the bashing he had endured since the events of that day had become public knowledge. Scott admitted that this was a "liberal construction" of what might "be considered as contemporaneous testimony," but he made the concession and focused his energies on preventing the printing of the postwar material Wallace had submitted in 1883.[53]

Eventually, Scott suggested a revised rule that would permit the publication of "papers prepared after the war was over" as long as they were "strictly official and complementary," meaning related to wartime occurrences that were settled only after the end of hostilities. Scott had two categories of papers in mind: first, the war's final reports, which "were necessarily made after the war was over, but they are essential to the completion of the Record"; and second, the postwar reinstatements of officers who "have been dismissed for cowardice or other misconduct in the field." Scott was clearly second-guessing his own decision-making, since he had authorized the printing of postwar documents in the case of Fitz John Porter, including the report of the board exculpating the general in 1879. "This seemed to me at the time a strictly impartial disposal of an extraordinary case," he explained in an unusually contemplative memorandum.[54] The War Records Office settled on using footnotes to add information in cases where postwar proceedings cleared the names of men who had been court-martialed and found guilty during the war. Lew Wallace, who never stood trial and fought his battle in the court of public opinion, would not find absolution in the *OR*.[55]

During the quarter of a century it took to make the *OR*, compilers were steadfast in their insistence on contemporaneity as the only way to prevent their work from becoming a useless collection of memoirs and distorted accounts. As Scott once recounted in a report to the secretary of war, he had "had a Union colonel apply for permission to retract a statement *never made* in his report of Ball's Bluff . . . [A] general officer has complained that his report of Shiloh was garbled, but when shown his original report he acknowledged that it was correctly printed. Again, a Confederate major-general denied ever having made a report that he saw noted in our catalogue, and on inspection it was found to be in his own handwriting, and he so acknowledged."[56] What Scott failed to mention and perhaps chose to ignore was that even documents qualifying as contemporaneous were not always created when they were supposed to have been created and were not necessarily reflections of events on the ground. As the vicissitudes of Fitz John Porter and Gouverneur Warren made clear, wartime documents were filled with misleading and manipulated accounts. The fact that they were created between 1861 and 1865 offered little guarantee that they could furnish the historical truths the staff held so dear.

Another fundamental issue was the WRO's authentication process, which also handed considerable power to the authors of records. Though compilers did their best to obtain originals, they often had to make do with copies officers sent in. When that was the case, only a simple statement was required to validate a document: "I certify the above to be a true copy of the original report in my possession, as made at the time."[57] Certifying that a copy was true to the original turned it into an official record and endowed it with the same legitimacy as a document that had been stored in the War Department all along. It is impossible to tell today whether authors who sent copies tampered with their contents and to what extent. But there are indications that even at the time the staff noticed inconsistencies. In one instance, Robert N. Scott inquired of an officer directly whether he had edited the text of a memorandum originally written in 1865, published in Frank Moore's *Rebellion Record*, and copied by Scott for publication in the *OR*. Scott had sent the copy to the officer for verification and received an amended text that immediately raised suspicion: "It is important that I should know whether or not the alterations made by your notes have simply corrected errors in the printed copy, or have added new matter."[58]

At other times, though, officers received permission to vet wartime records and to make "corrections" when they were asked to approve the veracity of records that were not originally on file in the War Department but were printed elsewhere. This left considerable leeway. In one instance, when three officers were asked to verify reports, one sent his back after making "a few corrections on the copy sent him, and as *thus signed* accepts the report." Another "also signs the copy sent him but asks that a statement accompanying it may be filed with the same."[59] Thomas Jordan, the Confederate officer who was leery of his private letters going public, demanded that if "their publication is not to be suppressed, then I claim the right to proof read them, for I have noticed several evident misprints." Permission was granted. "As you will see," he wrote when returning the proofed galleys, "I have been careful not to subtract, add, or change a word that could alter meaning or the style of these letters, or soften their matter but several of the corrections of words + punctuations are material to the correct meaning." Not exactly. Two corrected sheets, of a letter written to his commanding general, Pierre G.T. Beauregard, from Tupelo, Mississippi, on July 7, 1862, remain in the records of the WRO and are attached to the correspondence. Some revisions Jordan made are indeed merely technical, and some are corrections of words copied poorly from his rather illegible handwriting. Yet two interventions Jordan tried to make in the record were clearly attempts to alter the meaning of his original wording, if only slightly. In a sentence reading, "I shall be at your service whenever you take the field, a day near at hand I earnestly hope," Jordan replaced "hope" with "trust." This may not come across as a significant modification, but in a letter from a subordinate officer to his commander, it is not devoid of meaning. Apparently, Scott thought so too, since in the published volumes the sentence appears in its original wording. Whether Jordan was particularly brazen in attempting to shape his legacy or whether he is simply on record doing so is impossible to tell. What is clear, though, is that the compilation process was highly susceptible to the editing of documents at different stages.[60]

There is also considerable evidence that for all their devotion to official records, WRO staff were willing to bend their own rules when they were particularly motivated to locate documents. In general, it seems, the more illustrious a Civil War actor, the greater flexibility the War Records Office showed about including his records. When it came to Ulysses S. Grant, George B. Davis was hunting down letters he had written to personal friends like Elihu B. Washburne, the Illinois congressman who launched Grant's career as a Civil War commander and who continued to support him throughout the war. Addressing his son, Chicago mayor Hempstead Washburne, Davis wrote: "Your father was so close and constant a friend to General Grant that he may have written him quite fully in relation to the operations which he proposed to carry on against the enemy, in front of Richmond and elsewhere in the Confederate States, and such letters would probably throw great light upon General Grant's intentions as to those operations." Whether these letters were official, if written to a close friend who was not in the army, seemed beside the point. Both men were dead, and Davis was eager to fill in the gaps.[61]

While compiling the critical Gettysburg volumes, the staff could not locate a report by General Gouverneur Warren, the same officer who was ousted from his command in the final days of the war. At Gettysburg, Warren performed admirably and won wide public acclaim. Considering his later troubles, Davis may have been eager to ensure that his actions received proper recognition. "We had to build up something to replace his report out of his journals and dispatches," he told a correspondent. "This often happens and has from the first." Indeed, Davis solicited personal journals from veterans like Daniel H. Reynolds, a Confederate general who had served in the Western theater in the latter part of the war, a time and place for which there was scant documentation on the Confederate side. "I have been informed that it was your practice, throughout the greater part of the war, to keep a diary of the events in which yourself and your command participated," Davis wrote in January 1892, as the staff was working on the final volumes of the first series. "Will you not kindly allow me to copy your diary, with a view to its publication in the Official Records of the Rebellion? I am sure that it will be a valuable contribution to the work."[62]

Given this enthusiasm for acquiring personal diaries, it is hardly surprising that the War Records Office made the mistake of publishing a document that has been conclusively shown to be a postwar narrative masquerading as a wartime record. In the early 1970s, historian Richard M. McMurry discovered that what appears in volume 38 of the *OR* as "Journal of the Army of Tennessee, May 14–June 4, 1864," allegedly kept at headquarters by Confederate staff officer Thomas B. Mackall, was an expanded and revised version of the actual field diary. The fraudulent text, McMurry has persuasively shown, was meant to enhance the reputation of General Joseph E. Johnston, who commanded Confederate forces in Tennessee and Georgia in the summer of 1864. In the aftermath of the war, he was involved in a bitter dispute with one of his subordinates, John Bell Hood, over the string of debilitating defeats they had suffered while trying to stave off William T. Sherman's March to the Sea. McMurry happened to discover the original diary in an archival collection of Johnston's personal papers and pointed out two crucial and revealing differences between the two versions. In the *OR*, the "diary" includes longer and more detailed entries, some of which do not exist in the original and seem out of place in a field diary kept by a busy staff officer. The late additions suspiciously support Johnston's version of the events, which stood at the heart of the controversy between him and Hood. To make matters worse, the published version is accompanied by a footnote saying that it was "furnished by General J.E. Johnston." McMurry did not find any correspondence of the WRO with Johnston about this particular document, and it seems to have been accepted for publication without much debate. Without knowing whether Johnston was unique in rewriting documents, McMurry's discovery certainly shows that such tampering was possible.[63]

Perhaps the greatest leverage the War Department gave officers in the making of the *OR* was in determining which records they wanted to make public. In essence, every submission of records by a veteran or an heir was a voluntary act, which left substantial room for decision-making on their part. But at times, the license to send whatever one wanted was made explicit. Senior commanders in particular seemed to enjoy this privilege: "I will be glad to see any official documents that you may desire to have published in the compilation under my charge," Robert N. Scott wrote John C. Frémont, a famous officer, explorer, and politician. To George B. McClellan, his former commander in the Army of the Potomac, Scott wrote in a tone becoming a subordinate: "If there is any correspondence in your possession, strictly official, or that influenced your official action, not already furnished in your report on Army of the Potomac and that you would desire to have placed among the war records, I will gladly receive it." William T. Sherman was allowed to make his own call as to whether documents "taken from books containing private as well as official letters . . . should be considered as 'official.' " Even lesser celebrities, like Major General Henry W. Slocum, were invited to send in "rough drafts" of dispatches the War Department was missing. It is impossible to say, based on the available documentation, what these men did with the license to choose which records would be published. But it is important to keep in mind that the War Department did not treat them as subjects of its work, the way a modern scholar would, but as partners in the publication project.[64]

Civil War veterans, high-ranking or not, exerted their influence on the collection simply by being its presumed audience. The demand by veterans for the publication was made explicit through the lobbying efforts that propelled the project from the outset and was articulated even by celebrity generals who could and did publish their own narratives. As early as 1875, William T. Sherman complained at the opening of his memoirs that "no satisfactory history" of the war had been published, "nor should any be attempted until the Government has published, and placed within the reach of students, the abundant materials that are buried in the War Department at Washington." Others followed suit. "When will the publication of your War Correspondences probably commence?" asked General Joseph Hooker, a former commander of the Army of the Potomac, during an exchange with Robert N. Scott in July 1878. "It will be voluminous I know, but will be the only work which will contain the data necessary for the historian to write a truthful history of our great war, made much more necessary by the volumes of *trash* that has already been placed in the hands of the public."[65]

On occasion, the editors of the *OR* were explicit about the extent to which work was driven by the knowledge that the same men who fought in the war were also going to be the ones who would use the collection. As George B. Davis put it in 1889, "[I]f we cannot convince participants of its accuracy the value of the work would be small indeed." Eight years later, as the ranks of Civil War veterans were thinning, George W. Davis recommended prioritizing the publication of volumes covering battles and campaigns while suspending publication of all other matter, since they were of particular "interest to a very much larger number of survivors than any other portion of the work."[66]

Most critically, the interests of veterans shaped the massive effort of indexing the *OR*. The importance of indexing was understood by all who were familiar with the scope and complexity of Civil War paperwork. When Sherman was prodding the War Department to make progress on the project, he specified that the compilation should come out "with full indexes to enable the historian to make a judicious selection of the materials."[67] Every compiler who worked on the collection agreed. Robert N. Scott adopted a uniform indexing plan early in his tenure, and it was consistently adhered to until the project was finished, perhaps because one person, John S. Moodey, filled the position of indexer throughout the process. When Congress in 1885 failed to appropriate money for Moodey's salary, Scott remonstrated, stating that "such provision is in my judgment more important than any other single item in the appropriation"; not only that, but Moodey had been "specially commended by the students of the war." In line with the notion that veterans would be the compilation's primary users, both as aging men reminiscing about their pasts and as historical writers requiring research material, indexing of individuals was extraordinarily detailed, and included the name of every person and every unit mentioned in the compilation, down to the company level.[68]

The capstone of the *OR* was its General Index, a two-volume, 2,250-page behemoth that required the labor of two years and was compiled from 500,000 index cards.[69] This was a departure from the original plan, which stipulated a two-volume index for the first series. The decision to create a single index for the entire work was made by Fred C. Ainsworth, the chief of the Record and Pension Division, who by then had assumed control of the work. Ainsworth was driven, in all probability, by the urge to speed up work on the project and bring it to completion. Yet even under the new plan, the guiding principle remained the same: creating an index in which every single person appearing in the compilation could be found. Later scholars have found this scheme mind-boggling. In the era before computerized search, it made the compilation extraordinarily difficult to use as it prevented effective searching for events and places.[70]

And yet these concerns belonged to the twentieth century. Back in the postwar era, when memories were still fresh and wartime actors still alive, the WRO's nearly single-minded focus was on the veterans. As Moodey and his assistants were transitioning from working on volume indexes to the General Index, they endeavored to identify the first names of men who were represented by initials in the original records. Though they would eventually be criticized for their rudimentary professional practices and ignorance of modern indexing methods, they could not be blamed for laziness. They sent dispatches far and wide, trying to pinpoint individuals like a "Captain Smith, of the Confederate States Quartermaster's Department, who was associated with Colonel William M. Wadley in connection with the convention of railroad officers which met in the Masonic Hall, Augusta, Ga., December 15, 1862." Smith was anonymous even to Charles E. Jones, a historian of Civil War Georgia.[71] The effort to create an entirely comprehensive index was driven by the sense that it was the heart of the project. Ainsworth was confident it would "no doubt be used to a much greater extent in the consultation of these records than any other portion of the work." He tried to ensure that the General Index would be printed on thicker paper, "hand sewd and bound (as strongly as possible) in black silk cloth, using for this purpose design No. 44 of the Interlaken Mills book cloth patterns, with head bands. It is also requested that the boards for the covers be somewhat heavier than those used in the other volumes, and a strong tar board is suggested."[72]

Once *OR* volumes started rolling off the press, veterans from every walk of life left no doubt as to their unbridled enthusiasm for the compilation, voicing insistent demands to receive copies. Like other governmental publications at the time, the *OR* was distributed through Congress, which had initiated and funded the project and whose members were fond of doling out published documents as special favors to constituents. In August 1882 lawmakers mandated the printing of 11,000 copies: each member of the House of Representatives received 21, and each senator received 26, to be distributed in their respective states. Another 1,000 copies were parceled out among the executive departments, and an additional 1,000 were allotted to active-duty officers and contributors to the work. Unclaimed volumes were sold by the War Department at the cost of printing plus 10 percent. Over time, Congress legislated the printing of additional sets for newly elected members and ordered the public printer to supplement incomplete sets lying around in the War Department and the congressional documents room. All in all, 1,500,000 individual volumes from *OR* sets were distributed across the country.[73]

Veterans certainly had an edge when it came to obtaining a set of the *OR*. Institutions for veterans—posts of veterans' organizations and homes for aging or infirm veterans—were often selected by congressmen as recipients.[74] By 1894, 600 posts of the Grand Army of the Republic were on the War Department's list as regular recipients, and others were receiving volumes through additional channels.[75] Occasionally, the staff of the WRO loaned out copies to veterans engaged in their own historical projects.[76] And when staffers had access to a very limited number of copies for independent distribution, priority was given to GAR posts in areas that were heavily populated by veterans and where no *OR* sets could be found, like the Far West.[77]

Yet these arrangements were hardly sufficient for men who felt the *OR* was both about and for them. In their adamant letters to their representatives in Congress or directly to the War Department, enlisted men and junior officers who were not defined as "contributors to the work" and were therefore not entitled to personal copies demonstrated a clear sense of ownership over the project.[78] In November 1880, a few months after the first volume was published, Charles Rice, chairman of the library committee at the College of Pharmacy in New York City, wrote to ask that his library be supplied with a book, arguing that "a great number of the members of this college have themselves taken active part in the War of the Rebellion, and they would greatly appreciate the favor of a copy." Major D.M. Vance, an officer in the regular army, wrote in 1885 from his post in New Mexico asking how he could obtain the publication, as he had "been informed that all field officers are entitled to them." The same year, the Illinois branch of the Military Order of the Loyal Legion of the United States praised the *OR* as a project of "great importance to the country at large, and especially to the veterans of the war," and demanded that it be completed as quickly as possible "in order that those who bore a part in the suppression of the Rebellion may have an opportunity to read and study the narrative of the operations in which they were participants." The commander of one unlucky GAR post tried to guilt the WRO into providing a copy: "It seems that arrangements can be made whereby this organization, whose members helped *make the history* might be so far recognized, especially when we know that many copies have been placed in the hands of those whose part in 61–65 were neither so creditable or so deserving of the favor as the comrades whom I represent."[79]

Since the *OR* was published over the course of twenty years, its editors were in constant communication with readers even as the work was still in progress. A few months after the first volume was published, the War Department heard from a veteran of the 23rd Ohio Infantry who was working as superintendent of the public schools in Coshocton, Ohio. He asked for copies, as "our public school library in this *democratic-rebel* town, need such lessons daily, as the history of the rebellion contains." Requests such as these would continue to pour in for decades, impressing on the staff the excitement among veterans about the publication. In 1890, George B. Davis informed the secretary of war that "demand for the work—already great—steadily increases, as its existence becomes generally known, and as the volumes appear which relate to the great campaigns of the war. It is proper that this demand should be supplied, and that those who took part should have the privilege of reading the official narrative of their services."[80]

Veterans were also early users of the *OR* for published works of history. Francis W. Palfrey, a U.S. general who published a study of the Antietam and Fredericksburg battles in 1882, thanked Robert N. Scott for providing him advance sheets of the compilation, which he defined as "by far the largest assistance" he had received in researching the book. In 1891, George B. Davis was reading General William F. Smith's newly published study on a certain episode in the history of the U.S. army during the war and could barely contain his excitement. "It was a revelation to me of the manner in which the truth can be extracted from the correspondence volumes of the War Records with no other comment or criticism than is necessary to point out a line of thought or action as each despatch bears upon it." Davis asked for a dozen more copies to send to West Point and other military schools as an example of how the *OR* could be used for the teaching of military history. In 1901, Thomas L. Livermore, who had served as a colonel in the war, published his monumental *Numbers and Losses in the Civil War in America*, a massive statistical work based largely on a close reading of the *OR*.[81] Another veteran by the name of Livermore, William Roscoe, who spent the Civil War as a cadet at West Point and joined the army in June 1865, noted that, despite the limitations of individual documents, the *OR* enabled a military expert to "learn where almost every regiment was from the beginning to the end of a campaign or a battle. This is almost the only great war for which this would be possible."[82]

All told, the *OR* was created in tandem with a large, energetic, and self-entitled constituency whose partnership was absolutely indispensable to the compilation process and whose expectations were never far from compilers' minds. Yet veterans also reciprocated, by giving the compilation an enthusiastic welcome, putting it into use, and pressuring congressmen to keep funding the work and bring it to completion.

In a study of General Douglas Haig, who commanded Great Britain's forces on the Western front during the First World War, historian Denis Winter offers an astounding description of the efforts by the British government to fabricate the history of the war and cover up the disastrous mistakes of its leaders. First, the compiler,

Brigadier General Sir James E. Edmonds, crafted a version of events as favorable as possible to the army's high command and circulated it among relevant parties to get their approval; next, he compiled for publication only those documents that agreed with this narrative scheme; finally, he made sure that only a small fraction of the available documentation be deposited in Britain's Public Records Office, concealing and destroying untold papers so to prevent skeptical researchers from piecing together a different story. As Winter puts it, "The end product of Edmonds' work was therefore an Official History which presented a fraudulent account of the Western Front, supported by documents mischievously selected and leaks maliciously planted in the path of writers pressing too hard on the truth."[83]

Seen in comparison, the compilation work of the War Department comes across as impartial, fact-based, and honest. There are no sinister mandarins, no overarching attempts to falsify the record and mislead historians into recounting the government's version of events. Those actually seem rather foreign to the nineteenth-century American state, before it grew into a gargantuan machine equipped with sophisticated mechanisms for hiding information. Yet the work of compilation was also profoundly shaped by men whose wartime careers were going to be represented in the government's official history and who had every reason to be concerned about what would be published. The latitude they received in determining which records to send in, the dependence of the WRO on their active collaboration at virtually every step, and the close camaraderie that developed between compilers and contributors were all baked into the editorial process and must be understood as integral to its output.

Amazingly, active collaboration came not only from the men who fought in the ranks of the United States but also from the men who took up arms against it. For they, too, exerted a powerful influence on the making of the *OR* in ways that ultimately had far-reaching and unexpected consequences for the fitful process of remaking the nation after the Civil War.

CHAPTER SEVEN

The Archive and Sectional Reconciliation

The first sign that the publication of the government's Civil War records would play a role in the country's complex process of reunification was already visible during the brief congressional discussion of the $15,000 appropriation that allowed the War Department to begin work on the project. The date was June 12, 1874, and the man speaking was Representative John Coburn of Indiana, a Republican and the chairman of the Committee on Military Affairs. As Congress debated a standard Miscellaneous Appropriations Bill, Coburn brought up an amendment "to enable the Secretary of War to begin the publication of the official records of the war of the rebellion, both of the Union and of the confederate armies."[1]

On the face of it, the amendment was merely a routine matter of military administration, tucked between an appropriation for purchasing additional office space in Washington and an appropriation for building a prison in Kansas. In the absence of a Federal archiving apparatus, Coburn was fulfilling his duty as an elected official by trying to salvage precious war records from destruction. He was also, conceivably, acting as a historically minded veteran. A brigadier general in the U.S. volunteer army, he had commanded the 33rd Indiana Infantry, spent time in Libby Prison, participated in Sherman's March to the Sea, and was the officer who officially accepted the surrender of Atlanta from its Confederate mayor in September 1864. After the war, he participated in veterans' commemorative activities, giving fiery speeches glorifying the men who had died "to put down this slave-holding confederacy, to blot forever the ideas of disunion and secession, to establish on firmer foundations this great Republic." In short, this was a man who had devoted himself to the Union war effort, endured some of its harshest trials, and remained committed to its legacy.[2]

The chamber Coburn was addressing was largely sympathetic to a former officer arguing in favor of preserving war records and to the lobbying of veteran organizations on behalf of the same cause. In 1874, Reconstruction had not yet ended, and postwar animosities were still running high. The House of Representatives was heavily dominated by the Republican Party at a moment when it was reaping electoral benefits from leading the country in wartime. The long shadow of the war was evident in the language of the amendment, which casually used the term "war of the rebellion," reflecting the standard position of loyal Americans that the war had been an illegal insurrection against the Federal government and implicitly rejecting the counterargument that it was a legitimate conflict between sovereign states.[3]

The case Coburn made for publishing Confederate records along with those of the United States was first and foremost archival. The records of both governments could be destroyed, taken, or lost "and thus a most important part of the history of the country may at any time, for want of proper protection of these records, be utterly annihilated." But then, rather suddenly, Coburn shifted gears and made an emotional plea to his colleagues, speaking in a language of national unity and nonpartisanship. "Everybody in the land, whether he may have been engaged on one side or the other in the late rebellion, every lover of his country, every one who delights in the preservation of its history, is interested in this matter . . . it seems to me useless to reason with the House in favor of a proposition so manifestly calculated for the benefit of the entire nation."[4]

Coburn was trying to convince his colleagues to allocate money for a project he believed was both important and urgent.

Yet his remarks reflect the first signs of a budding sentiment that would grow increasingly powerful as time went by, and shape culture and society in America for decades to come. Sectional reconciliation was the process through which the United States was reconstituted as a single nation in the aftermath of a war that had torn it apart. To some extent, it had always been inherent to the logic behind the Federal government's pursuit of victory in the war. What was the point of fighting to subjugate the rebellious states, after all, if not to bring them back into the fold? For this and other reasons, a strong undercurrent of leniency toward white Southerners was evident in the policies enacted by the United States even before the war was over, and was reinforced once active fighting stopped.[5]

Over the next few decades, this sentiment grew as white Southerners were reintegrated into the American union, acquiring a plethora of different guises in multiple realms. Popular writers were producing highly romanticized and deeply nostalgic tales of the Old South; Northern editors made a profit off publication projects like *Century Magazine*'s highly marketable and deeply reconciliationist Battles and Leaders of the Civil War series; historians were crafting a master narrative that presented the war as an unfortunate but unavoidable stage in the evolution of the United States as a modern nation; the Federal government organized commemorative activities that brought veterans across the sectional divide into shared spaces and communal commemoration rites. Modern scholars have debated the nature, scope, and depth of this process fiercely. Some, like David Blight, have argued for its monumental importance in shaping postbellum American society, chiefly in marginalizing the memory of slave emancipation as the war's end and meaning.[6] Others, like Caroline Janney, have produced convincing evidence that reconciliation was always profoundly limited by Americans' core beliefs in the righteousness of their respective causes, whether secession and slavery or Union and abolition.[7] Yet as Nina Silber has put it, for all the nuance and complexity introduced by contemporary scholarship into our understanding of how Americans contended with the memory of the war, there is simply no other paradigm than reconciliation for understanding sectional relations in the post–Civil War era.[8]

The work of making the *OR* would play a crucial role in propelling this process forward. Once Congress mandated the publication of Confederate records along with those of the United States, the exigencies of archival work created a set of new conditions for the interaction between the Federal government and its erstwhile enemies. The relationship between the archive and the culture of which it was a part worked both ways: the processes of collecting, arranging, and proofing Confederate records were shaped by a broader climate but were also instrumental in fostering it by making the Southern military leadership a partner in the War Department's historical work and reforming its relationship with the government it had sought to destroy.

Although Congress mandated in 1874 that Confederate records be published, it gave no further instructions on how the publication should be designed. It fell to Secretary of War William W. Belknap to make that decision. Belknap, a Republican lawyer and politician from Iowa, had served notably in the Civil War, fighting under the command of the no-nonsense William T. Sherman and reaching the rank of brigadier general. After the war, he took part in veteran activities, giving rousing speeches in his baritone voice. But he was also deeply unsympathetic to African Americans and was the secretary of war who closed down the Freedmen's Bureau and humiliated its chief, Oliver O. Howard. In August 1875, right before embarking on a long trip to the Far West, Belknap gave a verbal order that his chief clerk made sure to write down in an official letter book. The secretary of war, the clerk stated, "expressed his wish that the rebel archives should be prepared for publication under the act of June 23, 1874, *pari-passu*, with the Federal records now being prepared for publication."[9] Belknap, whose own record-keeping practices were extremely slipshod, left no written explanation for why he chose to have Confederate records printed side by side with those of the United States. Was it a recommendation by a subordinate, Belknap's own vision for a user-friendly collection, or a political calculation meant to ingratiate him with Democrats and former Confederates at a moment when they were regaining national power? The available evidence does not provide an answer.[10]

In many ways, however, Belknap's motivations are immaterial compared to the profound impact of his order. In practical terms, placing the records of both sides on an equal footing meant that the space allocated to each had to be at least comparable. This posed an extraordinary challenge for the War Department. The government's collection of Confederate documents, housed in the Archive Office, was tiny compared to its holdings of U.S. records. "As it now is," Belknap wrote Congress in 1875, "these confederate records are so incomplete that the result of their compilation will necessarily be very unsatisfactory to all concerned."[11] Untold papers were in private hands, kept by former Confederate officers and politicians who took them home at the end of the war and had never been required to report their existence or hand them over. Nominally, of course, these records were as much the property of the Federal government as were the ruins of Confederate forts, but no one in Washington seems to have entertained the possibility of obtaining them by force. The reality of archival scarcity would demand a massive effort of reaching out to former rebels and coaxing them into granting the government access to their private collections. When it came to the publication of official records, the once-victorious Federal War Department was at the mercy of its fallen enemies.

The task was never going to be easy, owing to the level of hostility among white Southerners toward the government that had conquered them in war. But it was made even harder by the fact that some ex-Confederates were particularly livid about the very existence of the Archive Office, which remained a symbol of their subjugation even when other manifestations of Federal power in the former Confederacy had gradually disappeared. The repository was a source of humiliation both because it was used to defeat Southern claims and because it was a storehouse of Confederate history closed to the same people who cared about it most. To make matters worse, though the official name of the bureau was "Archive Office, War Department," it was commonly known as the "Rebel Archives," a term ex-Confederates still perceived as an explicit offense, especially when employed by Federal officials.[12]

For years, different parties attempted to gain access to the records stored in the Archive Office, but to no avail. Individuals were told that the "Rebel archives are not in a condition to admit of their examination" or that they were "not accessible for information except of an official nature."[13] State administrations hoping to retrieve records required for governance were also turned down. In 1869 the government of Virginia asked to receive its executive journals from the war years, which were taken by the U.S. army when it occupied Richmond in April 1865. The chief clerk of the Archive Office, Bezalel Wells, presented a persuasive case that the books were of great historical import and should not be given up. In 1877, John Letcher, the wartime governor of Virginia, applied for a considerable number of his own papers and was told that the staff in the Archive Office were too busy looking up material for claims commissions and could not assist him. Perhaps knowing what he was up against, Letcher submitted his application through the secretary of the navy, Richard Thompson, but that made no difference. The request was denied by the secretary of war, whose chief clerk openly admitted that giving back records was bad policy in an era of intense legal disputes between Southerners and the Federal government over claims. As he put it, "[I]n general it is thought that a compliance with such requests in a measure impairs the advantage of the Government of possessing the Rebel Archives."[14]

One person holding a particular grudge against the Archive Office was Zebulon Vance, the Confederate governor of North Carolina who had been reelected to the same office in 1876. A few months after his reelection, he received a standard request from the War Department to provide wartime records from the state's Adjutant General's Office for the *OR.* Vance refused for reasons he was happy to expound on at length. The letter books of his state, he argued, had been illegally confiscated to begin with, since hostilities had already ceased when they were discovered in Greensboro and shipped to Washington, never to be seen again. "Permission has been asked again and again to return them, or to obtain copies for the State Archives, which has been persistently refused." Worse still, in 1871 Vance had required access to the records of the War Department in order to respond to a newspaper article charging him with cruelty toward Federal prisoners of war who were interned in North Carolina. "The refutation of this calumny was contained in certain official letters recorded in those books. I went in person to the War Department, stated my object, and asked permission to copy two letters, which contained my full vindication, and was refused on the ground, as was assigned, that no copies could be given without the authority of Congress." Five years later, while running for election as governor, Vance discovered his Republican opponent was "supplied with an armful of *garbled* and *mutilated* copies of these same official letters, certified as *true* copies by yourself, as Secretary of War, with the great seal duly attached." Vance had applied to Congress for access to the originals in the archive, but the Republican-controlled Senate ignored his request, which prompted Vance's refusal to supply more records. "Under this state of things, therefore I should deem myself wanting both in self-respect and in appreciation of the office, which I have the honor to fill, were I to comply with your request."[15]

Vance's resentment was widely shared by those Southerners who devoted their postwar lives to keeping the memory of the Confederacy alive. This was by no means a large group. During the first postwar decades, most ex-Confederates were preoccupied with putting their lives back together in a deeply altered social, economic, and political landscape. While memorial activities for fallen soldiers had begun before the war was over and continued in its aftermath, most men and women who had been involved in the Confederate war were eager to set aside the trauma of defeat or simply had more pressing concerns.[16] Amidst what seemed like willful amnesia, a few former officers in the Confederate army stepped forward and volunteered to serve as professional gatekeepers of its history. In 1869 they founded the Southern Historical Society (SHS) and began collecting documents in an attempt to create an archive for the nation that died in the war. In 1876 the society launched its own publication project, *The Southern Historical Society Papers*, a mix of original documents from the war period with speeches, essays, and reminiscences from the postwar period. In all of its endeavors, the society's goal was one and the same: propagating the Confederate version of the Civil War, according to which the South had fought nobly for its traditional way of life and lost, through no fault of its own, given the U.S army's overwhelming advantage in men and matériel. In time, this Lost Cause narrative would gain immense traction in

American public life. The diehards acting under the auspices of the Southern Historical Society were crucial actors in cementing its underpinnings.[17]

Though the SHS enjoyed little popular following and was in constant financial trouble, it positioned itself as the rightful heir of the Confederacy's written record. Founded in New Orleans, it quickly moved its headquarters to Richmond, still the South's sentimental capital, where it was allotted office space in the Virginia General Assembly. The fact that a vast cache of Confederate documents existed under lock and key in Washington was both an affront to these ardent believers and an impediment to the society's goal of shaping how the history of the Confederacy would be written. The society's secretary, J. William Jones, a Baptist minister and Lost Cause author, decried the "outrage of keeping these documents locked up to Confederates" and confessed that the occasional morsels of information trickling out of the Office "have only served to sharpen the appetite of those interested in such matters, and to make them all the more anxious to have access to the rich store of material."[18]

The decision to undertake the publication project under the terms dictated by Belknap recast the relationship between the government and historically inclined ex-Confederates. As it became apparent that the holdings of the Archive Office would fall short of sustaining the Confederate portion of the compilation, the War Department was compelled to modify its stance toward the same white Southerners who had played important roles in the rebellion, since they were the ones who were most likely to possess official documents. And so Edward D. Townsend, the famously anti-Southern adjutant general, sent around letters looking for the members of the retinue that had escorted Jefferson Davis when he fled Richmond in April 1865, in search of a fictional "train of eight wagons containing records of the Confederate States which were hidden in the swamps."[19] Belknap, for his part, ordered the return of "a large amount of the papers and all the personal effects" belonging to Jefferson Davis that had been found on his person and among his belongings in the spring of 1865 and kept in the War Department ever since.[20] As the 1870s advanced, the War Department was also responding more positively to requests by states for their executive records, sending them boxes of papers that were not deemed historically essential and authorizing the making of copies, the only exceptions being those records that could potentially help the Federal government defeat claims.[21] In a communication with Zebulon Vance in November 1877, the secretary of war pointed out that North Carolina's state records were "in the possession of the United States as property captured in war," but for the first time the state was allowed to make copies of the records stored in the Archive Office.[22]

The lengths to which the War Department was willing to go in order to obtain the Confederate records it was missing was most visible in its new approach toward the Southern Historical Society. In January 1876, Secretary Belknap wrote an extraordinary letter to SHS secretary J. William Jones, which was widely printed in newspapers across the country. Belknap was following up on "conversations" his private secretary, William T. Barnard, had held with Jones and "other gentlemen" which revealed the "existence, in different sections of the country, many records, such as battle reports, official correspondence, etc. etc., relating to the late war, and . . . intimations have been given that it would be practicable for the War Department to secure these either permanently or temporarily, for use in connection with the publication of the Records of the war now in hand." Belknap, by his own admission, was induced to write Jones because he had learned "that an impression prevails, to a greater or less extent in some localities of the country, that a disposition exists, on the part of the administration, to make a distinction between the Confederate and Federal Archives, as regards the thoroughness of their compilation." Belknap wanted to ensure Jones that was far from true: "[T]he Department is not only willing but anxious to secure every official report, letter, telegram, or order, emanating from either side during the late War, and has no thought whatever of discriminating in favor of one section as against another, in their publication."[23]

Jones responded a week later, expressing his "great satisfaction" that the War Department was about to start publishing war records, since the Southern Historical Society aspired "to place our Confederate people right upon the record" and was therefore "ready to co-operate most heartily in any effort which shall tend to secure that result." Jones did not deny that Southerners were highly suspicious of the Federal government's archiving policies: "To be frank, there *has* been, as you intimate, a wide spread fear at the South that few of the captured Confederate Records would ever see the light, and a general feeling that their suppression, and a refusal to give us access to them would be a great wrong to the cause of justice, and truth." Yet for all his enthusiasm about justice and truth, Jones set clear terms for the "hearty co-operation" he promised: "We will have furnished you properly authenticated copies of such as are in our possession, and will assist you in procuring others—it being understood, of course, that your Department will afford us similar facilities in the prosecution of our work."[24] Jones, in short, was offering the society's services on the condition of reciprocity with the War Department, a proposition Belknap could not accept. The rules of the War Department, he explained to Jones in response, "forbid all access to papers on its files, except for official purposes." Though he had "every desire and intention" of furnishing Congress with the most complete compilation possible, he was unable to meet the society's condition, and the publication would have to move forward regardless. Belknap's response did not allude to the fact that the records in the SHS archive were actually the property of the Federal government, or that Jones and his partners were rebels who had been defeated in war. Whether it was the dire state of the government's Confederate holdings or a deep-seated kinship with white Southerners, or a little of both, Belknap, while holding the line on War Department policy, did not seem either shocked or perturbed by the attempt of an ex-Confederate heading a small and cash-strapped historical society to dictate terms to the Federal government.[25]

It is therefore not entirely surprising that a year later Barnard approached Jones again. Belknap was no longer in office, having been impeached by Congress on charges of corruption and forced to resign. The new secretary, J. Donald Cameron, a Republican businessman from Pennsylvania with no previous political experience, placed Barnard in charge of the compilation project. Barnard reminded Jones of their previous exchanges and asked him to consider his letter as "exhibiting the desire of the Department to make as fair and perfect a record of the Southern military operations, compared with those of the North . . . I trust you will unite with me in desiring to make this work as national and unpartisan as it can be made." The department was still unable to grant nonofficial personnel access to its files, but Barnard was offering another concession instead. The Southern Historical Society would receive advance copies of the volumes produced by the War Department, simultaneously with their submission to Congress. As this preliminary edition was only printed in twelve copies, receiving one in advance seemed exceptionally desirable to Barnard: "This concession has never before been made or proposed by the Department and I trust you will unite with me in securing its acceptance."[26] In response, Jones told Barnard he had introduced his offer to the SHS executive committee, where it was summarily rejected. Though its members were "anxious that your publication of Confederate reports, documents, etc. shall be as full and accurate as possible" the leaders of the SHS felt "that our Society should receive some equivalent benefit for what we may be able to furnish the Department."[27] By that point, Barnard had had enough. In his response he reminded Jones that the Society "had as its object the dissemination of the knowledge contained in its archives among the people," which is why the War Department had approached it in the first place, something that it was not required to do. The department, "of course as an official matter, would not feel called upon to publish anything beyond what its files contained, or go beyond them in seeking for official material, but, as its representative in the matter, I am solicitous that the motives and actions of neither side should remain in doubt or be misconstrued" because records still in existence could not be obtained. "If your Society does not practically unite in this desire, it would be a source of personal regret, but not as a matter of concern to the Department, whose rules have been stretched to the utmost in allowing me to make the proposition now before your Society."[28] Jones and his colleagues did not waver. Two months later, after discussing the matter again in a meeting of the executive committee, Jones wrote Barnard to say he did not see "that we would derive the slightest advantage from your proposition to furnish us your material" a few weeks earlier than the general public received it, and reiterated "our *ultimatum*, that there must be some *reciprocity* in the matter."[29]

Barnard never responded, and he resigned his position a few weeks later. Though he did not cave in to the demands of the SHS, the attempt he made to persuade its leaders to collaborate with the War Department is striking in and of itself. His promise that the compilation would be "as national and unpartisan as it can be made" and the offer to share volumes of widely coveted documents from the government's archives before any veteran of the U.S. army could see them reveal the impact of the desire to close the gaping holes in the archive and to produce a complete collection. Barnard, a senior War Department bureaucrat serving a Republican administration, was making concessions to unrepentant former rebels that would have been unthinkable a decade earlier.

J. Donald Cameron left his position as secretary of war in March 1877, following the tumultuous presidential election of November 1876, and was replaced by George McCrary. McCrary was a politician from Iowa who had played a major part in the contested election the country had just endured by forming the electoral commission that eventually handed over the presidency to the Republican nominee, Rutherford B. Hayes. Hayes rewarded McCrary by appointing him secretary of war, and it was under his administration that the last U.S. troops retreated from the South, bringing an end to Federal intervention in the governance of former rebellious states. Though the move was largely symbolic, as the great majority of U.S. troops had departed years earlier, it was nevertheless a potent expression of the Federal government's new priorities and its compliance with the notion that white Southerners had both the right and the ability to rule their own states.[30]

The existing evidence does not allow for a reliable reconstruction of McCrary's decision-making when it came to the relationship between the War Department and the Southern Historical Society. Partly this is the fault of Barnard's successor as superintendent of the *OR*, another War Department bureaucrat, Thomas J. Saunders, who was even sloppier when it came to keeping a written record of his own work. In addition, there is reason to believe that a Letters Sent book from this period has disappeared in the storage spaces of the National Archives.[31] Yet there are some hints showing that the entrance of McCrary into office changed the tenor of the relationship with the SHS, which is not surprising considering the broader policy of coming to terms with white Southern home rule and McCrary's specific role in achieving the compromise that settled the chaotic presidential election of 1876 at the price of relinquishing Federal involvement in the region. On December 6, 1877, the executive committee of the Southern Historical Society unanimously adopted "a memorial to Congress to vote ample appropriations to the War Records Office in view of the pleasant relations now established between that office and our society."[32] No explanation is offered for how the "pleasant relations" came about. Yet regardless of what exactly had been agreed on with Saunders or Secretary McCrary, the relationship between the War Department and the men who fought it was about to undergo a wholesale transformation with the departure of Saunders on December 8, 1877, and the appointment of Robert N. Scott the following week.[33]

Scott had served honorably in the U.S. army during the Civil War, but under different circumstances he might have easily joined the other side. Born in Tennessee and raised in Louisiana, at the beginning of the war he was arrested for voicing pro-Southern sentiments in public.[34] In 1865 he ascribed his difficulty in winning a promotion to his Southern roots and applied to the governor of Louisiana for help in making his case to the secretary of war. He also used his father's Tennessee connections to get the attention of President Andrew Johnson, the Tennessean who came into power after Lincoln's assassination. In a political culture suffused with patronage and nepotism, ambitious men were impelled to muster whatever connections they could. For Scott, these connections were with men from the South.[35]

It is more than conceivable that some of this background was on Scott's mind when he made the forceful recommendation, early in his tenure, to abolish the separation between Federal and Confederate records in the compilation under his charge. "By all means," Scott wrote the secretary of war in his first annual report, "both the Union and the Confederate accounts of any event should be given in the same volume. This, to my mind, is a matter of vital importance to our national welfare." And so, more or less from the start, Scott conceived of the *OR* not only as a historically minded bureaucrat and legal thinker but also as an American with a complicated background who clearly considered his Southernness to have played a part in his life. In Scott's mind, the *OR* was to be part of the effort to heal the country following a terrible civil war.[36]

And yet, as head of the War Records Office, Scott also faced the very material challenge of closing the huge gaps in the government's Confederate holdings. Here, he was aided by the political interest in appointing a former Confederate as an agent for the collection of Civil War records. The files of the War Department do not offer a full picture of how the hiring came about, but enough can be gleaned to determine that Southern men drove the process. The agent hired on July 1, 1878, was Marcus J. Wright, an undistinguished brigadier general from Tennessee with a passion for historical writing and a considerable talent for self-promotion.[37] Struggling to make ends meet during Reconstruction, he identified an opportunity in the War Department's new interest in historical records following the 1874 appropriation. With the help of congressmen from Mississippi and Alabama, he approached the department in 1875 and offered to sell his private collection of wartime records, which earned him $2,000 and praise from Secretary Belknap for his service and the "generous spirit in which it has been done."[38] He then volunteered to search the South for additional records gratis, proclaiming "a very deep interest in the completeness of the publication." At a time when J. William Jones was exchanging caustic messages with Barnard, and other senior ex-Confederates seemed all but out of reach, Wright stood out as a willing and cheerful collaborator with the Federal government's historical efforts.[39]

And yet, by tendering his offices to the War Department, Wright was also playing a long game. Though it is quite plausible that as an inveterate believer in the Confederate cause he really did care about how it would be represented in the official history of the war, Wright was also perennially broke and clearly considered his budding relationship with the War Department from a pecuniary point of view.[40] In a communication with Congressman Casey Young, a Confederate veteran and Democrat representing Tennessee's 10th congressional district, Wright said he had hoped Congress would appoint a commission to make the compilation and that one of its members would be a Confederate, hinting that he would be an appropriate choice for the position. He reiterated his conviction that many valuable records were hidden in Southern archives but that he was too poor to work on obtaining them without compensation. Young was responsive and lobbied Secretary McCrary for greater attention to the collection of official Confederate records, which he guaranteed were widely available across the South and could be easily gathered, but were "constantly liable to loss or destruction." He also asked and received an estimate for how much funding would be required to assemble Confederate material, and pushed for a congressional appropriation to pay for it. Professing to feel "much interest" in the matter, Young stressed it would be impossible to tell the story of the war "fully and fairly" without the assistance of a Southerner to collect material. In the spirit of Washington politics, he repeatedly brought Wright up as the perfect candidate for the position, declaring that "in all the qualities that fit him for such a work as this, I am sure he has no superior." The War Department welcomed the idea, having already considered putting one of its own staff in charge of resolving the problem of scarcity in the Confederate archive. "Probably the appointment of such a gentleman thus to represent the Confederate side would be acceptable," wrote an unnamed staffer, "and a substitute for the former proposed plan of associating someone with the officer at present compiling the work." Wright's was the only name mentioned in connection with the opening. And so, at this crucial juncture, the devotion of certain ex-Confederates to the history of their cause intersected with the exigencies of the archive and created the opportunity Wright had been trying to engineer for three years. On July 1, 1878, he received his letter of appointment.[41]

Wright's arrival on the scene launched a new era in the relationship between the Federal government and its former adversaries. From his first day on the job, he worked tirelessly to assemble the remnants of the Confederate official archive scattered across the former rebellious states and, by one estimate, was personally responsible for three quarters of the Confederate material appearing in the *OR*. He started out by issuing a form letter asking veterans for "the originals of all such records as may be valuable in illustrating the nature of the great struggle from which the country has emerged" and promising that placing them in government hands

Marcus J. Wright, agent for the collection of Confederate records, War Department. Image from Diary of Brigadier-General Marcus J. Wright, C.S.A.: April 23, 1861–February 26, 1863. *Courtesy of Wilson Special Collections Library, University of North Carolina at Chapel Hill.*

would preserve them from destruction.[42] He personally contacted numerous officers and family members, who sent in a wide variety of Confederate records that had remained in private hands since the end of the war. He traveled extensively across the South and Southwest, visiting private parties, historical societies, and state archives, and found records in expected and unexpected places ("We have struck we think a *bonanza* in a junk shop of old papers," he reported from Richmond on one occasion).[43] His monthly reports include meticulously detailed lists of the documents he had been able to procure: battle reports on engagements large and small, letter books, order books, telegrams, returns, muster rolls, congressional documents, medical records, and all other specimens of military paperwork. Among the contributors he recruited, meticulously listed in his monthly reports, are the famous, infamous, and unfamous, anyone from Jefferson Davis to Nathan Bedford Forrest to field officers whose names are familiar only to specialists. Though the documentary record of the rebellion would always remain smaller and more fragmentary than that of the United States side of the war, Wright's hard work, ambition, and good connections transformed the scope of the government's Confederate holdings and enabled the War Department to produce the collection both congressmen and Scott had in mind, in which the records appeared side by side and reflected how events were experienced by both armies.[44]

Wright's work, however, had far-reaching implications beyond the simple collection of records. From the moment he took office, he became a one-man outpost of the Confederate army in the Federal War Department, representing the interests of individuals and organizations, lobbying for expanded access to the material kept in the department's archival bureaus, and serving as a liaison between former rebels and the government that defeated them. Wright felt no compunction about his participation in the war, continuing to refer to himself as a "former *rebel* or *Confederate*" for as long as he worked in the War Department. He openly sought to use his position to promote the legacy of the Confederacy in more ways than by ensuring that the published compilation would offer as complete coverage as could be managed.[45]

One of Wright's first action items was to break the deadlock with the Southern Historical Society over copying privileges. In his first monthly report, submitted to Scott on July 31, 1878, he stated that if the secretary of war would authorize him to give permission to the SHS to copy whatever documents they may desire, "I believe I can get copies of all papers in these files which are desirable to attain; and they have many very valuable original papers, the absence of which from our archives, leaves them incomplete." Scott, his Southern heritage notwithstanding, was reluctant to agree. Reminding Secretary of War McCrary of the "unsatisfactory correspondence" held with the SHS, he also pointed out that McCrary had already "permitted prominent Confederate leaders to get from the Union archives such data as has enabled them to wage a supplemental war." Scott was hoping that the courtesies extended by the War Department would be reciprocated, but he was "averse to having any bargain made between the United States and any association of individuals, be they of Union or Confederate antecedents." Nevertheless, McCrary, who was willing to go much further for ex-Confederates than his predecessors were, assented to Wright's request despite Scott's objections. On August 5, Scott formally authorized Wright "to inform the Southern Historical Society and like associations, that duly accredited agents from them will be allowed access to . . . consult and take copies from such records as are of purely historical value and not bearing upon claims against or in behalf of the United States Government." Gloating in a statement to the *Richmond Dispatch*, Jones announced that the War Department's "offer, made voluntarily and without condition, was all that we had ever asked, and was in the highest degree gratifying to our committee."[46]

Feeling confident, Wright seized on the moment and submitted a list of documents from the Archive Office he wanted copied, without explaining why. This was such a brazen violation of traditional War Department policy that even the lenient McCrary was surprised. Adjutant General Townsend responded on the secretary's behalf that "the furnishing of such papers in advance of their publication is uniformly refused. Genl. Wrights' employment gives him no privileges in regard to the records of the war Dept. not enjoyed by any other person, but is confined specifically to collecting records from outside sources." Wright did not back down, arguing that the copying was required for individuals who had contributed papers and that he would be unable to perform his duties if he had "to ask Confederate officers for their military books and papers, to be placed in the Archives of the Dpt., and then inform them that while historical societies and other persons are permitted to have copies, they are to be excluded from this privilege." Once again, McCrary was convinced by Wright's logic, and the Archive Office flung open its doors to former rebels asking to peruse or copy records. And so, within a few weeks of his appointment, Wright's palpable achievements in collecting records were sufficient grounds for abandoning policies that dated back to 1865.

Wright also struck up a correspondence with Jefferson Davis, the bitter and brooding former president of the Confederacy, who was living on a Mississippi plantation and working on his own history of the war, which would come out in 1881 under the title *The*

Rise and Fall of the Confederate Government. Wright wrote Davis immediately upon his appointment and heard back that Davis was "glad for the sake of truth and courtesy" that he had been appointed. From that moment on, Wright was in regular touch with Davis and his assistant William T. Walthall, also a former Confederate officer. Davis still harbored ill feelings toward the U.S. army and in particular toward Adjutant General Townsend, whom he called "that poor snake" and whom he accused of intentionally retaining some of his private papers just for spite.[47] Yet Wright's personal appeal and his promise of full access to War Department files obviously made a difference. Davis agreed to give Wright copies of the official records in his private archive, which was far from complete but still contained a treasure trove of invaluable correspondence with other wartime actors. Walthall, who had tried and failed on several occasions to gain access to the Archive Office, immediately asked for certain documents he and Davis needed and took advantage of the license to visit the Archive Office within a year.[48]

Wright, however, offered much more than documents, and at times acted like Davis's personal emissary in his contacts with the Federal government. In an effort to overcome the fallen president's continued resentment toward the War Department, he applied for the return of some private papers that had been designated as historically valuable and retained when the bulk of Davis's belongings were sent to his lawyer in 1874. Wright argued that the records were "of no value whatever to the office" and emphasized that "Mr. Davis is and has been for some time furnishing us copies of all such papers in his possession as we request, and giving his assistance in procuring papers of value from other persons for the use of this office." Scott concurred and ordered their return, with Wright serving as middleman.[49] Davis would continue writing Wright to ask for information from the records and to complain about this or that aspect of the compilation process, to which he was closely attuned.[50]

For Davis and other ex-Confederates, Wright was the go-to person in the War Department, their representative in all matters relating to the archive in Washington. His presence on the staff facilitated contact with Southerners, but no less critically, he embodied the new approach of the War Department toward its onetime

Jefferson Davis, Beauvoir, Mississippi, ca. 1885. Photo courtesy of Library of Congress.

foes and offered an assurance that the Federal government would not use the *OR* to settle scores. It probably made some difference that Wright remained actively involved in Confederate memorialization efforts throughout his time as an employee of the War Department. He was intimately engaged in the internal affairs of the Southern Historical Society and corresponded frequently with its officers on a variety of institutional matters. He was also an active historical writer, publishing articles and books on a variety of subjects, from accounts of little-known battles to biographies of famous generals. Always on the lookout for more income, in 1893 he began publishing a magazine called *The Confederate War Journal*, a publication in competition with the better-known *The Confederate Veteran*. In it he referred to the conflict as "The War Between the States," the standard term among white Southerners for the Civil War and a counterbalance to the official term, "War of the Rebellion."[51] In more than one way, Wright's interstitial position personified the culture of reconciliation in the late nineteenth century: ex-Confederates had been welcomed back into the Union without having to relinquish their old beliefs or show remorse for the bloodbath they had caused. As long as one was cordial to old foes and committed to the project of American nationhood, the past could be, perhaps not entirely forgotten, but certainly set aside.

Even as Wright served as the linchpin of the new relationship between the government's archival bureaus and ex-Confederates, the transformation taking place in the War Department during the late 1870s was broader than any single person. Though the head of the War Records Office, Robert N. Scott, was initially suspicious of the rebellion's leadership, he was quick to change his mind once Wright opened lines of communication to previously indisposed Southern men. In September 1879, Scott approached Jefferson Davis directly and asked him for copies of telegrams the War Department did not have, spelling out that Davis was not required to submit any papers he did not so choose. In their exchanges, Scott employed a deferential tone that left no doubt as to who was in control of the records. "In arranging the Confederate correspondence covering operations in Virginia I find several letters from General Lee, answering or referring to communications from yourself that I cannot find," he wrote Davis on one occasion. "Is it asking too much to request that you furnish me with a list of such of your dispatches (letters or telegrams) to General Lee as you are willing to furnish for the compilation?"[52] When Scott thought that his office had mistakenly received "copies of some papers that you did not desire should be furnished," he invited Davis to "designate such dispatches and [if] they have not already been published I will return the copies to you."[53] Scott, in short, was offering Davis the same courtesy extended to other senior Civil War figures: a document he did not want published would be withheld. The particular role Davis had played in the war seemed beside the point. The former president was no longer a rebel, the commander in chief of an army that fought tooth and nail against the United States. He was now a highly valuable "contributor to the work"—furnishing papers, deciphering telegrams, and proofreading copies—and was thus entitled to the gratitude and consideration of the War Department.[54]

After Davis's death in 1889, the WRO established a relationship with his widow, Varina, by sending Wright to visit her in Louisiana. Mrs. Davis agreed to give compilers access to her late husband's papers, but the two made a verbal agreement to exclude certain papers, which were marked "not to be copied." The War Department clerk doing the copying in New Orleans, unsure how to proceed, noted in a letter to Washington that it was "generally understood here that there are some papers which would be of value, but which *Mrs. Davis does not wish printed.*" Compiler George B. Davis spoke with Wright, who assured him that such records "as have been put under that head ought not to be copied, either because they are immaterial, or because they are private and personal in character." Without asking further questions, George Davis ordered the copyist to "leave that matter out of question altogether, and deal with the rest" of the Jefferson Davis papers.[55] In the celebratory introduction attached to the final volume of the compilation and published in 1901, Secretary of War Elihu Root singled out Jefferson and Varina Davis for affording the government "access to his papers relating to the late war, and from this source were obtained copies of archives of the greatest historical value." The praise publicly bestowed was no empty gesture. The Davises had indeed proved crucial partners in making Civil War records publishable, a telltale sign if there ever was of the distance the War Department, and the United States, had traveled since the final days of the war, when the former president and his wife were hounded in the swamps of rural Georgia by Federal cavalry with orders to take them in.[56]

Though the Davises were particularly essential, the War Records Office became reliant on the assistance of any number of other ex-Confederates. Robert N. Scott asked General D.H. Hill "for any suggestions that you may care to make in connection with the report, herewith, of your corps at Chickamauga. I specially desire to get the names of all actual commanders during that battle." Other officers were asked to describe how the Confederate artillery was organized at Appomattox, which commands acted when at Gettysburg, or what direction and distance a certain force marched while on a little-known expedition in southwestern Virginia.[57] In July 1879, Scott hired a second former Confederate officer, this time as a clerk, to answer the need for "some one familiar with the *personnel* of the Confederate armies." The appointee's name was Edwin J. Harvie, and Scott assured the secretary of war that he was "specially qualified and was vouched for by distinguished men of both the great political parties."[58]

Soon after his appointment, Harvie approached Jubal Early, the man that historian Gaines Foster has called the "prototypical unreconstructed Rebel." Early had served under Robert E. Lee and fled to Mexico after the war, believing he could not live under United States rule. Returning to Virginia in 1869, he quickly emerged as a central figure in the early efforts to establish and promulgate the Southern narrative of the war, becoming president of the Southern Historical Society in 1873. Until his death in 1894, he waged a relentless campaign to uphold the reputations of Robert E. Lee, the Army of Northern Virginia, and the Lost Cause.[59]

An obsessive devotion to Confederate history was precisely what made Early such an asset for the War Department. Harvie, in his first letter, said he assumed the general had "seen some notice of my appointment" and told him that he was working on a "correct roster of General officers, senators, etc. for the Confed. States one that our people would recognize as satisfactory. Knowing your accuracy of statement and love of truth it occurred to me to write and ask your assistance in the matter . . . I would gladly mail you these papers, if it would be agreeable to you to look on and correct them." From then on, the War Records Office regularly turned to Early for help in examining and proofreading records and for hunting down absent papers. In return, Scott offered Early easy access to the records of the Archive Office, even voluntarily. "Did you ever see the correspondence in relation to yourself between Gov. Smith and Genl. Lee transmitted by the return to the War Dept. October 14 1864?" he asked at the end of a routine letter

Jubal Early, painting by John P. Walker, 1898. Courtesy of the Virginia Museum of History & Culture (1946.216).

searching for missing documents. "If you so desire I will send you copies."[60]

Scott's successors were equally dependent on the good offices of these former rebels as the Confederate paper trail grew ever thinner toward the end of the war. Writing to John B. Gordon, the leader of the newly founded United Confederate Veterans in 1889, George B. Davis pleaded that he ask members to send in their records for the volumes being compiled under his charge, since "in no other way can the full story be told, or exact justice be done to the services of the Confederate Armies."[61] In 1891, Davis sent an infantry officer, Lieutenant Lyman W.V. Kennon, to meet in person with Jubal Early in his Virginia home. Kennon, a future hero of the Spanish-American War, was working on an independent study of Civil War battles in which Early took part. Once in Lynchburg, he was instructed to try and obtain Early's "orders and correspondence relating to the operations conducted by him in the Valley of Virginia and in Maryland, between May 1st and December 31st 1864." Those operations were widely considered to have been some of the most notorious Confederate actions of the war. They included burning down the town of Chambersburg, Pennsylvania, kidnapping free African Americans, and extorting large sums of money from the residents of Hagerstown and Frederick in Maryland in exchange for sparing their towns. Now, however, since the War Records Office needed the records documenting these sensational events, they were cast in a different light. Davis asked Kennon to "represent to the General how little matter we have relating to his operations in Maryland, and how important it is that a campaign so ably conceived and brilliantly conducted should be fully reported."[62] Once Early granted permission to examine and copy the records, Davis procured the help of two of Early's staff officers "to look them over and select such as should be published." He made sure to return to Early records that he thought were of particular personal value and thanked him for his "great kindness." Communication with other former Confederate leaders also remained effusively cordial. Henry M. Lazelle, corresponding with General Edward Porter Alexander, addressed him as "my dear Alexander" and assured him that his "kind expressions are greatly appreciated, and that I take pleasure in doing you any favor."[63]

In 1892 the WRO embarked on an extensive venture of copying archival records from the New Orleans Historical Society, at first relying on the aid of the society's secretary, a former Confederate colonel, W. Miller Owen, and later stationing a full-time copyist in its offices. The holdings of the society helped complete the War Department's gravely deficient records of the Confederacy's Western armies, whose actions were poorly documented to begin with. Owen took an active interest in the work of the WRO, providing material from the society's files, disentangling illegible documents, and looking for those records still in private hands.[64] As George B. Davis was about to "close up" (as compilers used to call it) volume 38, covering the operations of the Atlanta campaign in 1864, he wrote Owen to ask, "[W]ill you not kindly make a special effort to see if you have any matter falling within that period, and pertaining to the operations of the armies of either General Johnston or General Hood?" By the fall of 1892, Owen was given authority to determine which papers from the Jefferson Davis collection would be copied, as the records were in the society's hands and Marcus J. Wright was unable to make another trip to New Orleans. "I suggest that you look them over yourself, and cause such to be copied as you think should appear in the War Records," Davis wrote. Leslie J. Perry, the two-time prisoner of war, invited Owen to visit Washington. "Had you not better shake off your provincialism and visit the capital? I will agree to fight the war all over again with you if you will come." George B. Davis lavished praise on the society's president, Colonel E.A. Palfrey, professing "the deep sense of personal obligation under which I am to you, for the great and thoughtful kindness" he had exhibited toward War Department officials. "It has been of the greatest service to me in the publication of the War Records, and has contributed, materially, to a complete presentation of the Confederate side."[65]

Meanwhile, the Southern Historical Society remained the WRO's most constant and reliable partner in the compilation process. The ill feelings that had informed the interactions between the two parties before 1878 seemed to have disappeared once the men involved met in person and examined each other's repositories. J. William Jones arrived in Washington in August 1878, less than three weeks after Secretary McCrary authorized reciprocal copying privileges, and reveled at finding collections thought to have been lost, like Robert E. Lee's confidential letter books. Later that fall, Marcus J. Wright together with Albert P. Tasker, the chief clerk of the Archive Office, visited the society's rooms in Richmond and "found a very large mass of very valuable and official matter which is not in the archives of the War Department."[66] Wright attended a meeting of the Southern Historical Society in Virginia's White Sulphur Springs shortly thereafter, and though his request to give a speech at the meeting was denied by the secretary of war, he met with the executive council. The meeting, he reported to Scott, "resulted in the unconditional tender by the Society to the War Department, of the privilege of taking copies of any and all records and papers belonging to the society." In December 1878, Scott sent the SHS the preliminary volumes of Confederate reports compiled in the department to prevent important records from being lost. An excited Jones reported to Early on their arrival, noting that "leading Northern libraries" were unable to secure the volumes. "These are the first copies that have been allowed to leave the Dept," he boasted, but asked for Early's discretion: "[T]his is only for our friends as it would probably raise a howl if known at the North."[67] In return, Scott asked Jones to conduct a form of peer review by going over the volumes and informing him "as to any errors that may be discovered in these preliminary prints, as of proper names, dates etc." Jones and other society officials tendered the War Department a range of other crucial services on an ongoing basis: they corrected the official roster of Confederate officers, helped in locating missing records, and tracked down elusive facts.[68]

The tone and substance of the frequent missives exchanged between Washington and Richmond leave no doubt as to the nature of the personal relationships that had developed between staffers on both sides as they became gradually enmeshed in a web of mutual obligations. Jones thanked Scott profusely for the "uniform courtesy with which you are treating our Society and for the many favors we are receiving from the War Records Office" and assured him he was "anxious to reciprocate so far as it may be in our power."[69] When a question arose about a payment owed by Jones for copying he had ordered from the Archive Office, Tasker noted he was "sure the Dept. is not disposed to be exacting towards you especially after your generosity to us." In another obvious act of consideration for ex-Confederate feelings, Scott selected as his copyist in Richmond the Kentucky-born Virginia Dade, a longtime employee of the War Department's archival bureaus who was known for her remarkable efficiency and for her strong links to the South. Back in 1877, when relations with former rebels were still tense, chief clerk Albert P. Tasker had asked that she be permanently positioned in the Archive Office, arguing that her "being acquainted with many Southern Members could do much to dispel the charges of unfairness which are being made."[70]

The institutional alliance that took shape in the 1870s proved remarkably resilient, carrying over into the 1890s, regardless of personnel turnover in both offices. In 1888, Henry M. Lazelle commiserated with Robert A. Brock, the new SHS secretary, over the burdens of editorial work: "I am sorry that you have so much to arrange and methodize, but from the amount of such work constantly before us I can readily understand it." Three years later, George B. Davis hired a founder and former president of SHS, Dabney H. Maury, to locate additional Confederate papers, a job Maury desperately needed for financial reasons.[71]

Compiling the Confederate portions of the *OR*, which began as a requisite of the publication project, took on a life of its own and thrust record keepers across the sectional divide into a close collaboration that would have seemed highly unlikely only a few years earlier. Naturally, the ease with which Federal bureaucrats embraced their erstwhile enemies was also the product of the broader trend of sectional reconciliation, which began to gather momentum in the late 1870s and fed on the shared interests and sensibilities of white Americans. But other manifestations of this cultural shift did not become prevalent before the mid-1880s: the funeral of Ulysses S. Grant, which Joan Waugh has identified as a "benchmark event for sectional reconciliation," took place in August 1885; *Century Magazine* began publishing its reconciliationist War Series in 1884, reissued in 1887 as Battles and Leaders of the Civil War; battlefield preservation reached a peak in the 1890s; and blue-gray reunions began in the mid-1880s.[72] The crucial turning points in the making of the *OR* preceded and presaged these highly publicized events. Though copying records and correcting rosters lacked the flare and drama of a battlefield reunion and largely took place outside the public eye, the impact of these seemingly dull and bureaucratic undertakings was in some ways greater. The Federal government's compilation work bound together the most unyielding ex-Confederates and War Department officials in a shared commitment to reassembling the written record of the rebellion. While battlefield reunions, captured in iconic photographs and rhapsodic newspaper reports, were singular events, the ongoing collaboration between War Department officials and Lost Cause advocates was sustained, lasting years and decades. Each side, of course, entered the process with a different agenda—Lost Cause warriors like Jones, Davis, and Early sought to commemorate their beloved Confederacy, while Washington bureaucrats aspired to produce a complete and accurate compilation befitting an official history published by the victor in the war. Yet ultimately the demands of the editorial process trumped the interests that record keepers on both sides brought to the work. The result was a compilation in which rebels received the same consideration as the government against which they fought. The *OR* was a portable monument to the great war the nation had gone through, even as it embodied the determination to leave that war behind.[73]

And portable it was. The dissemination by Congress ensured that the compilation would travel far and wide, reaching every state in the Union and nearly every type of community. To the War Department's annoyance, most sets ended up in private hands, probably an inevitable outcome of congressmen using the publication to curry favor with constituents.[74] But sets also reached public venues where they could serve multiple readers. Beyond soldiers' homes and local branches of veteran organizations, *OR* sets were most often sent to public libraries and the libraries of educational institutions, but they were also found in historical societies, YMCAs, jails, asylums, convents, hospitals, military barracks, and the offices of county clerks.[75] On August 4, 1900, a normal business day at the office, clerks sent out volumes to institutions as remote and diverse as the Aberdeen Public Library in South Dakota, the Gate Academy in Neligh, Nebraska, the *Birmingham News* in Birmingham,

Alabama, and the Female Seminary Library in Washington, Pennsylvania. Among the individuals waiting for volumes were Prof. J.W. Conger in Arkadelphia, Arkansas, Mrs. Martha B. Bohan in Los Angeles, California, and George Burns in Denmark, Mississippi.[76] Some of the applicants whose requests could not be immediately accommodated were the librarian of a small institution, the Leland Stanford Junior University in Palo Alto, California; an unnamed member of the English cabinet, who applied through a Washington lawyer; and a Philadelphian by the name of James W. Hendricks, who in 1890 wrote to the secretary of war, reassuring him that "I do not want an office, but I am desirous of obtaining a copy of the official record of the War of the Rebellion." Hendricks was hoping the secretary would remember that the two had met a decade earlier during a boat trip from Jacksonville to Savannah and spent their whole time playing cards. "My memory of it is very vivid," Hendricks recalled, "from the fact that you and your partner failed to win a single game."[77] If such appeals failed, and they usually did, a reader anxious to own a copy could resort to looking in secondhand book stores in America's big cities, where volumes commanded, according to Leslie J. Perry, "pretty stiff prices." Clearly, there was a receptive audience for the War Department's creed of "impartial" history, in which no one was right, no one was wrong, and everyone deserved to see their records published by the Federal government in a commemorative project. But it is worth considering the extent to which the national distribution of the *OR* did not just reflect a prevalent disposition across America but amplified it too.[78]

Appropriately, white Southerners shared in the excitement about the publication of the compilation. Congressman Randall L. Gibson, representing Louisiana, lobbied for the adjutant general of his state to receive a set, arguing that the officer was a "large contributor to the war records." By 1883, the prevalence of *OR* volumes in Southern libraries was enough of an established fact to move Henry S. Cohn, a veteran of Sherman's army living in Louisville, Kentucky, to write his old general and complain that he was unable to get a copy. "As you may well know you may find these very same official records on the shelves of hundreds of Confederate soldiers in the South, while hardly one of the soldiers that wore the blue is able to obtain any favors from those in Congress or Senate from the South." His own congressman told him he had already distributed his copies, as did the two senators of his state, "of which [the] last named Gentleman once served as General in the Rebel Army."[79] Finally, in 1885, Joseph Wheeler, representing Alabama in Congress, drafted a bill for the printing of additional *OR* volumes. During the Civil War he was known as the commander of Wheeler's Cavalry, a rowdy fighting force that was often feared by Southern civilians as much as it was by U.S. soldiers. Yet those were different times. Twenty years later, Wheeler was a respected "contributor to the work" and a member of the House of Representatives. Plainly feeling the *OR* did justice to the South, he wanted to get more copies off the press.[80]

The professional gatekeepers of Southern history shared the sentiment. Yates Snowden, a historian in Charleston, asked in 1881 that the South Carolina Historical Society be put on the list of recipients, reminding Adjutant General Townsend that he had lent the department some records. The Southern Historical Society celebrated the publication with a glowing review in its own organ, praising the importance of the work "so skillfully compiled under the able supervision of Colonel R.N. Scott (to whose courtesy we are indebted for continued favors)." J.W. Jones complimented "Colonel Scott and his assistants" for being "not only very competent to the discharge of their duties, but fair in their treatment of Confederate as well as Federal reports and documents."[81] Douglas Southall Freeman, the staunchly pro-Confederate historian who associated with veterans of Lee's army, including officers of the general's own staff, testified that "the *Official Records* amazed the South by their impartiality. Except for the fact that the ugly word 'Rebellion' appeared on the books, the only fact to indicate they were issued by the victors was that the Union reports and correspondence always preceded the Confederate."[82]

Outside the South, the *OR* offered historians the documentary basis for narratives that put both sides in the conflict on an equal footing and made battlefield drama the central interest of Civil War history. James Ford Rhodes wrote in *History of the United States from the Compromise of 1850 to the McKinley-Bryan Campaign of 1896* (1904–1919) that his "greatest obligation" for the Civil

War portions was to the government for the "unique publication" it had produced at great effort and expense. "Rarely has money for the behoof of history been better spent." Rhodes belonged to the nationalist school, whose members divided blame for the Civil War and Reconstruction evenly and offered a version of American history that stressed unity and continuity. Though Rhodes was a businessman who wrote history as a hobby, a new generation of university-trained scholars, writing in an age of virulent nationalism, were equally invested in a unifying narrative of American development. Bisectional and free of judgment, the *OR* was the ideal source material for historians writing in this vein.[83]

The reunionist bent of the compilation would continue to endear it to historians for generations. Clarence E. Carter, an Illinois-born historian of the West and president of the Organization of American Historians, who was also an expert on document editing, commended the "courageous work" of Robert N. Scott. "By associating former confederate officers on the staff, Scott was able to procure essential records of the confederate army, and by his policy of excluding irrelevant matter, especially non-contemporary materials, a work was produced which will never have to be redone."[84] Writing in the 1950s, Shelby Foote referred to the *OR* as the "most useful" source he consulted for his three-volume *The Civil War: A Narrative*, and praised the authentic feel of the documents, in which he "could hear the live men speak." Foote was a Mississippian, but his work enjoyed a national appeal, paving the way for his starring turn in the 1990 documentary *The Civil War* by Ken Burns. The visually irresistible series was not just a blockbuster but also a groundbreaking achievement in making documentary films. In some ways, it might be considered the *OR* on film. It told the story from both sides, focused overwhelmingly on military action, and conveyed a soothing message of national rebirth. And like the *OR*, it also seemed to bring the dead back to life.[85]

By the early twentieth century, the records first created as tools of war, enabling two gigantic armies to operate across a vast tract of land, had been transformed into vehicles of sectional peace. The process was fraught, but once underway, it was remarkably consistent. The War Department's work to remake the archive into a published collection created a demand for Confederate records and historical expertise that could be met only by teaming up with the people who could provide both. Archival labor brought the former enemies together in sustained contact in the service of a shared goal: the creation of a complete, accurate record of the Confederate armies, which would take its place alongside the records of the United States. The results have remained pertinent to students of Civil War history, and their audiences, to this day.

Coda

An Imperfect Story

In all likelihood, no one who lived in the twentieth century knew the Civil War records stored in Washington better than Dallas D. Irvine. A towering figure in the halls of the National Archives for decades, he was one of the institution's first professional employees, carrying the title of senior specialist for military archives. Irvine was also a trained historian holding a PhD from the University of Pennsylvania who played a prominent role in founding what became the Society for Military History and who published widely on the history of warfare in Europe and the United States.[1]

Irvine developed an expertise in the history of Civil War record management early in his career. He wrote a series of seminal articles on the subject in the 1930s based on published sources and preliminary research in the records of the War Department. Years later, he initiated the preparation of a comprehensive finding aid for the *OR*, which he defined as "badly needed" by "long suffering" users of the compilation. Irvine conceived *The Military Operations of the Civil War: A Guide-Index to the Official Records of the Union and Confederate Armies, 1861–1865* as a means to overcome the debilitating organization of the *OR*'s General Index, which was created with veterans in mind and therefore lists the name of every individual appearing in the volumes but largely omits the names of military operations.

Irvine's *Guide-Index* enabled researchers to locate every mention of virtually all military engagements appearing in the *OR* and provided important explanations on how the work was organized. Though it would be made largely obsolete less than two decades later by digitization and keyword search, the making of the five-volume reference tool entailed a fifteen-year effort by a team of archivists. When Irvine submitted volume 1 of the work, in 1966, the typescript totaled 1,536 double-spaced pages.[2]

Irvine, therefore, knew what he was talking about. He had gone through substantial portions of the *OR* with a fine-toothed comb and was disgusted by what he found. He blamed the compilers for producing unusable indexes, which forced researchers looking for information about a particular engagement to first find the names of every officer who had participated in it and filed a report. "After going through this process a sufficient number of times, the student of military operations in the Civil War will be tempted to find some easier field of scholarship or some less grueling form of recreation," Irvine wrote in the introduction to the published version of the *Guide-Index*. The compilers of the *OR* also strangely failed to add tables of contents to each volume and committed numerous editorial mistakes. Some were inconsequential, he conceded, "but others are egregious, the total of such mistakes is very large. The editorship was not rigorous in any scholarly or scientific sense; it was empirical and relatively uncritical."[3]

Irvine had another reason to seethe at the staff of the War Records Office: they had not left a written record of their own work. As he put it, "The compilers often failed to document their operations adequately and left no unofficial accounts of their activities. In addition, many of the pertinent records seem to have been lost." In a different internal memo, written while going through a collection of letters by early *OR* compilers, Irvine criticized William T. Barnard for being "pretty cavalier and very careless" in his record keeping, "conducting much correspondence of an official or semi-official nature 'off the record' " and taking home records belonging to the War Department. Though Irvine recognized that *OR* staff did not at first understand that their work deserved documentation, their failure to keep records was personally aggravating, denying him the ability to understand how the project evolved, but it also hindered his efforts to make the *OR* more legible to modern users contending with the "bootless obscurities" of the finished product. "Any real understanding of the nature of *Official Records, Armies,* requires some knowledge of the history of the publication project. That story, however, has never really been told and is now difficult to reconstruct."[4]

By all accounts, Irvine was a rather short-tempered character who was as easily irritated by his living colleagues as he was by the dead. (One younger colleague described him as "crusty," even in print.) Yet he was right that reconstructing the government's management of Civil War records is made enormously more complicated by the absence of regular documentation and by the loss of crucial records. Nineteenth-century archivists, as it turns out, were no better than other historical actors in preserving a written record of their work. The silences and gaps inherent in every archive are as present and as consequential in the archive of the archive. Writing *about* an archive is conditioned by the same epistemic problems as writing *with* the aid of an archive.[5]

What this means is that some questions remain unanswered: Who ordered Francis Lieber to abstain from publishing any of the information about the Confederacy stored under his charge? Who was really at fault for the chaos on the day the Freedmen's Bureau's records were moved? Why did Secretary of War William W. Belknap decide in 1874 that Confederate records should be printed *pari passu* with Federal records? What did Thomas J. Saunders promise the Southern Historical Society in 1877? Did Libbie Custer eventually succumb to the War Department's pleas and send in her husband's papers? Did compilers intentionally withhold embarrassing records from publication? Did the War Records Office ever reach an authorized estimate of how many prisoners of war died on either side of the war, and did the staff keep it from the public?

Then there are the missing documents. Some we know had existed but vanished over time, most crucially the Letters Sent book from the War Records Office's early years, when War Department officials first attempted to negotiate with the Southern Historical Society and other ex-Confederates for their records. Other documents were never created to begin with, like service records for the clerks who worked in the War Department. Their absence leaves us with precious little information on, for example, the identity of Bezalel Wells, the chief clerk of the Archive Office, who wielded the power of records against ex-Confederates trying to curry favor with the government during early Reconstruction. There is the tantalizing possibility that Robert N. Scott left personal reflections somewhere, perhaps in private letters, a forlorn diary, or even an official memorandum hiding somewhere in the bowels of the National Archives. Perhaps more plausibly, pertinent documents, not sufficiently utilized, are buried in the records of the offices of the secretary of war and the adjutant general. Some of these missing documents might someday emerge through sheer luck or through the efforts of a different researcher. Others will remain lost, like the other innumerable pieces of documentation historians must do without.

Nicholas Dirks, a historian of Britain's imperial archive, once critically remarked that "the archive is constituted as the only space that is free of context, argument, ideology—indeed history itself. Accordingly, historians can only really become historians or write history once they have been to the archive." Yet studying archival history raises the possibility that to become a historian, or remain one, it is essential, while *in* the archive, to stop and consider archival collections as creations of their time and place, as the products of both manipulation and circumstance. A historian *of* an archive might be sensitive to the vagaries of archival organization, to the personalities of archivists, and to the political and budgetary demands made on archival institutions. The challenge to a historian engaging with an archive—not as a subject of research but as an instrument—is to factor in all of these contingencies while using archival collections to construct other stories.[6]

In the end, Irvine was not entirely right. Even if a full and accurate story of the Federal government's archiving of Civil War records cannot be told, *a* story can be told. That story is fundamentally imperfect. It is based on fragmentary evidence and determined by how the sources were organized in various archives and through the efforts of different archivists. It is also shaped by the mundane imperatives of twenty-first century travel and access and reflects the historian's biases, blind spots, and errors. Yet *this* story has unearthed the forces shaping Washington's Civil War archive and has demonstrated how archival records figured in the fraught reality of the postbellum era. It has reconstructed the process through which records created as tools of war ended up serving as vehicles of sectional peace; it has revealed how some of the received wisdom in Civil War history has been shaped by decisions made in the archive; and it has demonstrated the extent to which archival labor—assembling, organizing, storing, and publishing records—is deeply rooted in specific cultural contexts. All this remains as true today as it was when War Department bureaucrats endeavored to master the written record of the Civil War.

Notes

Abbreviations

CMLS—Confederate Memorial Literary Society Collection, under the management of the Virginia Museum of History and Culture, Richmond, Virginia

EP—Jubal Anderson Early Papers, Manuscript Division, Library of Congress, Washington, D.C.

FLPHL—Francis Lieber Papers, Henry E. Huntington Library, San Marino, California

FLPLC—Francis Lieber Papers, Manuscript Division, Library of Congress, Washington, D.C.

GI1966—Dallas Irvine, "Military Operations of the Civil War: A Guide-Index to the Official Records of the Union and Confederate Armies, 1861–1865," vol. 1, Microfilm M1036, National Archives and Records Administration, Washington, D.C., 1966

GI1977—Dallas Irvine, *Military Operations of the Civil War: A Guide-Index to the Official Records of the Union and Confederate Armies, 1861–1865*, vol. 1: Conspectus (Washington, D.C.: National Archives and Records Service, General Services Administration, 1977)

HL—Henry E. Huntington Library, San Marino, California

HP—Burton Norvell Harrison Papers, Manuscript Division, Library of Congress, Washington, D.C.

JTP—John T. Pickett Papers, Manuscript Division, Library of Congress, Washington, D.C.

LC—Manuscript Division, Library of Congress, Washington, D.C.

LSAG—Letters Sent by the Office of the Adjutant General, Main Series 1800–1890, vol. 34, Jan. 23, 1882–Jan. 31, 1863, M565, roll 21, Record Group 94, National Archives and Records Administration, Washington, D.C.

NARA—National Archives and Records Administration, Washington, D.C.

OR—*War of the Rebellion: A Compilation of the Official Records of the Union and Confederate Armies*, 128 vols. (Washington, D.C.: Government Printing Office, 1880–1901)

RG 94—Records of the Adjutant General's Office, 1775–1928, National Archives and Records Administration, Washington, D.C.

RG 107—Records of the Office of the Secretary of War, National Archives and Records Administration, Washington, D.C.

RG 109—War Department Collection of Confederate Records, National Archives and Records Administration, Washington, D.C.

RG 159—Records of the Inspector General (Army) National Archives and Records Administration, Washington, D.C.

SP—Edwin McMasters Stanton Papers, Manuscript Division, Library of Congress, Washington, D.C.

SHC—Southern Historical Collection, Wilson Library, University of North Carolina at Chapel Hill

WSHC—Marcus J. Wright Papers, Southern Historical Collection, Wilson Library, University of North Carolina at Chapel Hill

Introduction

1. The term "Houses of Memory" is from Terry Cook, "What Is Past Is Prologue: A History of Archival Ideas since 1898, and the Future Paradigm Shift," *Archivaria* 43 (Spring 1997), 18. See also Arlette Farge, *The Allure of the Archives*, trans. Thomas Scott Railton (New Haven, Conn.: Yale University Press, 2013). In the foreword, Natalie Zemon Davis reminisces about her own archival travels and discoveries, describing sensations familiar to many an archival user. "I still recall the look of the important archival sources I've used: the large heavy volumes, with their leather thongs and sometimes their original binding; the bundles of papers tied with string, sometimes with a centuries-old pin holding pages together. In their handwriting, their occasional doodles and asides, and their registers, I have in my hands a link to persons long dead: it strengthens my historian's commitment to try to tell of the past with as much discernment, insight, and honesty as I can," xiv–xv.
2. Terry Cook, "The Archive(s) Is a Foreign Country: Historians, Archivists, and the Changing Archival Landscape," *The American Archivist* 74 (Fall/Winter 2011), 608, 617, doi.org/10.17723/aarc.74.2.xm04573740262424.
3. Alexandra Walsham, "The Social History of Archives: Record Keeping in Early Modern Europe," *Past and Present* 230 (suppl. 11), 11. The theoretical texts at the core of the archival turn are Michel Foucault, *The Archeology of Knowledge*, trans. A.M. Sheridan Smith (New York: Vintage, 2010 edn.); Foucault, *The Order of Things: An Archeology of the Human Sciences* (London: Routledge, 2002 edn.); Jacques Derrida, *Archive Fever: A Freudian Impression*,

trans. E. Prenowitz (Chicago: University of Chicago Press, 2001); Carolyn Steedman, *Dust: The Archive and Cultural History* (Manchester: Manchester University Press, 2001).

4. "The archival turn" has produced a vast literature spanning multiple disciplines. Useful overviews are in Marlene Manoff, "Theories of the Archive from Across the Disciplines," *portal: Libraries and the Academy* 4 (2004), 9–25, doi.org/10.1353/pla.2004.0015; Elizabeth Yale, "The History of Archives: The State of the Discipline," *Book History* 18 (2015), 332–359, doi.org/10.1353/bh.2015.0007; Alexandra Walsham, Kate Peters, and Liesbeth Corens, eds., *Archives and Information in the Early Modern World* (Oxford: Oxford University Press, 2018), 1–25. Important historical works include Nicholas B. Dirks, *Castes of Mind: Colonialism and the Making of Modern India* (Princeton, N.J.: Princeton University Press, 2001), 61–123; Antoinette Burton, ed., *Archive Stories: Facts, Fictions, and the Writing of History* (Durham, N.C.: Duke University Press, 2005); Verne Harris, *Archives and Justice: A South African Perspective* (Chicago: Society of American Archivists, 2007); Ann Laura Stoler, *Along the Archival Grain: Epistemic Anxieties and Colonial Common Sense* (Princeton, N.J.: Princeton University Press, 2009); Nupur Chaudhuri, Sherry J. Katz, and Mary Elizabeth Perry, eds., *Contesting Archives: Finding Women in the Sources* (Champaign: University of Illinois Press, 2010); Katherine Burns, *Into the Archive: Writing and Power in Colonial Peru* (Durham, N.C.: Duke University Press, 2010); Kirsten Weld, *Paper Cadavers: The Archives of Dictatorship in Guatemala* (Durham, N.C. : Duke University Press, 2014); Markus Friedrich, *The Birth of the Archive: A History of Knowledge*, trans. John Noël Dillon (Ann Arbor: University of Michigan Press, 2018); Randolph C. Head, *Making Archives in Early Modern Europe: Proof, Information, and Political Record-Keeping, 1400–1700* (Cambridge: Cambridge University Press, 2019); Jason Lustig, *A Time to Gather: Archives and the Control of Jewish Culture* (Oxford: Oxford University Press, 2021). Examples for how the idea of "the archive" is used by cultural and literary critics are Thomas Richards, *The Imperial Archive: Knowledge and the Fantasy of Empire* (New York: Verso, 1993); Diana Taylor, *The Archive and the Repertoire: Performing Cultural Memory in the Americas* (Durham, N.C.: Duke University Press, 2003).

5. Bonnie G. Smith, *The Gender of History: Men, Women, and Historical Practice* (Cambridge, Mass.: Harvard University Press, 1993); W. Fitzhugh Brundage, *The Southern Past: A Clash of Memory and Race* (Cambridge, Mass.: Harvard University Press, 2005), 105–137; Cheryl Beledoe, *The Import of the Archive: U.S. Colonial Rule of the Philippines and the Making of American Archival History* (Sacramento, Calif.: Litwin, 2013); Lisa M. Tetrault, *The Myth of Seneca Falls: Memory and the Women's Suffrage Movement, 1848–1898* (Chapel Hill: University of North Carolina Press, 2014), 112–144. Some recent work shows the field is beginning to evolve.

See Eric C. Stoykovich, "Public Records in War: Towards an Archival History of the American Civil War," *The American Archivist* 80 (2017), 135–162, doi.org/10.17723/0360-9081.80.1.135; Laura E. Helton, "On Decimals, Catalogs, and Racial Imaginaries of Reading," *PMLA* 134.1 (2019), 99–119, doi.org/10.1632/pmla.2019.134.1.99; Daniel Eric Cone, "The Cause Archived: Thomas Owen, the Alabama Archives, and the Shaping of Civil War History and Memory" (PhD dissertation, University of Alabama, 2020).

6. Laura Helton et al., "The Question of Recovery: An Introduction," *Social Text* 33, no. 4 (2015), 2 and the entire special volume, doi.org/10.1215/01642472-3315766. See also Brian Connolly and Marissa Fuentes, "Introduction: From Archives of Slavery to Liberated Futures?," *History of the Present* 6, no. 2 (2016), 105–116, and the entire special volume, doi.org/10.5406/historypresent.6.2.0105. The seminal text is probably Saidiya Hartman, "Venus in Two Acts," *Small Axe* 26 (2008), 1–14, doi.org/10.1215/-12-2-1. See also Marissa Fuentes, *Dispossessed Lives: Enslaved Women, Violence, and the Archive* (Philadelphia: University of Pennsylvania Press, 2018); Jewel Spangler, "Slavery's Archive, Slavery's Memory: Telling the Story of Gilbert Hunt, Hero of the Richmond Theater Fire, 1811," *Journal of the Early Republic* 39, no. 4 (2019), 677–708, doi.org/10.1353/jer.2019.0086. For a different argument, stressing the ways in which historians can discover the history of African Americans in archives despite the limitations inherent to repositories, see Leslie M. Harris and Daina Ramey Berry, "Researching Nineteenth-Century African American History," and the entire special issue of the *Journal of the Civil War Era* 12, no. 4 (December 2022).
7. Terry Cook and Joan Schwartz, "Archives, Records, and Power: The Making of Modern Memory," *Archival Science* 2 (2002), 12, doi:10.1023/a:1020826710510.
8. Eric Ketelaar, "Tacit Narratives: The Meaning of Archives," *Archival Science* 1 (2001), 138, doi.org/10.1007/bf02435644.
9. Francis X. Blouin and William G. Rosenberg, eds., *Archives, Documentation, and Institutions of Social Memory: Essays from the Sawyers Seminar* (Ann Arbor: University of Michigan Press, 2006), 2.
10. For examples of using this term, see Lurton Dunham Ingersoll, *A History of the War Department of the United States* (Washington, D.C.: Francis B. Mohun, 1879); B.W. Brice to E.M. Stanton, Nov. 1, 1864, in *OR*, ser. III, vol. IV, 870; Montgomery Meigs to E.M. Stanton, Nov. 3, 1864, in *OR*, ser. III, vol. III, 885.
11. On the scale of the Civil War, see James M. McPherson, *Drawn with the Sword: Reflections on the American Civil War* (New York: Oxford University Press, 1996), 66–86. For a critical view of the war's size and totality, see Wayne Wei-Siang Hsieh, "Total War and the American Civil War Reconsidered: The End of an Outdated 'Master Narrative,' " *Journal of the*

Civil War Era 1, no. 3 (2011), 394–408, doi.org/10.1353/cwe.2011.0045. For a useful overview of technological innovation and its limits during the Civil War see Andrew W. Bledsoe, "Technology and War," in *The Cambridge History of the American Civil War*, ed. Aaron Sheehan-Dean (Cambridge: Cambridge University Press, 2019), vol. 2, 141–158.

12. Graham Thompson, "From Mind to Matter: Paper, Pens, and the Materiality of Letter-Writing," *The Edinburgh Companion to Nineteenth-Century American Letters and Letter-Writing* (Edinburgh: Edinburgh University Press, 2016), 33. See also Lothar Müller, *White Magic: The Age of Paper*, trans. Jessica Spengler (London: Polity, 2014), 129–179. It is worth keeping in mind, though, that this was not the first age of exponential growth in the volume and ubiquity of paper. Early modern historians have exposed similar patterns, albeit on a smaller scale, from the sixteenth century onward. See Daniel Rosenberg, "Early Modern Information Overload," *Journal of the History of Ideas* 64 (2003), 1–9, doi.org/10.1353/jhi.2003.0017; Jacob Soll, *The Information Master: Jean-Baptiste Colbert's Secret State Intelligence System* (Ann Arbor: University of Michigan Press, 2009); Ann Blair, *Too Much to Know: Managing Scholarly Information Before the Modern Age* (New Haven, Conn.: Yale University Press, 2010); John C. Rule and Ben S. Trotter, *A World of Paper: Louis XIV, Colbert de Torcy, and the Rise of the Information State* (Montreal: McGill-Queen's University Press, 2014); Paul M. Dover, *The Information Revolution in Early Modern Europe* (Cambridge: Cambridge University Press, 2021).

13. Annual Report, Stanton to Lincoln, Dec. 5, 1863, in *OR*, ser. III, vol. III, 1137; Annual Report of the Quartermaster General's Office to Stanton, Nov. 3, 1864, in *OR*, ser. III, vol. III, 885; Ingersoll, *A History of the War Department of the United States*, 350; James Gregory Bradsher, "An Administrative History of the Disposal of Federal Records, 1789–1949," *Provenance, Journal of the Society of Georgia Archivists* 3, no. 2 (1985), 2, https://digitalcommons.kennesaw.edu/provenance/vol3/iss2/2.

14. There are several important studies of the *OR*, but none are comprehensive nor based on the full documentation available in the National Archives. See Dallas D. Irvine, "The Genesis of the Official Records," *Mississippi Valley Historical Review* 24 (Sept. 1937), 221–229, doi.org/10.2307/1892082; See also Irvine, GI1966, and Irvine, GI1977. An unpublished study of the *OR* was conducted in 1930–1931 by Warrant Officer Charles Franklin as part of a decision-making process about the possibility of compiling a collection of records on the First World War. It is available in Record Group 165, Records of the War Department General and Special Staffs, National Archives and Records Administration II, College Park, Maryland. Other scholarly treatments are Joseph L. Eisendrath Jr., "The Official Records—Sixty Three Years in the Making," *Civil War History* 1 (March 1955), 89–94; Stetson Conn, *Historical Work in the United States Army 1862–1954* (Washington, D.C.: U.S. Army Center of Military

History, 1980), 1–10; Harold E. Mahan, "The Arsenal of History: The Official Records of the War of the Rebellion," *Civil War History* 29 (Spring 1983), 5–27, doi.org/10.1353/cwh.1983.0071; Alan C. Aimone and Barbara A. Aimone, *A User's Guide to the Official Records of the American Civil War* (Shippensburg, Pa.: White Mane Publishing, 1993); Michael P. Musick, "Honorable Reports: Battles, Campaigns, and Skirmishes," *Prologue* 27, no. 3 (Fall 1995), 259–277; Noah Andre Trudeau, "To 'Mold the Judgement of History,' " in *The Ongoing Civil War: New Versions of Old Stories*, ed. Herman Hattaway and Ethan S. Rafuse (Columbia: University of Missouri Press, 2004); Joan Waugh, *U.S. Grant: American Hero, American Myth* (Chapel Hill: University of North Carolina Press, 2009), 169–170; Yael A. Sternhell, "The Afterlives of a Confederate Archive: Civil War Documents and the Making of Sectional Reconciliation," *Journal of American History* 102, no. 4 (March 2016), 1025–1050.

15. Eric Ketelaar, *Archiving People: A Social History of Dutch Archives* (The Hague: Stichtig Archiefpublicaties, 2019), 19a.
16. The term "invisible archive" is from Cook, "The Archive(s) Is a Foreign Country," 611. See also B.M. Watson, "Please Stop Calling Things Archives: An Archivist's Plea," *Perspectives on History* 59 (January 2021), https://www.historians.org/research-and-publications/perspectives-on-history/january-2021/please-stop-calling-things-archives-an-archivists-plea.

Chapter One. An Archive Made and Unmade

1. Mark R. Wilson, *The Business of War: Military Mobilization and the State, 1861–1865* (Baltimore: Johns Hopkins University Press, 2006), 36. See also Wayne Wei-siang Hsieh, *West Pointers and the Civil War: The Old Army in War and Peace* (Chapel Hill: University of North Carolina Press, 2009), 32; Clayton R. Newell and Charles R. Shrader, *Of Duty Well and Faithfully Done: A History of the Regular Army in the Civil War* (Lincoln: University of Nebraska Press, 2011), 5. "Bureaucracy" is a heavily theorized concept, going back to the foundational texts by Max Weber in the early twentieth century who valorized bureaucracy as a form of rational organization, intimately intertwined with the rise of the modern state. Peter Crooks offers a useful definition for bureaucracy as a category of analysis: "Bureaucracy describes a system of administration in which routine administrative activity is delegated to officeholders (who are often, but not always, professional career administrators), conducted on the basis of information (typically in the form of written records), with some differentiation and specialization of offices that are organized hierarchically and are reliant on systems of communication." Peter Crooks, "Bureaucracy," in *Information: A Historical Companion*, ed. Ann Blair et al. (Princeton, N.J.: Princeton University Press, 2021), 343. For Weber, see

his *Economy and Society: An Outline of Interpretive Sociology*, trans. Guenther Roth and Claus Wittich (Berkeley: University of California Press, 1978), 217–226, 956–1005. Another formative work is James C. Scott, *Seeing Like a State: How Certain Schemes to Improve the Human Condition Have Failed* (New Haven, Conn.: Yale University Press, 1999). On the growth of Western bureaucracies in the eighteenth and nineteenth centuries, see Martin Krygier, "State and Bureaucracy in Europe: The Growth of a Concept," in *Bureaucracy: The Career of a Concept*, ed. Robert Brown et al. (London: Edward Arnold, 1979), 1–10. For an important non-Western example of bureaucratization, see Edgar Kiser and Cai Yong, "War and Bureaucratization in Qin China: Exploring an Anomalous Case," *American Sociological Review* 68, no. 4 (2003): 511–539, doi.org/10.1080/13642529.2018.1489578. On paperwork, see Bruno Latour, *The Making of Law: An Ethnography of the Conseil d'Etat* (Cambridge, U.K.: Polity, 2009); Ben Kafka, *The Demon of Writing: Powers and Failures of Paperwork* (New York: Zone, 2012). The term "files" has also been the subject of analytical treatment. See Cornelia Vismann, *Files: Law and Media Technology*, trans. Geoffrey Winthrop-Young (Durham, N.C.: Duke University Press, 2008); Lisa Gitelman, *Paper Knowledge: Toward a Media History of Documents* (Durham, N.C.: Duke University Press, 2014). Recent special journal volumes on bureaucracy and its meaning for the production of historical knowledge are Barbara Brookes and James Dunk, eds., "Bureaucracy, Archive Files, and the Making of Knowledge," *Rethinking History: The Journal of Theory and Practice* 22, no. 3 (2018); Sebastian Felten and Christine von Oertzen, eds., "Histories of Bureaucratic Knowledge," *Journal for the History of Knowledge* 1, no. 1 (2020), doi.org/10.5334/jhk.18.

2. Lurton Dunham Ingersoll, *A History of the War Department of the United States with Biographical Sketches of the Secretaries* (Washington, D.C.: Francis B. Mohun, 1879), 140.
3. Lucille H. Pendell and Elizabeth Bethel, *Preliminary Inventory of the Records of the Adjutant General's Office* (Washington, D.C.: National Archives and Records Administration, 1949); War Department, *Instructions for Keeping the Records and Transacting the Clerical Business of the War Department* (Washington, D.C.: Government Printing Office, 1876).
4. Harvey Meyerson, *Nature's Army: When Soldiers Fought for Yosemite* (Lawrence: University of Kansas Press, 2001), 44.
5. *Regulations for the United States Army* (New York: Harper & Brothers, 1857), 57–63. Quotes on pp. 60, 59.
6. Wilson, *Business of War*, 39.
7. Hsieh, *West Pointers and the Civil War*, 32.
8. Newell and Shrader, *Of Duty Well and Faithfully Done*, 43.
9. M.C. Meigs to Sir, Nov. 28, 1861, in *OR*, ser. III, vol. I, 682. On war as a generator of records in a similar context, see Charlotte McDonald and

Rebecca Lenihan, "Paper Soldiers: The Life, Death, and Reincarnation of Nineteenth-Century Military Files across the British Empire," *Rethinking History* 22, no. 3 (2018), 375–402, doi.org/10.4324/9781003038542-6.

10. M.C. Meigs to the Secretary of War, Nov. 18, 1862, in *OR*, ser. III, vol. II, 789–790.
11. Geo. D. Ramsay to E.M. Stanton, Oct. 27, 1863, in *OR*, ser. III, vol. III, 935.
12. B.W. Brice to A. Stager, Oct. 31, 1864, in *OR*, ser. III, vol. IV, sec. 2, 870; Montgomery C. Meigs to Secretary of War, April 16, 1879, box 7, entry 710, Letters Received, RG 94; E.D. Townsend to Edwin M. Stanton, Oct. 31, 1864, in *OR*, ser. III, vol. IV, sec. 2, 807.
13. Much of the evidence for record-keeping practices in both the United States and the Confederacy comes from the voluminous correspondence between the Federal War Department and numerous officers asked to provide wartime documents to complete the Federal government's collection. The project of completing and publishing the Federal Civil War archive will be extensively treated in Chapters 5–7.
14. Grant quoted in Stephen Cushman, *The Generals' Civil War: What Their Memoirs Teach Us Today* (Chapel Hill: University of North Carolina Press, 2021), 96.
15. Geo. B. Davis to Emily F. Warren, May 5, 1891, book 10, entry 708, Letters Sent, RG 94.
16. W.S. Rosecrans to H.M. Lazelle, Feb. 1, 1888, box 9, entry 710, Letters Received, RG 94; Geo. B. Davis to George Meade, Jan. 15, 1897, book 12, entry 708, Letters Sent, RG 94.
17. Geo. B. Davis to Adjutant General, June 24, 1897, box 6, entry 713, General Correspondence, RG 94; Hugh Hastings to G.D. Ruggles, June 15, 1897, box 6, entry 713, General Correspondence, RG 94.
18. U.S. War Department, *Report of the Secretary of War; Being Part of the Message and Documents Communicated to the Two Houses of Congress at the Beginning of the First Session of the Forty-Fourth Congress* (Washington, D.C.: Government Printing Office, 1875), vol. I, 25. On this point see also Drew Gilpin Faust, *This Republic of Suffering: Death and the American Civil War* (New York: Vintage, 2008), 332–334.
19. Alan C. Aimone and Barbara A. Aimone, *A User's Guide to the Official Records of the American Civil War* (Shippensburg, Pa.: White Mane Publishing, 1993), 43; Irvine, GI1977, 5.
20. L. Thomas to E.A. Hitchcock, May 15, 1862, p. 186, LSAG.
21. Extracts of Inspection Reports, vol. 1, entry 3, RG 159. The book of extracts includes reports starting 1864, when The Inspector General became an independent department. Earlier reports were submitted to commanding generals or the adjutant general. See finding aid for RG 159, NARA.
22. Extracts of Inspection Reports, vol. 1, entry 3, RG 159, p. 462, pp. 483–484, p. 435.

23. Extracts of Inspection Reports, vol. 1, entry 3, RG 159, p. 329.
24. Extracts of Inspection Reports, vol. 1, entry 3, RG 159, p. 325, p. 637, quote appears on p. 292.
25. Chelsey D. Bailey to Geo. B. Davis, July 22, 1889, box 9B, entry 710, Letters Received, RG 94. See also Nelson Cross to Secretary of War, March 16, 1877, entry 715, Letters Received Relating to Missing Military Reports, RG 94.
26. Wm. Brooke Rawle to R.N. Scott, Dec. 24, 1885, box 7, entry 710, Letters Received, RG 94.
27. T. Seymour to Secretary of War, Sept. 18, 1876, entry 715, Letters Received Relating to Missing Military Reports, RG 94.
28. R.H. Milroy to J.D. Cameron, Sept. 22, 1876, entry 715, Letters Received Relating to Missing Military Reports, RG 94.
29. Geo. B. Davis to Guy E. Howard, June 19, 1890, box 11, entry 710, Letters Received, RG 94; Geo. B. Davis to P.T. Sherman, Sept. 26, 1891, book 11, entry 708, Letters Sent, RG 94. See also Thos. B. Van Horne to Robert N. Scott, Sept. 23, 1879, box 3, entry 710, Letters Received, RG 94.
30. Geo. B. Davis to J.W. Forsythe, June 13, 1892, book 13, entry 708, Letters Sent, RG 94; Geo. B. Davis to George Meade, Jan. 15, 1892, book 12, entry 708, Letters Sent, RG 94; Geo. B. Davis to E.C. Dawes, Jan. 5, 1892, book 11, entry 708, Letters Sent, RG 94.
31. For some examples, see J. Hartwell Butler to E.D. Townsend, Jan. 20, 1877, entry 715, L.P. Graham to Sec. of War, Sept. 2, 1876, entry 715, Letters Received Relating to Missing Military Reports, RG 94; Loomis L. Langdon to H.M. Lazelle, Feb. 25, 1888, box 9, entry 710, Letters Received, RG 94.
32. Geo. B. Davis to C.C. Andrews, Nov. 8, 1892, book 14, entry 708, Letters Sent, RG 94.
33. H.W. Slocum to H.M. Lazelle, May 6, 1888, box 9, entry 710, Letters Received, RG 94; G. Weitzel to Adjutant General, July 13, 1877, box 11, entry 710, Letters Received, RG 94.
34. Geo. B. Davis to J.W. Forsythe, June 13, 1892, book 13, entry 708, Letters Sent, RG 94; George B. Davis to Charles A. Clark, March 17, 1892, book 12, entry 708, Letters Sent, RG 94; M.T. McMahon to Geo. B. Davis, July 15, 1890, box 11, entry 710, Letters Received, RG 94.
35. S.S. Carroll to J.D. Cameron, Oct. 5, 1876, N.J.T. Dana to Secretary of War, Sept. 11, 1876, O.O. Howard to Secretary of War, Dec. 4, 1876, Z.B. Bower to Secretary of War, Oct. 16, 1876, entry 715, Letters Received Relating to Missing Military Reports, RG 94; W.G. Veazey to H.M. Lazelle, April 21, 1888, box 9, entry 710, Letters Received, RG 94.
36. Geo. B. Davis to L.A. Stockwell, Dec. 13, 1893, book 17, entry 708, Letters Sent, RG 94; Robert Lincoln to Geo. M. Robeson, Jan.19, 1882, box 7, entry 710, Letters Received, RG 94; Geo. B. Davis to Walter Clark, June 29, 1897, box 6, entry 713, General Correspondence, RG 94.

37. Some additional examples: The Department of the Gulf barely left a paper trail, as did the commands serving in West Virginia. See George B. Davis to Thomas H. Hubbard, June 29, 1892, book 13, entry 708, Letters Sent, RG 94; Geo. B. Davis to W.R. Smedberg, March 28, 1891, book 10, entry 708, Letters Sent, RG 94; Adjutant General to W.H. Ludlow, March 30, 1880, box 7, entry 710, Letters Received, RG 94.
38. Catalogue of books belonging to the Rebel Departments, Francis Lieber Report, box 2, entry 451A, Record Books of the Archive Office, RG 109.
39. A.K. Lamar to Francis Lieber, Oct. 2, 1865, box 2, entry 438, Letters Received, RG 109; Francis Lieber Report to Judiciary Committee, Jan. 18, 1866, box 1, entry 436, Report of Francis Lieber, Chief of the Archive Office, RG 109. See Jno. C. Whitner to J.H. Wilson, June 18, 1865, box 4, entry 438, Letters Received, RG 109; Paul P. Van Riper and Harry N. Scheiber, "The Confederate Civil Service," *Journal of Southern History* 25, no. 4 (1959), 448–470.
40. John Beauchamp Jones, *A Rebel War Clerk's Diary at the Confederate States Capital* (Philadelphia: J.B. Lippincott & Co., 1866), vol. 1, May 27, 1861, 45; July 24, 1861, 66. On the Confederate War Department, see Stephen V. Ash, *Rebel Richmond: Life and Death in the Confederate Capital* (Chapel Hill: University of North Carolina Press, 2019), 21–22.
41. *OR*, ser. IV, vol. I, sec. 2, 962. See also *OR*, ser. IV, vol. II, 1059.
42. Francis Lieber Report to Judiciary Committee, Jan. 18, 1866, box 1, entry 436, Report of Francis Lieber, Chief of the Archive Office, RG 109. On the records of the Provisional Congress, see John C. Whitner to J.H. Wilson, June 18, 1865, box 4, entry 438, Letters Received, RG 109. On state records, see Mr. Stone to G. Norman Lieber, May 11, 1866, box 3, entry 438, Letter Received, RG 109.
43. William A. Crocker, "Army Intelligence Office," *Confederate Veteran* 8 (1900), 118–119. This is a highly curious case of archival loss, since not only were the bureau's own records lost, but references to it in other contemporary sources are also few and far between. See also report by Secretary of War, in *OR*, ser. IV, vol. III, 945; W.W. Lester and William J. Bromwell, "A Digest of Military and Naval Laws of the Confederate States, from the Commencement of the Provisional Congress to the End of the First Congress under the Permanent Constitution" (Columbia, S.C.: Evans and Cogswell, 1864), 127, https://docsouth.unc.edu/imls/digest/digest.html.
44. T.C. Hindman, *OR*, ser. I, vol. XIII, 30; Munroe Crane, *The Great Panic: Being Incidents Connected with Two Weeks of the War in Tennessee* (Nashville, Tenn.: Johnson & Whiting, 1862), 11.
45. J.C. Pemberton to John J. Pettus, *OR*, ser. I, vol. XXIV, pt. III, 821. See also Eric C. Stoykovich, "Public Records in War: Towards an Archival History of the American Civil War," *The American Archivist* 80 (2017), 146–147.
46. S.H. Lockett to Marcus J. Wright, May 12, 1883, box 7, entry 710, Letters Received, RG 94; Ro. Ould to Marcus J. Wright, March 22, 1880,

box 3, entry 710, Letters Received, RG 94. Samuel H. Stout to Marcus J. Wright, July 22, 1878, folder 10B, ser. 5, WSHC.

47. There is no definite number for the size of Johnston's collections. One enumeration is 6,336; another is 8,000–10,000 documents. Wm. Preston Johnston to Randal L. Gibson, Feb. 28, 1878, box 2, entry 438, Letters Received, RG 109.

48. S. Cooper to James A. Seddon, Dec. 16, 1863, in *OR*, ser. IV, vol. II, 1059; Irving A. Burt to L.H. Mangum, April 23, 1888, box 9, entry 710, Letters Received, RG 94; V.D. Groner to S. Cooper, Sept. 30, 1861, in *OR*, ser. IV, vol. I, sec. 2, 626; Jno. D. Ashmore to C.D. Melton, Aug. 7, 1863, in *OR*, ser. IV, vol. II, 771.

49. Faust, *This Republic of Suffering*, 104, 118, 128. The image of chaos in recording casualties stands in stark contrast to Crocker's description of the care and competence employed in the reporting of casualties. The discrepancy may be the result of Faust describing the reality in the field, and Crocker describing the work to systematize data in an office. It may also be the result of Crocker exaggerating the efficiency of the agency he had established. See Crocker, "Army Intelligence Office."

50. Geo. B. Davis to William Coggswell [*sic*], March 5, 1894, book 17, entry 708, Letters Sent, RG 94.

51. Keith Bohannon, " 'Many Valuable Records and Documents Were Lost to History': The Destruction of Confederate Military Records during the Appomattox Campaign," in *Petersburg to Appomattox: The End of the War in Virginia*, ed. Caroline E. Janney (Chapel Hill: University of North Carolina Press, 2018), 170–191.

52. Geo. B. Davis to J.B. Gordon, Dec. 21, 1889, book 8, entry 708, Letters Sent, RG 94.

53. W.C. Falkner to Marcus J. Wright, March 24, 1879, box 2, entry 710, Letters Received, RG 94; H.M. Lazelle to C.C. Augur, Jan. 25, 1888, book 6, entry 708, Letters Sent, RG 94; C.C. Augur to H.M. Lazelle, Jan. 26, 1888, box 9, entry 710, Letters Received, RG 94.

54. C.G. Memminger to Marcus J. Wright, Feb. 27, 1879, box 2, entry 438, Letters Received, RG 109. On Union destruction of local archives across the South, see Stoykovich, "Public Records in War," 150–152.

55. See, e.g., the April 4 entry in the J.E. Whitehorne Diary, no. 3116-z, SHC; Edward A. Moore, *The Story of a Cannoneer under Stonewall Jackson* (Lynchburg, Va.: J.P. Bell Company, 1910), 301. Bohannon, "Many Valuable Records and Documents Were Lost to History," 172–174.

56. Robert E. Lee to O. Latrobe, April 11, 1865, box 5, Robert E. Lee Headquarter Papers, Virginia Historical Society, Richmond, Virginia; R.E. Lee to Jefferson Davis, April 12, 1865, in *OR*, ser. I, vol. XLVI, pt. I, sec. 2, 1265–1267; see also Bohannon, "Many Valuable Records and Documents Were Lost to History."

57. James M. Pomeroy to Secretary of War, March 17, 1877, box 1, entry 710, Letters Received, RG 94; M.L. Bonham to Geo. B. Davis, Aug. 12,

1889, box 9B, entry 710, Letters Received, RG 94; Alexander Ramsey to H.M. Corkell, Feb. 11, 1880, book 3, entry 435, Letters Sent, RG 109.

58. Henry C. Wayne to Geo. W. McCrary, May 12, 1877, box 1, entry 710, Letters Received, RG 94; John McIntosh Kell to Marcus J. Wright, Feb. 6, 1888, box 9, entry 710, Letters Received, RG 94. On the absence of records in Alabama, see A.B. Garland Jr. to H.M. Lazelle, March 12, 1888, box 9, entry 710, Letters Received, RG 94.

59. William J. Bromwell to Judah Benjamin, April 5, 1865; William J. Bromwell Affidavit, Sept. 3, 1872, vol. 3, JTP; Stephen R. Mallory Diary and Reminiscences, SHC, 43.

60. Jones, *A Rebel War Clerk's Diary*, vol. 2, March 2, 4, 6, 7, 1865, 437–443; Dallas D. Irvine, "The Fate of the Confederate Records: Executive Office," *The American Historical Review* 44 (July 1939), 828, doi.org/10.2307/1844406; Nelson Lankford, *Richmond Burning: The Last Days of the Confederate Capital* (New York: Penguin, 2002), 72.

61. *The Diary of Robert Garlick Hill Kean*, ed. Edward Younger (New York: Oxford University Press, 1957), June 1, 1865, 205. John S. Wise, *The End of an Era* (Boston and New York: Houghton, Mifflin and Company, 1899), 415.

62. Robert Garlick Hill Kean, *Inside the Confederate Government: The Diary of Robert Garlick Hill Kean* (Baton Rouge: Louisiana State University Press, 1993), 205–207; Franklin A. Stratton to Adjutant General, Oct. 21, 1865, box 3, entry 438, Letters Received, RG 109; R.G.H. Kean to Jubal A. Early, Nov. 15, 1873, in *Southern Historical Society Papers* (Richmond, Va., 1876–1959), vol. 2, July 1876, 56–57.

63. Irvine, "Fate of the Confederate Archives," 833, 836, 837, 829; J. Morton Callahan, "The Confederate Diplomatic Archives—The 'Pickett Papers,' " *South Atlantic Quarterly* 2, no. 1 (Jan. 1903), 2–4.

64. Albert H. Campbell, "The Lost War Maps of the Confederates," *Century Magazine* 35, no. 3 (Jan. 1888), 481; Albert H. Campbell to H.M. Lazelle, Jan. 8, 1888, box 9, entry 710, Letters Received, RG 94; Irvine, "Fate of the Confederate Records," 830. It should be noted that some records of the Ordnance Bureau were eventually recovered and sent to Washington. On this, see Francis Lieber Report to Judiciary Committee, Jan. 18, 1866, box 1, entry 436, Report of Francis Lieber, Chief of the Archive Office, RG 109.

65. William Harwar Parker, *Recollections of a Naval Officer: 1841–1865* (New York: Charles Scribners' Sons, 1883), 358; A. Roane to Hugh McCullough, July 27, 1865, vol. 2, JTP; Eugenia C. Babcock, "Personal Recollections of the War between the States," in *South Carolina Women in the Confederacy: Records Collected by Committee from South Carolina State Division, U.D.C.* (Columbia, S.C.: The State Company, 1907), vol. 2, 144. See also Irvine, "Fate of the Confederate Archives," 831; Elizabeth Bethel, *Preliminary Inventory of the War Department Collection of Confeder-*

ate Records (Washington, D.C.: National Archives and Records Service, 1957), 8.

66. Lankford, *Richmond Burning*, 73.
67. Clayton G. Coleman, Letter to Wife Anna, Richmond, Va., April 9, 1865, CMLS; Lankford, *Richmond Burning*, 96–146; Edward A. Pollard, *Southern History of the War* (New York: Charles B. Richardson, 1866), vol. 2, 492–497.
68. Alan C. Aimone and Barbara A. Aimone, *A User's Guide to the Official Records of the American Civil War* (Shippensburg, Pa.: White Mane Publishing, 1993), 31; Irvine, "Fate of the Confederate Archive." For what was later found in Richmond of these departments' records, see Richd. D. Cutts to C.A. Dana, May 5 1865, box 2, entry 438, Letters Received, RG 109. For a comprehensive guide to the availability of Confederate records, see Henry Putney Beers, *Guide to the Archives of the Government of the Confederate States of America* (Washington, D.C.: The National Archives, 1968).
69. Charles A. Page, *Letters of a War Correspondent*, ed. James R. Gilmore (Boston: L.C. Page & Company, 1899); Constance Carry Harrison, *Recollections Grave and Gay* (New York: Charles Scribner, 1911), 211.
70. Richd. D. Cutts to C.A. Dana, May 5, 1865, May 12, 1865, box 2, entry 438, Letters Received, RG 109.
71. Burton N. Harrison to Jefferson Davis, May 24, 1877, Jefferson Davis Folder, box 6, HP. On Varina Davis, see Joan E. Cashin, *First Lady of the Confederacy: Varina Davis's Civil War* (Cambridge, Mass.: Harvard University Press, 2006), 156–157. John Taylor Wood Diary, April 2, 1865, vol. 3, folder 9, John Taylor Wood Papers, 1858–1915, SHC; Micajah H. Clark to W.T. Walthall, Aug. 28, 1877, Jefferson Davis Folder, Box 6, HP.
72. Israel Vodges to E.M. Stanton, June 17, 1865, folder 231, box 4, entry 1, RG 109; Burton N. Harrison to Jefferson Davis, May 24, 1877, Jefferson Davis Folder, box 6, HP.
73. On the retreat of the Confederate government from Richmond, see William C. Davis, *An Honorable Defeat: The Last Days of the Confederate Government* (New York: Harcourt, 2001), 62–75; Herman Hattaway and Richard E. Beringer, *Jefferson Davis, Confederate President* (Lawrence: University Press of Kansas, 2002), 391–393; William J. Cooper, *Jefferson Davis, American* (New York: Knopf, 2000), 523–524; Lankford, *Richmond Burning*, 77–79, 91, 104–105; Burke Davis, *The Long Surrender* (New York: Random House, 1985), 30–32, 44–53; Michael B. Ballard, *A Long Shadow: Jefferson Davis and the Final Days of the Confederacy* (Jackson: University Press of Mississippi, 1986), 43–49; Yael A. Sternhell, *Routes of War: The World of Movement in the Confederate South* (Cambridge, Mass.: Harvard University Press, 2012), 179–192.
74. Micajah H. Clark to Burton Harrison, Feb. 20, 1866, folder 4, box 6, HP; John Taylor Wood Diary, May 2, 1865, vol. 3, folder 9, John Taylor

Wood Papers, 1858–1915, SHC; Jefferson Davis to Philip Phillips, Sept. 24, 1874, in *The Papers of Jefferson Davis*, ed. Lynda Lasswell Crist (Baton Rouge: Louisiana State University Press, 2012), vol. 13: 1871–1879, 241; Burton N. Harrison to Jefferson Davis, May 24, 1877, Jefferson Davis Folder, box 6, HP; M.H. Clark to Mrs. Jefferson Davis, Nov. 27, 1865, folder 3, box 6, HP; C. Wickliffe Yulee, *Senator Yulee of Florida: A Biographical Sketch* (Jacksonville: Florida Historical Magazine, 1909), 29–30.

75. Israel Vodges to E.M. Stanton, June 17, 1865, folder 231, box 4, entry 1, Jefferson Davis Papers, RG 109; Benjamin Pritchard Deposition, May 27, 1865, folder 231, box 4, entry 1, Jefferson Davis Papers, RG 109; Harrison to Davis, May 24, 1877, Jefferson Davis Folder, box 6, HP; Christ, ed., *Papers of Jefferson Davis*, vol. 13, 55.
76. Micajah Clark to W.T. Walthall, Aug. 28, 1877, Jefferson Davis Folder, box 6, HP.
77. Burton Harrison to Jefferson Davis, May 24, 1877, Jefferson Davis Folder, box 6, HP. For a complete history of Lee's resignation letter, see William Harris Bragg, "Charles C. Jones, Jr., and the Mystery of Lee's Lost Dispatches," *Georgia Historical Quarterly* 72, no. 3 (Fall 1988), 429–462.

Chapter Two. Revenge in the Archive

1. Edwin M. Stanton to G. Weitzel, April 5, 1865, in *OR*, ser. I, vol. XLVI, pt. III sec. 1, 584; Edwin M. Stanton to C.A. Dana, April 5, 1865, box 25, reel 9, SP; C.A. Dana to Edwin M. Stanton, April 6, 1865, box 25, reel 9, SP; E.D. Townsend, General Orders no. 60, April 7, 1865, in *OR*, ser. III, vol. IV, sec. 2, 1259; Charles A. Dana, *Recollections of the Civil War: With the Leaders at Washington and in the Field in the Sixties* (New York: D. Appleton and Company, 1902), http://www.gutenberg.org/files/42892/42892-h/42892-h.htm; Carl J. Guarneri, *Lincoln's Informer: Charles A. Dana and the Inside Story of the Civil War* (Lawrence: University Press of Kansas, 2019), 350–353; Dallas Irvine, "The Archive Office of the War Department: Repository of Captured Confederate Archives, 1865–1881," *Military Affairs* 10, no. 1 (Spring 1946), 93–97; Carl L. Lokke, "The Captured Confederate Records under Francis Lieber," *The American Archivist* 9, no. 4 (Oct. 1946), 277–278, doi.org/10.17723/aarc.9.4.c736554789t63013.
2. John F. Marszalek, *Commander of All Lincoln's Armies: A Life of General Henry W. Halleck* (Cambridge, Mass.: Harvard University Press, 2004), 222.
3. H.W. Halleck to Ord, April 22, 1865, in *OR*, ser. I, vol. XLVI, pt. III, 896; J.C. Kelton, General Orders no. 3, April 25, 1865, in *OR*, ser. I, vol. XLVI, pt. III, 944; Marszalek, *Commander of All Lincoln's Armies*, 230–231.
4. H.W. Halleck to E.M. Stanton, May 11, 1865, in *OR*, ser. I, vol. XLVI, pt. 3, 1132.

5. Richard D. Cutts memorandum, box 2, entry 438, Letters Received, RG 109; Richard D. Cutts to Charles A. Dana, May 2, 3, 4, 5, 6, 10, 13, 19, 26, 27, 1865, box 2, entry 438, Letters Received, RG 109; Robert N. Scott to Charles A. Dana, May 31, 1865, and June 7, 1865, box 2, entry 438, Letters Received, RG 109.
6. J.C. Babcock to M.R. Patrick, May 14, 1865, box 2, entry 438, Letters Received, RG 109; H. W. Halleck to E.M. Stanton, May 15, 1865, in *OR*, ser. I, vol. XLVI, pt. III, 1152.
7. John M. Schofield to Charles A. Dana, May 17, 1865, box 3, entry 438, Letters Received, RG 109; Morris C. Runyan, *Eight Days with the Confederates and the Capture of Their Archives, Flags & c. by Company "G" Ninth New Jersey Vol.* (Princeton, N.J.: Wm. C.C. Zapf, 1896).
8. Edwin M. Stanton to Halleck, May 16, 1865, in *OR*, ser. I, vol. XLVII, pt. III, 510; H.W. Halleck to Schofield, May 16, 1865, in *OR*, ser. I, vol. XLVII, pt. III, 510–511; J.M. Schofield to Halleck, May 17, 1865, in *OR*, ser. I, vol. XLVII, pt. III, 519.
9. Geo. L. Hartsuff to Weitzel, April 10, 1865, in *OR*, ser. I, vol. XLVI, pt. III, sec. 1, 698; J. Kilpatrick to Campbell, May 20, 1865, in *OR*, ser. I, vol. 47, pt. III, 545; J.D. Cox to Campbell, May 22, 1865, in *OR*, ser. I, vol. XVII, pt. III, 560; G. Weitzel to Hartsuff, April 8, 1865, in *OR*, ser. I, vol. XLVI, pt. III, sec. 1, 659; Jno. A.J. Creswell to W.W. Belknap, April 21, 1871, box 1, entry 451A, Memoranda on Archive Office, RG 109.
10. J.M. Schofield to E.M. Stanton, in *OR*, ser. I, vol. XLVII, pt. III, 631; F.T. Sherman to E.D. Townsend, July 21, 1865, box 2, entry 438, Letters Received, RG 109; P.H. Sheridan to E.D. Townsend, July 19, 1865, box 4, entry 438, Letters Received, RG 109; J.H. Wilson to E.D. Townsend, June 24, 1865, box 4, entry 438, Letters Received, RG 109; J.C. Whitner to J.H. Wilson, June 18, 1865, box 4, entry 438, Letters Received, RG 109.
11. Invoice of property turned over by Lt. Col. B.W. Thompson, Provost Marshall General D.S., June 17, 1865, folder 230, box 4, entry 1, Jefferson Davis Papers, RG 109.
12. J.M. Schofield to E.M. Stanton, June 6, 1865, in *OR*, ser. I, vol. XLVII, pt. III, 631; William Hartsuff to Schofield, June 23, 1865, in *OR*, ser. I, vol. XLVII, pt. III, 661; G. Weitzel to Hartsuff, April 8, 1865, in *OR*, ser. I, vol. XLVI, pt. III, sec. 1, 659.
13. Israel Vodges to E.M. Stanton, June 17, 1865, folder 231, box 4, entry 1, Jefferson Davis Papers, RG 109. On the contents of the Waldo trunk, see Q.A. Gilmore to L. Thomas, June 24, 1865, folder 230, box 4, entry 1, Jefferson Davis Papers, RG 109; Inventory of private property of Jefferson Davis captured at Waldo, June 17, 1865, folder 230, box 4, entry 1, Jefferson Davis Papers, RG 109.
14. Nelson A. Miles to C.A. Dana, May 24, 1865, folder 233, box 4, entry 1, Jefferson Davis Papers, RG 109; B.D. Pritchard statement, May 30, 1865, folder 236, box 4, entry 1, Jefferson Davis Papers, RG 109.

15. Edwin M. Stanton to Gillmore, June 25, 1865, in *OR*, ser. I, vol. XLVII, pt. III, 663–664.
16. E.D. Townsend to Vodges, June 30, 1865, box 27, reel 10, SP; I. Vodges to E.D. Townsend, July 7, 1865, in *OR*, ser. I, vol. XLVII, pt. III, 677.
17. W.L.M. Burger to John P. Hatch, May 21, 1865, in *OR*, ser. I, vol. XLVII, pt. III, 552; Q.A. Gillmore to Secretary of War, June 30, 1865, in *OR*, ser. I, vol. XLVII, pt. III, 672; quote appears in *Daily Intelligencer* (Wheeling, W.Va.), May 8, 1865.
18. Horatio Woodman to Edwin M. Stanton, May 22, 1865, box 27, reel 10, SP; Edwin M. Stanton to George Bancroft, May 30, 1865, box 27, reel 10, SP; U.S. Grant to E.M. Stanton, May 29, 1865, box 27, reel 10, SP; U.S. Grant to E.M. Stanton, June 6, 1865, box 27, reel 10, SP.
19. On Lieber, see Francis Friedel, *Francis Lieber: Nineteenth-Century Liberal* (Baton Rouge: Louisiana State University Press, 1947); Peter W. Becker, "Prologue: Lieber's Place in History," in *Francis Lieber and the Culture of the Mind*, ed. Charles R. Mack and Henry H. Lesesne (Columbia: University of South Carolina Press, 2005), 1–7; Michael O'Brien, "The Stranger in the South" in Mack and Lesesne, *Francis Lieber and the Culture of the Mind*, 33–41.
20. Patrick Roughen, "Francis Lieber and the South Carolina College Library: An Examination of a Scholar's Academic Library Use," *ANZLH-E Journal* 3 (2013), http://138.25.65.22/au/journals/ANZLawHisteJl/2013/4.pdf; Hartmut Kiel, "Francis Lieber's Attitudes on Race, Slavery, and Abolition," *Journal of American Ethnic History* 28, no. 1 (Fall 2008), 13–33.
21. Friedel, *Francis Lieber*, 342–359. See also Paul Finkleman, "Francis Lieber and the Modern Law of War (reviewing *Lincoln's Code: The Laws of War in American History* by John Fabian Witt)," *The University of Chicago Law Review* 80, no. (2013), 2078–2086, https://chicagounbound.uchicago.edu/uclrev/vol80/iss4/12.
22. John Fabian Witt, *Lincoln's Code: The Laws of War in American History* (New York: Free Press, 2012), 234; D.H. Dilbeck, " 'The Genesis of This Little Tablet with My Name': Francis Lieber and the Wartime Origins of General Orders No. 100," *Journal of the Civil War Era* 5, no. 2 (June 2015), 247, doi.org/10.1353/cwe.2015.0037; Stephanie McCurry, *Women's War: Fighting and Surviving the American Civil War* (Cambridge, Mass.: Harvard University Press, 2019), 45. Historians agree about the importance of Lieber's code both at the time and in laying the groundwork for the rules agreed upon in the Hague Conventions of 1899 and 1907. However, there are substantial disagreements about the origins of the code and what issues were foremost on Lieber's mind when he wrote it.
23. Francis Lieber Memorandum, July 15, 1865, "Reasons why Jefferson Davis Ought not to be tried by Military Commission for complicity in the unlawful raiding, burning, etc.," book 3, FLPLC. Lieber's earlier

statement is in Francis Lieber, *The Miscellaneous Writings of Francis Lieber*, ed. Daniel C. Gilman (Philadelphia: J.B. Lippincott, 1880), vol. 2: Contributions to Political Science, including Lectures on the Constitution of the United States, 293–297. See also Friedel, *Francis Lieber*, 362; Witt, *Lincoln's Code*, 318.

24. Friedel, *Francis Lieber*, 306, 324–326. Quote on p. 325.
25. Francis Lieber to Karl Josef Anton Mittermaier, March 1, 1866, box 38, FLPHL.
26. Marszalek, *Commander of All Lincoln's Armies*, 218; Francis Lieber to Matilda Lieber, July 14, 1865, box 36, FLPHL; Edward D. Townsend to Francis Lieber, July 15, box 65, FLPHL.
27. War Department, General Orders no. 127, July 21, 1865, box 1, entry 441, Order and Regulations of the Archive Office, RG 109; E.D. Townsend, Regulations for the Archive Office of the War Department, Aug. 23, 1864, box 1, entry 441, Orders and Regulations of the Archive Office, RG 109. See also G. Norman Lieber, Instructions for the Sergeant of the Guard, Sept. 20, 1865, book 1, entry 435, Letters Sent, RG 109.
28. Francis Lieber Report to Judiciary Committee, Jan. 18, 1866, box 1, entry 436, Report of Francis Lieber, Chief of the Archive Office, RG 109; G. Norman Lieber to W.S. Kilchum, March 22, 1867, book 1, entry 435, Letters Sent, RG 109.
29. Francis Lieber to Henry Halleck, Sept. 10, 1865, box 28, FLPHL.
30. Francis Lieber to Sir, Sept. 15, 1865, book 1, entry 435, Letters Sent, RG 109; Catalogue of Books Belonging to the Rebel Departments, Oct. 3, 1865, box 2, entry 451A, Record Books of the War Records Office, RG 109.
31. G. Norman Lieber to Francis Lieber, Sept. 8, 1865, book 1, entry 435, Letters Sent, RG 109; G. Norman Lieber to Francis Lieber, Sept. 22, 1865, book 1, entry 435, Letters Sent, RG 109; Francis Lieber to E.M. Stanton, Sept. 15, 1865, book 1, entry 435, Letters Sent, RG 109; Francis Lieber to Henry Halleck, Sept. 10, 1865, box 28, FLPHL.
32. Francis Lieber to Judge Holt, Sept. 15, 1865, book 1, entry 435, Letters Sent, RG 109.
33. James F. Wilson to Francis Lieber, June 22, 1866, book 2, entry 438, Letters Received, RG 109; Francis Lieber to James F. Wilson, June 28, 1866, book 1, entry 435, Letters Sent, RG 109; G. Norman Lieber to T.T. Eckert, Dec. 18, 1865, book 1, entry 435, Letters Sent, RG 109; Jno. P.C. Shanks to J.M. Schofield, Jan. 1, 1869, and endorsements by E.D. Townsend, B. Wells, box 3, entry 438, Letters Received, RG 109. On the prisoner of war camps commanders' trials, see Witt, *Lincoln's Code*, 298–304.
34. Francis Lieber to Henry Halleck, March 20, 1866, box 28, FLPHL; Francis Lieber to Henry Drisler, Oct. 18, 1865, box 24, FLPHL; Francis Lieber to Henry Halleck, Nov. 17, 1865, box 28, FLPHL.

35. Francis Lieber to Henry Halleck, Sept. 10, 1865, box 28, FLPHL.
36. James F. Wilson to Francis Lieber, May 4, 1866, box 2, entry 438, Letter Received, RG 109.
37. Francis Lieber Report to Judiciary Committee, May 4, 1866, box 30, reel 11, SP; Francis Lieber to Henry Halleck, May 19, 1866, box 28, FLPHL.
38. Francis Lieber to Henry Halleck, May 19, 1866, box 28, FLPHL. Cynthia Nicoletti, *Secession on Trial: The Treason Prosecution of Jefferson Davis* (Cambridge: Cambridge University Press, 2017). See also, Witt, *Lincoln's Code,* 318–322; Guarneri, *Lincoln's Informer,* 374. On the failure to indict Robert E. Lee, see Elizabeth Varon, *Appomattox: Victory, Defeat, and Freedom at the End of the Civil War* (New York: Oxford University Press, 2013), 183–207.
39. Francis Lieber to Karl Josef Anton Mittermaier, March 1, 1866, box 38, FLPHL; Francis Lieber to Henry Halleck, May 19, 1866, box 28, FLPHL. See also F.L. to Unknown, July 13, 1866, FLPLC; Francis Lieber to Sir, Nov. 6, 1867, FLPLC.
40. Francis Lieber to Henry Halleck, March 20, 1866, box 28, FLPHL.
41. "Special Dispatch to the Boston Daily Advertiser," *Boston Daily Advertiser,* Aug. 27, 1867; Robert N. Scott, Memorandum for the Adjt. General, June 16, 1880, book 2, entry 707, Letters Sent, RG 94; E.D. Townsend to Francis Lieber, Aug. 17, 1867, box 65, FLPHL; Francis Lieber to U.S. Grant, Aug. 30, 1867, box 26, FLPHL.
42. Frank W. Klingberg, *The Southern Claims Commission* (New York: Octagon, 1978), 21–24.
43. Susanna Michele Lee, *Claiming the Union: Citizenship in the Post–Civil War South* (Cambridge: Cambridge University Press, 2014), 20–21.
44. Lee, *Claiming the Union,* 23.
45. James G. Randall, "Captured and Abandoned Property During the Civil War," *The American Historical Review* 19, no. 1 (Oct. 1913), 65–79, doi.org/10.2307/1834807; Stanton J. Peelle, "History and Jurisdiction of the United States Court of Claims," *Records of the Columbia Historical Society* 19 (1916), 1–21; Klingberg, *Southern Claims Commission,* 34–35.
46. Lee, *Claiming the Union,* 23.
47. President to Appoint Three Commissioners of Claims, March 3, 1871, sec. 2, ch. 116, Forty-First Congress, Third Session, in *Statutes at Large and Proclamations of the United States of America from December 1869 to March 1871,* ed. George P. Sanger (Boston: Little, Brown, and Company, 1871), vol. 16, 524.
48. Lee, *Claiming the Union,* 24–25.
49. Lee, *Claiming the Union,* 37.
50. Convention between United States and Mexico, July 4, 1868, in *Treaties and Other International Agreements of the United States of America, 1776–1949,* ed. Charles I. Bevans (Washington, D.C.: Department of State Publication, 1972), vol. 9: *Iraq-Musqat,* 826–830, https://tile.loc.gov/storage-services

/service/ll/lltreaties//lltreaties-ustbv009/lltreaties-ustbv009.pdf; A.H. Feller, *The Mexican Claims Commissions, 1923–1934: A Study in the Law and Procedure of International Tribunals* (New York: The Macmillan Company, 1935), 6.

51. Mixed Commission on British and American Claims, List of claims of British subjects against the United States, and American citizens against Great Britain: Before the Mixed Commission under the Twelfth Article of the Treaty of Washington of May 8, 1871. Foreign and Commonwealth Office Collection (Washington, D.C.: Judd & Detweiler, 1873), https://www.jstor.org/stable/60235910; John Bassett Moore, *History and Digest of the International Arbitrations to Which the United States Has Been a Party* (Washington, D.C.: Government Printing Office, 1898), vol. 3, 2201–2211.
52. B. Wells to E.D. Townsend, March 19, 1869, book 2, entry 435, Letters Sent, RG 109; B. Wells to E.D. Townsend, Sept. 26, 1868, book 2, entry 435, Letters Sent, RG 109; see also B. Wells to E.D. Townsend, May 27, 1869, book 2, entry 435, Letters Sent, RG 109.
53. E.D. Townsend to W.W. Belknap, Feb. 14, 1872, box 4, entry 438, Letters Received, RG 109; W.W. B. to Sec. of Treasury, March 4, 1872, box 4, entry 438, Letters Received, RG 109; W.W. B. to Sec. of Treasury, Feb. 20, 1872, box 4, entry 438, Letters Received, RG 109; George W. McCrary to John Sherman, April 16, 1878, book 3, entry 435, Letters Sent, RG 94; E.D. Townsend to George W. McCrary, May 28, 1878, book 3, entry 435, Letters Sent, RG 94; A.P. Tasker to J.S. Moodey, May 22, 1878, book 4, entry 438, Letters Received, RG 109; a Joint Resolution by Congress, passed June 21, 1870, authorized the Secretary of the Treasury to "collect wrecked and abandoned property, derelict claims, and dues belonging to the United States." See Joint Resolution No. 75, June 21, 1870, in Sanger, ed., *Statutes at Large and Proclamations of the United States of America*, vol. 16, 380.
54. Thomas H. Talbot to Wm. W. Belknap, Oct. 6, 1870, box 2, entry 438, Letters Received, RG 109; Thomas H. Talbot to Wm. W. Belknap, Sept. 1, 1870, box 2, entry 438, Letters Received, RG 109; Rbt. S. Hale to B. Wells, May 17, 1870, box 2, entry 438, Letters Received, RG 109.
55. Lee, *Claiming the Union*, 26–27.
56. B. Wells to E.D. Townsend, April 28, 1871, book 2, entry 435, Letters Sent, RG 109; Chas. F. Benjamin to Office of the Commissioners of Claims, May 1, 1871, box 3, entry 438, Letters Received, RG 109; B. Wells to E.D. Townsend, May 5, 1871, book 2, entry 435, Letters Sent, RG 109; E.D. Townsend to W.W. Belknap, Nov. 18, 1872, book 2, entry 435, Letters Sent, RG 109; E.D. Townsend to M.C. Meigs, Dec. 8, 1879, book 3, entry 435, Letters Sent, RG 109; A.P. Tasker to E.D. Townsend, June 12, 1871, book 2, entry 435, Letters Sent, RG 109.
57. E.D. Townsend to A.O. Aldis, Dec. 10, 1872, book 2, entry 435, Letters Sent, RG 109; Fold3.com has digitized the entire collection of disbarred claims:

https://www.fold3.com/title/12/southern-claims-barred-and-disallowed. The following footnotes include some examples from the collection Comprising 13,461 claims.

58. Adjt. Genl. to A.O. Aldis, July 16, 1872, book 2, entry 435, Letters Sent, RG 109. Most reports appear in the records of the Archive Office without details about their contents. See, e.g., Thos. M. Vincent to A.O. Aldis, July 31, 1874, book 3, entry 435, Letters Sent, RG 109; E.D. Townsend to A.O. Aldis, March 31, 1876, book 3, entry 435, Letters Sent, RG 109.
59. Claim of Jonas P. Levy, claim no. 135, roll 001, M1407, Southern Claims Commission—Barred and Disallowed, NARA, https://www.fold3.com/image/2505177. See in particular pages 19, 38, 52, and 75 in claim; Wm. D. Whipple to Prest. of the Southern Claims Commission, June 14, 1871, book 2, entry 435, Letters Sent, RG 109.
60. "Case in the Court of Claims," unattributed newspaper clipping, entry 444, Newspaper Clippings, RG 109. An identical segment is in the *Weekly Star*, Wilmington, North Carolina, June 9, 1871; see also B. Wells to E.D. Townsend, July 24, 1871, box 4, entry 438, Letters Received, RG 109.
61. E.D. Townsend to M.C. Meigs, Dec. 8, 1879, book 3, entry 435, Letters Sent, RG 109; Claim of James A. Jones, submitted by his widow Eliza Jones, Oct. 18, 1872, claim no. 17078, p. 9, no roll number, M1407, Southern Claims Commission, NARA, https://www.fold3.com/image/27/665294; Claim of Amos Windel, no. 1047, p. 20, roll 006, M1407, Southern Claims Commission, NARA, https://www.fold3.com/image/27/8739; Claim of James M. Montgomery, no. 19311, p. 6, roll 047, M1407, Southern Claims Commission, NARA, https://www.fold3.com/image/27/4251199.
62. E.D. Townsend to A.O. Aldis, Oct. 18, 1873, book 2, entry 435, Letters Sent, RG 109; E.D. Townsend to E.B. French, Sept. 18, 1877, book 3, entry 435, Letters Sent, RG 109; E.D. Townsend to Thos. H. Talbot, Feb. 18, 1871, book 2, entry 435, Letters Sent, RG 109; B. Wells to E.D. Townsend, Dec. 20, 1870, book 2, entry 435, Letters Sent, RG 109; Thomas H. Talbot to W.W. Belknap, Oct. 11, 1870, box 2, entry 438, Letters Received, RG 109.
63. E.D. Townsend to W.W. Belknap, Dec. 5, 1871, book 2, entry 435, Letters Sent, RG 109; E.D. Townsend to A.O. Aldis, Jan. 18, 1873, book 2, entry 435, Letters Sent, RG 109; E.D. Townsend to George W. McCrary, Dec. 8, 1877, book 3, entry 435, Letters Sent, RG 109; E.D. Townsend to R.S. Hale, June 10, 1872, book 2, entry 435, Letters Sent, RG 109.
64. Joseph McKenna, *British Blockade Runners in the American Civil War* (Jefferson, N.C.: McFarland & Company, 2019), 39; Craig L. Barry and David C. Burt, *Suppliers to the Confederacy II: Isaac Campbell & Co., London, Peter Tait & Co., Limerick* (Fairfield, Ohio: Stainless Banner Publications, 2014). The two firms jointly filed a claim in 1863 for the cargo of the

bark *Springbok*, which was captured by a U.S. ship. United States District Court (New York: Southern District). *The United States vs. the Bark Springbok and Her Cargo: In Prize: Opinion of the Court* (New York: John W. Amerman, 1863), www.jstor.org/stable/60235340.

65. Copy of J. Gorgas to Sec. of War, Feb. 3, 1863, box 2, entry 438, Letters Received, RG 109; Copy of Contract with Thomas Stirling Begbie, undated, box 2, entry 438, Letters Received, RG 109; Rob. S. Hale to E.D. Townsend, Sept. 25, 1873, box 2, entry 438, Letters Received, RG 109; A.P. Tasker to E.D. Townsend, Aug. 16, 1872, book 2, entry 435, Letters Sent, RG 109.

66. H.R. 3573, 42 Cong., 3 sess., Jan. 20, 1873, LC, https://memory.loc.gov/cgi-bin/ampage?collId=llhb&fileName=042/llhb042.db&recNum=12399; H.R. 1133, 42 Cong., 2 sess., Jan. 22, 1872, LC, https://memory.loc.gov/cgi-bin/ampage?collId=llhb&fileName=042/llhb042.db&recNum=3778; H.R. 3448, 42 Cong., 3 sess., Jan. 13, 1873, LC, https://memory.loc.gov/cgi-bin/ampage?collId=llhb&fileName=042/llhb042.db&recNum=12109.

67. W.W. Belknap to J.A.J. Creswell, March 7, 1872, book 2, entry 435, Letters Sent, RG 109. At the end of the letter, Tasker noted that the copy was made "from memory of the contents of this letter—therefore may not be exact." E.D. Townsend to Wm. W. Belknap, April 2, 1872, book 2, entry 435, Letters Sent, RG 109; Jn. A.J. Creswell to Wm. W. Belknap, March 23, 1872, box 3, entry 438, Letters Received, RG 109.

68. Probably Albert P. Tasker to W.W. Belknap, Jan. 14, 1874, book 2, entry 435, Letters Sent, RG 109.

69. E.D. Townsend to S.J.R. McMillan, Jan. 14, 1879, box 3, entry 438, Letters Received, RG 109.

70. "Using the Confederate Archive," *New York Times*, March 9, 1878, 1; *Congressional Record*, 45 Cong., 2 sess., March 8, 1878, p. 1594–1600; *Congressional Record*, 47 Cong., 1 sess., June 14, 1882, p. 4877–4881. The newspaper stories are in a scrapbook in entry 444, Newspaper Clippings, RG 109.

71. Jeffrey E. Vogel, "Redefining Reconciliation: Confederate Veterans and the Southern Responses to Federal Civil War Pensions," *Civil War History* 51, no. 1 (March 2005), 67–92, doi.org/10.1353/cwh.2005.0019; Theda Skocpol, *Protecting Soldiers and Mothers: The Political Origins of Social Policy in the United States* (Cambridge, Mass.: Harvard University Press, 1992), 143. See also James Marten, *Sing Not War: The Lives of Union & Confederate Veterans in Gilded Age America* (Chapel Hill: University of North Carolina Press, 2011), 217. Recent scholarship has put a spotlight on Black families' struggles for Federal pensions and the myriad ways in which the government attempted to deny veterans and their dependents their due payments. See Brandi Clay Brimmer, *Claiming Union Widowhood: Race, Respectability, and Poverty in the Post-Emancipation South* (Durham, N.C.: Duke University Press, 2020); Holly M. Pinheiro, *The Families' Civil War: Black Soldiers and the Fight for Racial Justice*

(Athens: University of Georgia Press, 2022); Tera Hunter, *Bound in Wedlock: Slave and Free Black Marriage in the Nineteenth Century* (Cambridge, Mass.: Harvard University Press), 274–279; Hilary Green, "Black Widows and the Struggle for Pensions after the Civil War," in "#FamiliesCivilWar: A Roundtable," Black Perspectives Blog, published by the African American Intellectual History Society, Jan. 12, 2023, https://www.aaihs.org/black-widows-and-the-struggle-for-pensions-after-the-civil-war/.

72. Caty Shaw to H. Van Arman, March 8, 1871, box 3, entry 438, Letters Received, RG 109; F.A. Worlfley, copy of statement, July 13, 1871, box 3, entry 438, Letters Received, RG 109; Statement by Frank Morey, July 14, 1871, box 3, entry 438, Letters Received, RG 109; J.D. Baker to W.W. Belknap, July 21, 1871, box 3, entry 438, Letters Received, RG 109; B. Wells to E.D. Townsend, July 26, 1871, book 2, entry 435, Letters Sent, RG 109; J.H. Baker to W.W. Belknap, March 29, 1872, box 3, entry 438, Letters Received, RG 109. For other petitions discovered in the Archive Office, see, e.g., E.D. Townsend to J.H. Baker, March 30, 1872, book 2, entry 435, Letters Sent, RG 109.

73. J.H. Baker to Adjutant General, May 27, 1873, box 3, entry 438, Letters Received, RG 109; E.D. Townsend to J.H. Baker, May 28, 1873, book 2, entry 435, Letters Sent, RG 109. For additional examples of signature comparisons, see E.D. Townsend to W.W. Belknap, April 5, 1872, book 2, entry 435, Letters Sent, RG 109; T.H. Talbot to Wm. W. Belknap, Jan. 23, 1871, box 2, entry 438, Letters Received, RG 109.

74. For example, Robert Boon (pension certificate 6403) and Jacob Ray (pension certificate 6250) were both discovered to have served in the 6th North Carolina Volunteers. E.D. Townsend to J.H. Baker, Feb. 26, 1874, book 2, entry 435, Letters Sent, RG 109; E.D. Townsend to J.H. Baker, Feb. 26, 1874, book 2, entry 435, Letters Sent, RG 109.

75. E.D. Townsend to J.A. Bentley, March 2, 1878, book 3, entry 435, Letters Sent, RG 94; J.H. Baker to E.D. Townsend, March 20, 1875, box 3, entry 438, Letters Received, RG 109; E.D. Townsend to J.H. Baker, March 17, 1865, book 3, entry 435, Letters Sent, RG 109; E.D. Townsend to Commissioner of Pensions, April 7, 1875, book 3, entry 435, Letters Sent, RG 109. On occasion, ex-Confederates applied to the Archive Officer to ask for documents to support their claims for pensions from Southern states. See, e.g., Monroe McClurg to Marcus J. Wright, July 23, 1888, box 9, entry 710, Letters Received, RG 94.

76. B. Wells to E.D. Townsend, Feb. 7, 1870, book 2, entry 435, Letters Sent, RG 109; B. Wells to E.D. Townsend, Dec. 10, 1870, book 2, entry 435, Letters Sent, RG 109.

77. "A Startling Revelation," unattributed newspaper clipping, entry 444, Newspaper Clippings, RG 109; "General Caleb Cushing," *National Republican*, Jan. 15, 1874.

78. Judith F. Gentry, "White Gold: The Confederate Government and Cotton in Louisiana," *Louisiana History* 33, no. 3 (summer 1992), 233, https://resolver.scholarsportal.info/resolve/00246816/v33i0003/229_wgtcgacil.xml.
79. Sec. of War to G.S. Boutwell, Jan. 25, 1872, box 3, entry 438, Letters Received, RG 109; B.F. Flanders to War Department, undated, box 3, entry 438, Letters Received, RG 109; A.P. Tasker to E.D. Townsend, Nov. 17, 1871, book 2, entry 435, Letters Sent, RG 109; Doc. No. 86, Aug. 16, 1872, box 1, entry 441, Orders and Regulations of Archive Office, RG 109; A.P. Tasker to E.D. Townsend, Aug. 20, 1872, book 2, entry 435, Letters Sent, RG 109; Thomas M. Vincent to Sec. of War, Jan. 10, 1872, box 3, entry 438, Letters Received, RG 109.
80. M.M. Broadwell to A.P. Tasker, Feb. 15, 1873, box 3, entry 438, Letters Received, RG 109; A.P. Tasker to E.D. Townsend, March 12, 1873, box 3, entry 438, Letters Received, RG 109; E.D. Townsend to M.M. Broadwell, March 14, 1873, box 3, entry 438, Letters Received, RG 109; A.P. Tasker to J.P. Broadwell, May 2, 1873, box 3, entry 438, Letters Received, RG 109.
81. Geo. Williamson to A.P. Tasker, Feb. 8, 1873, box 3, entry 438, Letters Received, RG 109; E.D. Townsend to Wm. A. Richardson, April 11, 1873, box 3, entry 438, Letters Received, RG 109; E.D. Townsend to George Williamson, March 12, 1873, box 3, entry 438, Letters Received, RG 109.
82. Robert N. Scott and A.P. Tasker to E.D. Townsend, Jan. 13, 1879, box 2, entry 438, Letters Received, RG 109; Geo. McCrary to Speaker of the House of Representatives, Jan. 16, 1879, box 2, entry 438, Letters Received, RG 109.
83. "The Rebel Archives: Their Importance to the Government—The Authority for Purchasing Them," entry 444, Newspaper Clippings, RG 109. An identical newspaper story appeared in the *Boston Globe*, Aug. 7, 1872.
84. John T. Pickett, Memorandum, June 27, 1872, vol. 3, JTP; Thomas O. Selfridge to Columbus Delany, July 2, 1872, vol. 3, JTP; "Collection of captured, &c., property." June 10, 1872, ch. 415, Forty-Second Congress, Second Session in Sanger, ed., *Statutes at Large and Proclamations of the United States of America*, 350.
85. William J. Bromwell to Judah Benjamin, April 5, 1865, vol. 2, JTP; William J. Bromwell Affidavit, Sept. 3, 1872, vol. 3, JTP.
86. See Don E. Doyle, *The Cause of All Nations: An International History of the American Civil War* (New York: Basic Books, 2015), 120–121; On Bromwell and Benjamin see Finding Aid for Confederate States of America Records, p. 5, LC; "The Missing Confederate Records," Affidavit by John T. Pickett, JTP; Jno. T. Pickett to C.F. Henningsen, Sept. 15, 1872, vol. 3, JTP; for criticism of the purchase, see "The Rebel Archives—A Huge Joke or a Giant Swindle," unattributed newspaper clipping, p. 13, entry 444, Newspaper Clippings, RG 109.

87. "The Rebel Archives: Their Importance to the Government, The Authority for Purchasing Them," entry 444, Newspaper Clippings, RG 109. An identical newspaper clip appeared in the *Boston Globe*, Aug. 7, 1872.
88. "Special Dispatch to the Boston Daily Advertiser," *Boston Daily Advertiser*, Aug. 27, 1867; Francis Lieber to Henry Halleck, March 20, 1866, box 28, FLPHL. For a pro-Johnson view of the management of the Archive Office, see "The Rebel Archive," *Daily National Intelligencer*, Sept. 17, 1867, http://tinyurl.galegroup.com/tinyurl/rcoJo.
89. E.D. Townsend to Samuel J. Randall, March 13, 1876, book 3, entry 435, Letters Sent, RG 109 (though the letter eventually was sent through the Secretary of War Alphonso Taft).
90. *Congressional Record*, 44 Cong., 1 sess., April 26, 1876, p. 2772; *Congressional Record*, 44 Cong., 1 sess., March 16, 1876, p. 1753.

Chapter Three. Archiving without an Archive

1. H.W. Halleck to E.M. Stanton, May 11, 1865, in *OR*, ser. I, vol. XLVI, pt. III, sec. 2, 1132.
2. Francis Lieber Report to Judiciary Committee, Jan. 18, 1866, box 1, entry 436, Report of Francis Lieber, Chief of the Archive Office, RG 109; Francis Lieber to Lorenzo H. Whitney, Oct. 27, 1865, book 1, entry 435, Letters Sent, RG 109.
3. Francis Lieber to Henry Halleck, Sept. 10, 1865, box 28, FLPHL; G. Norman Lieber to E.D. Townsend, Nov. 9, 1865, book 1, entry 435, Letters Sent, RG 109.
4. Jacob Soll, *The Information Master: Jean-Baptiste Colbert's Secret State Intelligence System* (Ann Arbor: University of Michigan Press, 2009), 14.
5. On Spain, see Arndt Brendecke, " 'Arca, Archivillo, Archivo': The Keeping, Use and Status of Historical Documents about the Spanish Conquista," *Archival Science* 10 (2010), 267–283, doi.org/10.1007/s10502-010-9124-z; Geoffrey Parker, *The Grand Strategy of Philip II* (New Haven, Conn.: Yale University Press, 1998), 22–66; Lothar Müller, *White Magic: The Age of Paper*, trans. Jessica Spengler (London: Polity, 2014), 32–33. On France, see Soll, *The Information Master*. On archiving in early modern Europe generally, see, among other works, Peter Burke, *A Social History of Knowledge: From Gutenberg to Diderot* (London: Polity, 2000), 138–141; Alexandra Walsham, Kate Peters, and Liesbeth Corens, eds., *Archives and Information in the Early Modern World* (Oxford: Oxford University Press, 2018); Markus Friedrich, *The Birth of the Archive: A History of Knowledge*, trans. John Noël Dillon (Ann Arbor: University of Michigan Press, 2018); Randolph C. Head, *Making Archives in Early Modern Europe: Proof, Information, and Political Record-Keeping, 1400–1700* (Cambridge: Cambridge University Press, 2019); Eric Ketelaar, "Records Out and Archives In: Early Modern Cities as Creators of Records and as

Communities of Archives," *Archival Science* 10 (2010), 201–210, doi.org/10.1007/s10502-010-9123-0; Filippo De Vivo, "Ordering the Archive in Early Modern Venice 1400–1650," *Archival Science* 10 (2010), 231–248, doi.org/10.1007/s10502-010-9122-1; Paul M. Dover, *The Information Revolution in Early Modern Europe* (Cambridge: Cambridge University Press, 2021), 91–148. Useful syntheses of the field of early modern archival turn are in Alexandra Walsham, "The Social History of the Archive: Record-Keeping in Early Modern Europe," *Past and Present* 230, suppl. 11 (2016), 9–48; Philippo de Vivo, Andrea Guidi, and Alessandro Silvestri, "Archival Transformations in Early Modern European History," *European History Quarterly* 46, no. 2 (2016), 421–434. On information management among scientists in this era, see Ann M. Blair, *Too Much to Know: Managing Scholarly Information before the Modern Age* (New Haven, Conn.: Yale University Press, 2010); Elizabeth Yale, "With Slips and Scraps: How Early Modern Naturalists Invented the Archive," *Book History* 12, no. 1 (2009), 1–36, doi.org/10.1353/bh.0.0013. While this brief overview begins in the early modern period and is limited to Europe, the study of archives neither starts nor ends there. For earlier periods, see M.T. Clanchy, *From Memory to Written Record: England 1066–1307* (Cambridge, Mass.: Harvard University Press, 1979); Patrick Geary, *Phantoms of Remembrance: Memory and Oblivion at the End of the First Millennium* (Princeton, N.J.: Princeton University Press, 1994); Marina Rustow, *The Lost Archive: Traces of a Caliphate in a Cairo Synagogue* (Princeton, N.J.: Princeton University Press, 2020).

6. Lara Jennifer Moore, *Restoring Order: The École des Chartes and the Organization of Libraries and Archives in France, 1820–1870* (Duluth, Minn.: Litwin, 2008); Jennifer S. Milligan, "The Problem of *Publicité* in the Archives of Second Empire France," in *Archives, Documentation, and Institutions of Social Memory*, ed. Francis X. Blouin and William G. Rosenberg (Ann Arbor: University of Michigan Press, 2006), 20–35; Wolfgang Ernst, "Archival Action: The Archive as ROM and Its Political Instrumentalization under National Socialism," *History of the Human Sciences* 12, no. 2 (1999), 13–34, doi.org/10.1177/09526959922120225; Peter Fritzsche, "The Archive," *History & Memory* 17, no. 1–2 (Spring–Winter 2005), 15–44, doi.org/10.2979/his.2005.17.1-2.13; Andreas Estefane, "Imperial Uncertainties and Republican Conflicts: Archives, Diplomacy, and Historiography in Nineteenth-Century Chile," *Early American Studies: An Interdisciplinary Journal*, 11, no. 1 (2013), 192–207, doi.org/10.1353/eam.2013.0005; Ernst E. Posner, "Some Aspects of Archival Development since the French Revolution," in *A Modern Archives Reader: Basic Readings on Archival Theory and Practice*, ed. Maygene F. Daniels and Timothy Walch (Washington, D.C.: National Archives and Records Service, 1984), 3–14.

7. Nicholas Dirks, *Castes of Mind: Colonialism and the Making of Modern India* (Princeton, N.J.: Princeton University Press, 2001), 106–107. Other

important work on colonial archives includes but is far from limited to Ann Laura Stoler, *Along the Archival Grain: Epistemic Anxieties and Colonial Common Sense* (Princeton, N.J.: Princeton University Press, 2009); Anjali R. Arondekar, *For the Record: On Sexuality and the Colonial Archive in India* (Durham, N.C.: Duke University Press, 2009); Tony Ballantyne, "Archive, Discipline, State: Power and Knowledge in South Asian Historiography," *New Zealand Journal of Asian Studies* 3, no. 1 (2001), 87–105, https://www.nzasia.org.nz/uploads/1/3/2/1/132180707/archive.pdf; Gayatri Charkavorty Spivak, "The Rani of Sirmur: An Essay in Reading the Archives," *History and Theory* 24 (Oct. 1985), 247–272, doi.org/10.2307/2505169; Indrani Chatterjee, "Testing the Local against the Colonial Archive," *History Workshop* 44 (Autumn 1997), 215–224, doi.org/10.1093/hwj/1997.44.215. The colonial archive lives on in the aftermath of imperial breakdown, presenting grave challenges for those seeking to write the histories of the lands and peoples documented in its files. On this, see "AHR Roundtable: The Archive of Decolonization," *American Historical Review* 120, no. 3 (June 2015), 844–950.

8. Moore, *Restoring Order*, 144–154; Peter Horsman, Eric Ketelaar, and Theo Thomassen, "New Respect for the Old Order: The Context of the Dutch Manual," *The American Archivist* 66, no. 2 (Winter 2003), 249–270, doi.org/10.17723/aarc.66.2.452235k813568872; Terry Cook, "What Past is Prologue: A History of Archival Ideas since 1898, and the Future Paradigm Shift," *Archivaria* 43 (Spring 1997), 17–63, https://archivaria.ca/index.php/archivaria/article/view/12175; John Ridener, *From Polders to Postmodernism: A Concise History of Archival Theory* (Duluth, Minn.: Litwin, 2009), 21–68.
9. Randall C. Jimerson, "Documents and Archives in Early America," *Archivaria* 60 (Fall 2005), 235–258, https://archivaria.ca/index.php/archivaria/article/view/12522.
10. Victor Hugo Paltsits, "Tragedies in New York's Public Records," in *Annual Report of the American Historical Association for the Year 1909* (Washington, D.C.: Government Printing Office, 1911), 376–377.
11. Harold Holzer, ed., *The Union Preserved: A Guide to Civil War Records in the New York State Archives* (New York: Fordham University Press, 1999), 17–22.
12. R.A. Halley, "The Preservation of Tennessee History," *American Historical Magazine* 8, no. 1 (Jan. 1903), 55–56, https://www.jstor.org/stable/45331989; Philip M. Hamer, "The Preservation of Tennessee History," *The North Carolina Historical Review* 6, no. 2 (April 1929), https://www.jstor.org/stable/23515194. See also E. Merton Coulter, "What the South Has Done about Its History," *The Journal of Southern History* 2, no. 1 (Feb. 1936), 6–7, doi.org/10.2307/2191556; W. Fitzhugh Brundage, *The Southern Past: A Clash of Race and Memory* (Cambridge, Mass.: Harvard University Press, 2005), 106–107.

13. Morey Rothberg and Jacqueline Goggin, eds., *John Franklin Jameson and the Development of Humanistic Scholarship in America*, vol. 1: *Selected Essays* (Athens: University of Georgia Press, 1993), 319, 320; Waldo Gifford Leland, "The National Archives: A Programme," *American Historical Review* 18, no. 1 (Oct. 1912), 7, doi.org/10.1086/ahr/18.1.1; Waldo Gifford Leland, "American Archival Problems," in *Annual Report of the American Historical Association for the Year 1909* (Washington, D.C.: Government Printing Office, 1911), 343.
14. Leland, "The National Archives," 9–10. See also Dunbar Rowland, "The Concentration of State and National Archives," in *Annual Report of the American Historical Association for the Year 1910* (Washington, D.C., 1912), 295. On the loss of Revolutionary War records see Geo. B. Davis to S.B. Elkins, Jan. 20, 1892, book 12, entry 708, Letters Sent, RG 94.
15. Victor Gonds Jr., *J. Franklin Jameson and the Birth of the National Archives, 1906–1926* (Philadelphia: University of Pennsylvania Press, 1981), 6; James Gregory Bradsher, "An Administrative History of the Disposal of Federal Records, 1789–1949," *Provenance, Journal of the Society of Georgia Archivists* 3, no. 2 (Jan. 1985); Craig Robertson, *The Passport in America: The History of a Document* (Oxford: Oxford University Press, 2010), 113.
16. Charles M. Andrews, "Archives," in *Annual Report of the American Historical Association for the Year 1913* (Washington, D.C.: Government Printing Office, 1915), vol. 1, 264.
17. H.M. Lazelle to Secretary of War, June 4, 1888, book 6, entry 708, Letters Sent, RG 94; Elihu Root, "Preface," *OR* General Index, iii–v; *Congressional Record*, 43 Cong., 1 sess., June 12, 1874, p. 4931.
18. Robert N. Scott to Secretary of War, Sept. 7, 1878, book 1, entry 708, Letters Sent, RG 94; Charles S. Cudlip to Robert N. Scott, April 25, 1879, box 2, entry 710, Letters Received, RG 94; Robert N. Scott to Secretary of War, July 7, 1886, book 5, entry 708, Letters Sent, RG 94.
19. "Property and papers turned over to other Departments and to Individuals," undated, box 1, entry 441, Orders and Regulations of Archive Office, RG 109; E.D. Townsend to A.P. Tasker, Aug. 7, 1873; quote in A.P. Tasker to Adjutant General, Aug. 11, 1873, box 1, entry 451A, Memoranda on Archive Office, RG 109. See also A.P. Tasker to E.D. Townsend, Dec. 17, 1879, box 4, entry 438, Letters Received, RG 109.
20. G. Norman Lieber to General, Nov. 6, 1865, book 1, entry 435, Letters Sent, RG 109; A.P. Tasker to E.D. Townsend, April 3, 1878, book 3, entry 435, Letters Sent, RG 109; C.J. Davis to E.D. Townsend, Aug. 12, 1878, book 3, entry 435, Letters Sent, RG 109. See also H.M. Lazelle to Secretary of War, June 4, 1888, book 6, entry 708, Letters Sent, RG 94.
21. George R. Bentley, *A History of the Freedmen's Bureau* (Philadelphia: University of Pennsylvania Press, 1955), 212; Oliver O. Howard, *Autobiography of Oliver Otis Howard: Major General United States Army* (New York: The Baker & Taylor Company, 1907), vol. 2, 445–455; E.D. Townsend to

Commissioner of the Bureau of Refugees, Freedmen, and Abandoned Lands, June 29, 1872, box 26, entry 18, Secretary of War Letters Received, RG 107. For personal reflections on contemporary work with Freedmen's Bureau records, see Thavolia Glymph, "Black Women and Children in the Civil War: Archive Notes," and Jim Downs, "Emancipating the Evidence: The Ontology of the Freedmen's Bureau Records," in *Beyond Freedom: Disrupting the History of Emancipation*, ed. David W. Blight and Jim Downs (Athens: University of Georgia Press, 2017).

22. Leland, "The National Archives," 11–12; Lucille H. Pendell and Elizabeth Bethel, *Preliminary Inventory of the Records of the Adjutant General's Office* (Washington, D.C.: National Archives and Records Administration, 1949), 107.
23. Thomas M. Vincent to the Adjutant General, Oct. 7, 1872, H.R. Doc. No. 109, 42nd Cong., 3rd sess. Quote on p. 3.
24. O.O. Howard to the Chairman of the Military Committee of the House of Representatives, Feb. 7, 1873, H.R. Mis. Doc. No. 87, 42 Cong., 3 sess., 2, 3.
25. O.O. Howard to the Chairman of the Military Committee, H.R. Mis. Doc. No. 87, 42 Cong., 3 sess., 2; Howard, *Autobiography*, vol. 2, 448–449.
26. Thomas M. Vincent to Adjutant General, Feb. 20, 1873, box 26, entry 18, Secretary of War Letters Received, RG 107.
27. O.O. Howard to the Chairman of the Military Committee, H.R. Mis. Doc. No. 87, 42 Cong., 3 sess., 10; Jno. S. Moodey to Thomas M. Vincent, Feb. 20, 1873, box 26, entry 18, Secretary of War Letters Received, RG 107.
28. O.O. Howard to the Chairman of the Military Committee, H.R. Mis. Doc. No. 87, 42 Cong., 3 sess., 3, 2, 13; Howard, *Autobiography*, vol. 2, 206–228.
29. Bentley, *A History of the Freedmen's Bureau*, 213, including quote; Howard, *Autobiography*, vol. 2, 449–452.
30. War Department, General Orders no. 60, April 7, 1865, box 1, entry 438, Letters Received, RG 109. For additional orders stipulating that officers should have unit records ready for handoff, see General Orders no. 24, May 16, 1865, in *OR*, ser. I, vol. XLVI, pt. III, 1159; General Orders no. 94, May 15, 1894, in *OR*, ser. I, vol. XLVI, pt. III, 1153.
31. Geo. B. Davis to J.C. Bush, Oct. 5, 1892, book 13, entry 708, Letters Sent, RG 94.
32. Geo. B. Davis to James H. Wilson, July 25, 1892, book 13, entry 708, Letters Sent, RG 94; Geo. B. Davis to A.C. Ducat, Dec. 15, 1892, book 14, entry 708, Letters Sent, RG 94.
33. H.M. Lazelle to Fitz John Porter, Jan. 24, 1889, book 7, entry 708, Letters Sent, RG 94. Porter, who had been discharged from the army in ignominy following a dispute with Pope, was not convinced of Pope's account, and suspected him of concealing his record books. Fitz John

Porter to George B. Davis, Sept. 15, 1890, box 11, entry 710, Letters Received, RG 94.

34. Francis E. Pinto to G.W. McCrary, Oct. 6, 1877, entry 715, Letters Received Relating to Missing Military Reports, RG 94; John R. Brooke to Geo. B. Davis, Jan. 30, 1891, box 13, entry 710, Letters Received, RG 94; Geo. B. Davis to C.H. Ingalls, Feb. 9, 1894, book 17, entry 708, Letters Sent, RG 94.
35. W.T. Sherman to E.D. Townsend, June 25, 1865, in *OR*, ser. I, vol. XLVII, pt. III, 663; W.T. Sherman to J.D. Cameron, Aug. 31, 1876, entry 715, Letters Received Relating to Missing Military Reports, RG 94.
36. Ebenezer Hazard, ed., *Historical Collections: Consisting of State Papers, and Other Authentic Documents; Intended as Materials for An History of the United States of America*, 2 vols. (Philadelphia: T. Dobson, 1792–1794); Ebenezer Hazard to Thomas Jefferson, Aug. 23, 1774, microfilm reel 1, ser. 1, Thomas Jefferson Papers at the Library of Congress, Manuscript Division, LC, https://www.loc.gov/resource/mtj1.001_0290_0294/?sp=1; Clarence E. Carter, "The United States and Documentary Historical Publication," *Mississippi Valley Historical Review* 25, no. 1 (June 1938), 4–5, doi.org/10.2307/1892322; Fred Shelley, "Ebenezer Hazard: America's First Historical Editor," *William and Mary Quarterly* 12, no. 1 (Jan. 1955), 44–73, doi.org/10.2307/1923095.
37. Carter, "The United States and Documentary Historical Publication," 3–24; David D. Van Tassell, *Recording America's Past: An Interpretation of the Development of Historical Studies in America, 1607–1884* (Chicago: University of Chicago Press, 1960), 103–110; Randall C. Jimerson, "Documents and Archives in Early America," *Archivaria* 60 (Fall 2006), 235–258, https://archivaria.ca/index.php/archivaria/article/view/12522; Oz Frankel, *States of Inquiry: Social Investigations and Print Culture in Nineteenth Century Britain and the United States* (Baltimore: Johns Hopkins University Press, 2006), 72–103; Eliza Tamarkin, *Anglophilia: Deference, Devotion, and Antebellum America* (Chicago: University of Chicago Press, 2007), 87–89.
38. *Keeping America Informed: The U.S. Government Printing Office* (Washington, D.C.: Government Printing Office, 2011), 4–10.
39. Oz Frankel treats this topic exhaustively in *States of Inquiry*.
40. Peter Burke, *A Social History of Knowledge*, vol. 2: *From the* Encyclopédie *to Wikipedia* (London: Polity, 2012), 195.
41. *Congressional Globe*, 39 Cong., 1 sess., May 24, 1866, p. 2806.
42. Lorraine Daston, "The Immortal Archive: Nineteenth-Century Science Imagines the Future," in *Science in the Archives: Pasts, Presents, Futures*, ed. Lorraine Daston (Chicago: University of Chicago Press, 2017), 161.
43. Lisa Tetrault, *The Myth of Seneca Falls: Memory and the Women's Suffrage Movement, 1848–1898* (Chapel Hill: University of North Carolina Press, 2014), 112–144. Tetrault's story becomes even more interesting as it

turns out that the actual goal of the authors/editors was to construct a master narrative of the movement that would highlight their own contributions and push aside their rivals. In this context, though, the main issue is how *History of Woman's Suffrage* fits in with a broader trend of editing and publishing original records.

44. United States Surgeon General, *The Medical and Surgical History of the War of the Rebellion (1861–65)* (Washington, D.C.: Government Printing Office, 1870–1883), vol. 1, iv; War Department, Surgeon General's Office, Circular No. 6, Nov. 1, 1865 (Philadelphia: J.B. Lippincott, 1866), 1–2.
45. Shauna Devine, *Learning from the Wounded: The Civil War and the Rise of American Medical Science* (Chapel Hill: University of North Carolina Press, 2014), 13–52. As part of the effort to make use of this vast trove of knowledge, the Surgeon General also established the Army Medical Museum, which housed pathological specimens and became a leading institution for medical research and education.
46. *Medical and Surgical History of the War of the Rebellion*, vol. 1, viii.
47. H.W. Halleck to E.M. Stanton, November 15, 1863, *OR*, ser. III, vol. III, 1039; Alan C. Aimone and Barbara A. Aimone, *A User's Guide to the Official Records of the American Civil War* (Shippensburg, Pa.: White Mane Publishing, 1993), 1. On the faults in the printed records, see also *Congressional Globe*, 39 Cong., 1 sess., May 16, 1864, p. 2279.
48. John F. Marszalek, *Commander of All Lincoln's Armies: A Life of General Henry W. Halleck* (Cambridge, Mass.: Harvard University Press, 2004), 63–64, 76.
49. *Congressional Globe*, 38 Cong., 1 sess., April 21, 1864, p. 1771, May 12, 1864, p. 2249, 2279; *Statutes at Large*, 43 Cong., 1 sess., p. 222.
50. Elihu Root, "Preface," *OR* General Index, vi; *Congressional Globe*, 39 Cong. 1, sess., May 24, 1866, p. 2804, 2805; Aimone and Aimone, *User's Guide to the Official Records*, 2.
51. General Orders no. 127, July 21, 1865, box 1, entry 441, Orders and Regulations of the Archive Office, 1865–1880, RG 109; "Archive Office of the War Department," unsigned memorandum, box 1, entry 438, Letters Received, RG 109.
52. *Congressional Globe*, 39 Cong., 1 sess., May 24, 1866, p. 2804. A recent perspective on Wilson's historical work is in William A. Blair, "A Modern Sensibility in Older Garb: Henry Wilson's Rise and Fall of the Slave Power and the Beginnings of Civil War History," in *Civil War Witnesses and their Books: New Perspectives on Iconic Works*, ed. Gary W. Gallagher and Stephen Cushman (Baton Rouge: Louisiana State University Press, 2021).
53. *Congressional Globe*, 39 Cong., 1 sess., May 24, 1866, p. 2805, 2806.
54. The 1866 Senate debate is in *Congressional Globe*, 39 Cong., 1 sess., May 24, 1866, p. 2804–2807.

55. *Statutes at Large*, 39 Cong., 1 sess., p. 369; Elihu Root, "Preface," *OR* General Index, vi–vii.
56. U.S. War Department, *Annual Report of the Secretary of War* (Washington, D.C.: Government Printing Office, 1870), vol. 1, xv; *Congressional Record*, 43 Cong., 1 sess., June 12, 1874, p. 4931.
57. Stetson Conn, *Historical Work in the United States Army 1862–1954* (Washington, D.C.: U.S. Army Center of Military History, 1980), 3; J.N. Larned, ed., *The Literature of American History* (Boston: American Library Association, 1902), 214; Dallas D. Irvine, "The Genesis of the Official Records," *Mississippi Valley Historical Review* 24 (Sept. 1937), 225; Aimone and Aimone, *User's Guide to the Official Records*, 2; Harold E. Mahan, "The Arsenal of History: The Official Records of the War of the Rebellion," *Civil War History* 29 (Spring 1983), 10.
58. *Congressional Record*, 43 Cong., 1 sess., June 12, 1874, p. 4931.

Chapter Four. Official Records and the Search for Truth

1. David E. Shi, *Facing Facts: Realism in American Culture 1850–1920* (New York: Oxford University Press, 2008), 1. See also Leslie Schwalm, "A Body of Truly Scientific Work: The U.S. Sanitary Commission and the Elaboration of Race in the Civil War Era," *Journal of Civil War Era* 8, no. 4 (Dec. 2018), 653, doi.org/10.1353/cwe.2018.0073; Susan Schulten, *Mapping the Nation: History and Cartography in Nineteenth Century America* (Chicago: University of Chicago Press, 2012), 187. On the Civil War as a catalyst for literary realism, see Ian Finseth, "The Realists' Civil War," in *A History of American Civil War Literature*, ed. Coleman Hutchinson (Cambridge: Cambridge University Press, 2016), 62–76.
2. Yael A. Sternhell, "Communicating War: The Culture of Information in Richmond during the American Civil War," *Past & Present* 202 (Feb. 2009), 175–205, doi.org/10.1093/pastj/gtn022. For an earlier example of publishing original documents in newspapers as a means to quell an agitated readership, see David Paul Nord, *Communities of Journalism: A History of American Newspapers and their Readers* (Urbana: University of Illinois Press, 2001), 199–244. On the role of rumors in the Confederacy, see Jason Phillips, "The Grapevine Telegraph: Rumors and Confederate Persistence," *Journal of Southern History* 72 (2006), 753–788, doi.org/10.2307/27649232.
3. Frank Moore, ed., *The Rebellion Record: A Diary of American Events, with Documents, Narratives, Illustrative Incidents, Poetry, Etc.*, 12 volumes (New York, 1861–1868); Alice Fahs, *The Imagined Civil War: Popular Literature of the North & South, 1861–1865* (Chapel Hill: University of North Carolina Press, 2001), 51–52. Quote on p. 52.
4. United States War Department, *Exchange of Prisoners* (Washington, D.C.: Government Printing Office, 1865); United States War Department,

Letter of the Secretary of War: Transmitting Report of the Organization of the Army of the Potomac, and of its Campaigns in Virginia and Maryland, under the Command of Maj. Gen. George B. McClellan, from July 26, 1861, to November 7, 1862 (Washington, D.C.: Government Printing Office, 1864); United States War Department, *Murder of Union Soldiers in North Carolina. Letter from Secretary of War, in Answer to a Resolution of the House of Representatives, of April 16, Transmitting the report of Judge Advocate Holt, relative to the Murder of Certain Union Soldiers Belonging to the 1st and 2nd North Carolina Loyal Infantry* (Washington, D.C.: Government Printing Office, 1866). Most documents were produced by executive departments and then transmitted and printed by Congress. As Oz Frankel has shown, Congress controlled the publication of state records as a matter of course. See Oz Frankel, *States of Inquiry: Social Investigations and Print Culture in Nineteenth-Century Britain and the United States* (Baltimore: Johns Hopkins University Press, 2006).

5. United States Congress, *Supplemental Report of the Joint Committee on the Conduct of the War*, 2 vols. (Washington, D.C.: Government Printing Office, 1866); Carl Schurz, *Report on the Condition of the South*, Ex. Doc., 39 Cong., Senate, 1st sess., no. 2, 76; David D. Van Tassell, *Recording America's Past: An Interpretation of the Development of Historical Studies in America, 1607–1884* (Chicago: University of Chicago Press, 1960), 156.
6. Both pensions and claims and their relationship to Civil War records are treated in Chapter 2.
7. Edwin M. Stanton, June 21, 1864, Ex. Doc. 155, 38 Cong., 1 sess., 5–6.
8. Sallie A. Brock, *Richmond during the War: Four Years of Personal Observation* (New York: Carlton & Co., 1867), 362; Thomas De Leon, *Four Years in Rebel Capitals* (Mobile, Ala.: The Gossip Printing Company, 1892), 111, 124–125.
9. William A. Crocker, "Army Intelligence Office," *Confederate Veteran* 8 (1900), 119; See also Henry Putney Beers, *Guide to the Archives of the Government of the Confederate States of America* (Washington, D.C.: The National Archives, 1968), 233.
10. Sarah Chenoweth to Sir, Sept. 28, 1865, box 1, entry 438, Letters Received, RG 109.
11. H.V. Lucas to W.W. Belknap, Feb. 28, 1876, box 2, entry 438, Letters Received, RG 109; Anastasia O'Boyle to W.H. Belknap, May 5, 1875, box 3, entry 438, Letters Received, RG 109; W.W. Rollins to Adgt General, Jan. 16, 1875, box 3, entry 438, Letters Received, RG 109.
12. B. Wells to Francis Lieber, April 18, 1870, book 2, entry 435, Letters Sent, RG 109.
13. Wade Keyes to Francis Lieber, Sept. 4, 1865, box 2, entry 438, Letters Received, RG 109; Josephine LeConte to Francis Lieber, Nov. 8, 1865, box 2, entry 438, Letters Received, RG 109; M.J. Smead to Francis Lieber, Sept. 20, 1865, box 3, entry 438, Letters Received, RG 109.

14. G. Norman Lieber to Adjutant General, May 14, 1866, box 3, entry 438, Letters Received, RG 109.
15. My evidence for families writing the War Department's archival bureaus comes from the records of the Archive Office. It seems safe to assume that the bureaus keeping the records of the United States were similarly inundated with requests for information, but I have not done this research. For evidence of African Americans searching for family members in the aftermath of enslavement and war, see Heather Andrea Williams, *Help Me to Find My People: The African American Search for Family after Slavery* (Chapel Hill: University of North Carolina Press, 2012).
16. On United Confederate Veterans membership see Gaines M. Foster, *Ghosts of the Confederacy: Defeat, the Lost Cause, and the Emergence of the New South 1865–1913* (New York: Oxford University Press, 1987), 107. On GAR membership, see Stuart McConnell, *Glorious Contentment: The Grand Army of the Republic 1865–1900* (Chapel Hill: University of North Carolina Press, 1992), 54.
17. On veterans and commemorative activities, see Foster, *Ghosts of the Confederacy;* David W. Blight, *Race and Reunion: The Civil War in American Memory* (Cambridge, Mass.: Harvard University Press, 2001); Donald R. Shaffer, *After the Glory: The Struggles of Black Civil War Veterans* (Lawrence: University Press of Kansas, 2004); Robert Hunt, *The Good Men Who Won the War: Army of the Cumberland Veterans and Emancipation Memory* (Mobile: University of Alabama Press, 2010); Barbara Gannon, *The Won Cause: Black and White Comradeship in the Grand Army of the Republic* (Chapel Hill: University of North Carolina Press, 2011); Caroline Janney, *Remembering the Civil War: Reunion and the Limits of Reconciliation* (Chapel Hill: University of North Carolina Press, 2013); M. Keith Harris, *Across the Bloody Chasm: The Culture of Commemoration Among Civil War Veterans* (Baton Rouge: Louisiana State University Press, 2014); Brian Matthew Jordan, *Marching Home: Union Veterans and their Unending Civil War* (New York: Liveright, 2014); Robert J. Cook, "Hollow Victory: Federal Veterans, Racial Justice, and the Eclipse of the Union Cause in American Memory," *History & Memory* 33, no. 1 (Spring 2021), 3–33, doi.org/10.2979/histmemo.33.1.02.
18. Steven E. Sodergen, "Exposing False History: The Voice of the Union Veteran in the Pages of the *National Tribune*" in *The War Went On: Reconsidering the Lives of Civil War Veterans*, ed. Brian Matthew Jordan and Even C. Rothera (Baton Rouge: Louisiana State University Press, 2020), 137–156. On the post–Civil War publishing boom, see Stephen Cushman, *The Generals' Civil War: What Their Memoirs Teach Us Today* (Chapel Hill: University of North Carolina Press, 2021), 3–8.
19. Blight, *Race and Reunion*, 186. The opposing view is in Sodergen, "Exposing False History." See also Jordan and Rothera's introduction to the same volume, *The War Went On*, especially p. 4.

20. This brief summary is based on the records in boxes 1–13, entry 710, Letters Received, RG 94.
21. On Scott, see H.V. Boynton, "A Just Man and a Great Historical Work," *Century Magazine* 34 (July 1887), 467–468. Scott will be an important protagonist in Chapter 5, and his story will be told in greater detail there. On Lazelle, see James Carson, *Against the Grain: Colonel Henry M. Lazelle and the U.S. Army* (Denton: University of North Texas Press, 2016); Joseph W. Kirkley, *Historical Record of First Regiment Maryland Infantry* (Washington, D.C.: Gibson Brothers, Printers, 1871); Henry V. Boynton and Joseph W. Kirkley, *The National Military Park, Chickamauga—Chattanooga An Historical Guide, with Maps and illustrations* (Cincinnati, Ohio: The Robert Clarke Company, 1895); Joseph W. Kirkley, *Itinerary of the Army of the Potomac and Co-operating forces in the Gettysburg Campaign, June and July, 1863* (Washington, D.C.: Government Printing Office, 1886).
22. On Davis, see Frederic L. Borch, "From Frontier Cavalryman to the World Stage: The Career of Army Judge Advocate General George B. Davis," *Army History* 74 (Winter 2010), 6–19, https://www.jstor.org/stable/26296025. See also Geo. B. Davis to Henry Stone, Sept. 26, 1892, book 13, entry 708, Letters Sent, RG 94; Geo. B. Davis to Bureau Bros., May 9, 1894, box 18, entry 708, Letters Sent, RG 94; Geo. B. Davis to R. Snowden Andrews, May 9, 1894, box 18, entry 708, Letters Sent, RG 94; Geo. B. Davis to James M. Brown, June 5, 1894, box 18, entry 708, Letters Sent, RG 94; Geo. B. Davis to Geo. C. Rounds, June 7, 1894, box 18, entry 708, Letters Sent, RG 94. On Marcus J. Wright, see Brig. Gen. Marcus J. Wright, CSA, folder 6, ser. 3, WSHC; John Sharp Williams, "Gen. Marcus J. Wright, A Tribute," *Confederate Veteran* 31 (Feb. 1923), 49–50.
23. John Bresnahan to H.M. Lazelle, Sept. 10, 1888, box 9, entry 710, Letters Received, RG 94; Oliver O. Howard to Robt. N. Scott, Dec. 21, 1885, box 7, entry 710, Letters Received, RG 94; H.M. Lazelle to Theodore A. Dodge, Nov. 25, 1887, box 6, entry 708, Letters Sent, RG 94.
24. Thos. L. Rosser to Robt. N. Scott, Aug. 23, 1884, box 5, entry 710, Letters Received, RG 94; Saml. Hodgkins to Col. Jones, Oct. 4, 1884, box 5, entry 710, Letters Received, RG 94; Robert Lincoln to Thos. L. Rosser, Oct. 17, 1884, box 5, entry 710, Letters Received, RG 94; Thos. L. Rosser to Col., Oct. 23, 1884, box 5, entry 710, Letters Received, RG 94; Thos. L. Rosser to Robert N. Scott, Oct. 30, 1884, box 5, entry 710, Letters Received, RG 94. On Rosser's exploits after Lee's surrender, see Caroline E. Janney, *Ends of War: The Unfinished Fight of Lee's Army after Appomattox* (Chapel Hill: University of North Carolina Press, 2021).
25. Michael Zakim, "The Political Geometry of Statistical Tables," *Journal of the Early Republic* 38, no. 3 (Fall 2018), 445–449, doi.org/10.1353/jer.2018.0047. See also Patricia Cline, *A Calculating People: The Spread of Numeracy in Early America* (Chicago: University of Chicago Press, 1983).

26. Drew Gilpin Faust, *This Republic of Suffering: Death and the American Civil War* (New York: Vintage, 2008), 331. See also Susan Schulten, "The Cartography of Slavery and the Authority of Statistics," *Civil War History* 56, no. 1 (March 2010), 3–32, doi.org/10.1353/cwh.0.0141.
27. Quote from *Richmond Examiner*, July 8, 1863, is in Sternhell, "Communicating War," 198.
28. Robert E. Lee, General Order no. 9, April 10, 1865, Encyclopedia Virginia, https://encyclopediavirginia.org/280hpr-5d67b64c8310b0b.
29. Jordan, *Marching Home*, 95; Jonathan Shay, *Odysseus in America: Combat Trauma and the Trials of Homecoming* (New York: Scribner, 2002), 92–95.
30. W.E. Simonds to War Records Office, Feb. 16, 1888, box 9, entry 710, Letters Received, RG 94; Judson W. Bishop to Geo. B. Davis, Aug. 15, 1889, box 9B, entry 710, Letters Received, RG 94; H. Capehart to Major Davis, March 4, 1890, box 10, entry 710, Letters Received, RG 94; E.C. Dawes to A.V. Rice, March 4, 1878, box 1, entry 438, Letters Received, RG 109; H.B. McClellan to Robert N. Scott, Dec. 30, 1884, box 5, entry 710, Letters Received, RG 94.
31. Geo. B. Davis to Benj. F. Butler, June 4, 1891, book 10, entry 708, Letters Sent, RG 94; Geo. B. Davis to B.H. Hartogenses, Feb. 9, 1892, box 12, entry 708, Letters Sent, RG 94; W. Allan to Marcus J. Wright, Feb. 6, 1888, box 9, entry 710, Letters Received, RG 94; Geo. B. Davis to A.W. Fenton, Jan. 18, 1894, book 17, entry 708, Letters Sent, RG 94. See also Geo. B. Davis to John S. Billings, April 6, 1894, book 17, entry 708, Letters Sent, RG 94.
32. Geo. B. Davis to W.R. Holloway, Feb. 26, 1892, book 12, entry 708, Letters Sent, RG 94; Geo. B. Davis to Andrew Cowan, March 17, 1894, book 17, entry 708, Letters Sent, RG 94; Geo. B. Davis to M.S. Bolles, June 12, 1894, book 18, entry 708, Letters Sent, RG 94; Geo. B. Davis to B.H. Hartogenses, Feb. 9, 1892, book 12, entry 708, Letters Sent, RG 94; Geo. B. Davis to A.W. Fenton, Jan. 18, 1894, book 17, entry 708, Letters Sent, RG 94.
33. On public perceptions of Civil War prisoners of war, see Blight, *Race and Reunion*, 183–185; Jordan, *Marching Home*, 131–150. On prisoners' narratives, see Ann Fabian, *The Unvarnished Truth: Personal Narratives in Nineteenth Century America* (Berkeley: University of California Press, 2000), 117–158.
34. W.H. Newbin to Colonel Scott, Oct. 22, 1880, box 4, entry 710, Letters Received, RG 94.
35. Geo. B. Davis to A.W. Fenton, Jan.18, 1894, book 17, entry 708, Letters Sent, RG 94. See also Geo. B. Davis to John S. Billings, April 6, 1894, book 17, entry 708, Letters Sent, RG 94.
36. Francis Amasa Walker, "General Hancock and the Artillery at Gettysburg," *Battles and Leaders of the Civil War* (New York: The Century Company, 1887–1888), 385–386, https://ehistory.osu.edu/books/battles/vol3/

385; Francis Amasa Walker, *History of the Second Army Corps in the Army of the Potomac* (New York: Charles Scribner's Sons, 1886), iv. A second and revised edition appeared in 1891. See Allen C. Guelzo and Brianna Kirk, "The Hancock-Walker Correspondence on Gettysburg," *Gettysburg Magazine* 56 (Jan. 2017), 53–55. Scott's response is in Robert N. Scott to F.A. Walker, Sept. 22, 1886, book 5, entry 708, Letters Sent, RG 94.

37. Jordan, *Marching Home*, 84.
38. C.C. Andrews to the officer in charge of the Official Records, War of the Rebellion, Dec. 30, 1889, box 10, entry 710, Letters Received, RG 94. Geo. B. Davis to C.C. Andrews, Jan. 11, 1892, book 11, entry 708, Letters Sent, RG 94; On the battle, see Mark K. Christ, " 'A Hard Little Fight': The Battle of Fitzhugh's Woods," April 1, 1864, *The Arkansas Historical Quarterly* 64, No. 4 (Winter, 2005), 381–393.
39. A.L. Gusman to Marcus J. Wright, Sept. 3, 1888, box 9, entry 710, Letters Received, RG 94.
40. John M. Corse to Henry M. Lazelle, April 7, 1888, box 9, entry 710, Letters Received, RG 94; E.C. Dawes to A.V. Rice, March 4, 1878, box 1, entry 438, Letters Received, RG 109; endorsements by W.T. Sherman, Archive Office, and Secretary of War, March 28, box 1, entry 438, Letters Received, RG 109.
41. Geo. B. Davis to H.A. Hambright, June 27, 1891, book 10, entry 708, Letters Sent, RG 94; Geo. B. Davis to Garnett Andrews, Feb. 14, 1891, book 10, entry 708, Letters Sent, RG 94; E.D. Townsend to P.H. Sheridan, March 1, 1878, box 1, entry 710, Letters Received, RG 94.
42. E.E. Marvin to J.W. Kirkley, Sept. 13, 1888, box 9, entry 710, Letters Received, RG 94; William E. Merrill to My Dear Davis, Jan. 22, 1890, box 10, entry 710, Letters Received, RG 94; H.B. McClellan to Robert N. Scott, July 9, 1885, box 6, entry 710, Letters Received, RG 94.
43. Wm. E. Potter to Sir, Dec. 26, 1881, box 7, entry 710, Letters Received, RG 94; E.C. Walthall to Robt N. Scott, Jan. 1, 1886, box 7, entry 710, Letters Received, RG 94; E.C. Walthall to Robt N. Scott, Jan. 9, 1886, box 7, entry 710, Letters Received, RG 94.
44. Robert McAllister to H.M. Lazelle, April 26, 1888, box 9, entry 710, Letters Received, RG 94; Geo. B. Davis to C.S. Sargeant, March 28, 1891, book 10, entry 708, Letters Sent, RG 94.
45. On early attitudes toward Gettysburg, see Blight, *Race and Reunion*, 33–34.
46. W.R. Bond to Genl., Feb. 26, 1876, box 1, entry 438, Letters Received, RG 109; E.D. Townsend to R.B. Vance, March 20, 1876, book 3, entry 435, Letters Sent, RG 109. On the postwar infighting between Virginians and North Carolinians, see Carol Reardon, "Pickett's Charge: The Convergence of History and Myth in the Southern Past," in *The Third Day of Gettysburg and Beyond*, ed. Gary W. Gallagher (Chapel Hill: University of North Carolina Press, 1994), 56–92.

47. CSA officers to Honorable Senate and House of Representatives, Dec. 1879, box 3, entry 710, Letters Received, RG 94.
48. Geo. B. Davis to E.P. Alexander, Oct. 25, 1897, box 7, entry 713, General Correspondence, RG 94; E.P. Alexander to War Records Office, Jan. 12, 1898, box 7, entry 713, General Correspondence, RG 94; Geo. B. Davis to E.P. Alexander, Jan. 31, 1898, box 7, entry 713, General Correspondence, RG 94; Gary G. Gallagher, ed. *Fighting for the Confederacy: The Personal Recollections of General Edward Porter Alexander* (Chapel Hill: University of North Carolina Press, 1989), xvii. See also Gary G. Gallagher, "The Best Confederate Memoirist: Edward Porter Alexander's Unrivaled Military Accounts," in *Civil War Writing: New Perspectives on Iconic Texts*, ed. Gary W. Gallagher and Stephen Cushman (Baton Rouge: Louisiana State University Press, 2019), 259–280.
49. Peter Novick, *That Noble Dream: The "Objectivity Question" and the American Historical Profession* (Cambridge: Cambridge University Press, 1988); Bonnie G. Smith, *The Gender of History: Men, Women, and Historical Practice* (Cambridge, Mass.: Harvard University Press, 1998); Joyce Appleby, Lynn Hunt, and Margaret Jacob, *Telling the Truth about History* (New York: W.W. Norton & Company, 1994). See also Ellen Fitzpatrick, *History's Memory: Writing America's Past, 1880–1980* (Cambridge, Mass.: Harvard University Press, 2002); Michael Kraus, *The Writing of American History* (Norman: University of Oklahoma Press, 1953); Dorothy Ross, *The Origins of American Social Science* (Cambridge: Cambridge University Press, 1991); John Higham, *History: Professional Scholarship in America* (Baltimore: Johns Hopkins University Press, 1989).
50. Appleby, Hunt, and Jacob, *Telling the Truth about History*, 73; Novick, *That Noble Dream*, 37. On objectivity, see Lorraine Daston and Peter Galison, "The Image of Objectivity," *Representations* 40 (1992), 81–128, doi.org/10.2307/2928741.
51. Smith, *The Gender of History*, 128, 121; See also Julie Des Jardins, *Women and the Historical Enterprise in America: Gender, Race, and the Politics of Memory, 1880–1945* (Chapel Hill: University of North Carolina Press, 2003); James Turner, *Philology: The Forgotten Origins of the Modern Humanities* (Princeton, N.J.: Princeton University Press, 2014).
52. Anthony Grafton, *The Footnote: A Curious History* (Cambridge, Mass.: Harvard University Press, 1997); Suzanne Marchand, "Ancient History in the Age of Archival Research," in *Science in the Archives: Pasts, Presents, Futures*, ed. Lorraine Daston (Chicago: University of Chicago Press, 2017). See also Lorraine Daston and Glenn W. Most, "History of Science and History of Philologies," *Isis* 106 (June 2015), 385, doi.org/10.1086/681980. For contemporary views of Ranke, see Kasper Risbjerg Eskildsen, "Inventing the Archive: Testimony and Virtue in Modern Historiography," *History of the Human Sciences* 26, no. 4 (2013), 8–26, doi.org/10.1177/0952695113496094; Kasper Risbjerg Eskildsen, "Leopold

Ranke's Archival Turn: Location and Evidence in Modern Historiography," *Modern Intellectual History* 5, no. 3 (2008), 425–453, doi.org/10.1017/s1479244308001753. On Ranke in America, see Dorothy Ross, "On the Misunderstanding of Ranke and the Origins of the Historical Profession in America," *Syracuse Scholar* 9, no. 1 (1988), Article 6, https://surface.syr.edu/suscholar/vol9/iss1/6.

53. Eileen Ka-May Cheng, *The Plain and Noble Garb of Truth: Nationalism and Impartiality in Historical Writing, 1784–1860* (Athens: University of Georgia Press, 2008). Cheng's nuanced study distinguishes between the different meanings of "impartial," but identifies one of its uses as being close to the idea of "objectivity," which would become popular later in the century. See also Higham, *History*, 92.

54. Peter Luebke has identified similar patterns in his work on unit histories. See " 'To Perpetuate the Fruits of This Victory': Union Regimental Histories and the Great Rebellion in Immediate Retrospect" (paper, 2018 biannual meeting, Society for Civil War Historians, Pittsburg, Pa.).

55. Richd. B. Irwin to Henry M. Lazelle, Sept. 28, 1888, box 9A, entry 710, Letters Received, RG 94; Luis F. Emilio to Robt. N. Scott, Dec. 14, 1884, box 5, entry 710, Letters Received, RG 94; Jos. R. Hawley to Henry M. Lazelle, April 9, 1888, box 9, entry 710, Letter Received, RG 94.

56. Robert McAllister to H.M. Lazelle, April 26, 1888, box 9, entry 710, Letters Received, RG 94. Robert McAllister to H.M. Lazelle, July 11, 1888, box 9, entry 710, Letters Received, RG 94. See also James I. Robertson, ed., *The Civil War Letters of General Robert McAllister* (Baton Rouge: Louisiana State University Press, 1998).

57. E.V.D. Miller to M.J. Wright, Dec. 12, 1884, box 5, entry 710, Letters Received, RG 94. On Van Dorn, see Derek Clements, "Earl Van Dorn," Encyclopedia of Arkansas, accessed May 17, 2021, https://encyclopediaofarkansas.net/entries/earl-van-dorn-2367.

58. Emily Van Dorn Miller, *A Soldier's Honor: With Reminiscences of Major-General Earl Van Dorn* (New York: Abbey Press, 1902). Van Dorn's remarks also appear in the original transcript of the court martial. See *OR*, ser. I, vol. XVII, pt. I, 458.

59. Wm. Preston Johnston to Randal L. Gibson, Feb. 28, 1878, box 2, entry 438, Letters Received, RG 109.

60. Dozier G. Herbert to H.A. McArdle, Oct. 28, 1875, The Battle of San Jacinto Notebook, The McArdle Notebooks, Archives and Information Services Division, Texas State Library and Archives Commission, accessed Sept. 12, 2022, https://www.tsl.texas.gov/mcardle/sanjac/sanjac063.html; Dozier G. Herbert to Marcus J. Wright, Jan. 2, 1880, and Dozier Herbert to E.D. Townsend, Aug. 24, 1879, box 2, entry 438, Letters Received, RG 109; Dozier Herbert to Marcus J. Wright, Dec. 24, 1879, box 2, entry 438, Letters Received, RG 109; Dozier Herbert to Marcus J. Wright, Feb. 26, 1880, box 2, entry 438, Letters Received, RG 109.

61. On John Johnson, see "John Johnson," Fort Sumter and Fort Moultrie, National Parks Service, accessed May 17, 2021, https://www.nps.gov/fosu/learn/historyculture/john-johnson.htm; Jno. Johnson to Robt. N. Scott, June 24, 1885, box 6, entry 710, Letters Received, RG 94; Jno. Johnson to Robt. N. Scott, Aug. 27, 1885, box 6, entry 710, Letters Received, RG 94; Jno. Johnson to Robert N. Scott, Sept. 4, 1885, box 6, entry 710, Letters Received, RG 94.
62. John Johnson, *The Defense of Charleston Harbor, Including Fort Sumter and the Adjacent Islands, 1863–1865* (Charleston, S.C.: Walker, Evans & Cogswell, 1890), 3.
63. On the Southern Historical Society, see Foster, *Ghosts of the Confederacy*, 47–62; Blight, *Race and Reunion*, 261–267; Richard D. Starnes, "Forever Faithful: The Southern Historical Society and Confederate Historical Memory," *Southern Cultures* 2 (Winter 1996), 177–194, doi.org/10.1353/scu.1996.0006.
64. Southern Historical Society, *Southern Historical Society Papers* (Richmond: Southern Historical Society, Jan.–June 1876), vol. 1, 41, 42–43.
65. *Southern Historical Society Papers*, vol. 1, 41.
66. Thomas S. Townsend to Marcus J. Wright, July 15, 1878, folder 10B, ser. 5, WSHC.
67. Report No. 1240, May 29, 1890, 51 Cong., 1 sess. On Townsend's newspaper selection, see the catalog entry in Columbia's University library: https://clio.columbia.edu/catalog/4079410?counter=1.
68. Thomas S. Townsend, *Townsend's Library of National, State, and Individual Records, 1860–1870* (New York: Styles and Cash, 1888), 3, https://babel.hathitrust.org/cgi/pt?id=loc.ark:/13960/t4zg7d66m&view=1up&seq=19; on Cogswell, see finding aid for Astor Library Records, The New York Public Library, accessed Sept. 7, 2022, http://archives.nypl.org/nypla/5975.
69. J. Henry Hager, "A History of the Library," *The Townsend Library of National, State, and Individual Civil Records at Columbia University* (New York: Columbia University, 1899), 13, https://archive.org/details/townsendlibrary00colu/page/12/mode/2up.
70. Report no. 1240, May 29, 1890, Senate, 51 Cong., 1 sess.; Thomas S. Townsend, *The Honors of the Empire State in the War of the Rebellion* (New York: A. Lovell & Co., 1899).
71. Townsend, *Townsend's Library*, 4.

Chapter Five. "Simply the Facts"

1. Elihu Root, "Preface," *OR* General Index, xvi–xvii.
2. Elihu Root, "Preface," *OR* General Index, xviii.
3. Bruce Catton, *A Stillness at Appomattox: The Army of the Potomac Trilogy* (New York: Random House, 1953), 330; Thavolia Glymph, *The Women's*

Fight: The Civil War's Battles for Home, Freedom, and Nation (Chapel Hill: University of North Carolina Press, 2020), e.g, pp. 312–313, and throughout.

4. United States Naval War Records Office, *Official Records of the Union and Confederate Navies in the War of the Rebellion*, 30 vols. (Washington, D.C.: Government Printing Office, 1894–1922); Janet B. Hewett et al., eds., *Supplement to the Official Records of the Union and Confederate Armies*, 100 vols. (Wilmington, N.C.: Broadfoot, 1994–2001).
5. "Records of the Rebellion," *National Tribune*, May 23, 1901, p. 5, in *Chronicling America: Historic American Newspapers*, July 24, 2022, LC, https://chroniclingamerica.loc.gov/lccn/sn82016187/1901-05-23/ed-1/seq-5/.
6. Stephen Cushman, *The Generals' Civil War: What Their Memoirs Teach Us Today* (Chapel Hill: University of North Carolina Press, 2021), 111. See, e.g., the methodological preoccupation with using the collections of slave narratives assembled in the 1930s by New Deal interviewers. John W. Blassingame, "Using the Testimony of Ex-Slaves: Approaches and Problems," in *The Slave's Narratives*, ed. Charles T. Davis and Henry Louis Gates Jr. (New York: Oxford University Press, 1985), 78–98.
7. *OR*, ser. I, vol. XIV, 224; D. Hunter to E.M. Stanton, April 22, 1862, in *OR*, ser. I, vol. XIV, 337; D. Hunter to E.M. Stanton, May 31, 1862, in *OR*, ser. I, vol. XIV, 348.
8. Report of the Secretary of War, House Exec. Doc., 44 Cong., 1 sess., 1875, pt. 2, p. 25; E.D. Townsend to R.A. Hatcher, Dec. 19, 1874, book 3, entry 435, Letters Sent, RG 109; H.T. Crosby to James A. Garfield, Jan. 13, 1875, book 1, entry 707, Letters Sent, RG 94; William W. Belknap to H.T. Crosby, March 3, 1875, book 1, entry 707, Letters Sent, RG 94.
9. W.T. Barnard to Secretary of War, May 16, 1877, book 1, entry 707, Letters Sent, RG 94; W.T. Barnard to Secretary of War, March 12, 1877, box 1, entry 710, Letters Received, RG 94; W.T. Barnard to Chief Clerk Bureau of Military Justice, Oct. 11, 1876, book 1, entry 707, Letters Sent, RG 94.
10. Elihu Root, "Preface," *OR* General Index, viii.
11. In his official War Department biography, published during his tenure, McCrary was described as having "a special interest" in the work of "arranging and printing the rebel archives and records in the control of the Department . . . The inestimable value of this vast mass of historical material is fully appreciated by the Secretary." Lurton Dunham Ingersoll, *A History of the War Department of the United States* (Washington, D.C.: Francis B. Mohun, 1879), 585.
12. George M. McCrary to Chiefs of Bureaus of the War Department, June 16, 1877, box 3, entry 438, Letters Received, RG 109; Thomas J. Saunders to Secretary of War, Dec. 8, 1877, book 1, entry 707, Letters Sent, RG 94.

13. Robert N. Scott, *The Soldier's Book: A Pocket Diary for Accounts and Memoranda, for non-commissioned officers and privates of the U.S. Volunteer and Regular Army* (New York: D. Appleton & Co., 1863); D. Appleton & Co., *The Soldier's Book* advertisement, (2) 5786.F.103c (McAllister), The Library Company of Philadelphia, accessed June 29, 2021, https://digital.librarycompany.org/islandora/object/Islandora%3A7086.
14. Robert N. Scott to Adjutant General, April 10, 1866. Information about Scott's service is in his personal file, 330 ACP 1873, RG 94.
15. Robert N. Scott, *An Analytical Digest of the Military Laws of the United States: A Compilation of the Constitutional and Statutory Provisions Concerning The Military Establishment, in all its Branches and Relations, accompanied by Judicial and Executive Decisions Explanatory of the Text* (Philadelphia: J.B. Lippincott & Co., 1873). See also Robert N. Scott, Fort Ontario, N.Y., November 3d, 1876 (New York: publisher unknown, 1876).
16. Robert N. Scott to Secretary of War, Sept. 30, 1878, book 1, entry 707, Letters Sent, RG 94. Senator Henry Wilson, the historian and Republican leader who pushed work on the *OR* forward in the 1860s, also suggested a similar organization. *Congressional Globe*, 39 Cong., 1 sess., May 24, 1866, p. 2804.
17. Robert N. Scott to Secretary of War, Dec. 21, 1878, book 1, entry 707, Letters Sent, RG 94; Robert N. Scott to Secretary of War, Sept. 30, 1880, book 2, entry 707, Letters Sent, RG 94. Serialization was a defining feature of nineteenth-century print culture, and perhaps an obvious choice for Scott. See Linda K. Hughes and Michael Lund, *The Victorian Serial* (Charlottesville: University of Virginia Press, 1991).
18. *Statutes at Large*, 43 Cong., 1 sess., June 23, 1874, vol. 18, pt. 3, p. 222; Robert N. Scott to Secretary of War, Jan. 26, 1878, book 1, entry 707, Letters Sent, RG 94.
19. Robert N. Scott, Memorandum, undated, book 3, entry 708, Letters Sent, RG 94; Robert N. Scott to D.C. Buell, March 5, 1880, book 2, entry 707, Letters Sent, RG 94; Robert N. Scott to Secretary of War, Sept. 1, 1879, book 2, entry 707, Letters Sent, RG 94; Robert N. Scott, endorsement on Wm. E. Chandler to Robert Lincoln, Nov. 25, 1882, box 5, entry 710, Letters Received, RG 94; Robert N. Scott to Secretary of War, Jan. 26, 1878, book 1, entry 707, Letters Sent, RG 94.
20. John Fabian Witt, "Making the Fifth: The Constitutionalization of American Self-Incrimination Doctrine, 1791–1903," *Texas Law Review* 77, no. 4 (1999): 851, 860–866, http://hdl.handle.net/20.500.13051/3434. See also John H. Langbein, "Historical Foundations of the Law of Evidence: A View from the Ryder Sources," *Columbia Law Review* 96, no. 5 (1996): 1199–1200, doi.org/10.2307/1123403; Eileen Ka-May Cheng, *The Plain and Noble Garb of Truth: Nationalism and Impartiality in Historical Writing, 1784–1860* (Athens: University of Georgia Press, 2008), 9. Oz Frankel has also argued for the affinity between nineteenth-century

congressional procedures and common law methods. Oz Frankel, *States of Inquiry: Social Investigations and Print Culture in Nineteenth-Century Britain and the United States* (Baltimore: Johns Hopkins University Press, 2006), 13.

21. H.M. Lazelle to Richard B. Irwin, June 4, 1888, book 6, entry 708, Letters Sent, RG 94; Wyllys Lyman to Geo. W. Harrison, March 15, 1887, book 5, entry 708, Letters Sent, RG 94.
22. Robert N. Scott to Secretary of War, Sept. 1, 1879, book 2, entry 707, Letters Sent, RG 94.
23. One letter, on p. 129, LSAG, has been stamped twice, showcasing the difference between the two stamps.
24. Elihu Root, "Preface," *OR*, General Index, v.
25. This analogy is from Clayton R. Newell and Charles R. Shrader, *Of Duty Well and Faithfully Done: A History of the Regular Army in the Civil War* (Lincoln: University of Nebraska Press, 2011), 85.
26. Mark K. Christ, " 'They Will Be Armed': Lorenzo Thomas Recruits Black Troops in Helena, April 6, 1863," *The Arkansas Historical Quarterly* 72, no. 4 (2013): 366–383, https://www.jstor.org/stable/24477388. On Townsend, see Chapter 3.
27. L. Thomas to Genl. Buell, Feb. 6, 1862, p. 21, LSAG; L. Thomas to C.P. Buckingham, Feb. 14, 1862, p. 32, LSAG; L. Thomas to D. Hunter, April 12, 1862, p. 133, LSAG; L. Thomas to B.F. Butler, Feb. 20, 1862, p. 44, LSAG; L. Thomas to J.W. Clayton, April 17, 1862, p. 141, LSAG; L. Thomas to Geo. Wright, May 21, 1862, p. 193, LSAG. Michael P. Musick, a NARA archivist, offers useful reflections on the selection process for the *OR* in "Honorable Reports: Battles, Campaigns, and Skirmishes," *Prologue* 27, no.3 (Fall 1995), 259–277.
28. L. Thomas to A.E. Burnside, March 10, 1862, p. 62, LSAG; L. Thomas to Gideon Welles, March 13, 1862, p. 69, LSAG; also in *OR*, ser. I, vol. V, 751.
29. Bryce Benedict, *Jayhawkers: The Civil War Brigade of James Henry Lane* (Norman: University of Oklahoma Press, 2009); Christopher Phillips, "Lane, James Henry," Civil War on the Western Border: The Missouri-Kansas Conflict, 1854–1865, Kansas City Public Library, accessed Oct. 10, 2021, https://civilwaronthewesternborder.org/encyclopedia/lane-james-henry.
30. Adjutant General to D. Hunter, Jan. 24, 1862, p. 3, LSAG. The letter appears in *OR*, ser. I, vol VIII, 525.
31. A couple of these unpublished exchanges relate to major operations in March 1862, and may have been left out since they had already been published elsewhere: a long, congratulatory letter to General Ambrose Burnside following his successful occupation of the North Carolina shore, and Abraham Lincoln's War Order No. 3, announcing crucial changes in the army's high command. L. Thomas to A.E. Burnside,

March 22, 1862, p. 90, LSAG; L. Thomas, President's War Order no. 3, March 31, 1862, p. 105–106, LSAG.

32. L. Thomas to James W. Denver, April 11, 1862, p. 139–140, LSAG. Important work showcasing the centrality of the West in the Civil War includes Ari Kelman, *A Misplaced Massacre: Struggling Over the Memory of Sand Creek* (Cambridge, Mass.: Harvard University Press, 2013); Megan Kate Nelson, *The Three Cornered War: The Union, The Confederacy, and Native Peoples in the Fight for the West* (New York: Scribner, 2020); Adam Arensen and Andrew R. Graybill, eds., *Civil War Wests: Testing the Limits of the United States* (Oakland: University of California Press, 2015); Steven Hahn, "Slave Emancipation, Indian Peoples, and the Projects of a New American Nation-State," *The Journal of the Civil War Era* 3, no. 3 (Sept. 2013), 307–330, doi.org/10.1353/cwe.2013.0053.

33. Drew Gilpin Faust, *This Republic of Suffering: Death and the American Civil War* (New York: Vintage, 2008). Death looms large in contemporary Civil War scholarship. See also Mark S. Schantz, *Awaiting the Heavenly Country: The Civil War and America's Culture of Death* (Ithaca, N.Y: Cornell University Press, 2008); J. David Hacker, "A Census-Based Count of Civil War Dead," *Civil War History* 57, no. 4 (Dec. 2011): 307–348, doi.org/10.1353/cwh.2011.0061; Nicholas Marshal, "The Great Exaggeration: Death and the Civil War," *The Journal of the Civil War Era* 4, no. 1 (March 2014), 3–27, doi.org/10.1353/cwe.2014.0010.

34. L. Thomas to Daniel Agnew, March 24, 1862, p. 89, LSAG; L. Thomas to John B. Alley, April 18, 1862, p. 144, LSAG; L. Thomas to William Hargrave, April 26, 1862, p. 155–156, LSAG.

35. L. Thomas to Charles E. Sherman, Feb. 25, 1862, p. 51, LSAG; Petition of Charles E. Sherman, 28 June 1862, Civil War Washington, accessed Oct. 13, 2021, https://civilwardc.org/texts/petitions/cww.00795.html.

36. L. Thomas to Colonel Geary, March 14, 1862, p. 75, LSAG; L. Thomas to N.P. Banks, April 22, 1862, p. 147–148, LSAG. It bears mentioning that I searched for the records from the letter book online by typing in samples from each missive. I did not read through entire volumes looking for them. This leaves room for the possibility that the digitization process missed certain words and thus that a record I did not find online exists in the hard copies. Even if so, I have searched for enough individual documents from the letter book and have failed to find them to support my overall argument about the *OR*'s editorial policy.

37. Historians have struggled to explain and work around the archival silence about rape in the Civil War. See, e.g., Crystal N. Feimster, " 'What If I Am a Woman': Black Women's Campaigns for Sexual Justice and Citizenship," in *The World the Civil War Made*, ed. Gregory P. Downs and Kate Masur (Chapel Hill: University of North Carolina Press, 2015), 249–268; Crystal N. Feimster, "How Are the Daughters of Eve to Be Punished? Rape during the American Civil War," in *Writing Women's History: A*

Tribute to Ann Firror Scott, ed. Elizabeth Ann Payne (Jackson: University Press of Mississippi, 2011), 64–80.

38. Irvine, GI1977, 4; Irvine, GI1966, 36; Contract between Robert N. Scott and The Bell Telephone, May 25, 1880, box 3, entry 710, Letters Received, RG 94; H.M. Lazelle to Secretary of War, July 13, 1887, book 5, entry 708, Letters Sent, RG 94.
39. Annie Heloise Abel, *The American Indian as Participant in the Civil War* (Cleveland: Arthur M. Clark Company, 1919), 361. Marilyn Elizabeth Perry, "Abel-Henderson, Annie Heloise (1873–1947), historian and author," American National Biography, Feb. 1, 2000, https://www.anb.org/view/10.1093/anb/9780198606697.001.0001/anb-9780198606697-e-1400002.
40. Geo. B. Davis to J. Scott Payne, Oct. 5, 1892, book 13, entry 708, Letters Sent, RG 94.
41. It bears mentioning that some reports do begin by stating that things are quiet. For example, on May 3, 1862, Brigadier General H.G. Wright of the U.S. army, writing from his headquarters on Edisto Island, South Carolina, began his report saying that "nothing of interest has occurred within the limits of my command since the date of my last communication." But he then went on to describe "a very dashing and successful reconnaissance of the Dawho River in the gunboat Hale" as well as convey important information about the enemy's positions. *OR*, ser. I, vol. XIV, 339–340.
42. See Chapter 4.
43. Lorien Foote, "Prisoners of War," in *The Cambridge History of the American Civil War*, ed. Aaron Sheehan-Dean (Cambridge: Cambridge University Press, 2019), vol. 2, 293–316. See also William B. Hesseltine, *Civil War Prisons: A Study in War Psychology* (Columbus: Ohio State University Press, 1930); Charles W. Sanders, Jr., *While in the Hands of the Enemy: Military Prisons of the Civil War* (Baton Rouge: Louisiana State University Press, 2005).
44. L. Thomas to J. Dimick, May 16, 1862, p. 187, LSAG; L. Thomas to John E. Wool, May 16, 1862, p. 188, LSAG. Both dispatches are printed in *OR*, ser. II, vol. III, 539.
45. Geo. W. Davis to Secretary of War, June 14, 1897, box 6, entry 713, General Correspondence, RG 94.
46. F.C. Ainsworth to Secretary of War, Aug. 12, 1898, box 7, entry 713, General Correspondence, RG 94 and Memorandum 1614/6, enclosed.
47. "Leslie J. Perry Dead," *La Cygne Weekly Record*, May 5, 1910, p. 4; "Death Calls Leslie J. Perry," *The Washington Herald*, April 26, 1910, p. 7, accessed through newspapers.com.
48. Some glimpses into Perry's pre–War Department days are in "Recent History," *The Paola Times*, April 20, 1882, p. 2; "To the Members of the Legislature of Kansas," *The Miami Republican*, Jan. 12, 1877, p. 5. On Perry's appointment, see "Leslie J. Perry Appointed," *The Topeka State Journal*, July 16, 1889, p. 1, accessed through newspapers.com.

49. Geo. W. Davis to Secretary of War, June 14, 1897, box 6, entry 713, General Correspondence, RG 94.
50. William P. Dole to C.B. Smith, June 5, 1862, in *OR*, ser. II, vol. IV, 8. The entire set of documents is on 2–13.
51. Geo. B. Davis to Secretary of War, July 31, 1891, book 10, entry 708, Letters Sent, RG 94.
52. Leslie J. Perry to E.H. Funston, April 4, 1892, book 12, entry 708, Letters Sent, RG 94; Geo. W. Davis to Secretary of War, June 14, 1897, box 6, entry 713, General Correspondence, RG 94.
53. On Davis's career path, see a widely reprinted newspaper report from 1902, "Will Relieve Chaffee," *The Aberdeen Democrat,* Nov. 21, 1902, p. 7, accessed through newspapers.com.
54. Geo. W. Davis to Secretary of War, June 14, 1897, box 6, entry 713, General Correspondence, RG 94.
55. Leslie J. Perry to F.C. Ainsworth, July 22, 1898, box 1, entry 720, Papers Relating to Distribution of Members of the 56th and 57th Congress, 1903–1904, RG 94.
56. Mabel Evelyn Deutrich, *Struggle for Supremacy: The Career of General Fred C. Ainsworth* (Washington, D.C.: Public Affairs Press, 1962); Siert F. Riempa, "A Soldier-Archivist and His Records: Major General Fred C. Ainsworth," *The American Archivist* 4, no. 3 (1941): 178–187, doi.org/10.17723/aarc.4.3.ou42qj751847175.
57. While Ainsworth's innovations emerged from an attempt to resolve the monumental challenges facing an ossified and overburdened military bureaucracy, they were very much aligned with a broader transformation in information management taking place in other realms. On this point, see Markus Krajewski, *Paper Machines: About Cards & Catalogs, 1548–1929,* trans. Peter Krapp (Cambridge, Mass.: MIT Press, 2011). See also Alex Wright, *Cataloging the World: Paul Otlet and the Birth of the Information Age* (New York: Oxford University Press, 2014); JoAnne Yates, *Control through Communication: The Rise of System in American Management* (Baltimore: Johns Hopkins University Press, 1989), chapters 2–3. For an important meditation on the meaning of filing, see Bruno Latour, *The Making of Law: An Ethnography of the Conseil d'Etat,* trans. Marina Brilman and Alain Pottage (Cambridge, U.K.: Polity, 2009).
58. Quote in Deutrich, *Struggle for Supremacy,* 143n26; Leslie J. Perry to Geo. C. Gorham, Feb. 14, 1894, book 17, entry 708, Letters Sent, RG 94.
59. F.C. Ainsworth to Secretary of War, Aug. 12, 1898, box 7, entry 713, General Correspondence, RG 94.
60. G.D. Meiklejohn, Orders, Sept. 21, 1898, box 7, entry 713, General Correspondence, RG 94.
61. G.D. Meiklejohn, Orders, Dec. 1, 1898, Record Card 1614/12, box 7, entry 713, General Correspondence, RG 94; F.C. Ainsworth to Secretary

of War, Aug. 12, 1898, box 7, entry 713, General Correspondence, RG 94; "Record of the Rebellion," *New York Times*, May 7, 1899, p. 4.

62. Carol Reardon, *Soldiers and Scholars: The U.S. Army and the Uses of Military History, 1865–1920* (Lawrence: University Press of Kansas, 1990), 147–151.
63. Irvine, GI1966, 3.
64. H.M. Lazelle to Secretary of War, June 4, 1888, book 6, entry 708, Letters Sent, RG 94; George B. Davis, response to Senate Resolution, May 28, 1890, box 8, entry 708, Letters Sent, RG 94.
65. E.D. Townsend to Marcus J. Wright, Dec. 12, 1878, folder 10B, series 3, WSHC.
66. Elihu Root, "Preface," *OR*, General Index, xii. The point about veterans lobbying Congress is from Noah Andre Trudeau, "To 'Mold the Judgement of History,' " in *The Ongoing Civil War: New Versions of Old Stories*, ed. Herman Hattaway and Ethan S. Rafuse (Columbia: University of Missouri Press, 2004), 145.
67. Annual Reports of the War Department for the Fiscal Year Ending June 30, 1901: Reports of Bureau Chiefs (Washington, D.C.: Government Printing Office, 1901), vol. 1, pt. 2, 1106. On the expanding agency of Congress in the late nineteenth century and its limits, see Williamjames Hull Hoffer, *To Enlarge the Machinery of Government: Congressional Debates and the Growth of the American State, 1858–1891* (Baltimore: Johns Hopkins University Press, 2007), x–xii; Jerry L. Mashaw, *Creating the Administrative Constitution: The Lost One Hundred Years of American Administrative Law* (New Haven, Conn.: Yale University Press, 2012), 240–244. William J. Novak, "The Myth of the Weak American State," *American Historical Review* 113 (June 2008), 752–772, doi.org/10.1086/ahr.113.3.752; Susan J. Pearson, "A New Birth of Regulation: The State of the State after the Civil War," *Journal of the Civil War Era* 5, no. 3 (2015), doi.org/10.1353/cwe.2015.0057. On the involvement of Congress in publication projects, see Frankel, *States of Inquiry*. On the complicated ways in which the Federal state wielded power in the nineteenth century, see Brian Balogh, *A Government Out of Sight: The Mystery of National Authority in Nineteenth-Century America* (Cambridge: Cambridge University Press, 2009). A recent intervention is Cameron Blevins, *Paper Trails: The US Post and the Making of the American West* (Oxford: Oxford University Press, 2021).
68. James Carson, *Against the Grain: Colonel Henry M. Lazelle and the U.S. Army* (Denton: University of North Texas Press, 2016), 264–283. Quote on p. 282. Dallas Irvine described Lazelle's troubles as resulting from a revenge campaign orchestrated by one of his clerks, who had been removed from the project after having been accused of drunkenness and dereliction of duty. Irvine, GI1966, 4, 51n8.
69. H.M. Lazelle to Secretary of War, Dec. 4, 1888, book 7, entry 708, Letters Sent, RG 94.

70. For use of the term "great work," see, e.g., "Records of the Rebellion," *The National Tribune* (Washington, D.C.), May 23, 1901, p. 5, accessed through newspapers.com. Memorandum for General Ainsworth, Aug. 29, 1901, box 7, entry 713, General Correspondence, RG 94; F.C. Ainsworth to Elihu Root, Aug. 29, 1901, box 7, entry 713, General Correspondence, RG 94.
71. Geo. W. Davis, Memorandum, May 12, 1897, box 6, entry 713, General Correspondence, RG 94; The precise number of pages is from F.C. Ainsworth, Memorandum, Jan. 28, 1901, box 7, entry 713, General Correspondence, RG 94.
72. Irvine, GI1977, 4.
73. As Julie Des Jardins has argued, "the historian's reverence for the 'official' had a devastating effect on the reconstruction of women's 'unofficial' past experience." This applies to other archivally underrepresented populations. Julie Des Jardins, *Women and the Historical Enterprise in America: Gender, Race, and the Politics of Memory, 1880–1945* (Chapel Hill: University of North Carolina Press, 2003), 22.
74. For a similar conclusion, see Alan C. Aimone and Barbara A. Aimone, *A User's Guide to the Official Records of the American Civil War* (Shippensburg, Pa.: White Mane Publishing, 1993), 39. For an important critique of scholars studying the war, see Drew Gilpin Faust, " 'We Should Grow Too Fond of It': Why We Love the Civil War," *Civil War History* 50, no. 4 (Dec. 2004), 368–383, doi.org/10.1353/cwh.2004.0068.
75. Douglas Southall Freeman, *The South to Posterity: An Introduction to the Writing of Confederate History* (New York: Scribner, 1939), 90–95. Freeman's enthusiasm about the *OR*, however, may very well have been enhanced by his desire to focus attention on the rebellion's martial aspects, rather than on its political grounding in the defense of slavery. Gary W. Gallagher argues that Lost Cause writers "helped create an interpretive framework within which military elements of the Confederate war would receive far more attention than any nonmilitary dimension. This proved immensely useful in presenting the white South's wartime experience in the best possible light. Far more attractive personally than Jefferson Davis, Lee could be examined within a martial setting largely free of the blighting influence of slavery." Considering Freeman's devotion to the Lost Cause, this characterization might very well apply to him as much as it applied to nineteenth-century writers. See "Shaping Public Memory of the Civil War: Robert E. Lee, Jubal A. Early, and Douglas Southall Freeman," in *The Memory of the Civil War in American Culture*, ed. Alice Fahs and Joan Waugh (Chapel Hill: University of North Carolina Press, 2004), 45.
76. Irvine, GI1977, 5; Irvine, GI1966, 48; Irvine, "Rootstock of Error," *Prologue: The Journal of the National Archives* 2, no. 1 (Spring 1970), 10. It bears mentioning that there is a rich and growing literature on irregular

warfare in the Civil War, which is becoming increasingly prominent in the historiographical discourse. See, e.g., Michael Fellman, *Inside War: The Guerrilla Conflict in Missouri During the American Civil War* (New York: Oxford University Press, 1989); Daniel E. Sutherland, *A Savage Conflict: The Decisive Role of Guerillas in the American Civil War* (Chapel Hill: University of North Carolina Press, 1999); Matthew Christopher Hulbert, *The Ghosts of Guerilla Memory: How Civil War Bushwhackers Became Gunslingers in the American West* (Athens: University of Georgia Press, 2016).

77. See, e.g., Thomas J. Brown, *Civil War Monuments and the Militarization of America* (Chapel Hill: University of North Carolina Press, 2019). There has been an explosion of writing in recent years about contemporary meanings of Civil War memory, much of it directed toward a general public. See, e.g., Catherine Clinton, ed., *Confederate Statues and Memorialization* (Athens: University of Georgia Press, 2019); Karen L. Cox, *No Common Ground: Confederate Monuments and the Ongoing Fight for Racial Justice* (Chapel Hill: University of North Carolina Press, 2021).

Chapter Six. Missing Links

1. See, e.g., J.D. Cameron to E.W. Hinks, Aug. 18, 1876, entry 715, Letters Received Relating to Missing Military Reports, RG 94.
2. H.M. Lazelle to H.A. Axline, Feb. 6, 1888, book 6, entry 708, Letters Sent, RG 94; Geo. B. Davis to W.F. Smith, June 18, 1891, book 10, entry 708, Letters Sent, RG 94; Geo. B. Davis to George W. Coffin, March 21, 1892, book 12, entry 708, Letters Sent, RG 94; Robert N. Scott to James McDonald, May 13, 1878, book 1, entry 707, Letter Sent, RG 94.
3. M.C.M. to R.N. Scott, July 1, 1880, box 4, entry 710, Letters Received, RG 94; R. Macfeely to R.N. Scott, March 11, 1878, box 1, entry 710, Letters Received, RG 94.
4. R.H. Orton to H.M. Lazelle, March 22, 1888, box 9, entry 710, Letters Received, RG 94. For examples of states that had no information to offer see R.R. Henney to H.M. Lazelle, March 13, 1888, box 9, entry 710, Letters Received, RG 94; W.L. Alexander to Geo. B. Davis, Aug. 29, 1889, box 9b, entry 710, Letters Received, RG 94.
5. Robert N. Scott to Secretary of War, Sept. 30, 1878, book 1, entry 707, Letters Sent, RG 94. The issue of collecting Confederate records will be dealt with in great detail in Chapter 7.
6. H.M. Lazelle to W.T. Sherman, Dec. 2, 1887, book 6, entry 708, Letters Sent, RG 94; Robert N. Scott to General Sherman, Nov. 13, 1886, box 9, entry 710, Letters Received, RG 94; Geo. B. Davis to P.T. Sherman, Oct. 2, 1891, Sept. 26, 1891, book 11, entry 708, Letters Sent, RG 94.
7. Robert N. Scott to Joseph Hooker, May 11, May 29, 1878, book 1, entry 708, Letters Sent, RG 94; Joseph Hooker to Robert N. Scott, May 28, 1878, box 2, entry 710, Letters Received, RG 94.

8. W.C. Prime to Lieut. Col. Lazelle, Jan. 10, 1888, box 9, entry 710, Letters Received, RG 94; H.M. Lazelle to William C. Prime, Jan. 17, 1888, box 6, entry 708, Letters Sent, RG 94; Geo. B. Davis to H.G. Wright, Sept. 13, 1892, book 13, entry 708, Letters Sent, RG 94.
9. Geo. B. Davis to George Meade, May 21, 1891, book 10, entry 708, Letters Sent, RG 94.
10. Geo. B. Davis to George Meade, May 8, 1891, book 10, entry 708, Letters Sent, RG 94; H.M. Lazelle to George Meade, May 14, 1888, book 6, entry 708, Letters Sent, RG 94; Robert N. Scott to George Meade, March 14, 1879, book 1, entry 708, Letters Sent, RG 94. Quotation appears in H.M. Lazelle to George Meade, May 8, 1888, book 6, entry 708, Letters Sent, RG 94.
11. Geo. B. Davis to Alexander Moore, April 19, 1890, book 8, entry 708, Letters Sent, RG 94.
12. Geo. B. Davis to O.O. Howard, Dec. 3, 1891, book 11, entry 708, Letters Sent, RG 94; see also Geo. B. Davis to D.E. Sickles, April 19, 1890, book 11, entry 708, Letters Sent, RG 94.
13. Geo. B. Davis to Mrs. Delos B. Sacket, June 26, 1897, box 6, entry 713, General Correspondence, RG 94.
14. Geo. B. Davis to Mrs. Godfrey Weitzel, Nov. 16, 1891, book 11, entry 708, Letters Sent, RG 94; Geo. B. Davis to Mrs. Godfrey Weitzel Dec. 21, 1891, book 11, entry 708, Letters Sent, RG 94; Geo. B. Davis to Samuel F. Hunt, Dec. 19, 1891, book 11, entry 708, Letters Sent, RG 94; Geo. B. Davis to S.F. Hunt, Jan. 5, 1892, book 11, entry 708, Letters Sent, RG 94.
15. Geo. B. Davis to Ella M. Grover, Sept. 22, 1892, book 13, entry 708, Letters Sent, RG 94.
16. Elizabeth B. Custer to Major Davis, Nov. 26, 1890, box 12, entry 710, Letters Received, RG 94; George B. Davis to Mrs. George A. Custer, Sept. 13, 1892, book 13, entry 708, Letters Sent, RG 94. For a recent assessment of Libbie Custer as an important author in her own right, see Cecily N. Zander, "One Widow's Wars: The Civil War, Reconstruction, and the West in Elizabeth Bacon Custer's Memoirs," in *Civil War Witnesses and Their Books: New Perspectives on Iconic Works*, ed. Gary W. Gallagher and Stephen Cushman (Baton Rouge: Louisiana State University Press, 2021), 229–260.
17. On Tasker's estimate, see A.P. Tasker to Cockrell Garfield and Williams, March 20, 1878, box 2, entry 438, Letters Received, RG 109. On the purchase see E.D.T. [Edward D. Townsend] to Wm. Preston Johnston, June 21, 1878, book 3, entry 435, Letters Sent, RG 109; On Johnston offering Elise Bragg to serve as her agent, see W.T. Walthall to Marcus J. Wright, Oct. 1, 1880, folder 10E, ser. 5, WSHC. On Johnston's threat see Robert N. Scott to Sec. of War, March 19, 1880, book 2, entry 707, Letters Sent, RG 94. On the reluctance to purchase see Alex Ramsey to

President of the United States Senate, Dec. 8, 1880, box 4, entry 710, Letters Received, RG 94. For more on Johnston's dealings with the Federal government, see Chapter 4.

18. Stapled Clipping, J.T. King to Geo. B. Davis, July 16, 1889, box 9B, entry 708, Letters Sent, RG 94. For examples of Davis's public call, see "Missing War Records," *The Sentinel*, Milwaukee, July 15, 1889; "War Records Wanted," *Wisconsin State Journal*, Madison, July 15, 1889; "Some Records Wanted," *The Pittsburg Dispatch*, Pittsburg, July 15, 1889; "Records of Chickamauga," *The Indiana State Sentinel*, Indianapolis, July 17, 1889. Accessed through newspapers.com.
19. Robert Burns to Geo. B. Davis, July 19, 1889, box 9B, entry 710, Letters Received, RG 94; Albert Eads to Geo. B. Davis, July 15, 1889, box 9B, entry 710, Letters Received, RG 94; A. McD. McCook to G.B. Davis, Sept.15, 1889, box 10, entry 710, Letters Received, RG 94.
20. Geo. B. Davis to E.C. Dawes, Nov. 21, 1891, book 11, entry 708, Letters Sent, RG 94.
21. For examples, see Robert N. Scott to D.C. Buell, Feb. 18, 1880, book 2, entry 707, Letters Sent, RG 94; Geo. B. Davis to J.P. Cotton, Feb. 7, 1891, book 10, entry 708, Letters Sent, RG 94.
22. Geo. B. Davis to Eugene Griffin, Dec. 23, 1891, book 11, entry 708, Letters Sent, RG 94; Geo. B. Davis to P.T. Sherman, Sept. 26, 1891, book 11, entry 708, Letters Sent, RG 94.
23. Robert N. Scott to D.C. Buell, Feb. 18, 1880, book 2, entry 707, Letters Sent, RG 94; Geo. B. Davis to A. McD. McCook, Dec. 19, 1889, book 8, entry 708, Letters Sent, RG 94.
24. Geo. B. Davis to Allen R. Adams, March 31, 1894, book 17, entry 708, Letters Sent, RG 94; see, e.g., Geo. B. Davis to J.P. Cotton, May 16, 1894, box 18, entry 708, Letters Sent, RG 94; Geo. B. Davis to J.G. Nicolay, June 5, 1891, book 10, entry 708, Letters Sent, RG 94; Geo. B. Davis to J.D. Cox, Dec. 2, 1891, book 11, entry 708, Letters Sent, RG 94.
25. Robert N. Scott to D.N. Couch, Nov. 8, 1885, box 7, entry 710, Letters Received, RG 94; Geo. B. Davis to N.A. Miles, Dec. 28, 1889, book 8, entry 708, Letters Sent, RG 94; Robert N. Scott to Thos. T. Eckert, April 20, 1878, box 2, entry 710, Letters Received, RG 94.
26. See, e.g., Worth G. Ross to H.M. Lazelle, May 19, 1888, box 9, entry 710, Letters Received, RG 94; H.M. Lazelle to Alfred H. Campbell, Jan. 6, 1888, book 6, entry 708, Letters Sent, RG 94.
27. E.D. Townsend to Unknown, Sept. 19, 1879, box 7, entry 710, Letters Received, RG 94.
28. The title page of the work says as much. Thomas B. Van Horne, *History of the Army of the Cumberland, Its Organization, Campaigns and Battles, Written at the Request of Major-General George H. Thomas, Chiefly from His Private Military Journal and Official and Other Documents Furnished by Him* (Cincinnati, Ohio: Robert Clarke & Co., 1875).

29. Robert N. Scott to Thos. B. Van Horne, Feb. 15, 1879, book 1, entry 708, Letters Sent, RG 94.
30. Geo. B. Davis to E.C. Dawes, Jan. 5, 1892, book 11, entry 708, Letters Sent, RG 94; H.B. McClellan to Robt. N. Scott, Dec. 26, 1884, box 5, entry 710, Letters Received, RG 94; Geo. B. Davis to Henry Stone, April 1, 1891, book 10, entry 708, Letters Sent, RG 94; Geo. B. Davis to Henry Stone, Sept. 26, 1892, book 13, entry 708, Letters Sent, RG 94.
31. Robert N. Scott, endorsement, Feb. 9, 1886, box 7, entry 710, Letters Received, RG 94.
32. Richd. B. Irwin to Geo. B. Davis, May 9, 1890, box 10, entry 710, Letters Received, RG 94; Richd. B. Irwin to H.M. Lazelle, June 1, 1888, box 9, entry 710, Letters Received, RG 94.
33. Wm. F. Smith to H.M. Lazelle, Feb. 29, 1888, box 9, entry 710, Letters Received, RG 94; R. Ransom to H.M. Lazelle, April 12, 1888, box 9, entry 710, Letters Received, RG 94; H.M. Lazelle to D.E. Sickles, Sept. 7, 1887, book 5, entry 708, Letters Sent, RG 94. W. Lyman to James Longstreet, May 31, 1887, book 5, entry 708, Letters Sent, RG 94.
34. J.H. Mauzy to G.S. Davis [George B. Davis], July 27, 1889, box 9B, entry 710, Letters Received, RG 94; J.H. Mauzy to George B. Davis, Aug. 24, 1889, box 9B, entry 710, Letters Received, RG 94; Geo. E. Dolton to Geo. B. Davis, Sept. 12, 1889, box 9B, entry 710, Letters Received, RG 94; G.A. Wood to Geo. B. Davis, Oct. 24, 1889, box 10, entry 710, Letters Received, RG 94.
35. G. Weitzel to Adjutant Genl., July 13, 1877, box 1, entry 710, Letters Received, RG 94.
36. A.J. Miller to Geo. B. Davis, Sept. 4, 1889, box 9B, entry 710, Letters Received, RG 94; Geo. B. Davis to H. Seymour Hall, Oct. 3, 1892, book 13, entry 708, Letters Sent, RG 94; H.M. Lazelle to Francis E. Pinto, July 6, 1887, book 5, entry 708, Letters Sent, RG 94.
37. Lewis Merril to Robert N. Scott, Oct. 19, 1885, box 7, entry 710, Letters Received, RG 94; E.D. Townsend to Col. Scott, Sept. 19, 1879, box 7, entry 710, Letters Received, RG 94.
38. Bradley T. Johnson to M.J. Wright, Nov. 12, 1884, box 5, entry 710, Letters Received, RG 94; On Johnson, see "Bradley T. Johnson," American Battlefield Trust, accessed Sept. 8, 2022, https://www.battlefields.org/learn/biographies/bradley-t-johnson.
39. H.A. Hambright to Major, Aug. 6, 1889, box 9B, entry 710, Letters Received, RG 94; Geo. B. Davis to John P. Nicholson, Sept. 16, 1891, book 11, entry 708, Letters Sent, RG 94; see also Geo. B. Davis to W.U. Hensel, June 27, 1891, book 10, entry 708, RG 94.
40. F.J. Porter to H.M. Lazelle, Jan. 29, 1888, box 9, entry 710, Letters Received, RG 94; Geo. B. Davis to F.J. Porter, March 16, 1891, book 10, entry 708, Letters Sent, RG 94. More examples for the warm relationship between the WRO and Porter are in Geo. B. Davis to F.J. Porter,

June 4, 1891, book 10, entry 708, Letters Sent, RG 94; Geo. B. Davis to F.J. Porter, April 20, 1891, book 10, entry 708, Letters Sent, RG 94.

41. F.J. Porter to Geo. B. Davis, Sept. 15, 1890, box 11, entry 710, Letters Received, RG 94; F.J. Porter to H.M. Lazelle, Jan. 29, 1888, box 9, entry 710, Letters Received, RG 94.
42. Geo. B. Davis to J.P. Cotton, May 26, 1891, book 10, entry 708, Letters Sent, RG 94.
43. Loraine Ferris, "Gouverneur Kemble Warren, the Man," *Nebraska History* 19 (1938): 353; Emily F. Warren to Geo. B. Davis, Feb. 1, 1891, box 13, entry 710, Letters Received, RG 94. On Warren see "Gouverneur Kemble Warren (1830–1882)," US Army Corps of Engineers, accessed Sept. 8, 2022, https://www.usace.army.mil/About/History/Army-Engineers-in-the-Civil-War/Engineer-Biographies/Gouverneur-Warren.
44. W. Lyman to A.F. Devereux, May 9, 1887, book 5, entry 708, Letters Sent, RG 94; Dominick Emminger to George B. Davis, Aug. 23, 1889, box 9B, entry 710, Letters Received, RG 94; Geo. B. Davis to H.A. Hambright, Aug. 30, 1889, book 7, entry 708, Letters Sent, RG 94; H.M. Lazelle to J.W. Pollock, March 1, 1888, book 6, entry 708, Letters Sent, RG 94.
45. Geo. H. Gordon to Sec. of War, Nov. 18, 1876, entry 715, Letters Received Relating to Missing Military Reports, RG 94.
46. "Shiloh's Scapegoats," *National Tribune*, Oct. 4, 1883, accessed through newspapers.com.
47. Robert N. Scott to Secretary of War, Nov. 16, 1883, book 3, entry 708, Letters Sent, RG 94; Robert T. Lincoln to Lewis Wallace, Nov. 21, 1883, reel 21, series 1, Papers of Lew and Susan Wallace, Lew and Susan Wallace Multi-institution Microfilm Project, Indiana Historical Society. Original reference to this source was found in William M. Ferraro, "A Struggle for Respect: Lew Wallace's Relationship with Ulysses S. Grant and William Tecumseh Sherman after Shiloh," *Indiana Magazine of History* 104, no. 2 (June 2008), 145, https://www.jstor.org/stable/27792885.
48. Eli J. Sherlock to George B. Davis, Aug. 15, 1893, box 2, entry 713, General Correspondence, RG 94; Julius White to Secretary of War, March 31, 1877, box 1, entry 710, Letters Received, RG 94.
49. Thomas Jordan to Marcus J. Wright, July 14, 1885, box 6, entry 710, Letters Received, RG 94; Wm. E. Chandler to Robert T. Lincoln, Nov. 23, 1882, box 5, entry 710, Letters Received, RG 94.
50. Robert N. Scott to Secy. of War, endorsement, Nov. 25, 1882, book 2, entry 707, Letters Sent, RG 94.
51. Wm. F. Smith to Col., Jan. 28, 1884, box 7, entry 710, Letters Received, RG 94; General Orders no. 84, Oct. 4, 1866, in *OR*, ser. III, vol. V, 1012; H.M. Lazelle to Secretary of War, Sept. 26, 1888, box 9A, entry 710, Letters Received, RG 94.

52. Robert N. Scott to Secretary of War, Nov. 16, 1883, book 3, entry 708, Letters Sent, RG 94; George W. Davis Memorandum, May 12, 1897, box 6, entry 713, General Correspondence, RG 94.
53. Robert N. Scott to Secretary of War, Nov. 16, 1883, book 3, entry 708, Letters Sent, RG 94.
54. Robert N. Scott, Memorandum, undated, book 3, entry 708, Letters Sent, RG 94.
55. H.M. Lazelle to Adjutant General, July 14, 1887, book 5, entry 708, Letters Sent, RG 94. For an example of postwar reckoning in the Wallace case, see Ulysses S. Grant, "Memoranda on the Civil War," *The Century* 30 (1885), 776.
56. Scott quoted in Elihu Root, "Preface," *OR*, General Index, xii.
57. Robert McAllister to W. Lyman, July 23, 1888, box 9, entry 710, Letters Received, RG 94; W. Lyman to Robert McAllister, July 31, 1888, book 6, entry 708, Letters Sent, RG 94.
58. H.M. Lazelle to Wheelock G. Veazey, April 17, 1888, book 6, entry 708, Letters Sent, RG 94; Robert N. Scott to G.V. Fox, Dec. 19, 1879, book 2, entry 707, Letters Sent, RG 94. Noah Andre Trudeau also questions this practice in "To 'Mold the Judgement of History,' " in *The Ongoing Civil War: New Versions of Old Stories*, ed. Herman Hattaway and Ethan S. Rafuse (Columbia: University of Missouri Press, 2004), 148.
59. E.D. Townsend to Robert N. Scott, Sept. 19, 1879, box 7, entry 710, Letters Received, RG 94.
60. Thomas Jordan to Marcus J. Wright, July 14, 1885, box 6, entry 710, Letters Received, RG 94; Thomas Jordan to Robert N. Scott, July 16, 1885, box 6, entry 710, Letters Received, RG 94; Thomas Jordan, corrected proofs, attached to Thomas Jordan to Marcus J. Wright, July 14, 1885, box 6, entry 710, Letters Received, RG 94; the published Jordan letter is in *OR*, ser. I, vol. XVII, pt. II, 640.
61. Geo. B. Davis to Hempstead Washburne, May 17, 1892, book 13, entry 708, Letters Sent, RG 94.
62. Geo. B. Davis to George Meade, May 21, 1891, book 10, entry 708, Letters Sent, RG 94; Geo. B. Davis to D.H. Reynolds, Jan. 8, 1892, book 11, entry 708, Letters Sent, RG 94. On journals, see also Geo. B. Davis to J.D. Cox, Feb. 27, 1892, book 12, entry 708, Letters Sent, RG 94.
63. Richard M. McMurry, "The Mackall Diary and its Antecedents," *Civil War History* 20.4 (Dec. 1974), 311–328, doi.org/10.1353/cwh.1974.0095. While I read this article after I had finished researching the collections at NARA and could no longer access the archive because of COVID-19, there is no trace of Mackall in the thousands of War Department documents in my possession. As far as I can tell, it was simply accepted for publication with other records.
64. Robert N. Scott to John C. Fremont, Aug. 30, 1880, book 2, entry 707, Letters Sent, RG 94; Robert N. Scott to Geo. B. McClellan, May 29, 1879,

book 1, entry 708, Letters Sent, RG 94; Robert N. Scott to W.T. Sherman, Sept. 30, 1881, book 2, entry 707, Letters Sent, RG 94; Geo. B. Davis to H.W. Slocum, Dec. 22, 1892, book 14, entry 708, Letters Sent, RG 94.

65. William T. Sherman, *Memoirs of General William T. Sherman, Written by Himself* (New York: D. Appleton, 1875), vol. 1, 1; J. Hooker to Robert N. Scott, July 1, 1878, box 2, entry 710, Letters Received, RG 94.
66. Geo. B. Davis to Major W.A. Hotchkiss, Oct. 22, 1889, book 7, entry 708, Letters Sent, RG 94; Geo. W. Davis to Secretary of War, June 14, 1897, box 6, entry 713, General Correspondence, RG 94.
67. Sherman, *Memoirs*, 1.
68. "Special Index for the Principal Armies, Army Corps, Military Divisions and Departments," *OR*, ser. IV, vol. IV, xliii; Robert N. Scott to Secretary of War, Jan. 18, 1885, book 4, entry 708, Letters Sent, RG 94; Robert N. Scott to J. Warren Keifer, Feb. 7, 1885, book 4, entry 708, Letters Sent, RG 94; Robert N. Scott to Wm. B. Allison, June 19, 1886, book 5, entry 708, Letters Sent, RG 94.
69. J.S. Moodey to F.C. Ainsworth, Aug. 21, 1898, box 7, entry 713, General Correspondence, RG 94.
70. Irvine, GI1977, iii, 1. Ainsworth's decision is also the reason there are two volumes missing from the series, numbered 112 and 113. The *OR* has sometimes been described as comprising 130 volumes.
71. John Tweedale to Charles E. Jones, Dec. 9, 1899, box 7, entry 713, General Correspondence, RG 94.
72. F.C. Ainsworth to the Public Printer, Aug. 29, 1901, box 7, entry 713, General Correspondence, RG 94. The most systematic critique of *OR* indexing is by Dallas Irvine, in both versions of the *Guide-Index*, e.g., in GI1966, 15.
73. On laws governing the distribution of the *OR*, see *Annual Reports of the War Department for Fiscal Year Ended June 30, 1901, Reports of Chiefs of Bureaus* (Washington, D.C.: Government Printing Office, 1901), vol. I, pt. 2, 1118–1123. On congressional distribution of publications more broadly, see Oz Frankel, *States of Inquiry: Social Investigations and Print Culture in Nineteenth-Century Britain and the United States* (Baltimore: Johns Hopkins University Press, 2006), 19.
74. Record and Pension Office, War Department, *List of Libraries, Organizations, and Educational Institutions in the Several States and Territories of the United States supplied with the Official Records of the Union and Confederate Armies* (Washington, 1903).
75. Geo. B. Davis to Lewis D. Apsley, May 16, 1894, box 18, entry 708, Letters Sent, RG 94. The total number of GAR posts in 1894, as reported by Davis, was 7,671. See Geo. B. Davis to Lewis D. Apsley, May 12, 1894, box 18, entry 708, Letters Sent, RG 94. For examples of senators sending sets to GAR posts, see Thor A. Pine to Henry M. Lazelle, Feb. 16, 1888, box 9, entry 710, Letters Received, RG 94.

76. Geo. B. Davis to C.C. Andrews, Jan. 4, 1892, book 11, entry 708, Letters Sent, RG 94; Isaac R. Lane to George B. Davis, (?) Nov. 1889, box 10, entry 710, Letters Received RG 94.
77. Geo. B. Davis to L.S. Mortimer, July 16, 1890, book 8, entry 708, Letters Sent, RG 94; Geo. B. Davis to T.H. Grisham, April 30, 1890, book 8, entry 708, Letters Sent, RG 94; Geo. B. Davis to J.H. Mitchell, Sept. 4, 1891, book 11, entry 708, Letters Sent, RG 94.
78. On the definition of "contributor," see Geo. B. Davis to C.E. Wesche, March 10, 1892, book 12, entry 708, Letters Sent, RG 94.
79. Charles Rice to Alexander Ramsey, Nov. 26, 1880, box 4, entry 710, Letters Received, RG 94; D.M. Vance to R.N. Scott, Nov. 24, 1885, box 7, entry 710, Letters Received, RG 94; Charles W. Davis to William M. Springer, May 19, 1890, box 11, entry 710, Letters Received, RG 94; A.J. DeLong to George E. Adams, Feb. 9, 1890, box 10, entry 710, Letters Received, RG 94.
80. Edward E. Henry to J.H. Ramsey, Nov. 20, 1880, box 4, entry 710, Letters Received, RG 94; Geo. B. Davis to Secretary of War, Feb. 5, 1890, book 8, entry 708, Letters Sent, RG 94.
81. Francis Winthrop Palfrey, *The Antietam and Fredericksburg* (New York: Scribner's, 1882), vii; Geo. B. Davis to W.F. Smith, Sept. 23, 1891, book 11, entry 708, Letters Sent, RG 94. Thomas L. Livermore, *Numbers and Losses in the Civil War in America 1861–1865* (Boston and New York: Houghton, Mifflin and Co., 1901), iii–iv.
82. William Roscoe Livermore, *The Story of the Civil War: A Concise Account of the War in the United States of America between 1861 and 1865, in Continuation of the Story by John Codman Ropes* (New York: Putnam's, 1913), v. Livermore also noted in the same place that the *OR* "is extensively consulted at home and abroad, and of late years especially in England, where its value is now fairly understood." Carol Reardon offers a different reading of this source; see her *Soldiers and Scholars: The U.S. Army and the Uses of Military History, 1865–1920* (Lawrence: University Press of Kansas, 1990), 160.
83. Denis Winter, *Haig's Command: A Reassessment* (Barnsley, U.K.: Pen & Sword Military Classics, 2004, reprint edition), 240–257. Quote on p. 254–255.

Chapter Seven. The Archive and Sectional Reconciliation

1. *Congressional Record*, 43 Cong., 1 sess., June 12, 1874, p. 4931.
2. John Coburn, *An Address Delivered by General John Coburn, on Memorial Day, May 30, 1905* (Indianapolis: Jacobs Stationery and Printing Company, 1905), 9. On Coburn's wartime history, see "John Coburn," Encyclopedia of Indianapolis, accessed Jan. 27, 2022, https://indyencyclopedia.org/john-coburn.

3. On the 43rd Congress, see "43rd Congress (1873–1875)," History, Art & Archives, U.S. House of Representatives, accessed Dec. 05, 2021, https://history.house.gov/Congressional-Overview/Profiles/43rd. On the term "rebellion" see John M. Coski, "The War Between the Names: What Should the American War of 1861 to 1865 Be Called?" *North and South* 8, no. 7 (Jan. 2006), 67; Gaines M. Foster, "What's Not in a Name: The Naming of the American Civil War," *Journal of the Civil War Era* 8, no. 3 (Sept. 2018), 416–454, doi.org/10.1353/cwe.2018.0049.
4. *Congressional Record*, 43 Cong., sess. 1, June 12, 1874, p. 4931.
5. On clemency toward Southerners, see William A. Blair, *With Malice Toward Some: Treason and Loyalty in the Civil War Era* (Chapel Hill: University of North Carolina Press, 2014), 24–25, 234–267; Gregory P. Downs, *After Appomattox: Military Occupation and the Ends of War* (Cambridge, Mass.: Harvard University Press, 2015), 94–95. For a case study of early reconciliationist views by a former abolitionist, see Lawrence B. Glickman, "James Redpath, Rebel Sympathizer," in *Reconstruction and Empire: Legacies of Abolition and Union Victory for an Imperial Age*, ed. David Prior (New York: Fordham University Press, 2022), 136–160.
6. David W. Blight, *Race and Reunion: The Civil War in American Memory* (Cambridge, Mass.: Harvard University Press, 2001); Nina Silber, *The Romance of Reunion: Northerners and the South, 1865–1900* (Chapel Hill: University of North Carolina Press, 1993); Michael Fellman, *The Making of Robert E. Lee* (Baltimore: Johns Hopkins University Press, 2000); Timothy B. Smith, *The Golden Age of Battlefield Preservation: The Decade of the 1890s and the Establishment of America's First Five Military Parks* (Knoxville: University of Tennessee Press, 2008); Michele A. Krowl, " 'In the Spirit of Fraternity': The United States Government and the Burial of Confederate Dead at Arlington National Cemetery, 1864–1914," *The Virginia Magazine of History and Biography* 111, no. 2 (2003), 151–186, https://www.jstor.org/stable/4250101; Karen L. Cox, *Dixie's Daughters: The United Daughters of the Confederacy and the Preservation of Confederate Culture* (Gainesville: University of Florida Press, 2003), 141–158; Michael Kammen, *Mystic Chords of Memory: The Transformation of Tradition in American Culture* (New York: Vintage, 1991), 93–131.
7. Caroline E. Janney, *Remembering the Civil War: Reunion and the Limits of Reconciliation* (Chapel Hill: University of North Carolina Press, 2013); John R. Neff, *Honoring the Civil War Dead: Commemoration and the Problem of Reconciliation* (Lawrence: University of Kansas Press, 2005); Robert Hunt, *The Good Men Who Won the War: Army of the Cumberland Veterans and Emancipation Memory* (Tuscaloosa: University of Alabama Press, 2010); Barbara Gannon, *The Won Cause: Black and White Comradeship in the Grand Army of the Republic* (Chapel Hill: University of North Carolina Press, 2011); Gary W. Gallagher, *The Union War* (Cambridge, Mass.: Harvard University Press, 2011).

8. Nina Silber, "Reunion and Reconciliation, Reviewed and Reconsidered," *Journal of American History* 103, no. 1 (June 2016), 83, doi.org/10.1093/jahist/jaw008.
9. H.T. Crosby to E.D. Townsend, Aug. 17, 1875, book 1, entry 707, Letters Sent, RG 94. The paper trail for those years in the War Records Office files is almost nonexistent. See book 1, entry 707, Letters Sent, RG 94. On the missing book, see Lucille H. Pendell and Elizabeth Bethel, *Preliminary Inventory of the Records of the Adjutant General's Office* (Washington, D.C.: National Archives and Records Administration, 1949), 134.
10. William S. McFeely, *Grant: A Biography* (New York: Norton, 1981), 376, 427–8; Thomas Gaard, "William Worth Belknap, Fallen Hero," *Military Images* 26, no. 3 (Nov./Dec. 2004): 26–31. On Belknap's record-keeping practices, see Dallas Irvine, "Analysis of This Register," Nov. 23, 1962, entry 716, Letters Received Relating to Missing Military Reports, RG 94. It is worth remembering that, in the 1866 debate in the Senate, William P. Fessenden, Republican Senator of Maine and co-chairman of the Joint Committee on Reconstruction, also suggested publishing Federal and Confederate records together. See *Congressional Globe*, 39 Cong., sess. 1, May 24, 1866, p. 2804–2807.
11. U.S. War Department, *Report of the Secretary of War; Being Part of the Message and Documents Communicated to the Two Houses of Congress at the Beginning of the First Session of the Forty-Fourth Congress* (Washington, D.C.: Government Printing Office, 1875), vol. 1, 26.
12. For one example, see an exchange between James L. Kemper, governor of Virginia, and James D. Cameron, the secretary of war, in which the word "rebellion" was mentioned. "I must express my surprise at the employment of a term, deemed by most Southern citizens to be reproachful and offensive, in an official communication from a National functionary to the Executive of a Southern State." James L. Kemper to J.D. Cameron, Jan. 30, 1877, box 1, entry 451A, Memoranda on Archive Office, RG 109.
13. H.T. Crosby to Charles C. Jones, July 3, 1875, box 2, entry 438, Letters Received, RG 109; E.D. Townsend to W.T. Walthall, June 11, 1877, book 3, entry 435, Letters Sent, RG 94; W.T. Walthall to George W. McCrary, May 24, 1877, box 4, entry 438, Letters Received, RG 109. The records suggest that there were some exceptions. In 1869, a historian of the Confederate signal corps was allowed to enter, though it is not clear why. See E.D. Townsend to Mr. Wells, Feb. 9, 1869, box 1, entry 438, Letters Received, RG 109.
14. H.T. Crosby to R.N. Thompson, Aug. 16, 1877, box 2, entry 438, Letters Received, RG 109. See also A.P. Tasker endorsement, May 28, 1877, on James L. Kemper to Geo. W. McCrary, May 23, 1877, box 1, entry 451A, Memoranda on Archive Office, RG 109.
15. Z.B. Vance to J.D. Cameron, Feb. 6, 1877, box 1, entry 710, Letters Received, RG 94.

16. On early commemorative activity in the South, see Charles Reagan Wilson, *Baptized in Blood: The Religion of the Lost Cause, 1865–1920* (Athens: University of Georgia Press, 1980); Caroline E. Janney, *Burying the Dead but Not the Past: Ladies' Memorial Associations and the Lost Cause* (Chapel Hill: University of North Carolina Press, 2008); Robert J. Cook, *Civil War Memories: Contesting the Past in the United States Since 1865* (Baltimore: Johns Hopkins University Press, 2017).
17. On the Southern Historical Society, see Gaines M. Foster, *Ghosts of the Confederacy: Defeat, the Lost Cause, and the Emergence of the New South, 1865 to 1913* (New York: Oxford University Press, 1987), 47–62; Richard D. Starnes, "Forever Faithful: The Southern Historical Society and Confederate Historical Memory," *Southern Cultures* 2 (Winter 1996), 177–194, doi.org/10.1353/scu.1996.0006; Blight, *Race and Reunion*, 261–267.
18. *Annual Report of the Executive Committee of the Southern Historical Society, for the year ending October 25, 1875*, box 1, entry 710, Letters Received, RG 94; "Editorial Paragraphs," *Southern Historical Society Papers* 5, no. 5 (May 1878), 255.
19. E.D. Townsend to O. Tilghman, March 15, 1876, book 3, entry 435, Letters Sent, RG 109; E.D. Townsend to B.W. Brice, March 1, 1876, book 3, entry 435, Letters Sent, RG 109; E.D. Townsend to Jno. W. Scott, March 15, 1876, book 3, entry 435, Letters Sent, RG 109.
20. W.W. Belknap to J.B. Gordon, March 15, 1875, book 3, entry 435, Letters Sent, RG 109; Inventory of books, papers, and effects of Jefferson Davis, returned to him by Adjutant General E.D. Townsend, Sept. 9, 1874, folder 230, box 4, entry 1, Jefferson Davis Papers, RG 109.
21. Adam's Express Company voucher, June 26, 1877, Jas. McDonald to Geo. W. McCrary, June 30, 1877, box 1, entry 451A, Memoranda on Archive Office, RG 109; Geo. W. McCrary to Z.B. Vance, Nov. 6, 1877, box 2, entry 438, Letters Received, RG 109; Geo. W. McCrary to O.R. Singleton, Feb.14, 1878, box 2, entry 438, Letters Received, RG 109.
22. Geo. W. McCrary to Z.B. Vance, Nov. 6, 1877, box 2, entry 438, Letters Received, RG 109.
23. Secretary of War Belknap to J. William Jones, Jan. 22, 1876, box 1, entry 710, Letters Received, RG 94.
24. J. Wm. Jones to Wm. W. Belknap, Feb. 3, 1876, box 1, entry 710, Letters Received, RG 94.
25. Wm. W. Belknap to J. William Jones, Feb. 9, 1876, box 1, entry 710, Letters Received, RG 94.
26. W.T. Barnard to J.W. Jones, Jan. 26, 1877, box 311, Robert Alonzo Brock Collection, HL.
27. J. Wm. Jones to W.T. Barnard, Feb. 14, 1877, box 1, entry 710, Letters Received, RG 94.
28. W.T. Barnard to J.W. Jones, Feb. 23, 1877, box 8, Southern Historical Society Records, 1873–1887, CMLS.

29. J. Wm. Jones to W.T. Barnard, April 25, 1877, box 1, entry 710, Letters Received, RG 94; Southern Historical Society Minute Books, book 2, p. 5, Southern Historical Society Records, CMLS.
30. On the retreat of the Federal government from the South in 1877, see Eric Foner, *Reconstruction: America's Unfinished Revolution, 1863–1877* (New York: Harper, 1988); Douglas R. Egerton, *The Wars of Reconstruction: The Brief, Violent History of America's Most Progressive Era* (New York: Bloomsbury, 2014); Mark Wahlgren Summers, *The Ordeal of the Reunion: A New History of Reconstruction* (Chapel Hill: University of North Carolina Press, 2014).
31. On the missing book, see note 9 in this chapter.
32. Southern Historical Society Minute Books, book 2, p. 15, Southern Historical Society Records, CMLS. J. William Jones, in his editorial page in May 1878, remarked in relation to "The Archive Bureau" in Washington that ex-Confederates were no longer denied entry and that "a more liberal spirit seems to prevail with the present Secretary of War, and some of our friends have recently been allowed to inspect important documents." *Southern Historical Society Papers* 5, no. 5 (May 1878), 255.
33. Thomas. J. Saunders to Secretary of War, Dec. 8, 1877, book 1, entry 708, Letters Sent, RG 94.
34. On Scott's early life and arrest, see Harold E. Mahan, "The Arsenal of History: The Official Records of the War of the Rebellion," *Civil War History* 29 (Spring 1983), 10–12.
35. Robert N. Scott to J. Madison Wells, May 22, 1865, file 330, ACP 1872, RG 94; W.A. Scott to President Johnson, Dec. 5, 1865, file 330, ACP 1872, RG 94.
36. Robert N. Scott to Sec. of War, Sept. 30, 1878, book 1, entry 707, Letters Sent, RG 94. Scott's Southern background may have also aided his appointment at a moment in which the compilation required intensive communications with Southerners. I have not been able to find evidence for this, but as ever, it is worth considering as a possibility on which the archive is silent.
37. On Marcus J. Wright's life, see Brig. Gen. Marcus J. Wright, CSA, folder 6, ser. 3, WSHC; John Sharp Williams, "Gen. Marcus J. Wright, A Tribute," *Confederate Veteran* 31 (Feb. 1923), 49–50.
38. E.D. Townsend to M.J. Wright, Sept. 18, 1875, book 3, entry 435, Letters Sent, RG 109; Other correspondence on Wright's early contacts with the War Department are: W.C. Whitthorne to W.W. Belknap, April 22, 1875, box 4, entry 438, Letters Received, RG 109; E.D. Townsend to Marcus J. Wright, May 11, 1875, box 4, entry 438, Letters Received, RG 109; E.D. Townsend to M.J. Wright, Aug. 13, 1875, book 3, entry 435, Letters Sent, RG 109; Charles Hays to W.W. Belknap, Aug. 27, 1875, box 4, entry 438, Letters Received, RG 109.

39. Marcus J. Wright to E.D. Townsend, Aug. 9, 1875, Jan. 19, 1876, box 4, entry 438, Letters Received, RG 109.
40. Wright's financial troubles would become a nuisance for the War Department. Throughout the 1880s his creditors repeatedly approached the secretary of war demanding that he make Wright pay his old debts out of his government salary. For some documents, see R.M. Henderson to Fillmore Beall, May 29, 1882, box 6, entry 710, Letters Received, RG 94; Fillmore Beall to Robert T. Lincoln, June 2, 1882, box 6, entry 710, Letters Received, RG 94; Fillmore Beall to W.C. Endicott, May 1, 1885, box 6, entry 710, Letters Received, RG 94; Will W. Douglas to Wm. C. Endicott, May 7, 1888, box 9, entry 710, Letters Received, RG 94; Saml. Hodgkins to H.M. Lazelle, June 1, 1888, book 6, entry 708, Letters Sent, RG 94.
41. Marcus J. Wright to Casey Young, May 3, 1878, box 4, entry 438, Letters Received, RG 109; Casey Young to Geo. W. McCrary, May 20, 1878, box 4, entry 438, Letters Received, RG 109; Casey Young to Geo. W. McCrary, June 25, 1878, box 4, entry 438, Letters Received, RG 109; unsigned memorandum attached to Young to McCrary, May 20, 1878, box 4, entry 438, Letters Received, RG 109; Geo. W. McCrary to Marcus J. Wright, July 1, 1878, box 1, entry 445, Papers of Marcus J. Wright, RG 109. Wright's appointment propelled others to try and win employment as record collectors. Mrs. H.C. Hathaway was a schoolteacher in southwestern Arkansas between 1855 and 1864 and, according to her testimony, had assembled a large collection of Southern newspapers she was now offering to the government. Having read about Wright's appointment, she was asking for a similar arrangement: "I would also esteem as a *signal favor*, the privilege of making a tour through Arkansas under the auspices of Government, to visit localities and collect from living witnesses the unwritten history of the War in that section of the Confederacy." Hathaway was making an important point that little was known about the intensity of the war in the Southwest and claimed that she could help amend this. But she also attached a letter from her pastor in Hillsdale, Michigan, who left no doubt that she needed the job. "She lost all her buildings and school property amounting to some $15000 by the war and is now wholly dependent upon her own exertions." H.C. Hathaway to George McCrary, July 31, 1878, box 2, entry 710, Letters Received, RG 94; V. Leroy Lockwood endorsement on letter.
42. Williams, "Gen. Marcus J. Wright," 50; Marcus J. Wright, form letter, box 1, entry 445, Papers of Marcus J. Wright, RG 109.
43. Marcus J. Wright to R.N. Scott, April 25, 1879, box 2, entry 710, Letters Received, RG 94. On Wright's travels, see, e.g., Marcus J. Wright to R.N. Scott, Oct. 15, 1879, box 3, entry 710, Letters Received, RG 94.
44. For Wright's detailed reports, showing what records he collected every single month, see entry 447, Catalog of Confederate Military Records

Received by Marcus J. Wright, RG 109; Report by Marcus J. Wright, entry 446, RG 109.

45. Marcus J. Wright to James W. Eldridge, Aug. 9, 1898, box 66, James William Eldridge Collection, HL; Marcus J. Wright to James W. Eldridge, April 10, 1894, box 66, James William Eldridge Collection, HL.

46. Marcus J. Wright to Robert N. Scott, July 31, 1878, box 1, entry 445, Marcus J. Wright Papers, RG 109; R.N. Scott, endorsement on copy of Wright to Scott, July 31, 1878; Robert N. Scott to Marcus J. Wright, Aug. 5, 1878, box 3, entry 438, Letters Received, RG 109; "The Confederate Archives and the Southern Historical Society," *Richmond Dispatch*, Sept. 27, 1878, p. 1, accessed through newspapers.com.

47. Jefferson Davis to Marcus J. Wright, July 18, 1878, box 2, Jefferson Davis Papers, CMLS; Dunbar Rowland, ed., *Jefferson Davis, Constitutionalist: His Letters, Papers, and Speeches* (Jackson.: Mississippi Department of Archives and History, 1923), vol. 8, 293. W.T. Walthall to M.J. Wright, Sept. 3, 1879, Oct. 11, 1879, Wright Papers, folder 10C, ser. 5, WSHC.

48. W.T. Walthall to Marcus J. Wright, July 17, 1878, folder 10B, ser. 5, WSHC; W.T. Walthall to Marcus J. Wright, Oct. 11, 1879, folder 10C, ser. 5, WSHC. For a fuller treatment of the Davis archive after the war, see Yael A. Sternhell, "The Stuff of Defeat: Material Culture and the Downfall of Jefferson Davis," in *War Matters: Material Culture in the Civil War Era*, ed. Joan E. Cashin (Chapel Hill: University of North Carolina Press, 2018), 222–224.

49. Marcus J. Wright to R.N. Scott, May 11, 1880, folder 230, box 4, entry 1, Jefferson Davis Papers, RG 109; Robert N. Scott endorsement, May 11, 1880, A.P. Tasker endorsement May 31, 1880, both on letter.

50. Jefferson Davis to Marcus J. Wright, June 24, 1880, folder 10D, ser. 5, WSHC; Jefferson Davis to M.J. Wright, Nov. 6, 1884, folder 11, ser. 5, WSHC.

51. On Wright's meddling in SHS affairs, see Marcus J. Wright to Jubal Early, April 21, 1887, box 13, EP; J. Wm. Jones to Marcus J. Wright, Aug. 31, 1883, box 5, entry 710, Letters Received, RG 94. For Wright's published works, see, e.g., Marcus J. Wright, *General Scott* (New York: D. Appleton and Company, 1893); A.L. Long and Marcus J. Wright, *Memoirs of Robert E. Lee: His Military and Personal History, Embracing a Large Amount of Information Hitherto Unpublished* (New York: J.M. Stoddart and Company, 1886). *The Confederate War Journal* (New York: War Journal Publishing Company, 1893–1895) ran for two years.

52. Robert N. Scott to Jefferson Davis, Sept. 12, 1879, book 2, entry 708, Letters Sent, RG 94; Robert N. Scott to Jefferson Davis, Nov. 4, 1882, book 2, entry 707, Letters Sent, RG 94. See also Robert N. Scott to M.J. Wright, Jan. 8, 1880, book 2, entry 707, Letters Sent, RG 94.

53. Robert N. Scott to Jefferson Davis, Nov. 13, 1882, book 2, entry 707, Letters Sent, RG 94.

54. Robert N. Scott to Jefferson Davis, Jan. 10, 1884, book 3, entry 708, Letters Sent, RG 94; Robert N. Scott to Jefferson Davis, Oct. 8, 1884, book 3, entry 708, Letters Sent, RG 94. On the term "contributor to the work," see Chapter 6.
55. Geo. B. Davis to W. Miller Owen, Jan. 14, 1892, book 12, entry 708, Letters Sent, RG 94; Geo. B. Davis to W. Miller Owen, Jan. 26, 1892, book 12, entry 708, Letters Sent, RG 94; Allen R. Adams to Geo. B. Davis, Feb. 3, 1894, box 2, entry 713, General Correspondence, RG 94; Geo. B. Davis to Allen R. Adams, Feb. 7, 1894, book 17, entry 708, Letters Sent, RG 94.
56. Elihu Root, "Preface," *OR*, General Index, xi.
57. Robert N. Scott to D.H. Hill, Jan. 10, 1884, book 3, entry 708, Letters Sent, RG 94; Robert N. Scott to A.L. Long, Aug. 13, 1886, book 5, entry 708, Letters Sent, RG 94; Robert N. Scott to R.L. Walker, Aug. 31, 1886, book 5, entry 708, Letters Sent, RG 94; J.D. Imboden to R.N. Scott, Jan. 26, 1886, box 7, entry 710, Letters Received, RG 94; H.M. Lazelle to John S. Williams, March 16, 1888, book 6, entry 708, Letters Sent, RG 94.
58. Robert N. Scott to Secy. of War, Sept. 1, 1879, book 2, entry 707, Letters Sent, RG 94; Robert N. Scott to H.T. Crosby, Aug. 9, 1879, book 2, entry 707, Letters Sent, RG 94.
59. Foster, *Ghosts of the Confederacy*, 55. For widely disparate interpretations of Early's role and influence, see Thomas L. Connelly, *The Marble Man: Robert E. Lee and His Image in American Society* (Baton Rouge: Louisiana State University Press, 1977); Thomas L. Connelly and Barbara L. Bellows, *God and General Longstreet: The Lost Cause and the Southern Mind* (Baton Rouge: Louisiana State University Press, 1982); Gary W. Gallagher, *Jubal A. Early, the Lost Cause, and Civil War History: A Persistent Legacy* (Milwaukee, Wis.: Marquette University Press, 1995); Gary W. Gallagher, *Lee and His Generals in War and Memory* (Baton Rouge: Louisiana State University Press, 1998).
60. E.J. Harvie to Jubal Early, Aug. 9, 1879, box 10, EP; Robert N. Scott to Jubal Early, Oct. 10, 1883, box 12, EP.
61. Quote in Geo. B. Davis to J.B. Gordon, Dec. 21, 1889, book 8, entry 708, Letters Sent, RG 94. See also H.M. Lazelle to Holmes Conrad, Sept. 3, 1888, book 6, entry 708, Letters Sent, RG 94; Geo. B. Davis to W.E. Cameron, March 26, 1891, book 10, entry 708, Letters Sent, RG 94; Geo. B. Davis to Charles Marshall, March 3, 1891, book 10, entry 708, Letters Sent, RG 94.
62. Geo. B. Davis to L.W.V. Kennon, March 26, 1891, book 10, entry 708, Letters Sent, RG 94. On Early's raid, see James M. McPherson, *Battle Cry of Freedom: The Civil War Era* (New York: Oxford University Press, 1988), 756–758. On Kennon and Early, see Martin F. Schmitt, ed., "An Interview with General Jubal A. Early in 1889," *Journal of Southern History* 11, no. 4 (1945), 547–563, doi.org/10.2307/2198313.

63. Geo. B. Davis to D.H. Maury, Aug. 6, 1891, book 10, entry 708, Letters Sent, RG 94; Geo. B. Davis to J.A. Early, April 2, 1891, book 10, entry 708, Letters Sent, RG 94; H.M. Lazelle to E.P. Alexander, July 9, 1887, book 5, entry 708, Letters Sent, RG 94.
64. Geo. B. Davis to J.F. Huntington, July 22, 1891, book 10, entry 708, Letters Sent, RG 94; Geo. B. Davis to W. Miller Owen, Jan. 21, 1892, book 12, entry 708, Letters Sent, RG 94; Geo. B. Davis to W. Miller Owen Jan. 26, 1892, book 12, entry 708, Letters Sent, RG 94; Geo. B. Davis to W. Miller Owen Feb. 5, 1892, book 12, entry 708, Letters Sent, RG 94; Geo. B. Davis to W. Miller Owen April 7, 1892, book 12, entry 708, Letters Sent, RG 94; Geo. B. Davis to W. Miller Owen April 9, 1892, book 12, entry 708, Letters Sent, RG 94; Geo. B. Davis to W. Miller Owen, Dec. 19, 1893, book 12, entry 708, Letters Sent, RG 94.
65. Geo. B. Davis to W. Miller Owen, Jan. 14, 1892, book 12, entry 708, Letters Sent, RG 94; Geo. B. Davis to W. Miller Owen, Sept. 14, 1892, book 13, entry 708, Letters Sent, RG 94; Leslie J. Perry to W. Miller Owen, Sept. 6, 1892, book 13, entry 708, Letters Sent, RG 94; Geo. B. Davis to E.A. Palfrey, June 13, 1894, box 18, entry 708, Letters Sent, RG 94.
66. Marcus J. Wright to E.D. Townsend, Oct. 1, 1878, book 1, box 1, entry 447, Catalogs of Confederate Military Records Received by Marcus J. Wright, RG 109; J.W. Jones to Jubal Early, Jan. 7, 1879, box 10, EP; quote in Marcus J. Wright to E.D. Townsend, Nov. 8, 1878, book 1, box 1, entry 447, Catalogs of Confederate Military Records Received by Marcus J. Wright, RG 109. See also A.P. Tasker to E.D. Townsend, Oct. 14, 1878, box 3, entry 438, Letters Received, RG 109; J.W. Jones to A.P. Tasker, Nov. 20, 1878, box 3, entry 438, Letters Received, RG 109.
67. Marcus J. Wright to R.N. Scott, Sept. 19, 1878, box 1, entry 445, Papers of Marcus J. Wright, RG 109; J.W. Jones to Jubal Early, Dec. 28, 1878, box 10, EP.
68. Robert N. Scott to J. William Jones, Dec. 18, 1878, book 1, entry 708, Letters Sent, RG 94; J.W. Jones to Genl., Aug. 5, 1879, box 2, entry 710, Letters Received, RG 94; A.P. Tasker to J.W. Jones, Jan. 12, 1880, book 3, entry 435, Letters Sent, RG 109. On Confederate veterans and professional historical practices, see Kathryn Shively, " 'Duty to My Country and Myself:' The Jubal A. Early Memoirs," in *Civil War Writing: New Perspectives on Iconic Texts*, ed. Gary W. Gallagher and Stephen Cushman (Baton Rouge: Louisiana State University Press, 2019), 139–170.
69. J.W. Jones to R.N. Scott, June 27, 1879, box 2, entry 710, Letters Received, RG 94; J.W. Jones to R.N. Scott, Dec. 8, 1880, box 4, entry 710, Letters Received, RG 94.
70. Robert N. Scott to V.E. Dade, April 22, 1879, book 1, entry 708, Letters Sent, RG 94; Tasker to Kirkley, Dec. 17, 1877, box 1, entry 710, Letters Received, RG 94. Dade also did some freelance copying for Marcus J. Wright and ex-Confederate officer Bradley T. Johnson. See Marcus J.

Wright to Mr. Crosby, July 25, 1881, box 4, entry 438, Letters Received, RG 109; Marcus J. Wright to A.P. Tasker, Jan. 23, 1879, box 1, entry 445, Papers of Marcus J. Wright, RG 109. Dade was the most senior woman employed by the War Department's archival bureaus, and was later appointed as head copyist. On female employees of the Federal government in the Civil War era, see Jessica Ziparo, *This Grand Experiment: When Women Entered the Federal Workforce in Civil War–Era Washington, D.C.* (Chapel Hill: University of North Carolina Press, 2017).

71. A.P. Tasker to J.W. Jones, Sept. 23, 1879, book 3, entry 435, Letters Sent, RG 109; H.M. Lazelle, to R.A. Brock, May 4, 1888, book 6, entry 708, Letters Sent, RG 94; Dabney H. Maury to Jubal Early, July 28, 1891, box 14, EP.
72. Joan Waugh, *U.S. Grant: American Hero, American Myth* (Chapel Hill: University of North Carolina Press, 2009), 218; Blight, *Race and Reunion*, 173–176; Timothy B. Smith, *The Golden Age of Battlefield Preservation: The Decade of the 1890s and the Establishment of America's First Five Military Parks* (Knoxville: University of Tennessee Press, 2008), 5. However, William Blair has argued that the 1870s were a period of "mixed feelings," during which sectional animosities coexisted with a nascent reconciliationist sentiment. See *Cities of the Dead: Contesting the Memory of the Civil War in the South, 1865–1914* (Chapel Hill: University of North Carolina Press, 2004), 108–143.
73. This point also appears in Oz Frankel, *States of Inquiry: Social Investigations and Print Culture in Nineteenth-Century Britain and the United States* (Baltimore: Johns Hopkins University Press, 2006), 103.
74. On trying to get the *OR* to institutions, see Leslie J. Perry to E.J. Turner, Nov. 4, 1891, book 11, entry 708, Letters Sent, RG 94.
75. Record and Pension Office, War Department, *List of Libraries, Organizations, and Educational Institutions in the Several States and Territories of the United States supplied with the Official Records of the Union and Confederate Armies* (Washington, D.C.: no publisher, 1903).
76. Receipt, Aug. 4, 1900, Washington City Post Office Registry Division, box 1, entry 721, Reports on Financial Transactions as Regards Sales and Distribution, RG 94.
77. Leslie J. Perry to Edwin H. Woodruff, Aug. 23, 1892, book 13, entry 708, Letters Sent, RG 94; Geo. B. Davis to Robert Beall, April 13, 1894, book 17, entry 708, Letters Sent, RG 94; James W. Hendricks to Redfield Proctor, March 12, 1890, box 10, entry 710, Letters Received, RG 94.
78. Leslie J. Perry to Russell A. Alger, Aug. 10, 1891, book 10, entry 708, Letters Sent, RG 94. The military historian Robert M. Johnston, who was active in the early twentieth century and attempted to wrest control of historical editing of wartime records from the War Department, argued that many recipients of the *OR* sold them to book dealers. However, the very demand among booksellers for the volumes is in and of itself proof

of their popularity. See Carol Reardon, *Soldiers and Scholars: The U.S. Army and the Uses of Military History, 1865–1920* (Lawrence: University Press of Kansas, 1990), 161.

79. R.L. Gibson to R.N. Scott, Dec. 18, 1885, box 7, entry 710, Letters Received, RG 94; Henry S. Cohn to General William T. Sherman, June 5, 1883, box 7, entry 710, Letters Received, RG 94.
80. Jos. Wheeler to Robert N. Scott, Nov. 19, 1885, box 7, entry 710, Letters Received, RG 94. Wheeler was also an important contributor of records to the War Records Office and was in touch with Marcus J. Wright. See Jos. Wheeler to Marcus J. Wright, Jan. 21, 1880, folder 10D, ser. 5, WSHC.
81. Yates Snowden to E.D. Townsend, April 5, 1881, box 4, entry 710, Letters Received, RG 94; review of *"The War of the Rebellion"—Official Records of the Union and Confederate Armies, Southern Historical Society Papers* 11, no. 12 (Dec. 1883), 575–576.
82. Douglas Southall Freeman, *The South to Posterity: An Introduction to the Writing of Confederate History* (New York: Charles Scribner's Sons, 1939), 93; Freeman was born in Lynchburg, Virginia, the hometown of Jubal Early, in 1886. See Gary W. Gallagher's introduction to the 1998 edition of Freeman's book by Louisiana State University Press.
83. James Ford Rhodes, *History of the United States from the Compromise of 1850 to the McKinley-Bryan Campaign of 1896* (New York: The Macmillan Company, 1920), vol. 6, 111n1. On the professionalization of history and the rise of the nation-state, see Peter Novick, *That Noble Dream: The "Objectivity Question" and the American Historical Profession* (Cambridge: Cambridge University Press, 1988), 73–80. See also Michael Kraus, *The Writing of American History* (Norman: University of Oklahoma Press, 1953).
84. Clarence E. Carter, "The United States and Documentary Historical Publication," *Mississippi Valley Historical Review* 25, no. 1 (June 1938), 16.
85. Shelby Foote, *The Civil War: A Narrative* (New York: Vintage Books, 1958), vol. 1: *Fort Sumter to Perryville*, 813; Ken Burns et al., *The Civil War: A Film by Ken Burns* (Burbank, Calif.: PBS Home Video, 1990). For some responses to Burns by academic historians, see Robert Brent Toplin, ed., *Ken Burns's* The Civil War*: Historians Respond* (New York: Oxford University Press, 1996).

Coda

1. On Irvine as a scholar, see "Statement of Sherrod East for the National Archives and Records Service Oral History Project," National Archives Oral History Project, accessed Aug. 15, 2022, https://www.archives.gov/files/about/history/sherrod-east-final.pdf; Michael P. Musick, "Honorable Reports: Battles, Campaigns, and Skirmishes," *Prologue* 27, no. 3 (Fall

1995), 259–277. Some of Irvine's non–Civil War publications include "The Abbe Raynal and British Humanitarianism," *The Journal of Modern History* 3 (Dec. 1931), 564–577; "The French and Prussian Staff Systems Before 1870," *The Journal of the American Military Foundation* 2 (Winter 1938), 192–203; "The Origin of Capital Staffs," *The Journal of Modern History* 10 (June 1938), 161–179.

2. Dallas D. Irvine, "The Genesis of the Official Records," *Mississippi Valley Historical Review* 24 (Sept. 1937); "The Archive Office of the War Department: Repository of Captured Confederate Archives, 1865–1881," *Military Affairs* 10, no. 1 (Spring 1946), 93–97; "The Fate of Confederate Records: Executive Office," *The American Historical Review* 44, no. 4 (July 1939), 823–841. On Irvine's manuscript, see introductory remarks by Robert H. Gruber, Irvine, GI1966, i; Irvine, GI1966, 51; Irvine, GI1977, 1.
3. Irvine, GI1966, 2, 4.
4. Dallas Irvine, "Analysis of this Register," Nov. 23, 1862, entry 716, Register of Letters Received Relating to Missing Military Reports, RG 94; Irvine, GI1966, 39; Irvine, GI1977, 4.
5. Quote from Musick, "Honorable Reports."
6. Nicholas B. Dirks, "Annals of the Archive: Ethnographic Notes on the Sources of History," in *From the Margins: Historical Anthropology and Its Futures*, ed. Brian Keith Axel (Durham, N.C.: Duke University Press, 2002), 48.

Acknowledgments

A book about archives doesn't have to start in a conversation with an archivist, but this one did. In the summer of 2011, I walked into the National Archives in Washington, D.C., spurred by a rather vague notion that it would be interesting to examine how and why the ever-precarious Confederate government took care to preserve its records during the Civil War. Yet a passing comment by Jill Abrams-D'Andrea, an archivist in the reference room, propelled me to change course and look more deeply into the records of the Federal War Department bureaus that took charge of Civil War paperwork once the war was over. Since that day, archivists and librarians have remained essential partners in this endeavor. Staffers at the National Archives guided me through the intricate record groups of the War Department and pointed me to additional records hiding elsewhere. At the museum of the Confederacy (now the American Civil War Museum), John Coski provided crucial assistance in conceptualizing the project in its early stages and locating relevant records in the collections under his charge. At the Huntington Library, the Library of Congress, the Southern Historical Collection, and the Wissenschaftskolleg zu Berlin, librarians generously answered numerous queries and helped me find less-than-obvious sources I would never have located on my own (special thanks to Kirsten Graupner). At the very end of the process, veteran National Archives staffers—Michael P. Musick, Dale Floyd, and Rodney Ross—were kind enough to share their personal experiences managing Civil War records in the twentieth century. I am deeply grateful to all.

For funding, I am indebted to the Israel Science Foundation for two generous grants (813/13, 1368/17). The American Philosophical Society and a Mellon Fellowship from the Huntington Library provided funding for additional costly and necessary research trips. For institutional support that combined the financial, intellectual, and personal, I am grateful first and foremost to the Department of History at Princeton University. Though it has been a decade and a half since I walked out of Dickinson Hall, dissertation in hand, the department has continued to support my work in a variety of important ways. A 2013 invitation by Dirk Hartog to the American Studies colloquium generated advice and ideas I continued to draw on for years. A semester-long sabbatical at the Shelby Cullom Davis Center for Historical Studies in 2016 transformed this project and my life in more ways than can be explicated here. I am happily indebted to Philip Nord, a former teacher and the director of the Davis Center from 2012 to 2016, for extending the invitation and for the fellowship that came with it. A trio of great Princeton minds—James McPherson, Yaacob Dweck, and Daniel Rodgers—read the manuscript from cover to cover with painstaking care and offered invaluable insights and suggestions. It is hard to properly acknowledge Dan's full contribution to this project over the many years I have labored on it. Suffice it to say that I am an extraordinarily fortunate beneficiary of his limitless generosity and incomparable ability to make other people's work better than it could possibly have been otherwise.

A few years later, the Berlin Institute for Advanced Studies (Wissenschaftskolleg zu Berlin) helped me return to my research despite a newborn baby and a global pandemic and offered two extremely useful opportunities to present my work to a uniquely insightful audience. I am particularly grateful to Rektorin Barbara Stollberg-Rilinger for the warm welcome and for creating the conditions that allow even the most harried female scholar to get work done. Lorraine Daston, a permanent fellow at Wiko and a quintessential role model, offered her time and expertise in scientific archives and had exceptionally useful ideas for how to improve the manuscript. In both of these venerable institutions, the efficiency and professionalism of administrators—Jennifer Houle at Princeton and Andrea Bergmann, Vera Pfeffer, and their colleagues at Wiko—ensured that my stays were as productive as they could have possibly been. At Tel Aviv University, my home university, I am particularly indebted to Milette Shamir for her ongoing support of my efforts on every front and to my former dean, Leo Corry, for encouraging me to go to Germany.

Over the years I have received tremendously useful feedback from many colleagues, some of which became part of the book. These colleagues include audiences, fellow panelists, and commentators in meetings of the Society for Civil War Historians, the American Historical Association, and the Organization of American Historians. Also fruitful and enjoyable were talks at Boston University, Louisiana State University, University of Richmond, University of Virginia, and Tel Aviv University. For sage advice, hard questions, and thoughtful suggestions, I am deeply grateful to Alan Aimone, Alex Bevilacqua, Steven Berry, David Blight, Fitz Brundage, Angela Creager, Jim Downs, Gaines Foster, Oz Frankel, Luca Giuliani, Joseph Glatthaar, Judy Giesberg, Thavolia Glymph, Anthony Grafton, Dirk Hartog, David Henkin, Wayne Hsieh, Caroline Janney, Ari Kelman, Ed Linenthal and the anonymous readers at the *Journal of American History*, Noam Maggor, Suzanne Marchand, Matthew Mason, Stephanie McCurry, Megan Kate Nelson, Carol Reardon,

Hila Shamir, Aaron Sheehan-Dean, Kathryn Shively, Nina Silber, Will Slauter, and Joan Waugh.

A project of this scope requires assistance in research, and I was enormously lucky to find talented young scholars who helped me transcribe the thousands of handwritten records I brought back from the archives and who offered other important help. I am grateful to Olga Barenboim, Becca Dayan, Batel Levy, Ayelet Marron, Anat Ovadia-Rosner, Rebecca Sacks, Ophir Sloutsky, Daniel Youkilis, and, above all, Leonard Stein for their extraordinary work. Leonard reviewed the manuscript's research apparatus in its entirety and saved me from many embarrassing mistakes, a priceless service for which I am particularly grateful. When I was no longer able to travel to the archives as freely as I needed, Ellie Pallazolo and Jay Driskell stepped in and performed meticulous research on my behalf.

As long as I was still able to spend long periods of time in Washington, Nathan and Vered Guttman gave me a home away from home, and I am more than indebted to them for making my research trips cheerful and tasty on top of productive. Thanks also to Natan Sacks and Yoav Gery for hosting and entertaining me spectacularly. In New York, Erica Gilles had my back, and I am, as ever, deeply grateful to her and her family for their unmatched hospitality.

At Yale University Press, Adina Popescu Berk gave my book a home and pushed me to keep going amidst life's numerous distractions. Her firm guidance and editorial acumen were indispensable in bringing this book to life. Eric Stoykovich and an anonymous reader for the press offered helpful comments that materially improved the manuscript. Mary Pasti and freelancer Emma Johnson did a remarkable job reviewing, improving, and bringing this manuscript to the finish line. I am also grateful to Ash Lago and Eva Skewes for their skillful assistance in the process of book publishing. Working with Yale has been a great pleasure throughout.

Finally, heartfelt thanks to the people who were not involved in making this book directly but without whom I cannot imagine having had the peace of mind to write it: my friends Idit Froim, Tali Mentovitch, and Danielle Shani, who stood by me through thick and thin; my sister, Tali Gerber, and her family—Noah, Netta, Daphna, and Simi—who bring so much light into my life; my stepfamily—Racheli, Yoel, Tal, and Modi—who welcomed me with open arms and remain a constant source of great joy; my mother-in-law, Miriam Rosen-Zvi, who has done so much to sustain and support me; my daughters, Arielle and Shira, who have made me happier than I ever thought I could be; my better half, Ishay Rosen-Zvi, who champions and mentors me but more crucially, in the immortal words of Jessica Rabbit, makes me laugh; my beloved mother, Ziva, who throughout my life has remained an unbounded source of comfort, wisdom, affection, and good cheer; and my late father, Zeev, who instilled in me the faith that I too could be a historian and that being a historian is a worthwhile endeavor in a troubled world. I dedicate this book to him in grief, longing, and everlasting gratitude—for everything he gave me while he was still here.

Index

Page numbers in italics refer to figures.